Guiding Young Children

Ninth Edition

Patricia F. Hearron
Appalachian State University

Verna Hildebrand
Emerita, Michigan State University

PEARSON

Boston Columbus Indianapolis New York San Francisco Upper Saddle River
Amsterdam Cape Town Dubai London Madrid Milan Munich Paris Montréal Toronto
Delhi Mexico City São Paulo Sydney Hong Kong Seoul Singapore Taipei Tokyo

Vice President and Editorial Director: Jeffery W. Johnston
Senior Acquisitions Editor: Julie Peters
Editorial Assistant: Andrea Hall
Vice President, Director of Marketing: Margaret Waples
Senior Marketing Manager: Christopher D. Barry
Senior Managing Editor: Pamela D. Bennett
Project Manager: Linda Hillis Bayma
Production Manager: Laura Messerly
Senior Art Director: Jayne Conte

Cover Designer: Bruce Kenselaar
Full-Service Project Management: Sudha Balasundaram, Element LLC
Composition: Element/ Thomson
Text Printer/Binder: R.R. Donnelley & Sons/ Crawfordsville
Cover Printer: R.R. Donnelley & Sons/Crawfordsville
Text Font: ITC Galliard

Credits and acknowledgments for materials borrowed from other sources and reproduced, with permission, in this textbook appear on appropriate page within the text.

Every effort has been made to provide accurate and current Internet information in this book. However, the Internet and information posted on it are constantly changing, so it is inevitable that some of the Internet addresses listed in this textbook will change.

Photo Credits: Anthony Magnacca/Merrill, pp. 76, 243; David Mager/Pearson Learning Photo Studio, pp. 70, 211; Jacqueline Wood, pp. 68, 96, 206, 231; Karen Mancinelli/Pearson Learning Photo Studio, p. 132; Krista Greco/Merrill, p. 105; Lela Weems, p. 47; Merrill Education, p. 106; © Michael Newman/PhotoEdit, p. 192; Patricia Hearron, p. 120; Patricia Hearron/ Forest Early Childhood Center, Auburn MI, p. 202; Patricia Hearron/Lucy Brock Child Development Center, Appalachian State University, Boone, NC, pp. 79, 123, 127, 128, 262; Patricia Hearron/The Sandbox, Hickory, NC, pp. 17, 26, 27, 29, 46, 53, 86, 102, 110, 117, 126, 144, 181 (both), 182, 201 (top), 204, 228, 271; Scott Cunningham/Merrill, pp. 154, 236; Sheryl Zimmerman/Forest Early Child Development Center, Auburn, MI, pp. 6, 8, 11, 48, 50, 56, 78, 83, 101, 104, 157, 166, 168, 173, 188, 191, 200, 205, 226, 235, 276; Sheryl Zimmerman/Michigan Child Care Centers, Saginaw, MI, pp. 1, 4, 10, 63, 99, 100, 160, 201 (bottom), 216, 256; Sheryl Zimmerman/Webster Childcare Center, Bay City, MI, pp. 14, 15, 36, 40, 73, 124, 136, 139, 198, 203.

Library of Congress Cataloging-in-Publication Data

Hearron, Patricia F.
    Guiding young children / Patricia F. Hearron, Verna Hildebrand.—9th ed.
    p. cm.
Includes bibliographical references and index.
ISBN-13: 978-0-13-265713-6
ISBN-10: 0-13-265713-9
1. Education, Preschool. 2. Teacher-student relationships. 3. Child rearing. I. Hildebrand, Verna. II. Title.
LB1140.2.H52 2013
372.21—dc23

                                                                                        2011047132

PEARSON

ISBN-13: 978-0-13-265713-6
ISBN-10:   0-13-265713-9

We dedicate this book to the young children whose care is entrusted to all of us and to the early childhood professionals, present and future, whose commitment and hard work help those children develop their full potential.

About the Authors

Patricia Hearron teaches child development and early education at Appalachian State University where she has coordinated the Birth–Kindergarten teacher preparation program since 1994. Before coming to Appalachian, she worked with children and families in a variety of roles: as Child Life Specialist in a children's health clinic; a teacher and director of full- and part-day programs; a state child care licensing agent; and as a consultant, conducting professional development workshops for teachers and caregivers in Michigan, North Carolina and Texas. In addition to *Guiding Young Children*, she is co-author (with Verna Hildebrand) of *Management of Child Development Centers* and has published and presented on a wide variety of early childhood topics, including the importance of outdoor play, inclusion of children with disabilities in infant-toddler programs, the project approach, and aspects of the Reggio Emilia approach to early education and care.

Verna Hildebrand taught child development and early education in the College of Human Ecology at Michigan State University. She is recognized internationally as an expert in the field and has published several widely used textbooks, including an *Introduction to Early Childhood Education; Parenting: Rewards and Responsibilities;* and *Knowing and Serving Diverse Families*. In addition to *Guiding Young Children*, she is co-author (with Patricia Hearron) of *Management of Child Development Centers*.

Preface

Guiding Young Children, Ninth Edition, is designed for use by college students and others who are learning to work with young children in group settings. This is the only guidance text that provides an overview of the principles of guidance; detailed coverage of two broad strategies based on those principles—indirect and direct guidance; and several chapters explaining how to apply those principles to specific contexts.

OUR PHILOSOPHY: DEVELOPING HUMAN POTENTIAL

As in previous editions, our emphasis here is on the process of developing human potential in all children by consciously applying principles of guidance. Those principles are based on child development theory and research, as well as on the knowledge, beliefs, and values we have gained through many years of experience in our work with young children and their families, with early childhood professionals, and with students preparing for careers with young children.

Because our emphasis is on developing human potential, we view guidance as a concept that is broader and more complex than discipline or behavior management. **Guidance is more than getting children to do what we want them to do today; it is helping them to become everything they can become for all of their tomorrows.** It is important that even beginning caregivers and teachers understand, or at least think about, the ways in which their interactions can have an impact on those tomorrows. Thus, in addition to offering specific, concrete suggestions for adults who might be working with young children for the first time, we try to explain the reasoning behind those suggestions, and to offer general principles that can serve as a framework to guide—not to dictate—the reader's decisions and interactions with children.

As young children in this country spend more and more of their early lives in group settings, we note with alarm an ever-increasing emphasis on academic skills and a corresponding decrease in time for play, particularly outdoor play. Ironically, these trends exist amid reports that significant numbers of those children are being expelled from preschool programs because of behavior problems. Although bombarded on all sides with evidence that childhood has changed, we remain unwavering in our conviction that children continue to thrive best in settings that resemble the supportive and enriching aspects of home and family life rather than impersonal institutions. Our hope is that the guidance principles and strategies provided in this book will help early childhood professionals shift their focus from correcting or controlling behavior to providing the satisfying, joyful experiences and relationships that build a child's inner resources, providing a kind of immunity from the ill effects of life's challenges. We concur with Alison Gopnick that "Change and transience are at the heart of the human condition. But as parents [and caregivers] we can at least give our children a happy childhood, a gift that is as certain, as unchanging, as rock solid, as any human good" (2009, p. 201).

NEW TO THIS EDITION

While this ninth edition of *Guiding Young Children* retains many features that instructors have found useful in earlier editions, including provocative "Talk It Over" suggestions in each chapter, it has been extensively revised and updated. In addition to incorporating new information drawn from research and professional literature, we have added and clarified content in response to feedback from students, colleagues, and reviewers. We have also made a conscious effort to pedagogically structure the book to provide a better fit with expectations for online courses:

- *Expanded chapter on addressing challenging behavior.* We've expanded Chapter 11 to cover this topic in greater detail, adding more examples and tools while continuing to emphasize that challenging behavior cannot be effectively addressed without implementing all the strategies presented in this book.

- *New coverage of cutting-edge topics.* In addition to updating research throughout, we've

  - Expanded the section on brain development and the concept of self-regulation in Chapter 3.
  - Added a discussion of Response to Intervention (RtI) in Chapter 11.

- *New learning outcomes and realigned chapter content.* Learning outcomes are listed at the beginning of each chapter and have been aligned with primary headings and application activities. This supports teaching and learning online and in traditional settings.

- *New illustrations to help clarify key points.* These include a table listing warning signs of possible abuse and neglect in Chapter 4; charts and sample floor plans in Chapter 6; and a sample behavioral analysis and behavior plan in Chapter 11.

- *Concrete examples.* We've added or expanded examples and vignettes throughout to help students better understand concepts (e.g., conflict resolution example in Chapter 7).

- *Instructor ancillaries.* This edition is supported by an online Instructor's Manual, an online Test Bank, and online PowerPoint slides. All can be downloaded from the Instructor's Resource Center, at www.pearsonhighered.com.

As in the previous edition, Part I provides an overview of the principles of guidance; Part II presents a detailed examination of two broad strategies based on those principles—indirect and direct guidance; and Part III addresses the application of those principles to specific contexts, including caregiving routines, guiding children's play and learning indoors and outdoors, and understanding and responding to challenging behavior.

Although dealing with challenging behavior is the topic that students (and teachers!) often want to discuss first, we place that chapter at the end of Part III because we believe that early childhood professionals who conscientiously apply all the principles and strategies presented in this book will increase the likelihood of positive behavior, and they will avoid exacerbating challenging behaviors by setting unrealistic expectations for children's behavior or using ineffective guidance techniques. Thus, they will face fewer challenging behaviors in the long run and be better equipped to understand and address those that do occur in ways that promote children's self-direction.

We encourage all instructors who use *Guiding Young Children* to adjust this sequence of topics to suit their preferences, the needs of their students, and the constraints of their particular teaching situations. We have provided an extensive list of additional readings and Internet resources at the end of each chapter to help instructors enrich their courses and to make it easy for students to extend their exploration of the concepts in this book.

NEW CourseSmart eTEXTBOOK AVAILABLE

CourseSmart is an exciting new choice for students looking to save money. As an alternative to purchasing the printed textbook, students can purchase an electronic version of the same content. With a CourseSmart eTextbook, students can search the text, make notes online, print out reading assignments that incorporate lecture notes, and bookmark important passages for later review. For more information, or to purchase access to the CourseSmart eTextbook, visit www.coursesmart.com.

ACKNOWLEDGMENTS

We are grateful to the many early childhood professionals, including former students who have become our valued colleagues, who have contributed ideas, photographs, and feedback on the eight earlier editions of this book. We express our appreciation to the staff and children at the child development centers depicted in this book and to the parents who have permitted their children's photos to be used. Special thanks are due to Tom Hearron for his skill as an insightful reader and for his invaluable expertise in the creation of the Test Bank that accompanies this edition.

Laurel Anderson, Mira Costa College/Palomar College; Gayle J. Dilling, Olympic College; Amy M. Kay, University of Georgia; and Amanda Taintor, Reedley College provided helpful feedback in their reviews of the eighth edition. We are indebted to our editor at Pearson, Julie Peters, and to Andrea Hall, editorial assistant, for their unflagging encouragement and support. Finally, we appreciate the skillful assistance of Linda Bayma and Laura Messerly, project managers at Pearson, Sudha Balasundaram, project manager at Element, and Kitty Wilson, our copy editor.

Brief Contents

Brief Contents

Contents

CHAPTER 4 Collaborating with Families of Young Children   67

CHAPTER 5   Positive Guidance—*Building Human Resources*   94

PART II   STRATEGIES FOR GUIDANCE

CHAPTER 9 Guidance and Curriculum—*Interdependent Elements of Appropriate Practice*   197

CHAPTER 10   Guiding Young Children's Outdoor Play
and Learning   224

PART I

Principles of Guidance

PART 1

Principles of Guidance

CHAPTER 1

Guiding Young Children—
A Preview

Learning Outcomes

After studying this chapter you should be able to

- Provide a definition of *guidance* and describe how guiding children differs from controlling children.
- Describe factors that influence an individual's approach to guidance.
- List three major goals of guidance.
- Discuss what it means to approach guidance *developmentally* and *positively*.
- Identify the steps of the *learning cycle* in relation to your own professional development.

You watch, spellbound, as a teacher patiently helps three-year-old Mei-Li navigate the new climber and slide on the playground. "You can do it, Mei-Li. That's right, hold on to the rail and put your foot right here," directs the teacher. Mei-Li presses her lips together and knits her brows in concentration as she ascends the ladder slowly, one step at a time. The teacher stands nearby and offers encouragement when Mei-Li pauses at the top. Mei-Li sits down and hesitantly begins the descent, giggling with delight when she lands on her feet at the bottom. The teacher smiles broadly and says, "You did it!" Mei-Li runs around the structure to repeat the process several more times. As an observer, you ask yourself, "Could I be as patient as that teacher?"

Indoors, a little later that day, you watch the same teacher move quickly to the block corner, where four-year-old Randy is screaming and violently knocking down structures that other children have created. His face is red and contorted with rage, and the other children are cowering in fear. One of them tells the teacher that Randy became angry when Marissa accidentally bumped his block tower, causing it to topple over.

What would you do if you were the teacher? Would your answer change if you knew that Randy seems to be developing language skills more slowly than his peers and has been working with a therapist who visits the classroom several times a week?

On your first day as a student intern, you are asked to supervise children on the playground. The job seems easy enough, until you notice several children refusing to allow Rosa to play on the climber with them. Rosa happens to speak with a pronounced accent and have darker skin than the others. What do you think you should do?

UNDERSTANDING GUIDANCE

One of your goals as you study, practice, and gain experience interacting with young children will be to develop intentionality, a quality deemed important enough that leaders and mentors in the field devoted several days to discussing it at a recent National Professional Development Institute. Intentionality is "being planful and deliberate. Knowing what you are doing and why, and being able to explain it to others. Having a vision—as educators, as administrators, as a profession" (National Association for the Education of Young Children [NAEYC], 2007a, p. 2). What would you do if you were the adult in the episodes described above? What would you say? Why? How would you explain your choices to colleagues or parents? What is your vision for children? For yourself as an early childhood professional? Thinking ahead about your answers to these questions is an example of intentionality.

What Guidance Is

Infants come into the world endowed with the potential for growing, developing, and learning. The word *potential*, with its root word *potent*, means that there is energy or force for growing, developing, and learning. Children need guidance in order to feel secure and confident and to learn desirable ways of behaving. In short, they need guidance to become the kind of adults valued by the society in which they live. Guidance is defined as everything adults deliberately do and say, either directly or indirectly, to influence children's behavior, with the goal of helping the children become well-adjusted, self-directed, productive adults. It includes establishing appropriate expectations and setting the stage for those expectations to be fulfilled. It means supporting children so that they do the right thing and responding helpfully when they do not.

Infants come into the world full of potential for growing, developing, and learning.

Guidance requires knowledge of your own values as well as respect for those of the families whose children you hope to lead.

This textbook will help you use your own energy, or potential, in learning how to guide children toward achieving their full physical, social, emotional, and intellectual potential. Figure 1–1 provides a graphic overview of the way this textbook

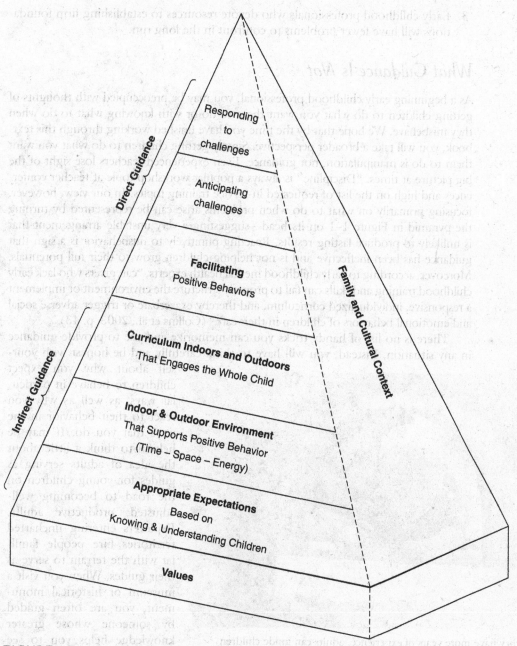

Direct Guidance

Responding
to
challenges

Anticipating
challenges

Facilitating
Positive Behaviors

Family and Cultural Context

Indirect Guidance

Curriculum Indoors and Outdoors
That Engages the Whole Child

Indoor & Outdoor Environment
That Supports Positive Behavior
(Time – Space – Energy)

Appropriate Expectations
Based on
Knowing & Understanding Children

Values

FIGURE 1–1 The guidance pyramid.

conceptualizes the topic of guidance. The image of a three-dimensional pyramid illustrates three fundamental concepts that underlie this textbook:

1. Each element of guidance creates a foundation for the one above.
2. All the elements depend upon—and reflect—family and cultural context, as well as personal and social values.
3. Early childhood professionals who devote resources to establishing firm foundations will have fewer problems to confront in the long run.

What Guidance Is Not

As a beginning early childhood professional, you may be preoccupied with thoughts of getting children to do what you want them to do or with knowing what to do when they misbehave. We hope that by the time you have finished working through this textbook, you will take a broader perspective. Simply getting children to do what you want them to do is manipulation, not guidance. Even experienced teachers lose sight of the big picture at times. "Discipline" is always a popular workshop topic at teacher conferences and high on the list of requested in-service training topics. In our view, however, focusing primarily on what to do when problems arise can be represented by turning the pyramid in Figure 1–1 on its head—suggesting a very unstable arrangement that is unlikely to produce lasting results. Reacting punitively to misbehavior is a sign that guidance has been ineffective and is not helping children grow to their full potentials. Moreover, according to early childhood mental health experts, "caregivers who lack early childhood training and skills can fail to properly structure the environment or implement a responsive, individualized curriculum, and thereby exacerbate or trigger adverse social and emotional behaviors of children in their care" (Collins et al., 2003, p. 43).

There is no list of handy tricks you can memorize and use to provide guidance in any situation. Instead, you will have to think carefully and be honest with yourself about why you expect children to behave in particular ways, as well as why you react to their behavior in the ways that you do. It may be helpful to think a little about the idea of adults serving as guides for young children on the road to becoming well-adjusted, productive adults. Explorers entering uncharted territories hire people familiar with the terrain to serve as their guides. When you visit a museum or historical monument, you are often guided by someone whose greater knowledge helps you to see and understand more of the

Because they have more years of experience, adults can guide children along the path to becoming well-adjusted, productive adults.

exhibit. In each case, the guide's greater knowledge and experience helps you reach your own goal. In a similar way, adults, who have more years of experience in a particular culture than children do, can help children do what they all desperately want to do: become powerful, independent "grown-ups."

Professional Concern for High-Quality Guidance

Within the early childhood profession, the need for high-quality, developmentally appropriate guidance is addressed at many levels. Licensing standards set by state governments establish a minimum acceptable level of quality to protect the safety and welfare of children in care. Guidance techniques are addressed in those standards, often in the form of prohibiting corporal punishment or other actions deemed harmful to children. Adherence to these standards is mandatory, and the law establishes penalties for failing to do so.

Programs may also elect to exceed these minimum requirements, using a variety of tools to assess and improve the quality of programs for young children (e.g., Harms, Clifford, & Cryer, 1998). Other standards are designed for specific types of programs, such as those serving young children with disabilities and their families (Hemmeter, Joseph, Smith, & Sandall, 2001), or family child-care homes (National Association for Family Child Care, 2003). In addition to standards for programs, some standards apply to individuals working with children; for example, the competencies required for the Child Development Associate (CDA) credential include many items related to child guidance. The CDA is a system that trains and provides credentials for persons who work in child-care centers.

The National Association for the Education of Young Children sets standards at two levels: for programs serving young children and for colleges and universities preparing candidates to work in such programs. Concepts related to appropriate guidance are woven throughout each set of standards. For example, early childhood teacher preparation programs at the associate, bachelor, and graduate levels must strive to ensure that candidates know how to use knowledge of child development to "create healthy, respectful, supportive, and challenging learning environments for young children" (NAEYC, 2010, p. 29) and to use a "broad repertoire of effective strategies and tools to help young children learn and develop well," including handling challenging behaviors appropriately (p. 34).

Center accreditation standards (NAEYC, 2007b) address guidance in the context of promoting "positive relationships among all children and adults" and requires programs to "encourage each child's sense of individual worth and belonging as part of a community and to foster each child's ability to contribute as a responsible community member" (2007b, p. 14). Specific criteria related to this standard call for staff to create a positive emotional climate and encourage children's appropriate expression of emotions. Other criteria prohibit corporal punishment, threats, or derogatory remarks.

WHAT SHAPES YOUR APPROACH TO GUIDANCE?

Effective guidance requires that you learn to consider many factors as you decide what to do and what to say to influence children's behavior. Your values derived from your own upbringing, your knowledge of what is considered best for children, and your personal beliefs will all be important factors. You may find that you have some habits that you would like to change. In fact, a frequent comment of early childhood students who have already reared their children is, "I wish I'd known these things when my children were growing up." These students discover—through the opportunity to study and through opportunities to work and observe under the guidance of an experienced early childhood education teacher—dimensions of child rearing that were not apparent to them in their earlier years.

Values

Values are your ideas about what is good or desirable. You acquire your personal values through life experiences, through exposure to the ideas of others, and through the teaching and example of important people in your life. While your particular set of values may not be identical to anyone else's, many of them are most likely shared with or derived from the values of the society in which you live; they include the goals or principles that people cherish. At the broadest level, a society's values are enshrined in both institutions such as Congress and fundamental documents such as the U.S. Constitution. For example, liberty, freedom, human dignity, and equality are basic values for Americans.

You translate these values into action for young children when you help them learn to make responsible choices and to act accordingly without ever-present authority persons. Although they might not use such abstract words, children will

Your values shape the guidance you provide young children. This teacher's obvious enthusiasm is reflected in the children's rapt attention and suggests a belief that learning should be joyful.

learn through practice to understand and to respect rights to liberty, freedom, human dignity, and equality for others. In fact, if you listen carefully, they may astonish you with the depth of their thinking about these subjects. Elizabeth Clarkson, a teacher at Boulder Journey School, found that the children's own values of freedom, movement, and safety were reflected in their ideas as they designed and constructed an elaborate "city" for their classroom hamster. Discussing the subject, they put themselves in the hamster's place and said, "If I was stuck in my cage and someone let me out, I would say that I appreciated it and I wouldn't bite anyone anymore." "I would say, 'Please let me out of this dumb cage'" (Hall & Rudkin, 2011, pp. 69–70).

Understanding Child Development

In the first episode at the opening of this chapter, it is obviously important to Mei-Li and the teacher that Mei-Li master the climber/slide. Do you suppose this skill will make Mei-Li feel more competent and develop a more positive self-concept? Are feelings of competence and confidence important for a child to have? Do other skills demand some of the muscle coordination learned in climbing and sliding? Does learning one skill facilitate learning other skills? You'll think about these questions and more as you study child guidance.

In the second example, do you think the fact that the child has a developmental delay should make a difference in how the teacher responds to the child's destructive behavior? What about the feelings of the other children in the episode?

Personal Beliefs

In the final example, do you think young children are capable of racial or ethnic prejudice? Do you think adults should talk to them about these matters? Does your own cultural and ethnic background make a difference in what you would do or say in this situation? What about your prior experiences of feeling left out or relating to people who are different from you?

Stop reading for a moment and think through these questions. Think of other situations that pose important questions about guidance and development. How much difference would children's ages make in what behavior you'd be willing to accept and what behavior you'd decide to stop or redirect? For example, we accept wetting in infants—we plan for it and adjust to it. However, wetting one's pants is not typically accepted behavior for a five-year-old with no mental or physical disability, and most people would want to find some guidance technique that would effectively teach a five-year-old to use the bathroom.

The primary focus in this textbook is on interacting with young children to support their social and emotional development. In other courses you may focus on the curriculum or on the administration of a center or on theories of child development. Just as it is impossible to completely separate social and emotional development from the physical and cognitive domains, you will see that there is a close relationship between guidance and these other areas of expertise.

GOALS OF GUIDANCE: CULTURAL AND INDIVIDUAL VARIATIONS

Effective guidance requires serious thought by parents, teachers, and caregivers. The adults you observe may seem to act spontaneously, but they probably have many ideas about the kind of people they want children to become. Those ideas come into play, often unconsciously, each time they interact with children. We begin to acquire our ideas about desirable behaviors and traits from earliest infancy. Often we are unaware that we hold a particular idea until we encounter someone who believes something that is different from what we believe.

Often such differences of opinion are a reflection of cultural differences. Early childhood educators have become more aware of, and developed a greater appreciation for, the important role these differences play in our work with children and families. For example, some parents and teachers, particularly those from an Anglo-European background, are eager to cultivate children's independence in feeding, toileting, and dressing themselves. They may be critical of adults who "do too many things" for children that children could do for themselves. Other cultures place a higher value on relationships and interdependence. A teacher in Italy, asked why she didn't teach her three-year-olds how to put on their own coats, responded that she would then be deprived of the opportunity to embrace each child individually.

The topic of cultural diversity will be addressed in greater detail in Chapter 4. It is important to note at this point that differences *within* particular groups can be as great as or greater than those *between* groups. To assume or act as if every member of a particular cultural group thinks in a particular way is to perpetuate stereotypes. You can probably see this for yourself by discussing the kinds of people you want young children to become with your classmates, friends, or family members. You may get responses such as these:

"I want my child to learn to make responsible decisions about how to behave without me being there all the time."

"I want a child to be a leader."

We begin to acquire our ideas about desirable behaviors and traits from earliest infancy, often following the model of the important adults in our lives.

Someone might say, "I don't want a child to be afraid or whiny." Often, as in this example, what you *don't* want in a child's behavior is easier to state than what you *do* want. A positive way of expressing the same idea might be, "I want a child to be courageous and confident and to speak up with assurance."

❀ Talk It Over ❀

What kind of people do you want today's children to become? Make a list of characteristics that you think are most important for young children to develop. List the characteristics in order of priority—the most important one first. Compare your list with those compiled by your classmates. Try to identify reasons for similarities and differences that might be due to your individual and cultural backgrounds.

There are many possible statements of desirable qualities in children. When you put together the statements, you get an idea of the kind of people you want guidance to help produce. This textbook assumes that many or most parents and teachers want children to learn the following:

1. To be able to take charge of their own behavior and to do the right thing when no one is watching (self-direction)

2. To care about and be able to get along with other people (relationships)

3. To be able to achieve satisfaction through work and make productive contributions to society (self-actualization)

These goals align with the "essential life skills" identified by Ellen Galinsky, whose recent exhaustive review of research on children and learning underscores the idea that social-emotional attributes or dispositions are as crucial as intellectual ability for achieving fulfillment in life (Galinsky, 2010).

Self-Direction

This goal is certainly consistent with values of freedom and liberty. In totalitarian states, citizens are under constant surveillance, and failure to conform to the expectations of authority is severely punished. A democratic society,

Most adults want children to care about and be able to get along with other people.

however, depends on citizens to act responsibly of their own free will, even questioning authority if it contradicts their notions of right and wrong. Helping children achieve this level of self-direction requires a view of guidance that goes far beyond the notion of getting children to comply with our wishes. It requires that adults gradually relinquish more and more control and responsibility to growing children.

Relationships

Italian educator Loris Malaguzzi (1998) said that relationship is the essence of education. Some might even say that relationship is the essence of a successful life: Consider its role in marriage, work, family, and community. Research shows us that children who cannot make friends by the time they get to elementary school are at serious risk of dropping out when they get to high school. The ability to form and maintain healthy, rewarding relationships is essential at every age. Early childhood educators have an important responsibility to help children feel connected to others.

Self-Actualization

According to psychologist Abraham Maslow (1968), human needs can be viewed in a hierarchy, beginning with physical survival needs and culminating in the highest need, that of self-actualization. Self-actualization means that a person finds meaning and fulfillment in using his or her potential to the fullest. Not every adult is fortunate enough to achieve this level of fulfillment, but even young children can experience a taste of it if they are supported by caring adults who take the time to learn what it is the children are trying to do and then help them to do it.

OUR APPROACH TO GUIDANCE

A Developmental Perspective

Starting at birth—some would argue even earlier—children learn continuously as they develop and mature. They have an instinctive inclination to become increasingly competent members of their society. As they achieve each milestone on the developmental ladder, they use that accomplishment to push themselves toward the next milestone or goal. Adults encourage this natural striving by setting the stage for children to experience the joy of practicing and exploring their new skills, thus helping them prepare to move forward. Ensuring the child's safety during the progression from one milestone to the next is part of guidance. An example of a milestone is an infant's ability to roll over. At about the fourth or fifth month, most infants will be able to roll over in bed. However, even before this time, babies become unsafe on an adult bed because they develop the ability to use their toes to move forward and can reach the edge, fall off, and get hurt. Responsible adults must always be sure the baby is safely in a crib with sides.

In your study of child guidance, you will learn to support children through the various stages of their development. Researchers have designated typical stages of development for parents and teachers to watch for as children grow. You'll have the benefit of this research without having to discover it all by yourself. Always remember, though, that each child is unique and reaches each developmental stage at his or her own rate. Your task will be to observe closely the children you work with to see just where each one is on the developmental ladder. When you recognize where each child is developmentally, you can use that information in planning your guidance and activities for the child. This is called developmentally appropriate planning, and it is very different from using knowledge of developmental stages to judge a particular child or group of children as deficient.

Developmentally appropriate planning means taking three factors into account: (1) what we know about children in general and how they develop; (2) what we know about the specific children in a particular setting or group; and (3) what we know about the beliefs, values, and customs of those children's families and communities.

For example, to be developmentally appropriate, the room and play yard for toddlers will be arranged and equipped differently from those used by kindergarteners. Also, the guidance and curriculum the teachers use will differ widely due to the social, mental, and motor skill differences of the two age groups. And for either age group, the materials and interaction styles should reflect the cultures of the families whose children are being taught. As you progress through your early childhood curriculum, you'll become increasingly aware of the stages of children's development, and you'll learn how to apply your knowledge of those stages to the guidance and curriculum planning in the school or center.

❋ Talk It Over ❋

Compare your childhood experiences with those of a classmate. How were you expected to behave at mealtimes? At what age were you expected to dress yourself? How were you expected to speak to adults? What was considered misbehavior? How was it dealt with? Discuss how your responses to these questions illustrate the influence of individual and cultural differences on guidance.

A Positive, Strengths-Based Approach

This book is grounded in an image of children as intelligent, strong, and capable, as citizens with rights and responsibilities (Malaguzzi, 1994/2005; Hall & Rudkin, 2011). It emphasizes recognizing and encouraging healthy, positive behavior in a child. Another, unfortunately prevalent, view of children as needy, deficient, and in need of shaping to become citizens of some future time often means that one episode of negative behavior—say, a fight between two children—gets much attention from observers and teachers, while hundreds of positive exchanges go unnoticed. In this book we approach the study of guidance for young children from a developmental perspective that involves a positive or wellness viewpoint rather than a negative or sickness viewpoint. This difference is important and will become clearer to you as your knowledge about child development and early childhood education progresses.

Every child is unique and reaches each developmental stage at his or her own rate.

Positive guidance means that you'll use your professional know-how to support children's growth and development; you will give them credit for having their own ideas and aspirations rather than simply imposing yours. Children should always be treated with respect and dignity. A positive approach to guidance makes children and others feel confident, competent, and happy. A positive approach does not include shaming, humiliation, ridicule, or pressure to compete, nor is it punitive, impatient, mean, or bossy.

Focusing on problems or sickness rather than on strengths or wellness is a negative approach that is seldom effective and, consequently, represents a misdirection of adult guidance. A person who focuses entirely on a child's negative or problem behavior, such as hitting, doesn't necessarily correct the problem behavior. In fact, by giving attention to the problem, one may be reinforcing the negative behavior, causing it to persist. On the other hand, recognizing the positive behavior of a child through respectful attention is likely to increase the occurrence of that behavior. As children begin to think more positively about themselves, problem behaviors tend to diminish. This leads to still more positive responses from other people, which will continue the cycle, contributing to improved self-image and increasingly improved behavior.

Here is an example of what we mean by seeing things from a wellness standpoint. A child who speaks Spanish in this English-speaking country might be deemed to have a problem or deficiency, and efforts might be made to eliminate the use of Spanish as quickly as possible. From the wellness standpoint, however, this child has language skills that can be the basis for learning more Spanish *and* for learning English, certainly an asset in a nation of rapidly expanding diversity and an increasingly globalized economy. The first approach, viewing a difference as a deficit or sickness, was typical in the United States before the more recent bilingual and bicultural approaches were developed and implemented for children using other languages. Bilingualism may not be feasible in every situation, but it is nearly always possible to make a child feel more comfortable by learning a few words of his or her home language.

An example of an issue that is best addressed using the wellness rather than sickness approach is thumb sucking. Some young children tend to keep their thumbs in their mouths for a variety of reasons. Using a wellness approach, adults accept or deliberately ignore such behavior and concentrate on giving the child interesting activities to do with the consequence that the thumb sucking diminishes. The sickness approach, however, focuses attention on the thumb sucking. Often the adult may shame or scold the child for such behavior. The resulting attention may actually encourage the persistence of the undesired behavior. In the process, parents may become unduly concerned and less effective in dealing with the behavior.

Just as children who are developing typically are helped through life's challenges by focusing on their strengths and competencies, children whose development may not be typical are best served when we see the child first, and then the disability. Children who use wheelchairs, for example, need to feel competent and part of the group, just as all other children do. Even children who seem cut off from human contact can be guided toward relationships if we focus on their strength and potential.

Psychiatrist Stanley Greenspan (1997), a recognized pioneer of new, effective ways of helping children with autism, advocates that therapists, instead of trying to eliminate peculiar or alarming behaviors, use those very behaviors as a way to open communication with the child. He tells the story of a two-year-old girl who never spoke or responded to others but stared into space, rubbing at a spot on the carpet for hours at a time. Through therapy, her mother learned to respond to this behavior in a playful way, repeatedly putting her hand on that particular spot and having her hand pushed away by the little girl. Not long after, the little girl's smiles showed that she enjoyed this interchange, and the therapist suggested that the mother add sound effects to their games, leading eventually to the girl making her own sounds. "Today," according to Greenspan, "at age seven, this girl has a range of age-appropriate emotions, warm friendships, and a lively imagination. She argues as well as her lawyer father, and scores in the low-superior IQ range" (pp. 16–17). Imagine the different outcome this story might have had if the therapist had, instead of focusing on the girl's potential, provided a regimen of reinforcements designed to extinguish her "deviant" behavior!

What you see and hear will always be only a partial picture of a particular child or event, and it will be filtered through the lenses of your particular background and experience.

Early childhood professionals in the United States who have long advocated such a positive approach have acquired eloquent support from Italy. The small northern Italian city of Reggio Emilia has become world renowned for the excellence of its infant-toddler and early childhood programs. Over and over, the educators responsible for those programs have been asked for the secret behind their excellence. The answer invariably begins with an image of the child as strong, competent, and full of potential—in contrast to a child seen as weak, needy, and full of deficits to be corrected.

Limits on Behavior.   Emphasizing children's power and potential does not mean that "anything goes." On the contrary, there will be many times when it will be up to you to set reasonable limits on children's behavior. The existence of such limits helps children feel secure and more able to focus their energy on growing and learning. Your study, observation, and practice will help you learn how to develop and enforce appropriate limits.

"Tyrone, kick the ball. It hurts Jamal when you kick him," is an example of an appropriate limit. Notice that it is stated in a positive way so that Tyrone knows what he *can* do as well as why he should stop what he was doing. Certainly adults will set limits, both in homes and in child development centers, to help children learn to respect other children's play space or learning environment, to respect their own and others' personal comfort and safety, and to respect furnishings and equipment.

You can expect to tell children what the limits are many times before the limits become part of the children's regular behavior. Always explain and enforce the limits in a spirit of preserving each child's dignity, in a manner that is nurturing and supportive rather than harsh or coercive. Many of the lessons children learn from your guidance will be applicable at home, in the community, and in interactions with older children as well.

Whose Problem Is It?   Some so-called behavior problems of children are actually adults' problems. That is, the "problems" really don't impede the child's development, but adults may feel that the behavior must be curtailed, stopped, or redirected. Noise is an example. Most children thrive in noisy settings, but grumpy neighbors, classes down the hall, or unsympathetic principals may require that children learn to use excessively "quiet voices" or "quiet feet." Inhibiting children's natural spontaneity then becomes the goal of some adult guidance. Adults should analyze the behaviors that bother them and that they have the impulse to stop. They should consider whether there are good reasons for stopping such behaviors in children.

✺   **Talk It Over**   ✺

Recall something you did as a child that bothered adults around you. What steps did they take to stop or change your behavior? How did you feel about that? What are things children do or say that bother some adults yet do not seem to bother the children?

As a student of child guidance, you'll develop skill in determining whether a "problem" belongs to children or adults, and you'll perhaps find ways of helping children and adults understand the difference. Finding legitimate outlets for children's spontaneity and avoiding placing heavy blame on children for acting like children are significant tasks that you will learn.

DEVELOPING YOUR GUIDANCE SKILLS

Your institution may have arranged a site where you can observe and interact with children and their teachers in action in order to learn the principles of guidance more thoroughly. This will give you an opportunity to put some of what you are learning into practice and gain a more practical understanding of theoretical concepts.

Participation

Participating with children while you are learning is a privilege for you, and you should treat it as such by showing respect for the center staff, children, and parents. They will expect you to be a learner, not a polished teacher; thus, you should learn from observing others, learn from asking questions, and learn from experimenting with the various techniques presented in your class and reading. If your instructor provides specific assignments or guidelines for your lab experiences, be sure to review them carefully before going to the center.

Be sure to attend as scheduled and to be prompt, just as the teaching staff is required to do. Call in as directed for an excused absence only when a serious illness prevents your attendance. Participate in any planned pre- or post-session conferences. Question the teacher about any instructions you don't understand thoroughly. Volunteer cheerfully for tasks. This shows your interest and your willingness to carry your share of the load. Ask for feedback on your participation, especially for suggestions for improvement. If you were perfect, you would not need the course!

When you are in a center, you are part of a team and should be supportive of the other team members. You should carry out your assigned duties as effectively as you can. Ask to work in all areas to gain a broad experience. Try to anticipate what your team members need and respond accordingly. Though you may

Participating with children while you are learning provides opportunities to enjoy one of the most rewarding aspects of this career: helping children achieve their potential and sharing their joy when they succeed.

be able to ask for direction, remember that the teachers have to give primary attention to the children, and your needs may have to be considered later—most likely at the end of the day.

Observation

You will learn many things through carefully observing children, teachers, and parents. Observation means that you look closely, watch for patterns of behavior, and see and hear subtle shades of differences in actions, words, and feelings of children and adults. In Chapter 3, you will find descriptions and examples of several different tools you can use to record your observations.

Learning to observe objectively, recording what you see and hear rather than your opinions and judgments, is an important goal, although it is one that is never fully achieved. What you see and hear will always be only a partial picture of a particular child or event, and it will always be filtered through the lenses of your particular background and experience. Knowing this should not discourage you but rather strengthen your resolve to become aware of your own biases and to seek information from more than one source before interpreting what a particular behavior means or deciding what, if anything, you should do about it.

Often you may need to make observation notes just when you are involved in helping with children's activities such as dressing, toileting, or painting. Thus, you may have to jot down reminders in a small notebook to be filled in more completely when the children don't require your attention. Remember to complete your notes at the earliest possible moment, before your memory fades.

As you progress through the chapters in this book, you will find suggestions for things to watch for as you observe. It is your privilege to be working with children. Protect that privilege by treating with confidentiality the things you see and hear. Discuss your observations only with the instructor of your course and the children's teachers. If you have a question about how to handle a child's behavior, your instructor and the child's teacher are the people to ask. If you observe practices that seem not to measure up to the standards described in this text, discuss them with your instructor and reflect on what you would do differently if you were in charge. Raising issues that concern you, professionally and in the appropriate context, will help you clarify your ideas and feelings and may help other students who have similar questions.

The Learning Cycle

Learning has been described as a cyclical process that continues throughout life. According to Bredekamp and Rosegrant (1992, p. 32), this cycle begins when you first become aware of a new concept or phenomenon and moves through phases of exploration and inquiry until you are able to use your new knowledge or skill. As you use what you have learned, you become aware of new areas in which you lack understanding, thus beginning the cycle over again.

Consider the example of infant LaToyah learning to speak. As she gradually becomes aware of patterns of sounds made by adults around her, she begins to explore her own ability to make a variety of sounds and, eventually, words. Anyone who has ever spent time with toddlers knows the joy they take in the next phase (inquiry), pointing to one object after another, looking up inquisitively, and pronouncing some approximation of "What's that?" Not long after, they are using language to relate stories, ask questions, make demands, and take full part in conversations around them—which opens up all sorts of new areas for the cycle to begin again.

Just as this cyclical pattern applies to young children, it applies to you as you study the concepts presented in this book. This book will raise your awareness of aspects of child development and guidance that you might not have considered before. By presenting explanations and examples of the concepts and by asking you to think about and respond to specific questions throughout the chapters, this book will help you move to the next step of exploration. Participating in a laboratory setting with young children will give you lots of opportunities to explore ways of supporting children's growing self-management. Your own unique life experiences and prior knowledge will come into play as you read, reflect, and interact with young children to form your own understandings of child guidance concepts.

The next step will be for you to compare your understandings with those of other people, to check your ideas against reality as you move from exploration to inquiry. Writing about your experiences with children and discussing ideas with your classmates and your instructor will help you do this. Finally, you will be able to use your new knowledge and skill with confidence as you interact with young children. This does not mean that you will wake up one day, ready to assume complete responsibility for guiding the development of young children. It means that you will gradually become more comfortable in an increasing variety of situations.

Perhaps the idea that it is sometimes an effective means of guidance to ignore children's behavior seems strange to you, or perhaps you remember times when you or someone you know has done just that and successfully influenced a child's behavior. In either case, at this point, you might be described as having awareness of this concept.

Next, reflect upon possible reasons why deliberately ignoring behavior might be an effective guidance tool. In other words, explore the idea. You might continue this exploration by watching for examples of adults ignoring children's behavior, either in a child-care facility or in public places, like shopping malls and playgrounds, or in other places where you can observe adults and children interacting.

Moving into the inquiry phase, you might begin to ask yourself questions about what you observe: Does ignoring behavior work with all children? If not, what might account for the differences in effectiveness? Is the age of the child a factor? What about the type of behavior that is being ignored? You might carry on your inquiry by discussing what you have observed with your classmates and your instructor. You might consult other books about child development and psychology to discover possible reasons for successes and failures of this technique.

Finally, you might gain enough confidence to begin to purposefully ignore certain types of behavior in certain situations. But your new knowledge and skill will also sensitize you to the many situations where ignoring is not appropriate, and, as you acquire awareness of those situations, you will begin the cycle again, exploring, inquiring, and using what you learn.

CONCLUSION

Infants come into the world endowed with tremendous human potential for growing, developing, and learning. As a parent, teacher, or caregiver, you have an exciting opportunity to become part of a team of adults who foster the development of that potential through careful, thoughtful guidance techniques. This book can help you learn some effective methods of interacting with children and influencing their behavior. Some of these methods have been discovered by parents and teachers through trial and error. Other methods have been developed and tested by researchers.

Expectations for children's behavior are shaped by what you believe children are capable of doing; the more you know about how children grow and develop, the more realistic and appropriate your expectations will be. Decisions about the ways in which behavior should be influenced are based upon values or ideas of what is right and good. As you strive to guide young children, you will need to think about how your values align with those of the families whose children you serve and find ways to negotiate differences.

You will be developing your own teaching and parenting style as you study, observe, and gain experience. Because you are a unique person with your own personality, cultural background, and life history, your style can be expected to differ somewhat from other people's—even if you share similar high standards concerning the understanding, nurturing, and teaching of young children. Your knowledge, your ability to think deeply and well, and your empathetic understanding of children are all essential. Being humble about what you know and using your best judgment will be helpful. When guiding children and helping parents, few rules apply 100 percent of the time. Because of the uniqueness of humans and human interaction, making hard-and-fast rules and prescriptions is unwise. What you study here is thus designed to help you become aware of possibilities and of methods that have worked for others. You can be observant and apply the information as creatively as possible. Child development, child guidance, and early childhood education are still young fields; even the experts have much to learn. Now that you have chosen to study child guidance, you can help with this exciting and forward-looking quest.

REVIEW: TEN THINGS TO REMEMBER ABOUT GUIDANCE

1. Guidance is defined as everything adults deliberately do and say, either directly or indirectly, to influence children's behavior, with the goal of helping the children become well-adjusted, self-directed, productive adults.

2. The study of guidance contributes to intentionality in professional practice: knowing what you are doing and why and being able to explain it to others.

3. An individual's approach to guidance is influenced by values, knowledge of child development, and personal beliefs.

4. Three commonly accepted goals of guidance are self-direction, ability to form and maintain positive relationships, and self-actualization.

5. Effective guidance is grounded in developmentally appropriate practice, reflecting knowledge of children in general and knowledge of individual children, their families, and communities.

6. Effective guidance is positive, emphasizing children's strengths and building on them.

7. Setting appropriate, reasonable limits for behavior is part of effective guidance.

8. Effective guidance requires self-awareness and the ability to recognize that some so-called "behavior problems" are actually examples of adults' personal peeves.

9. Licensing agencies and professional organizations (such as NAEYC) have established guidelines for appropriate guidance.

10. Participation and observation in settings for young children are important complements to the study of guidance concepts as you proceed through the cycle of learning from awareness, to exploration, to inquiry, and finally to application.

APPLICATIONS

1. Think about the teacher on the playground with Mei-Li in the vignette at the beginning of this chapter. What did she do and say? Why do you think she chose those actions and words? Did she demonstrate intentionality?

2. Review the definition of guidance and the example of Randy in the block corner at the beginning of the chapter. Describe how a teacher using a guidance approach would respond. How would that differ from what another teacher, more interested in controlling behavior, might do?

3. Recall the third example from the beginning of the chapter (about Rosa on the playground). Write down what you thought you would do in that situation. Reflect on your response: Explain how it reflects (a) values; (b) your knowledge of development; and (c) your personal beliefs.

4. Give examples of how knowledge of child development might influence a teacher's expectations for behavior at different ages (e.g., sharing toys, waiting for a turn, listening quietly at story time, using "good" table manners). How would knowledge of child development affect the way a teacher responds to children's behavior?

5. Write a paragraph describing your *image of the child* (i.e., your beliefs about what young children are like, what they are capable of, and what they deserve). Save this and review it from time to time to see whether (or how) your image changes as you continue to work with and learn about children.

RESOURCES FOR FURTHER STUDY

Websites

National Association for the Education of Young Children
naeyc.org
A national professional organization for individuals working with or on behalf of children ages birth through 8 years and their families. The site includes links to position statements (e.g., regarding professional preparation of early childhood educators), other organizations, and resources for early childhood educators.

The Division for Early Childhood of the Council for Exceptional Children

dec-sped.org

The early childhood division of the national professional organization for special educators. The site includes resources and position statements regarding programs for children with disabilities or developmental delays.

Mind in the Making

mindinthemaking.org

A website devoted to promulgating the ideas in the book *Mind in the Making: The Seven Essential Life Skills Every Child Needs* (Galinsky, 2010). Includes links to articles and videos related to each of the seven skills.

Readings

Copple, C., & Bredekamp, S. (eds.). (2009). *Developmentally appropriate practice in early childhood programs serving children from birth through age 8.* Washington, DC: National Association for the Education of Young Children.

Copple, C., & Bredekamp, S. (2005). *Basics of developmentally appropriate practice.* Washington, DC: National Association for the Education of Young Children.

Epstein, A. (2009). *Me, you, us: Social-emotional learning in preschool.* Ypsilanti, MI: HighScope Press.

Frost, J. L. (2007, Summer). The changing culture of childhood: A perfect storm. *Childhood Education, 83*(4), 225–230.

Gartrell, D. (2006). *A guidance approach for the encouraging classroom* (4th ed.). Albany, NY: Thomson Delmar Learning.

Hearron, P., & Hildebrand, V. (2011). *Management of child development centers* (7th ed.). Upper Saddle River, NJ: Pearson.

Kostelnik, M., Gregory, K., Soderman, A., & Whiren, A. (2012). *Guiding children's social development and learning* (7th ed.). Belmont, CA: Wadsworth.

CHAPTER 2

Values as a Basis for Guidance

Learning Outcomes

After studying this chapter you should be able to

- Understand the relationship between *values* and *guidance*.
- Explain how types of decisions are influenced by values.
- Identify values embodied in professional standards for practice.
- Discuss the relationship between *values* and *evaluation*.
- Explain the connection between *values* and *ethics*.
- Identify strategies for reconciling value differences.

Four-year-old Jamal struggles to get his arms into the sleeves of his coat, rejecting all offers of assistance with a vehement, "I can do it myself." The rest of the class is almost ready, and even though the teacher, Mr. Moore, is concerned that they will soon be waiting impatiently to head outdoors, he recognizes and wants to respect Jamal's fierce desire for independence. He is also worried because he thinks outdoor playtime is important, and teachers in this large program have worked out a schedule so each group gets a turn to use the playground. If Mr. Moore doesn't adhere to the plan, he will create a domino effect, disrupting his colleagues' plans for the day. Meanwhile, his group's scheduled 45-minute period is ticking away.

In this seemingly insignificant moment in the daily life of a child development program—one of hundreds that occur every day, if not every hour—Mr. Moore must decide among several competing values: respecting individuals' needs, respecting the rights of the group, following through on agreements with his colleagues, and adhering to institutional rules. What would you do if you were in Mr. Moore's shoes?

VALUES AND GUIDANCE

In Chapter 1 we defined *guidance* as "everything adults deliberately do and say, either directly or indirectly, to influence children's behavior, with the goal of helping the children become well-adjusted, self-directed, productive adults." In other words, we said guidance can be viewed as the process of helping children live up to society's expectations of its members. We said that if we are going to help children achieve these long-term goals, we need to know something about the sequence of development they are likely to pass through along the way. We may hope, for example, that children grow up to become caring, compassionate adults, considerate of others' feelings. If we have studied theories of emotional development, we don't expect these traits to blossom overnight. At the same time, mindful of the fact that theoretical knowledge must be evaluated and sometimes modified in light of experience, we can be alert for—and take delight in—exceptions, such as occasions when the youngest baby takes a favorite book to a crying playmate, clearly aware of and concerned about that child's feelings.

But how do we decide that caring, compassion, and consideration for others' feelings are part of being a "well-adjusted, self-directed, productive adult"? Who determines the expectations of a society? For that matter, in a pluralistic society, which group's expectations should be the norm by which individuals are judged? Answers to these complex questions require an understanding of the concept of values, and of the tightly interwoven relationship between values and culture.

VALUES—THE BASIS OF DECISIONS

Values are at the foundation of all adults' decisions regarding what to do with children. (See Figure 2–1.)

To value something is to consider it worthwhile or desirable. Values, which are often abstract ideals, are translated into the "oughts" and "shoulds" that guide our actions. People express values when they say things like the following:

- Children ought to obey adults.
- Teachers should treat all children equally.
- Families ought to participate in school activities.
- Society should provide safety nets for any family that is unable to earn a living wage.
- Children should be protected from images of war and violence on television or in video games.

These are all statements of values: for authority, fairness, education, social justice, and the right of vulnerable individuals to freedom from psychological or emotional harm.

Your values are reflected in your behavior and determine the goals you set and the actions that grow from your goals. Many values may be unconscious until you work at bringing them to the level of awareness or search for the implicit values on which your actions or the actions of others are, in fact, based. It may even surprise you to learn that your actions are not always consistent with your stated values.

Where do values come from in your own scheme of things? Actually, you've been acquiring them all your life, from your family, your friends, and your community,

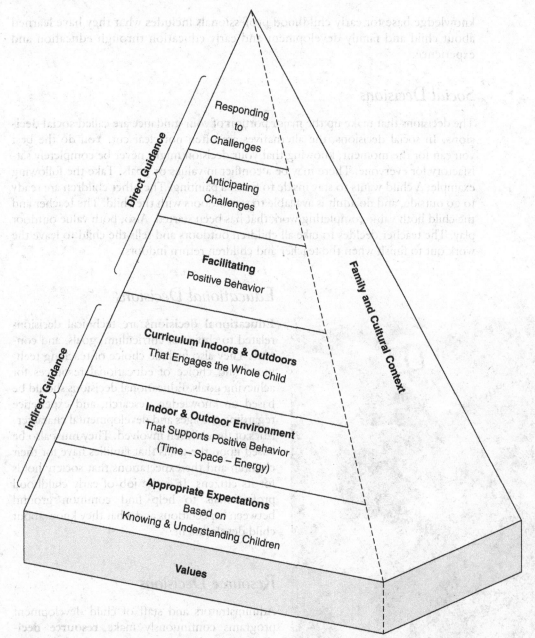

Direct Guidance

Responding
to
Challenges

Anticipating
Challenges

Facilitating
Positive Behavior

Curriculum Indoors & Outdoors
That Engages the Whole Child

Indoor & Outdoor Environment
That Supports Positive Behavior
(Time – Space – Energy)

Appropriate Expectations
Based on
Knowing & Understanding Children

Values

Indirect Guidance

Family and Cultural Context

FIGURE 2–1   The guidance pyramid: Values

including your schooling. Values get firmly set early in life and are difficult to change. They relate to such things as family, religion, economics, politics, work, play, health, freedom, individuality, order, and beauty. What are the "oughts" or "shoulds" related to each of these concepts that immediately come to your mind?

Professionals in every field are decision makers. They base decisions on specialized knowledge as well as on their personal and professional values. The knowledge base for early childhood professionals includes what they have learned about child and family development and early education through education and experience.

Social Decisions

The decisions that make up the major portion of your guidance are called **social decisions**. In social decisions, the alternatives are often not clear-cut. You do the best you can for the moment, knowing that your decision might never be completely satisfactory for everyone. There may be a conflict in values or goals. Take the following example: A child wants to stay inside to finish a painting. The other children are ready to go outside, and no adult is available to stay indoors with the child. The teacher and the child both value completing work that has been started. Also, both value outdoor play. The teacher decides to take all children outdoors and tells the child to leave the work out to finish when the teacher and children return indoors.

These children are checking to see if the eggplant growing in their garden is ready to harvest. What values are conveyed when adults help children care for plants and grow the food that they eat?

Educational Decisions

Educational decisions are technical decisions related to choice of curriculum, goals, and content. They also include choice of teaching technique and choice of educational resources for achieving goals. Educational decisions should be based on knowledge, research, and experience regarding the ages and developmental characteristics of the children involved. They must also be based upon the goals that families have for their children and the expectations that society holds for its citizens. It is the job of early childhood professionals to help find common ground between expectations and what they know about child development.

Resource Decisions

Administrators and staff of child development programs continuously make **resource decisions** when they allocate the means for achieving goals. Should we allocate the entire year's equipment budget for the purchase of a large fixed climbing structure on the playground, or should we look for inexpensive ways to provide more varied, nature-oriented experiences outdoors? Is it better to buy lots of commercially produced manipulative materials or to collect safe, clean materials recycled from community industries? How much time should be devoted to self-selected activity versus large group or circle time? How large an area should the block corner occupy in the classroom? Is there room in the budget to provide paid planning time for teachers? What items will have to be eliminated or reduced to do so? Will parent fees have to be raised?

In making decisions or choices, the decision maker must have enough information to recognize the alternatives. There is no opportunity for choice unless there are at least two alternatives. The consequences of classroom decisions will last a long time. Material or nonhuman resources are expendable and must be replenished. Human resources cannot be "used up," but the optimal time for their development and utilization may pass, never to occur again in the same way. A child's enthusiasm can be squelched instead of encouraged. One such instance may not seem earthshaking in itself, but the cumulative effect can be dispiriting for a child.

Is it wasteful of material resources for children to experiment with squeezing out more glue than an adult might think they need? What human resources (such as ingenuity, persistence, initiative, curiosity) might be fostered by allowing such experimentation?

❀   Talk It Over   ❀

What were the rules for sharing in your family? Were you expected to let brothers or sisters play with your toys? What about neighborhood children? What did your parents tell you you "ought" to do? What does this advice indicate about what your parents value? How did your parents teach you the rules? Compare your answers to these questions with your classmates' answers.

VALUES AND PROFESSIONAL STANDARDS

As an early childhood professional, you hold values; the families whose children you serve also hold values (which may be different from yours); and the children are developing their own values. Given the diversity of the U.S. population, the values within any single child development program are likely to be shaped by not one culture but by many cultures. Recent research (e.g., New, 1999) in international early childhood education has reemphasized the important role of culture in determining goals for children. All these viewpoints must be considered if you are to provide the best guidance for young children. Ironically, one of the values that characterizes our hypothetical "American culture" (which is more properly thought of as a conglomerate of many cultures) is awareness of and respect for differences (Szanton, 2001, p. 16). The U.S. Constitution, under which all U.S. professionals work, provides a framework for values and for actions. The concepts of equality, freedom, free speech, freedom of religion, and due process under the law are very strong value positions defined in the Constitution. The specific values that a profession might define must operate under all constitutional provisions. Any action of individuals working in any public service, such as an early childhood school or center, must respect these fundamental constitutional rights of the parents, children, or employees. According to Katz (1996, p. 141), "preparation for democracy may be one of the very few goals educators can still agree on."

Sometimes conflict arises between strongly supported values that seem incompatible with each other. Consider this example: Based on legal as well as moral and ethical grounds, an early childhood profession holds that children with disabilities should be included in programs with children who are developing typically. This value may come into conflict with the belief that all children should be served by high-quality programs if families have to choose between a segregated program set up to meet their child's particular needs with specialized equipment, smaller class size, and more highly trained teachers or an inclusive program with fewer of these benefits. Another potential values clash comes between the family-centered approach preferred by early interventionists and the child-centered approach that underlies many early childhood education programs. Thus, it is possible to hold one value contingent upon others; in the case of this example, for instance, it is possible to believe that children with special needs should be included in community-based programs only if they can receive high-quality, specialized, and family-centered services in those programs (Bailey, McWilliam, Buysse, & Wesley, 1998).

❈   Talk It Over   ❈

What professional values are implied in the following statement from a list of goals of early education for children who have special needs (Wolery, Strain, & Bailey, 1992, p. 96)?

> Children with disabilities ought to be able to participate in programs provided for children with typical development. In addition, teachers should use normal teaching strategies . . . and provide classrooms similar to those for normally abled children; and help children with disabilities learn skills that will promote transition into general classrooms.

Can personal values differ from constitutional and professional values? It may be theoretically conceivable for an individual manager or teacher to hold different personal values from the constitutional and agreed-upon professional values. However, the likelihood is that the individual would have many periods of discomfort and dissonance, since values determine so many interactions, decisions, and behaviors. Choosing to work in a particular profession generally means acceptance of that profession's widely held values.

Accreditation

The accreditation systems of the National Association for the Education of Young Children (NAEYC) and the National Association for Family Child Care (NAFCC) as well as the Council for Exceptional Children's Division for Early Childhood (CEC/DEC) Recommended Practices in Early Intervention/Early Childhood Education are highly developed statements of values held by members of the early childhood profession in the United States. To arrive at the final list of indicators or criteria of high quality in a program, each of these organizations consulted with a wide array of stakeholders (research experts, practitioners, parents, and advocates) to reach consensus on a list of criteria that could be field tested. Compromises were made to get agreement between the theoreticians and the practitioners. The resulting documents provide guidelines to which individuals both within and outside the profession can turn for measures of what programs "ought" to be.

The accreditation criteria of the NAEYC frequently mention the concept of *developmentally appropriate practice*—that is, practice that contributes to children's development. Like the accreditation criteria, the principles of developmentally appropriate practice are expressions of values held by the early childhood professionals who are members of NAEYC. Recommended practices of the CEC/DEC stem from explicitly stated values and beliefs about the rights of all children and families to be treated with respect and to have access to high-quality, comprehensive, coordinated, and family-centered services and supports. Children with disabilities or special needs are viewed as children first, with the right to participate meaningfully within their families and communities (Sandall, Hemmeter, Smith, & McLean, 2005, pp. 110–111). The accreditation standards of the NAFCC articulate the values placed on relationships, welcoming and comfortable environments, spontaneous play, developmentally appropriate learning goals, health and safety, and professionalism, with a goal of recognizing the special nature of high quality in the family child-care context.

As noted earlier, each professional organization's statement of values represents a consensus arrived at through years of discussion and debate among researchers and practitioners; each summarizes what the organization considers to be the best practices for children and families, based on what is known today. Members of the organizations agree to base their actions on those values, but they also have a voice

Good programs for children respect families and value their cultural heritage.

in reformulating these value statements as new knowledge and new ways of looking at things emerge.

The evolution of NAEYC's statement of *Developmentally Appropriate Practice* is an example of such reformulation. The first edition of this publication (1987) mentioned only age appropriateness and individual appropriateness in its definition of appropriate practice. Some argued that it gave the impression that there was only one right way to do things because of the way it contrasted appropriate and inappropriate practice. These criticisms prompted a great deal of dialogue among professionals, with the result that the revised edition (1997) referred to "developmentally appropriate practices," acknowledging that there can be many appropriate ways to help children grow and develop. The revised document also added the concept of social and cultural appropriateness to the ideas of age appropriateness and individual appropriateness, recognizing that good programs for children respect families and value their cultural heritages. Most recently, the document has undergone further revision in response to the ongoing dilemma of an academic "achievement gap" between poor children of color and their more advantaged peers. The third edition, greatly expanded, asserts that early childhood educators must address this gap and help children meet challenging, achievable goals, using practices based on evidence rather than assumptions (Copple & Bredekamp, 2009).

VALUES AND EVALUATION

When you examine the word *evaluation* ("to find the value of something"), you see that it is closely related to the concept of values. We have said that the values of parents, school, community, nation, and world all influence early childhood programs. Often values are implicit; that is, they are not specifically indicated. However, to evaluate programs or performance, values must be clearly stated. Values are often a source of much lively controversy, a healthy sign in a democratic society and the source of much progress. Differences and changing views in the area of values create fascinating problems for evaluation.

As if the challenges of articulating values and agreeing on them weren't enough, evaluation is further complicated by the fact that it seems to be human nature to feel uncomfortable or even fearful at the prospect of being evaluated or judged. Perhaps you have felt apprehensive when turning in a major class project for a grade or when meeting your future in-laws. Teachers feel nervous when the principal comes to observe their classrooms. Directors of child development centers worry when the licensing agent visits. Part of being professional is recognizing the importance of evaluation and approaching it calmly and objectively.

Who Evaluates? Who Needs Evaluation?

Managers Evaluate. The task of measuring program performance against standards most often falls to administrators. The managers, principals, and directors of early childhood programs act on behalf of their governing boards to ensure that program practices are living up to criteria or values that society holds for them. Where do the standards come from? They are established by the profession; they come from national, state, and local licensing and funding agencies; and they come from state departments of education and state departments of social services. Standards come from a parent board in a parent cooperative, a school board in public schools, or a board of directors in a private agency. Licensing bodies establish minimum standards in order to protect the safety and health of children in out-of-home settings. Professional organizations, such as NAEYC, CEC/DEC, and NAFCC, set higher benchmarks through their accreditation programs and recommended guidelines.

Practitioners Evaluate. Conscientious teachers and caregivers evaluate their practices all the time, every minute of the day. They make a decision, see the effects of the decision, and make adjustments—even in the immediate situation, if necessary—to remedy a situation that doesn't come up to standard. That's evaluation. Early childhood professionals set their own high standards and work to improve their practice, constantly searching for new ideas, new materials, and new ways to help children. They read professional journals, which give them new ideas to try and new standards to achieve. They go to school, take courses, read, and study. Actually, most good early childhood professionals do a far better job than minimum licensing standards require. If you have studied your state's licensing standards and the accreditation standards established by professional organizations such as NAEYC or NAFCC, you'll understand what you are working toward and what you'll be evaluated upon.

Children Evaluate. Children need evaluations of their child development programs because their day-to-day life experience, as well as their future, depend on the quality of those programs. Children evaluate the programs that serve them: They tell others by their behavior how things are going; they tell you, by the ways they use equipment and material, whether you have made appropriate selections; they tell you by coming to school happily or coming under protest. When children happily anticipate their arrival at school each day, you know that all is well.

Children's very lives and safety are at risk when programs don't meet minimum standards. Their human resources, skills, and knowledge will not flourish if they have substandard, mediocre programs day in and day out for all their early years.

Families Evaluate. Families want the best for their children, and they largely agree with professionals about what constitutes "the best." Families evaluate programs themselves: They ask their children what happens in school each day, and they ask other families when they meet them in the grocery store or at a ball game; they judge the way things are going by how happy or reluctant their children are to attend school; they judge the way things are going by the new ideas their children bring home, by their paintings, and by the things they see at school.

But families may lack the knowledge or access to information that goes beyond surface indicators of excellence, and they often overestimate the quality of the programs in which they place their children (Cryer & Burchinal, 1997). Families cannot inspect every nook and cranny of a facility to spot fire or sanitation hazards, nor can they spend all day at a program to assess whether adults are consistently responsive to their children's needs. Thus, they must rely on professional judgments of licensing agents or accreditation bodies to help them to evaluate programs. Informing families about these standards and the program's success in meeting them is an important step in the evaluation process.

Society Evaluates. Society needs evaluation of programs for young children, particularly because of the increasing numbers of children who attend them. As these programs serve more and more children, their influence on future generations grows. What types of people are they turning out? What values do they hold? What skills do they have? Program evaluation is a way of demonstrating accountability, of showing that a program is meeting its goal of building human resources. Early childhood programs represent considerable investments of resources, and society deserves to know if those resources are yielding desired results.

ETHICS: VALUES IN PRACTICE

Values define our idea of what is good. **Ethics** refers to the way we apply our values to our behavior. You have a set of personal values and a personal, informal code of ethics that determines how you act when confronted with choices for your behavior. Sometimes you have to make a choice between two or more competing values. If a friend asks you to provide answers for a take-home exam, for example, you will be faced with a dilemma involving the values of integrity and independence on the one hand and friendship and helpfulness on the other.

You might have difficulty responding if someone were to ask you to write out your personal code of ethics in detail. You might even be unable to give a reason for your actions in particular situations; you just know they "feel right." Deciding on a course of action in the line of duty, however, requires a more formal, professional code of ethics. Early childhood professionals have such a code.

This code, the Code of Ethical Conduct, which is the product of a special commission created by NAEYC (2011a; available online at naeyc.org/files/naeyc/file/positions/Ethics%20Position%20Statement2011.pdf), defines your professional responsibilities toward children, families, your colleagues, and society. It lists the ideals of the profession with regard to each of these groups and then lists principles or guidelines for action based upon those ideals. The code is not a recipe for correct behavior, however, and it cannot list every possible decision you might encounter during your work with children. You will have to think for yourself.

Although the code clearly states that one principle, "Above all, we shall not harm children" (p. 3), supersedes all others, you may occasionally be faced with a situation in which two or more principles apply. An ethical dilemma occurs, for example, when what seems best for a child is not what seems best for the child's family, as in the following scenario:

Kathryn Wilson is a single mother who works full time and receives support from the county social services agency to help cover the cost of the family child-care home her three-year-old daughter, Shannon, attends. Kathryn became very upset recently because Shannon had come home with a torn dress one day and purple paint (which did not wash out) on her blouse the next. Shelley Johnson, the family child-care provider, listens sympathetically to Kathryn's concerns and promises to try to help Shannon take better care of her clothing. She adds, however, that she does have five other children, including an infant and two toddlers, to supervise and that sometimes accidents will happen. She reminds Kathryn that her written policies emphasize the many active, creative, and messy experiences she believes children need, and asks parents to send children to her home in comfortable, washable "playclothes." At this point, Kathryn becomes even more upset and begins crying. "You don't understand," she says. "I only have a few outfits for Shannon and can't afford to buy more. If my former in-laws see her in shabby clothes when she spends weekends with her dad, they will think I'm a bad mother, that I can't take care of Shannon on my own. I'm doing the best I can, and I'm asking you to help me. Please don't let Shannon roughhouse or paint anymore."

Shelley has studied NAEYC's code of ethical conduct (2011a) and wholeheartedly accepts the responsibility of "supporting children's development and learning" and "promoting children's self-awareness, competence, self-worth, resiliency, and physical well-being" (p. 2). She is convinced that her rich array of activities does all these things, and that telling Shannon that she could not participate with other children in some activities would be harmful—a violation, she believes, of Principle P–1.1, which states "above all, we shall not harm children" (p. 3). Still, she also believes, with the authors of the code, that "families are of primary importance in children's development" (p. 3) and that she has a "primary responsibility to bring about collaboration between the home and school in ways that enhance the child's development" (p. 3). She is confident that she has followed Principle P–2.2, "we shall inform families of program philosophy, policies, and personnel qualifications, and explain why we teach as we do, which should be in accordance with our ethical responsibilities to children" (p. 4). She notes, however, that Principle P–2.4 states that "we shall involve families in significant decisions affecting their child" (p. 4).

Do you agree with Shelley that she is facing an ethical dilemma—a situation in which it seems impossible to meet both obligations to a child and obligations to the child's family? If so, what should Shelley do to resolve her dilemma?

❀ Talk It Over ❀

Refer to the NAEYC Code of Ethical Conduct (naeyc.org/files/naeyc/file/positions/Ethics%20Position%20Statement2011.pdf) and use it to guide your deliberations in the following role-playing activity. With your classmates, try to arrive at a solution that is agreeable to everyone (teacher, mother, and Sheldon):

Suppose that you work with a group of four-year-olds in a child development center. Every day, after nap and afternoon snack, you take the children outdoors to play, and the parents come to the playground to pick up their children. One day, Sheldon's mother tells you that she wants you to make Sheldon stay inside during this afternoon playtime. She explains that she has to rush from work to your center every day, and then hurry to finish some errands and get home to make supper before her husband and the older children arrive. She says that when she arrives at the center, she often has to spend precious minutes coaxing Sheldon to stop his play and then more time to brush sand from his clothing and hair before she can take him on her errands. She believes that if he played quietly by himself inside the center, things would go more smoothly at pick-up time. You believe very strongly that children need this outdoor play time.

What ideals and principles are involved here? Remember that there is usually no single "right" answer, so be sure to generate several possible approaches as you try to arrive at a fair and ethical solution.

RECONCILING VALUE DIFFERENCES

Values influence every aspect of your work with children. Values determine what behavior you expect from children as well as the methods that you find acceptable for encouraging (or enforcing) that behavior. The degree to which your values are in harmony with your colleagues' values and with the values of the families who send their children to you influences the amount of energy you must spend in raising your awareness of just what your values are and then explaining or defending your decisions.

Identifying Values: Your Own and Others'

Figure 2–2 contains brief profiles of nine teachers adapted from a series developed as part of some research conducted by Verna Hildebrand, one of the authors of this textbook. Each profile is designed to illustrate a particular value orientation. Try to identify and label what value orientation is predominant in each story and in the decisions the teacher is making in the classroom.

❀ **Talk It Over** ❀

In your opinion, which of the hypothetical teachers seems to be focusing on what is most important? Which is most like you? Which is least like you? Pick out the first- and second-ranking stories and the lowest-ranking story, according to the values you think are important in teaching. Can you explain your reasons for ranking the stories the way you did? If you can discuss the stories with a few parents, you may find that their views differ from yours. Where do these differences arise? How can you mediate the differences if you have the children in your classroom or family child-care home?

FIGURE 2–2   Nine hypothetical value orientations

1.	Socialization	4.	Morality	7.	Authority
2.	Aesthetics	5.	Academic success	8.	Freedom
3.	Health	6.	Economics	9.	Individuality

Teacher A thinks it is important for children to learn to get along with others. She feels children learn to help each other, and to share by having freedom to interact. Her classroom is usually a beehive of activity. She willingly puts off a science lesson if there is a spontaneous group activity in progress at that moment. Teacher A makes friends with children and parents and arranges situations so that each child will know and make friends with all the others. When difficulties arise, she prefers to let children work out the problem, intervening only as a last resort. She sometimes helps parents arrange their children's play groups during weekends or vacations.

Teacher B believes that children should be well prepared for "real school." His classroom schedule is arranged so that he gets lots of basic learning material covered each day. He avoids getting sidetracked during a class project; therefore, he is able to carry out lesson plans completely. He believes he must teach children a good deal of information, including ABCs, colors, shapes, and numbers. His children frequently achieve above-average scores on tests, which indicates to him that they are learning the material. His talks with parents focus on children's preparation for first grade. He participates in lectures and seminars to expand his own learning whenever he can.

Teacher C is concerned that children develop a sense of right and wrong. She often discusses with them how they ought to behave. She tells them her own views and introduces religious stories and ideas to the children. The children are taught classroom rules and are expected to behave accordingly. Fairness and consideration for others' feelings are stressed. Teacher C discusses any topic that is of interest to children, especially if she feels it will aid their character development. She encourages them to correct each other if they feel someone is doing something wrong.

Teacher D keeps her classroom looking attractive at all times. She takes special care that the colors are harmonious and that various artifacts are displayed in the room. Children's art objects and paintings are carefully mounted and labeled. Creative movement and music, including works of the great painters and composers, are a part of the program. Well-written children's literature is used regularly. Teacher D wears colorful and well-coordinated clothing. She helps children arrange their hair and clothing to look their best.

Teacher E's schedule and activities are outlined by the school's director, and he carefully follows these guidelines. He is grateful for the leadership of his school's director and values the opinions of fellow teachers and parents. At the beginning of each year the director distributes a list of policies and regulations that gives Teacher E a guide for administration in his classroom. He believes that the director is a competent administrator and knows a lot about running the class. He is pleased when the director brings in new learning programs for him to use.

Teacher F likes children to have lots of fresh air and sunshine. She makes sure her room has sufficient light, correct temperature, and chairs and tables of suitable height. Each morning she checks up on their habits of good breakfast, daily bath, tooth brushing, and proper rest. She checks throats for signs of contagious disease and has children taken home by parents when they seem ill. Routines of toileting and hand washing are frequent in her schedule. Nutritious foods are always available for snacks.

Teacher G feels that children should really plan their own program. He avoids thinking ahead about what children will be doing each day, emphasizing spontaneity and bringing toys out as children arrive and indicate their interests. He may choose an activity because he particularly wants to do it that day. He tries to respond to children's needs of the moment and avoids pushing them into organized learning tasks. His schedule is completely flexible, and rarely do the children follow the same schedule for two days in a row.

Teacher H believes that each child learns in a different way. She considers the child a person first and a student second. Her program is arranged so that each child can express his or her individuality. A supportive atmosphere prevails that allows the child to feel free to venture into new experiences, but is not one of indulgence. Teacher H strives to plan a rich variety of experiences with fresh views of familiar scenes, excursions to new places, or walks in parks. She uses many methods of motivation and novel ways of sparking children's imaginations.

Teacher I stresses protecting the school property and conserving materials. He teaches the children to use supplies such as paint, paper, and glue sparingly. He searches for "found" materials to supplement his supplies and utilizes all volunteer services available. He encourages the children to use both sides of the paper for drawing and coloring, rather than taking a new piece each time. Teacher I is also concerned with saving time, works at being efficient, and expects to teach children these traits. He thinks education is a way of improving one's station in life and leads to ways to make a good living.

Key: In these nine situations the primary value orientation is A.1, B.5, C.4, D.2, E.7, F.3, G.8, H.9, I.6

In real life, every teacher is probably a combination of several "stories." Each teacher places certain values in higher priority than others and therefore in decision-making situations chooses alternatives that reflect these values. For example, if the children have unloaded the entire shelf of blocks in the classroom, teachers who place a high value on order may be upset. However, they may be reconciled to the behavior when they notice that the blocks are being used in a creative manner because creativity is "good" in their value system. In the moment between when the teachers almost scold the children for unloading the blocks and when they actually compliment them for their interesting structure, they must weigh several value-based alternatives.

Importance of Listening

Because values stem from one's own cultural background, experiences, and beliefs, it is inevitable that you will encounter colleagues and parents whose values differ from yours. Although you may be uncomfortable talking about these disagreements, that is exactly what you need to do. The idea is not to convince the other person that you are right, or to give up your own values, but to try to understand some of the reasons behind the other person's beliefs and come to a solution that is acceptable to both of you. This means listening carefully, not just to the person's words but to the particular meaning of those words to that person, and restating what you think you heard so that any misunderstandings can be corrected. Usually, when people feel that they have been truly heard, they are more willing to listen to the other person's ideas. And once both parties have been able to clarify their ideas, they may be ready to strive for some common ground. As you might imagine, this process is not a "quick fix" for reconciling values differences. You may have to have several conversations around a particular topic before arriving at a compromise. One key to keeping the door open for continued discussion is acknowledging when you have reached an impasse and agreeing to set the matter aside for awhile.

A teacher who values creativity above all else, for example, might have a hard time sharing a classroom with a teacher who believes that children need a neat, orderly environment so they will learn to respect materials. The first teacher might feel stifled, while the second feels frustrated and irritated at what seems an unnecessary mess. Not only will their working relationship suffer, but the children are likely to become confused and begin to test both teachers in an attempt to find out what they can and cannot do with materials.

A teacher who values creativity and children's right to explore materials will be more comfortable with messy play than a teacher who values neatness and order.

If, however, the two teachers sit down and talk things over in a respectful, non-judgmental way, they might find a workable solution, such as setting aside an area of the classroom for messy, creative activities while keeping the rest of the space neat and orderly. They might even be surprised to find that each of them can learn from the other: that materials arranged in an orderly manner stimulate more creativity from the children, and that civilization does not fall if, on occasion, children fail to put every item back in its assigned place on the shelf.

Addressing Cultural Differences

If the values in conflict are rooted in culture, the solutions might require more talking, more respect, and more patience on everyone's part. You might not be able to arrive at an agreement, but you can at least agree to keep talking and learning from each other.

For example, most European Americans place a high value on independence and promoting the individuality of each child. Caregivers from this background may insist that children dress and feed themselves as soon as they are able, and praise them lavishly for each accomplishment in this regard. Caregivers from other cultural backgrounds, such as Asian Americans or Native Americans, may feel that it is more important for children to learn to be part of the group and to be helped to care for themselves even when they don't need help, so that they learn how to help others.

Janet Gonzalez-Mena (2007), an early childhood educator with a special interest in cultural aspects of development, suggests several areas where such conflicts are likely to arise between caregivers and parents (or other caregivers) from different cultural backgrounds. When and how to carry out toilet training, patterns of eating and sleeping, how much to hold a baby, sharing and ownership, expressing feelings—all can be grounds for disagreement as well as topics for healthy, productive discussions. Of course, when you think about it, differences of opinion about these topics can be just as strong between members of what appears on the surface to be the same culture.

When Compromise Is Possible . . . and When It Is Not

Regardless of whether the source of a conflict is personal or more broadly cultural, the key is open discussion, based on recognition that no one way is "right." Consider the following examples and think about what you would do in each case:

- A parent wants you to use stickers as a reward to speed up toilet-training for a two-year-old. You firmly believe that extrinsic rewards discount the child's own drive toward establishing inner controls.

- A mother makes a practice of bringing a peanut-butter sandwich for her four-year-old daughter on any day that she believes the child won't like what is being served for lunch. You know that the menu always includes a variety of foods so that a child who doesn't like one thing can find plenty of healthy alternatives and won't go hungry. You have observed that this child does eat reasonably well most days, but when she knows her mother has brought the sandwich, she announces, "My mom says I don't like . . . " and refuses even to taste anything on the menu. Furthermore, when other children see her sandwich, they ask why they don't have one. The cook is worried that soon she will have to prepare sandwiches for everyone and that the carefully planned lunch will go to waste. When you approach the subject with the mother, she says that she is actually providing the sandwich for her own peace of mind; she says she experienced difficulty breast-feeding this child, finally gave up after six months, and continues to fret over her eating.

- Suppose you believe that meals should be enjoyable times, full of lively conversation, while your co-teacher tells children that they should "eat, not talk." She tells you that because of her family's financial difficulties, she often went hungry as a child, and she just can't stand to see food wasted while children chatter and giggle.

There may be times when your disagreement with a parent, a colleague, or your employer is so great that compromise is not only impossible but would be a violation of your personal and professional ethics. In some instances, you will be able to appeal to the authority of state or federal laws to support your position. Let's look at a few examples:

Because you place a high value on fairness and equal opportunity, you might welcome into your classroom of three-year-olds a new child who has spina bifida and immediately set about learning what you need to know to make the inclusion work. (Children with spina bifida might need to use wheelchairs or leg braces and might have toileting issues that are more complicated than usual.) If your co-teachers do not share your values, and if they argue that the child will require too much help with toileting, for example, you will be able to respond that federal law requires child development centers to make every reasonable effort to accommodate children with disabilities.

Or, you might be faced with parents who want you to spank their child and argue that your methods are "too soft" to teach the child right from wrong. While you will certainly want to explain your reasons for using methods other than spanking, you will also be able to back up your viewpoint with state laws and licensing regulations that forbid corporal punishment.

❀ Talk It Over ❀

Imagine that parents or your supervisors demand that you use a curriculum or teaching methods that you believe are more suitable for much older children. In discussing the matter, you begin to understand that the parents sincerely want their children to be more adequately prepared for school or that your supervisors want to prove to the agency that funds your program that children are learning.

You tell parents or your supervisors that you wholeheartedly agree with their goal but that your methods for achieving it are different. No matter how much you discuss, however, you are unable to convince them or arrive at a compromise that you can accept. You are told that you must give up your ideas of developmentally appropriate practice if you want to keep your job. What would you do? Why?

However, you will not always have a law or policy to support your viewpoint. It is neither possible nor desirable to put every aspect of developmentally appropriate practice into a hard-and-fast law or rule. Thus, you may sometimes be asked to act in a way that, while perfectly legal, goes against what you know about children or violates your personal and professional ethics. If these demands are being made by persons in positions of authority over you and you are unable to convince them with arguments based on your professional knowledge, you may have to quit your job. Working day after day in a system that contradicts your values will have great psychological costs for you and for the children in your care.

THE COURAGE TO TEACH

By this point, you might be feeling somewhat overwhelmed by the enormous complexity of the field you have chosen. You have read that you must subscribe to a professional code of ethics based on commonly held values yet become sensitive to cultural differences among yourself, colleagues, and families. You may be tempted to think about a career that involves only inanimate objects, perhaps carpentry or accounting.

Parker Palmer (1998), a highly respected writer on issues of education, community, and social change, had university professors in mind when he wrote the following, but his ideas apply equally well to early childhood educators:

> I am a teacher at heart, and there are moments in the classroom when I can hardly hold the joy. When my students and I discover uncharted territory to explore, when the pathway out of a thicket opens up before us, when our experience is illumined by the lightning-life of the mind—then teaching is the finest work I know. (p. 1)

He goes on to describe other moments, what he calls "the tangles of teaching," when he loses his bearings and feels incompetent. He attributes those tangles to three causes: First, as teachers, our knowledge of the large and complex subjects we love (in our case, child development) can never be perfect and complete. Second, the students (in our case, children) we teach are even more complicated. The third factor that complicates our life as teachers is found in ourselves: "We teach who we are." He explains:

> Teaching holds a mirror to the soul. If I am willing to look in that mirror and not run from what I see, I have a chance to gain self-knowledge—and knowing myself is as crucial to good teaching as knowing my students and my subjects. (p. 2)

Lilian Katz wondered how teachers could strike a balance between awareness of how much is unknown (about child development) and the confidence to act anyway. Katz's proposed solution is that teachers need to forge ahead, confident that they are acting in children's best interests based on admittedly limited knowledge. Given that teachers are often faced with situations in which any action they take could result in a less than desirable outcome, they have to choose the "least worst error" (or "lesser of two evils") in light of what they truly value (Katz and Katz, 2009, pp. 13–16).

The teacher's philosophy of life, of human development, of family dynamics, and of education will all be reflected in the program that is developed for children and in the interaction that takes place between and among individuals. Teaching styles—all the unique ways that teachers make decisions and interact with children—develop out of the teacher's personality, knowledge, experience, and values.

Teachers need to forge ahead, confident that they are acting in children's best interests, based on admittedly limited knowledge.

CONCLUSION

Values and ethical positions are part of each person's life. Values indicate what "ought to" or "should" be done. You are reared with the values of your family and culture and gradually shape your own set of values throughout life. Ethics refers to the ways values are applied to behavior, though some values may not be consciously expressed. Adults can raise their awareness of the values underlying their behavior and think about the outcomes of various value positions. Although it takes effort, people *can* change values, given adequate reasons and time to practice new behaviors. With increased knowledge of child development, teachers and teachers-to-be can learn to adjust their expectations to fit children's developmental levels. Given alternatives to autocratic teaching styles, they can learn to be more democratic and person centered. Most importantly, a better understanding of alternative value systems and implications for children is gained.

As members of a profession that serves the public, early childhood practitioners have a special responsibility to follow the values set forth in the U.S. Constitution. In addition, they are expected to share the values, ideals, and principles of their profession and to subscribe to a code of ethics based on those values. Because of the great diversity of populations within the United States, you will no doubt work with many people whose values differ from your own. Respecting those differences is a value of the early childhood profession. Becoming aware of your own values is the first step toward that respect. Agreeing to join a profession obligates you to think seriously about values and ethics in your professional life.

REVIEW: TEN CHARACTERISTICS OF VALUES

1. Values are defined as concepts of the desirable.
2. Values are formed through experience, example, and instruction.
3. Values are transmitted as part of an individual's cultural heritage.
4. Values can be conscious or unconscious; unconscious values can be brought to a level of awareness.
5. Values guide the actions and decisions of individuals.

6. Values have been enshrined in the U.S. Constitution and in laws and regulations.
7. Values are rarely identical for two individuals.
8. Values are reflected in an early childhood program.
9. Values are the basis for regulations and standards in early childhood programs.
10. Values can be changed through the conscious effort of individuals.

APPLICATIONS

1. Write a definition of the terms *values* and *ethics* and explain how they are related.

2. List three types of decisions. Give an example of each and identify the values implied.

3. Write (or role-play) a scenario in which two people with different values try to reach a compromise, using the steps described in the text.

4. Locate an instrument for evaluating some aspect of a child development program (e.g., *Early Childhood Environmental Rating Scale* or *Preschool Outdoor Environments Measurement Scale*). Identify the values implicit in the items included.

5. Review the NAEYC Guidelines for Developmentally Appropriate Practice and your state standards for preschool. Identify similarities and differences in the values embodied in each.

RESOURCES FOR FURTHER STUDY

Websites

Division for Early Childhood of the Council for Exceptional Children
dec-sped.org
Provides information and resources for assessing programs and services and for implementing recommended practices in early intervention/early childhood special education.

National Association for Family Child Care
nafcc.org
Provides a link to the Accreditation Standards for Family Child Care Homes.

Teachers Resisting Unhealthy Children's Entertainment
truceteachers.org
Offers resources for understanding the impact of media violence on children and dealing with its reflection in classroom play.

Standards for Preschool Children's Learning and Development: Who Has Standards, How Were They Developed, and How Are They Used?
serve.org/FileLibraryDetails.aspx?id=78
Online source for a report of a 2003 survey of states' efforts to establish standards for early education.

Readings

Carlson, V. J., Feng, X., & Harwood, R. L. (2004 March). The "ideal baby": A look at the intersection of temperament and culture. *Zero to Three, 24*(4), 22–28.

Gonzalez-Mena, J. (2007). *Diversity in early care and education: Honoring differences.* Boston, MA: McGraw-Hill.

Kagan, S. L., Scott-Little, C., & Frelow, V. S. (2003, September). Early learning standards for young children: A survey of the states. *Young Children, 58*(5), 58–64.

Katz, L. G. (2007, May). Viewpoint: Standards of experience. *Young Children, 62*(3), 94–95.

Pelo, A., & Davidson, F. (2000). *That's not fair! A teacher's guide to activism with young children.* St. Paul, MN: Redleaf Press.

CHAPTER 3

Foundations of Guidance:
Understanding Development and Observing Children

Learning Outcomes

After studying this chapter you should be able to

- Explain the concept of *developmentally appropriate expectations*.
- List the principles of development.
- Explain why knowledge of brain development is crucial for effective guidance (especially in relation to *executive function* and *self-regulation*).
- Identify characteristics of *evidence-based practice* in early childhood care and education.
- Describe a variety of observation tools and strategies in early childhood education.

A licensing inspector was on the playground for three- to five-year-olds, checking for safety hazards. When she used the metal T-shaped probe to measure the depth of the wood chips cushioning the surface under the climber, Conner and Darnell became very interested. Both wanted a turn to push the probe into the ground themselves, and since it took some force to do so, were complimented by the consultant for being "strong." After two turns for each boy, the consultant retrieved the probe and said she had to go. Conner went back to playing on the slide, and Darnell, who whimpered and looked for a moment as though he were going to cry, followed suit. Their teacher, Ms. Henderson, had been watching the incident with interest. She smiled to herself as she jotted a few lines on a small notepad she kept in her pocket.

DEVELOPMENTALLY APPROPRIATE EXPECTATIONS

To understand what interested Ms. Henderson about this encounter and why it brought a smile to her lips, you would need to know how most four-year-old children are likely to behave and quite a bit about Conner and Darnell. Ms. Henderson found the incident significant because she knew that four-year-old children often have difficulty "de-centering," or changing their focus when involved in something they enjoy. She also knew that resistance to change was part of Darnell's temperament. In this instance, however, Darnell managed to control his feelings of frustration when he was not allowed to continue playing with the intriguing new tool. Under similar circumstances in the past, he had frequently responded to frustration of any sort by screaming and sometimes kicking or hitting the other person involved. His ability to regroup in this case was noteworthy.

In Chapter 1 we defined *guidance* as "everything adults deliberately do and say, either directly or indirectly, to influence children's behavior, with the goal of helping the children become well-adjusted, self-directed, productive adults." In other words, we might say that guidance is the process of helping children live up to society's expectations of its members. Translating those expectations into terms that are realistic and achievable for young children requires specialized knowledge of the ways children think, act, and develop. That is why we say that establishing appropriate expectations, based on understanding child development, provides an important part of the foundation for all of your other efforts to guide young children. (See Figure 3–1.)

Understanding Typical Patterns of Development: Knowing About Children

If you are going to guide young children as they journey from infancy toward adulthood, you will need a map that gives you some idea of where you are, what your destination is, and what signposts you will pass along the way. Fortunately, just such a map is available in the form of all the knowledge about child development that has been accumulated by researchers, parents, and teachers over the years. It is not a perfect map, and it changes over time as we gain new knowledge and insight about development, but it is helpful if you use it thoughtfully.

Building your knowledge of typical patterns of development is the first step toward a developmentally appropriate approach to guidance. This is the knowledge that lets you take it in stride when an infant suddenly starts screaming at the sight of strangers she has ignored previously, when a toddler begins balking at all your requests, or when a four-year-old blurts out some shocking new vocabulary words at the lunch table. Familiarity with typical stages of development will reassure you that none of these children are social deviants and that each of these behaviors is representative of a particular age. Not only are they typical behaviors, they are signs that children are moving along the path toward maturity. The infant's stranger anxiety is evidence that she can now remember familiar faces and compare new faces with those memories. The toddler's "no" is a sign of growing autonomy, of awareness that he is a separate person, not an appendage of his mother. The four-year-old's "bad" words are actually experiments with the social power of language, usually without real understanding of the words' meanings.

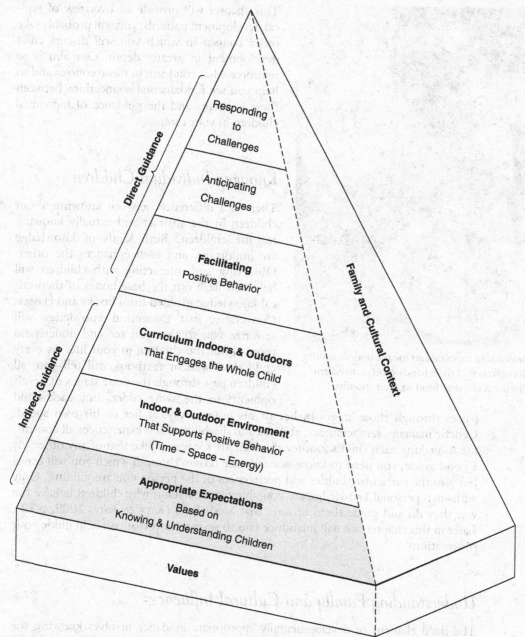

FIGURE 3–1 The guidance pyramid: Appropriate expectations

Knowing typical patterns of development will help you have reasonable expectations for children's behavior. You won't expect a toddler to comply willingly with every request or a three-year-old to sit through a half-hour circle time on the first day of school. Having this knowledge will also give you some basis for deciding when you need to look more closely at behaviors that are not typical within given ages.

Holding reasonable expectations means understanding that toddlers often find their hands more convenient than spoons for conveying food to their mouths.

This chapter will provide an overview of typical development patterns; you will probably take other courses in which you will discuss child development in greater depth. Our aim is to reinforce what you learn in those courses and to help you see fundamental connections between these concepts and the guidance of individual children in your care.

Knowing Individual Children

There is a difference between knowing about children in the abstract and actually knowing real-life children. Both kinds of knowledge are important, and each enhances the other. Observing and interacting with children will help you flesh out the bare bones of theoretical knowledge gleaned from books and classes. Conversely, that theoretical knowledge will sensitize you so that you see and understand more about the children in your life. As every child development textbook will tell you, all children pass through the same stages of development, in the same order, but each child passes through those stages in her or his unique way, at her or his own speed. Genetic makeup, temperament, abilities and disabilities, and experiences all contribute to making each child's journey through life's stages unlike that of any other. As a good guide, you need to know not only the terrain through which you will travel but also the particular abilities and preferences of the person you are guiding. Only with such personal knowledge are you able to understand why children behave the way they do and guide them in ways that are helpful (Katz & Katz, 2009, p.12). Later in this chapter, we will introduce you to several tools that will help guide your observations.

Understanding Family and Cultural Influences

The third element of developmentally appropriate guidance involves knowing the values and expectations of children's families and cultures. All children begin from infancy to absorb rules for how to talk, dress, and behave from their families and surrounding communities. They bring these ways of being into their child-care settings, where they may encounter very different sets of rules. Early childhood professionals must seek to understand each child's unique context in order to create an environment that is comfortable for all. This aspect of appropriate guidance will be discussed in detail in Chapter 4.

PRINCIPLES OF DEVELOPMENT

Development refers to the increasing complexity of various skills and attributes within the child—that is, the more complex motor, language, mental, social, and emotional responses. Several principles govern these changes in all children, and these principles form the basis for your decisions as you work with children and their families (Copple & Bredekamp, 2009).

First, development is not random; it follows predictable patterns, with each milestone building upon the previous ones. Second, development progresses from broad, generalized abilities to more refined, specific skills. For example, a baby can aim his arm toward the mobile over his crib long before he can use his finger and thumb to grasp a part of that mobile and put it in his mouth. Toddlers may play alongside each other, often in the same manner with the same materials, without much interaction other than occasional declarations of, "Mine!" Soon pairs of these solitary players, given experience and opportunity, begin enjoying elaborate pretend picnics with each other and their teddy bears. Young children scribble before they make recognizable letters. Their early written "words" consist of only initial consonants or perhaps a letter for each syllable they are trying to write. Later, they fill in letters to represent the sounds more completely.

Development follows predictable patterns. Children pull themselves up to stand and "cruise," holding on to furniture for support before they walk independently.

Third, although the sequence of development is the same for all children, the rate at which children progress through the sequence varies from one individual to another, and sometimes from one area to another within a single individual. A child who walks before her peers, for example, might not speak clearly until several months after they do. Or a child might experience sudden spurts of progress in a particular area from time to time, interspersed with what seem like lengthy plateaus. Adults who understand this will be cautious about making generalizations based on few observations, and they will support the repetition and practice that children need without trying to hurry them to the next milestone. Research gives no basis for concluding that faster-than-normal growth is necessarily desirable or that future success is thereby assured. In fact, the reverse could be true. An early academic bloomer may not reach any higher adult achievement level, and if subjected to excessive pressure to exceed more typical developmental rates, the child may experience stress levels that actually impede development.

A fourth principle concerns the integrated nature of development. Researchers in child development generally investigate particular types or domains of

Puzzle pieces with knobs are easier for children to manipulate as they acquire fine motor skills.

development. Physical, social, emotional, and intellectual development are commonly used categories, although some writers include perceptual, motor, aesthetic, language, and adaptive domains. The categories are created by researchers to describe aspects of development; they do not reflect actual entities within children, nor do they exist apart from one another. Some types of development might be seen as belonging to more than one category: Language, for example, requires physical development of the vocal tract, cognitive ability to understand and reproduce meaningful words, social skill to know when to use those words effectively, and the emotional qualities of motivation and confidence in one's ability to do so. Nevertheless, the categories are useful because they help us to focus more closely on children's development and notice things that we might have missed otherwise. Recognition of the connections across domains is what child development experts mean when they emphasize the need to consider the **whole child**. (See Figure 3–2.)

Each domain influences and is influenced by the others. For example, with each physical accomplishment—first raising the head, then sitting, standing, and walking—the infant acquires vast new territory to explore, resulting in new concepts and new feelings of competence. Recent research revealing connections between the physical, emotional, social, and cognitive domains in early brain development provides dramatic examples of integrated nature of development. The Center on the Developing Child at Harvard University (2010) summarizes what we now know:

> When developing biological systems are strengthened by positive early experiences, healthy children are more likely to grow into healthy adults. Sound health also provides a foundation for the construction of sturdy brain architecture and the associated achievement of a broad range of abilities and learning capacities. (p.2)

And the converse is also true: Excessive or prolonged stress (such as that caused by poverty or maltreatment) not only inhibits the transmission and storage of information within the brain (Willis, 2007) but is likely to lead to physical repercussions in adulthood, including severe depression, cardiovascular disease, and risk factors such as obesity, high cholesterol levels, and elevated blood pressure (Danese et al., 2009).

Historically, supporting the social-emotional development of children has been a major focus of the early childhood profession. Within the past decade or so, increasing emphasis on academic success has threatened to overshadow or supplant social-emotional goals. Teachers and caregivers who understand the interrelatedness of developmental domains will not be swayed by such an artificial distinction. The more we learn about brain development, in fact, the more we realize that social-emotional development provides the

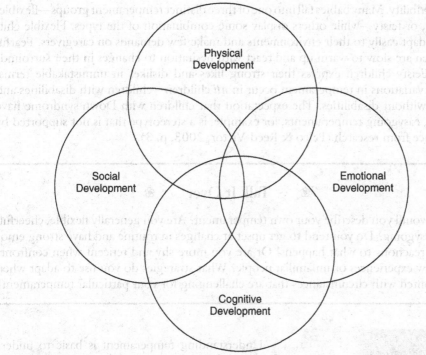

FIGURE 3-2 Interrelated areas of development

underpinning without which all learning will be impeded. Children need to feel secure, to experience pleasurable interactions with a few important people in their lives, and to possess sufficient self-control to focus their attention in order to learn (see, e.g., Epstein, 2009, and Galinsky, 2010). Conversely, persistent fear and chronic anxiety experienced in early childhood can alter the very structure of the developing brain and have lifelong adverse effects (National Scientific Council on the Developing Child, 2010).

FACTORS THAT INFLUENCE DEVELOPMENT

Maturation, motivation, experience, and temperament interact to influence a child's development. **Maturation** refers to the general tempo at which various biological, behavioral, and personality characteristics emerge. This tempo is largely dependent on the genetic makeup of the individual. **Motivation** refers to the child's incentive or desire to learn a behavior. **Experience** in practicing the skill can be provided by adults at strategic moments when the child shows readiness, thus enhancing development. Expert teachers are sensitive to children's readiness in many learning domains. Children seek ways to gain experience when they find a new skill fascinating. Watch them scramble up and down when they first learn to climb. Or listen to them practice words and sounds when they've started speaking. It often seems as though they have an inner drive to excel.

Temperament refers to the general way people respond to experiences, beginning in earliest infancy. It includes characteristics such as the intensity and duration of reactions, the tendency to approach or avoid new things, mood, perseverance, and distractibility. Many babies fall into one of three distinct temperament groups—flexible, fearful, or feisty—while others display some combination of the types. Flexible children adapt easily to their environments and make few demands on caregivers. Fearful children are slow to warm up and react with hesitation to changes in their surroundings. Feisty children express their strong likes and dislikes in unmistakable terms. These variations in temperament occur in *all* children—children with disabilities and those without disabilities. The expectation that children with Down syndrome have happy, easygoing temperaments, for example, is a stereotype that is not supported by evidence from research (Pelco & Reed-Victor, 2003, p. 3).

❀   **Talk It Over**   ❀

How would you describe your own temperament? Are you generally flexible, cheerful, and easygoing? Do you tend to get upset at changes in routine and have strong emotional reactions to what happens? Or are you more shy and reticent when confronting new experiences or unfamiliar people? What strategies do you use to adapt when confronted with circumstances that are challenging for your particular temperament?

A fearful child needs a familiar environment and a familiar supportive adult.

Understanding temperament is basic to understanding behavior, which is an essential component of guidance. Armed with this understanding, adults can think of ways to make the environment more comfortable for all children. A feisty child will need lots of opportunity for vigorous play and plenty of warning before transitions. A fearful child needs a predictable environment and a familiar supportive adult who gently encourages involvement with materials or other children and stays nearby until the child feels comfortable. Too much noise or harsh fluorescent lighting can be overwhelming to everyone, but particularly for a child who is extremely sensitive to such stimuli.

Occasionally an adult's temperament makes it difficult to relate well to a particular child. An adult who usually experiences very strong emotional responses and has difficulty adapting to change may find it especially difficult to tolerate a feisty child's angry outbursts at transition times. Generally, however, adults who cultivate self-awareness can adjust their interactions according to a child's temperamental needs. Feisty children need gentle guidance to learn acceptable ways of expressing their strong desires. Fearful children need calm support to try new experiences. And flexible children still need adequate attention, even though they are so undemanding it may be easy to overlook them. Whether adjusting the environment, fine-tuning your own interactions, or teaching the child to use coping strategies, the basic idea is to improve the "goodness of fit" between child and environment to facilitate positive development (Chess & Thomas, 1996).

Ideally, your professional preparation will have included one or more courses in child development prior to your study of guidance. If you have not had such coursework, or if you would benefit from refreshing your knowledge, you can find an excellent review of development at each age and across all domains in the revised edition of *Developmentally Appropriate Practice in Early Childhood Programs Serving Children Birth Through Age 8* (Copple & Bredekamp, 2009). Unrealistic expectations based on inadequate knowledge of typical patterns of development often lead to frustration for children, which may in turn be manifested as "misbehavior." We believe that if you know what children are like at each stage of development and how they are likely to behave, you will be better prepared to support them in their quest for self-direction.

❊ **Talk It Over** ❊

How would you evaluate a program for toddlers that expected all 18 children to sit quietly at tables and color a pre-drawn picture for a half hour? Cite examples of physical, social, emotional, and intellectual developmental characteristics of toddlers to explain your thinking.

THE BRAIN: INTEGRATING ALL DOMAINS OF DEVELOPMENT

While the brain is probably most closely associated with cognitive development in most people's minds, it actually represents the interplay of all domains. **Developmental cognitive neuroscience**, a relatively new area of study, brings together psychologists, biologists, and medical scientists in an attempt to understand the complex relationships between changes within the brain, what happens in the child's environment, and how the child functions in that environment. New technologies, such as the positron emission tomography (PET) scan, allow scientists to see what happens in a living brain as well as evidence of what doesn't happen when children are deprived of the security and stimulation needed to thrive. You may have seen the widely circulated images showing large dark gaps in the brain scans of Romanian orphans who had been raised in deplorable conditions contrasted with scans of the brain activity of their more fortunate peers. These images and other new information about brain development circulated in the popular media in the early 1990s, generating a great deal of public interest and providing strong evidence for the importance of high-quality child care. Some reactions were misguided, resulting in the proliferation of advice and products claiming to help build the baby's brain, "artificial interventions [that] are at best useless and at worst distractions from the normal interaction between grown-ups and babies" (Gopnik, Meltzoff, & Kuhl, 1999, p. 201).

When understood appropriately, the new findings of neuroscience do have powerful implications for guidance. Perhaps most importantly, they confirm what child development professionals have been saying for a very long time: that all domains of development are interwoven, that physical and mental health affect learning and behavior and vice versa. What you do to help a child feel secure and comfortable in your classroom will bear fruit in the child's ability to learn, to get along with others, and to exercise self-control for years to come. One study found that children's cortisol levels doubled or tripled over the course of days in child care when compared with days at home. The effects were greater when children were in large groups or spent more time in adult-directed activities. The girls became anxious and vigilant, while the boys became angry and aggressive (Gunnar, Dryzer, Van Ryzin, & Phillips, 2010).

To understand why this is important, you need to know that the physical structure of the brain begins forming before birth; it continues developing and changing throughout life, although the changes are most rapid during the first few years, when as many as 700 new synapses (connections between neurons) are formed every second. These earliest neural connections control breathing, heartbeat, and other systems necessary for life. As a baby encounters sights, sounds, and other sensations within her world, new synapses form, and the connections become stronger. Among many other tasks, the baby is literally learning to see, to focus, and to track objects in space.

Throughout the first few years, the network of connections explodes and becomes increasingly complex, providing concrete, visible evidence of the learning that is taking place. All this activity takes incredible amounts of energy (in the form of glucose used by the brain), which means babies need good nutrition and plenty of sleep to restore that energy (Chugani, 2004). After about age 6, the connections that are not used begin to be eliminated, in a process called "pruning."

If good nutrition, adequate rest, secure attachment, and an appropriate amount of stimulation provide the conditions for synapses to form, stress may impede those connections. Stress is the body's physiological response to discomfort. Stress affects the brain because it produces a hormone called cortisol that can slow or prevent neural connections. Researchers measure the amount of cortisol in saliva to assess the level of stress an individual may be experiencing in various conditions. It is impossible to eliminate all stress from a child's life, and in fact some stress stimulates development. When the stress is severe or ongoing, however, and the child has no adult support for coping, it becomes toxic, with the result the areas of the brain that govern learning and self-regulation are weakened. Instead of building healthy neural pathways, children living in violent or impoverished homes may develop patterns of responses that lead to harmful behaviors down the road.

In addition to requiring fulfillment of basic needs for food and rest, babies' brains are wired to seek reactions from the world. Babies expect responses to their babbling, smiles, and cries. When a baby doesn't get responses, or when a response doesn't match what the baby needs, the process of building the brain is interrupted or sidetracked, leading to problems functioning in school and in life. This means that neglect (absence of response) can be as harmful as abuse (sharply negative response). Researchers have adopted the term "serve and return" to describe this aspect of brain development (Levitt, 2009).

The degree to which children's needs for responsive caregiving and freedom from anxiety are met will affect the development of **executive function**, a capacity associated with the prefrontal cortex that has been likened to an air-traffic-control system for the brain (Center on the Developing Child at Harvard University, 2011). Components of executive function are the ability to remember, pay attention, control impulses, and adjust one's thinking to changing circumstances. These skills begin to emerge in early childhood but are not fully developed until adolescence or beyond, and then only if they are nurtured in environments where expectations match the child's growing abilities. As with all other aspects of brain development, adverse experiences (e.g., abuse or neglect, prenatal alcohol exposure, disrupted relationships with a primary caregiver) interfere with the process, making it harder for a child to pay attention, to think clearly, or to learn. Adults who

The best way for children to practice all types of self-regulation is through pretend play, where they take on roles requiring particular types of speech and make sure that their playmates stay in character.

want to help children develop executive function must realize that children do not misbehave because they are "bad" or are deliberately trying to break rules. They need time for their brains to develop the ability to remember and act on the rules; they need few, simple rules that are reasonable in light of their budding abilities; and they probably need several reminders.

Self-regulation, a concept closely related to executive function, spans all developmental domains. Whereas executive function broadly encompasses the way the brain manages and processes information, self-regulation represents the ability to control one's emotions and behavior. It begins in the physical realm, with the infant's ability to settle back to sleep during the earliest weeks of life. A little later in life, young children acquire the social-emotional skill of inhibiting certain behaviors, and they begin to master the cognitive challenge of purposefully focusing their attention on tasks at hand (National Research Council and Institute of Medicine, 2000). According to Bodrova and Leong (2007a), school readiness is more heavily influenced by self-regulation than by cognitive skills or family characteristics. They caution us not to confuse self-regulation with the ability to be regulated by others (i.e., to follow rules when someone is watching). Although that is a step in the right direction, a child also needs two other kinds of experience: regulating others (telling peers what the rules are and reporting infractions to authority) and regulating her own behavior by voluntarily following the rules. Based on their extensive study of the work of Vygotsky, Bodrova and Leong conclude that the best way for children to have lots of practice with all three types of regulation is through pretend play, where they take on roles requiring particular types of speech and make sure that their playmates stay in character. Unfortunately, this type of high-level play has become less and less common as children spend more time on computers or in front of television and have fewer occasions to play in mixed-age groups where older, more experienced children mentor the play of their younger peers.

EVIDENCE-BASED PRACTICE: CHILD DEVELOPMENT KNOWLEDGE IN PERSPECTIVE

As we noted earlier in this chapter, knowing about children in general is only part of a developmentally appropriate approach to guidance. You will soon learn that, even within a fairly homogeneous group, there can be a great deal of difference among individual children. Through study and experience, you will come to recognize and respect this range. Instead of glossing over differences or accepting generalizations based on race, ethnicity, gender, age, economic status, or disability, you will try to learn more about these aspects of diversity. Your goal will be to understand the individual children in your care, and their families, more fully. When you develop this understanding, you will be carrying on a long tradition of early childhood professionals who have worked to foster the development of *all* children and families. You will also be complying with federal laws that prohibit unequal treatment based on gender, race, ethnicity, or ability. And you will be helping the children in your care learn to appreciate their unique qualities while they respect and value differences in others.

The concept of child development research as a basis for early education has recently come under intense criticism by theorists and educators who say that it promises more than it delivers; that it cannot describe or predict development for all children because it reflects only white, relatively affluent, Western culture; and that it is too often based on artificially contrived situations with little resemblance—or relevance—to the everyday lives of children and families (Zimiles, 2000). For example, research suggests that African American children develop language in unique ways that are not accurately assessed using standardized vocabulary tests, which are based on patterns that are typical for their white peers who grow up speaking standard American-English (Horton-Ikard, 2006). Critics warn that generalized statements about what children typically do at certain ages can easily become prescriptions for what they *should* or *must* do, thereby creating unhealthy pressures on both children and teachers (Lubeck, 2000).

Theories and research are the products of human beings who exist within particular cultures and hold particular values. They must be examined in the light of your own experience and values as well as those of the families and children you serve. The concept of values and the relationship of values to guidance were discussed in Chapter 2. Does this mean that it is no use to study theory because there are no "right" answers? Hardly. In our view, child development theory and research provide a framework or skeleton that you will need to flesh out with your own experience and knowledge as you get to know the particular children and families you serve. We concur with Stott and Bowman (1996) that

> What makes theories worth reading and discussing is not the assumption that they mirror reality but that they serve as suggestions or estimations—they help us arrange our minds. . . . [T]hey organize and give meaning to facts, and they guide further observation and research. In so doing they provide guidance for our thinking. (p. 171)

Thinking about your own experiences and examining them in light of the theoretical approaches you study is part of reflective practice, a key to your own professional development (Perry & Gerard, 2002). *Evidence-based practice* is a term that you are likely to encounter as you continue your studies. Although it is widely used by early childhood professionals and others, many hold different ideas about its meaning.

For some, it suggests relying on research to find "right answers" that can then be applied in many situations. Researchers at the Frank Porter Graham Child Development Institute (Buysse & Winton, 2007) suggest that products of research in the form of general standards or guidelines don't always serve the best interests of children and families. They argue that the evidence upon which practice is based should include other forms and sources of knowledge, including professionals' "experiential learning, situated in practice, and influenced by one's personal beliefs and values as well as those of the families and communities served in early childhood programs" (p. 4).

❈ Talk It Over ❈

Suppose the director of a child development program where you work gives you a new form for reporting children's progress to families. The form lists various skills and abilities as well as the age at which children typically develop each. Several of the children in your classroom of three- and four-year-olds do not speak English at home, and although they chatter fluently in their home language while playing, you notice that they are "behind" the benchmarks listed on the form. Would you be comfortable using this form to report children's progress? Why or why not? What would you say to the director?

OBSERVATION: THE KEY TO KNOWING CHILDREN

As we pointed out in the previous chapter, developmentally appropriate guidance is based on knowing about children in general, knowing individual children in particular, and knowing about the families and communities where those children are growing up. You can learn about children in general by studying textbooks, but in order to know the individual children in your care, you will need to observe closely and reflect upon what you see. Through observation, you can learn what interests or challenges a child, how the child tackles problems or copes with frustration, who has friends in the classroom, and who seems to be isolated. Observation can help you build positive relationships with children: The more you observe, the better you understand why a child does what she does and the more sensitively you can respond. Observation tells you how effective your planning is—whether children are drawn to the interest centers you've created, whether they use the materials in the way you envisioned, and whether they remember things you have tried to teach them. Carefully recorded observations provide a basis for talking with families about what their children are learning and for showing your colleagues and administrators the good things that happen in your classroom.

Importance of Accuracy and Objectivity

Your observations will be most useful if you strive to make them *accurate* and *objective*. Look and listen closely. What appears on the surface to be one toddler shoving another could actually be an attempt at helpfulness that went awry because the helper did not have the muscular coordination to carry out an intention. Write only what you actually see or hear—not your opinion about a child's behavior or what you assume a child might be thinking. Compare the following two examples:

1. *Rasheeda was playing happily in the block center. Tonya and Jennifer came in, but Rasheeda didn't want them to play so she got mad and was mean to them.*

2. *Rasheeda had used the long unit blocks to create an enclosure with several compartments. She sorted the farm animals, placing horses in one compartment, sheep in another, and cows in a third. When she dropped a horse figure in with the cows, she giggled and picked it up, saying in a mock scolding tone, "You don't go in there, you naughty horse!" Tonya and Jennifer came into the block area, and Rasheeda told them not to mess up her farm. Tonya picked up one of the animals, and Rasheeda shouted at her to stop. When Tonya did not put the animal back, Rasheeda shoved her.*

Observation helps you know and understand children. The tender way this girl cuddles the doll and gazes into its face tells a lot about her understanding of the role of caregiver.

In the first example, the observer jumps to the conclusion that Rasheeda is "happy" and "doesn't want" company in the dramatic play area. Rasheeda's actual behavior is not described; we are just told she is "mean" to the others. The second example provides more concrete detail about what the observer actually saw and heard, and it allows us to understand Rasheeda's possible motivations more fully. It would also give a teacher more clues about how to intervene to help the three girls play together constructively.

In striving for objectivity, you will be trying to step outside the opinions and biases you have formed as a result of your past experiences. Of course, it will never be possible for you to do this completely. Nor would it be entirely desirable. After all, your knowledge of child development and your commitment to fostering that development for every child will make your observations different from those of someone who has no interest in children or in a particular child. While you cannot achieve complete objectivity, you can acknowledge your subjectivity, recognizing that the way you see a situation might not be the right way or the only way to see it.

It will help if you remember that your observations are always incomplete. The behaviors a particular child exhibits at the child development center may differ widely from the way that child behaves at home, at grandmother's house, or at the grocery store. Conferences with parents, visits in the home, and participation of the parents in the center's programs are ways to get to know children and their individual needs even further. You may know a lot about children in general, but family members are the experts when it comes to each particular child. It is important to respect that expertise and to show your respect by sharing information, asking for advice, striving to understand different viewpoints, responding to feelings and needs, and avoiding blame if problems arise.

Even two experts looking at the same behavior might focus on different aspects of that behavior. Imagine a physical therapist, a speech therapist, and a child development specialist all observing four-year-old Carlos at play. The physical therapist might be noticing the way the child coordinates his movements and the tenseness of his muscles, while the speech therapist is observing the way he pronounces certain sounds, and the child development specialist is watching the way he joins in block play with other children. This type of assessment is often used by teams of professionals working with children with disabilities. You can adapt this method in your own work with children, asking others—professionals and family members—to observe children and share their findings with you in order to build a more complete picture of the individual children in your care.

There are many different techniques for observation, and it will take practice for you to select and use each one effectively. We will describe and provide examples of several: checklists, narrative records, anecdotal records, time sampling, event sampling, and behavioral analysis, a particular type of event sampling. (Behavioral analysis will be discussed more fully in Chapter 11.) More important than the particular tool you use is a clear understanding that your purpose is to learn more about the children in your care, to understand them so that you can support their learning and growth more effectively.

Checklists

One very simple observation tool is the checklist. Two teachers in a half-day program wanted to determine how well the interest centers they had set up appealed to the children. They also wondered whether individual children were spending all their time in one or two centers, thus missing the learning opportunities afforded by the others. They constructed a simple checklist, consisting of a list of the children's names down the first column and an additional column for each interest center, labeled at the top with the center name. They made several copies of the checklist, and each day, after the children left, they took a few minutes to think back over the morning and put checkmarks in the appropriate column for each center that each child had visited that day.

Obviously, the power of the teachers' memory is a limitation to this method, but a checklist is helpful in providing an overview of classroom activity, especially in situations where two or more adults would each have only a piece of the picture. Completing the checklist together would fill in the gaps for each of them and give them an opportunity to share specific details about things that had occurred during the day.

Teachers can also construct more narrowly defined checklists and incorporate a simple notation system to indicate particular gradations of meaning. A clipboard in the block area could hold a list of children's names, with the days of the week across the top. Teachers could observe which children played in the block area and note the child's level of participation according to a key like this one:

1. Exploratory play: observed; carried and dumped; created rows or stacked, then "crashed"
2. Engaged, sustained, solitary construction
3. Collaborative construction; extended play

The reports that child development programs provide to families at various intervals throughout the year are often in the form of checklists. (See Figure 3–3.) Checklists can also be tools that let children participate in managing their classrooms. In one center, snack is available for a little over an hour each morning. Children serve themselves and then check off their names on the nearby clipboard, relieving their teacher of a clerical detail and practicing their literacy skills at the same time.

Narrative Records

As part of your work for this or other courses in child development, your instructor may ask you to compile several hours' worth of observations of a particular child. Because your goal is so broad—to learn everything you can about one particular

Child's Name _____ Program _____			
Birthdate _____ Age _____ Group_____			
Recorder _____ Role _____ Date _____			
Key: 0 = not observed 1 = with support 2 = consistently			
	0	1	2
Enters classroom willingly			
Chooses appropriate activities			
Sustains engagement with activities			
Responds to adults			
Approaches adults; communicates needs			
Responds to other children			
Initiates contact with other children			
Negotiates and resolves conflicts			
Participates in group activities			
Follows classroom rules			

FIGURE 3–3   An example of a checklist for observing an individual child

child—you may be asked to write down everything that child does during the periods that you observe. This is called a *running record*. Since it is humanly impossible to see and remember everything that happens, you will have to decide ahead of time to focus your observations on particular aspects of the child's behavior. While creating a running record may be a good way of capturing a wealth of detail about a particular child, it is probably not a practical method for a busy adult who is responsible for a group of children.

Anecdotal Records

Anecdotal records are brief vignettes that capture some aspect of a child's behavior or thinking. Deciding what should be recorded as an anecdote depends on your overall goals for the child and on your ability to recognize significant indicators of progress toward those goals. As your expertise and knowledge of individual children grows, you will no doubt record many things that would go unnoticed by the untrained observer. For example, the vignette at the opening of this chapter is an anecdote.

Anecdotes should always include the date, time, and circumstances of the event and as many concrete details as possible, including direct quotations of the child's actual words, so that readers (other teachers, parents, specialists, etc.) can picture the event for themselves and draw their own conclusions about its meaning. It is very important that anecdotal records be free of any derogatory or judgmental remarks that could cause readers to expect the worst of a child and thus create a self-fulfilling prophecy.

This is not to say that you will not interpret or analyze the anecdotes. It simply means that your comments or explanations of what you think the anecdote means should be clearly identified as such and recorded in a separate section. Those interpretations can consist of simply classifying an anecdote, such as the one on page 43 about Darnell, as part of emotional development, and identifying it as an example of "coping with frustration in acceptable ways." Or they can include more detailed reflections, comparing the incident described with what the observer already knows about the child and pondering possible explanations.

Anecdotal records, carefully collected and organized as part of a child's portfolio, will document change over time in all developmental domains. The information in anecdotal records is richer and more complete than that found in a checklist. Figure 3–4 is an example of an anecdotal record that depicts a child who chooses and pursues an activity, responds when another child approaches her, and negotiates a peaceful solution to a conflict.

Time Sampling

Suppose that four-year-old Charlie's parents complain to you that "all he does is play with trucks" at your center. They want you to forbid him to play with the trucks and to require him to make a picture or craft project to take home every day. Before taking such drastic action, you might begin by assuring the parents that you share their belief that Charlie needs to experience many types of activity. You have a vague impression that Charlie does spend a lot of time pushing the big trucks around the block area, but it seems to you that you have seen him do other things as well. You realize that

Child's Name: Kendra	Age: 4.6	Date of Observation 2/15/12
Recorder: Elisa Gomez		**Time Start:** 10:00 End: 10:20

Setting: ABC Child Development Center; 4-year-old classroom

Kendra is in the housekeeping center, humming quietly to herself as she bustles about, gathering dish and plastic food items to set the table. She has seated two dolls and a stuffed bear in three of the four available chairs, and she places a bowl and cup in front of each, saying, "There you go, baby. Here's your lunch." Micaela, another 4-year-old, enters the scene and starts to pick up one of the dolls. "No Kendra shouts. "That's my baby. I'm the mama." "I want to play, too," says Micaela, maintaining her grip on the doll. The two girls both tug on the doll, their voices becoming louder and more agitated "I was here first," says Kendra. She regains possession of the doll and plops it back in the chair with an air of finality. Micaela starts crying and says, "I won't be your friend. I'm gonna tell the teacher." Kendra moves close to Micaela, puts a hand on her shoulder and tells her, "Don't cry. You can play. You can be the big sister." She pulls out the fourth chair and says, "Here, Big Sister. Here's some lunch for you. Sit down and eat now." Micaela complies and pretends to eat the plastic food that Kendra puts before her.

Comments

Kendra's concentration and involvement in the doll play was in marked contrast to her behavior when she entered the classroom a few months ago. She frequently wandered from center to center, never real becoming engaged in anything. It was uncharacteristic of her to stand up to Micaela the way she did. In the past she has always given in when Micaela or any of the other more assertive children move into her space. She did seem genuinely concerned about Micaela's feelings, though. Her facial expression and tone of voice were very compassionate.

FIGURE 3–4 An example of an anecdotal record of social interactions

you don't have a complete picture of how he is spending his time, and you cannot say with certainty exactly what he is doing with the trucks. You devise a plan to observe Charlie more closely during free play for the next week.

Of course, you will not be able to just sit and watch Charlie for 90 minutes each morning, nor will you be able to record his every action. Besides, if you did follow him around, clipboard in hand, he might find your behavior a little strange, and you would not see his typical behavior. Instead, you could use a *time sampling* technique. This means that you will carry a notepad and pencil with you as you go about your regular routine of supervising the children each morning. Then, every five minutes you will make it a point to glance over at Charlie and jot a brief description of what he is doing. The more detail you can capture about what he is doing, how he is doing it, and with whom, the more useful your observations will be. Using a timer or wristwatch alarm will ensure that you make your observations at five-minute intervals.

At the end of the week, you can look over your notes and determine the accuracy of your initial impressions about how Charlie has been using his time. Often you will find that children who seem to spend all their time in one area are, in fact, managing to get around to several other areas over the course of the week. You can also develop a more accurate picture of the variety of ways Charlie is using the trucks. Is he exploring the physics of ramps and gravity, or is he demonstrating what he knows about various community helper roles? He might be learning something about being a leader and follower as the other children join him in his play. Perhaps you noticed him making road signs for his trucks, evidence of his emerging literacy.

You will be able to reassure yourself, as well as Charlie's parents, that he is having a rich variety of experiences at the center. And you will have avoided making choices for Charlie, depriving him of an activity that brings him great pleasure. If, on the other hand, you find that he has, indeed, spent the vast majority of each free play period with the trucks, and that he has played entirely alone, repeating the same motions and sounds over and over, you may want to think about ways to help him enrich his play by adding props, reading stories, or visiting a real truck, for example.

Event Sampling

Another way to focus your observations is the **event sampling** technique. Instead of recording what occurs at regular intervals, you record specific events whenever they happen to occur. In one center, for example, three-year-old Emily cried inconsolably every morning as her mother left her. This continued for over a month, well after her peers had happily adapted to their new school. A sensitive staff member began observing what happened during Emily's transition into the center each morning. She focused on this particular event and collected observations around it. After observing for a few days, she noticed a pattern: Emily's mother was usually occupied with the younger baby in her arms and in conversation with the center staff during the arrival. Emily seemed to hover in the background until the moment of good-bye, when she began her loud crying. Because the baby was still young enough to go to strangers willingly, the center staff devised a plan in which one of them took the baby for a few moments, freeing the mother to stoop down and focus her attention on saying good-bye to Emily. Soon, Emily's loud sobs became soft sniffles, and eventually they disappeared.

Behavioral Analysis

Behavioral analysis, a particular type of event sampling, is a technique frequently used to help deal with problematic behaviors. Suppose that Sarah, age two, has been pulling the hair of other children at your child development center. By carefully recording each time she pulls hair over a two-week period and noting what happens immediately before (the antecedent) and after (the consequence), you might discover patterns that help to explain the behavior.

You might see, for example, that Sarah always screamed when another child took a toy from her and that she pulled hair only after the child failed to respond to the scream. Furthermore, you may notice that she received a great deal of adult attention after each hair-pulling incident. As a result of your analysis, you could devise a plan to intervene before she pulls hair, perhaps by providing duplicate toys or positioning yourself so that you can move near quickly when another child approaches her. Or you might focus your effort on what happens after she pulls someone's hair, calmly attending to the injured child rather than giving Sarah a lot of attention. Figure 3–5 is an example of what that behavioral analysis record might look like.

Date/Time	Antecedent	Behavior	Consequence
11/9/12 8:50	Sarah has been playing alone with stuffed animals in the loft for about 20 minutes. Teacher A is helping a child tie his shoe and has her back to the loft. Koji crawls up the ramp and picks up one of the stuffed toys.	Sarah pulls on the toy and cries. When Koji doesn't release it, she pulls his hair.	Koji screams. Teacher A tells Sarah, "No! That hurts!" She picks up Koji to console him, continuing her reprimand to Sarah. "I don't like it when you hurt. Be nice to your friends," etc. Sarah sobs for a moment and then continues her play.
11/15/12 10:45	Teachers A and B are escorting the group from the playground back into the classroom. Sarah and Brandt both run ahead to get the play vacuum cleaner.	They each tug on it for a moment, yelling loudly, "Mine!" "No, mine!" Sarah drops her hold and grabs a fistful of Brandt's hair.	Brandt screams in protest but doesn't relinquish his hold on the toy. Teacher A hurries to the children and takes the toy away. "You have to share," she says, "or I will put it away." Both children cry and the teacher hugs them.
11/19/12 3:30	Some children are still napping. A few are awake and playing quietly with puzzles. Teacher A is diapering one child; Teacher B is supervising the puzzle players and doesn't see Sarah wake up.	Hallie toddles over and reaches for the teddy bear Sarah had cuddled during the nap. Sarah yells, "No!" and yanks Hallie's hair when she comes closer.	Teachers A and B both say, "No, Sarah. No hair pulling." Teacher B moves near the two girls and says to Hallie, "That's Sarah's bear, Hallie. She doesn't like it when you touch her bear."
11/29/12 11:00	Teachers A and B are both supervising children as they wash their hands before lunch. Sarah has finished and is sitting at the table. Hallie sits down next to her.	Sarah immediately places a protective arm between her placemat and Hallie's. "Mine," she says. Hallie moves to define her own space and Sarah pulls her hair.	Both teachers look over from the sink area and tell the girls to "Be nice."

FIGURE 3–5 An example of event sampling for behavioral analysis

DOCUMENTATION AND TEACHER AS RESEARCHER

For more than 20 years, since they were introduced to the United States in an article by Lella Gandini (1984), the early childhood programs of Reggio Emilia, Italy, have been providing inspiration and challenges to American educators. The concepts of **documentation** and **teacher as researcher** are two facets of their approach that have particular relevance for our discussion of observation and guidance. According to the educators in Reggio Emilia, documentation is more than a collection of notes, recordings, and artifacts to be examined and displayed after the fact. It is, instead, a dynamic process of searching for, or constructing, meaning. Adults seek to learn alongside children, asking themselves

> How can we help children find the meaning of what they do, what they encounter, what they experience? And how can we do this for ourselves?. . . We cannot live without meaning; that would preclude any sense of identity, any hope, any future. Children know this and initiate the search right from the beginning of their lives. (Rinaldi, 2001, p. 79)

Observation for purposes of documentation may seem more related to curriculum planning than the types of observation we have discussed thus far in this chapter. However, as suggested in our pyramid image (Figure 3–1, p. 45) and the discussion in Chapter 1, a curriculum that is deeply engaging to children and teachers is an essential component of guidance.

In brief, effort expended in igniting and sharing children's wonder often means less effort will be required to manage "misbehavior." Observation in this sense is the process of uncovering that wonder in order to build upon it. Palsha (2002) relates a beautiful example of the ways educators in Reggio Emilia used careful

A curriculum that is deeply engaging to children and teachers is an essential component of guidance.

observation and documentation to find a way of connecting with a three-year-old girl with autism. When she first entered the program, the child spent all her time racing around the perimeter of the classroom, and the teachers' first impulse was to find a way to stop that behavior. Encouraged to seek a deeper goal of getting to know the child—of finding the traces of her desire for a relationship—the teachers spent time observing and recording the child's running behavior. When they discovered that she was attracted to bright light, they offered her many opportunities to explore and play with light and enlisted the help of another child in the process. By the end of the school year, the child was able to work side-by-side with her companion and to concentrate for long periods of time.

CONCLUSION

Knowing children is the foundation of appropriate guidance. This means being familiar with the stages children typically pass through as they grow and develop physically, emotionally, socially, and cognitively—knowing what came before and what you can expect next. It means understanding how each of these domains influences and is influenced by the others and how factors in the environment affect them all. But knowing general characteristics and typical patterns of development give only part of the picture. Teachers and child caregivers must also know individual children and their families. By watching and listening closely, you can begin to notice little things that make up each child's personality. Observing carefully and recording those observations as carefully and accurately as possible will give you a firm basis for decisions you will need to make as you plan your program, and guide young children. Getting to know their families will help you understand children better and lay the foundation for the type of collaboration that is needed if guidance is to be effective. We have described several ways to observe and record children's behavior which will help you get to know individual children better. Chapter 4 will look at the next component of developmentally appropriate practice: understanding the families of children in your program and the cultural contexts of their lives.

REVIEW: TEN GUIDES FOR KNOWING CHILDREN

Understand how all children develop:

1. The general sequence of development is the same for all children; early development lays the foundation for what comes next, following a predictable pattern (from head to toe, midline to outer extremities, simple to more complex).

2. Rates of development vary from child to child and from one domain to another within an individual child.

3. Development is commonly studied as occurring within specific domains (e.g., physical, emotional, social, intellectual), but all the domains are interwoven; no area can be affected without affecting all the others.

4. Development is influenced by factors within the environment as well as factors within the child (e.g., temperament, the child's inborn way of responding to people and experiences).

5. A child's brain is under construction throughout the early years; chronic (toxic) stress and unmet needs for support and positive interaction can alter development of neuronal pathways (the architecture of the brain) and have lifelong consequences.

Observe closely to learn about individual children:

6. Strive for objectivity and accuracy.

7. Remember that the purpose of observation is to understand, not judge, children.

8. Practice using a variety of tools so that you can select the appropriate one for any given purpose.

9. Share observations with children's families and seek their input to make your observations more complete.

10. Use observation as the first step in documentation—a way to make sense of and communicate what happens in your classroom.

APPLICATIONS

1. Consider the following examples of expectations for the behavior of children in early childhood programs: sharing toys, waiting for a turn to use a swing, and putting away materials neatly after using them. Recall what you have learned about child development or locate information in a child development textbook to explain why each is (or is not) appropriate for two-year-old children. Repeat the process with four-year-old children in mind.

2. List the principles of development discussed in this chapter and give an example of each.

3. Identify domains of development and give examples of how they influence and are influenced by each other.

4. Define *self-regulation* and identify factors that contribute to its development.

5. Discuss characteristics of *evidence-based practice*.

6. Practice using each of the tools for observation described in this chapter.

RESOURCES FOR FURTHER STUDY

Websites

Center for Early Childhood Mental Health Consultation
ecmhc.org/temperament
A collaborative effort of university researchers developing strategies to help Head Start programs build a strong mental health foundation for their children, families and staff; includes a link to the *Infant-Toddler Temperament Tool*, an interactive self-assessment with suggestions for improving "goodness of fit" between children and their parents or caregivers.

National Scientific Council on the Developing Child
developingchild.net
A multidisciplinary collaboration of scientists and scholars from universities across the United States and Canada, established in 2003 to bring the science of early childhood and early brain development to bear on public policy decision making by generating, synthesizing, and communicating knowledge in the science of early childhood development and its underlying neurobiology. Includes a link to a short video, "Brain Hero," based loosely on such games as "Guitar Hero," "SimCity," and "The Game of Life," portraying how actions taken by parents, teachers, policymakers, and others can affect life outcomes for both a child and the surrounding community.

Center on the Social and Emotional Foundations for Early Learning(CSEFEL)
csefel.vanderbilt.edu
A national resource center funded by the Office of Head Start and Child Care Bureau for disseminating research and evidence-based practices for promoting the social emotional development and school readiness of young children birth to age five. Provides training materials, videos, and print resources for teachers, caregivers, and families.

Readings

Bowman, B., & Moore, E. K. (eds.). (2006). *School readiness and social-emotional development: Perspectives on cultural diversity.* Washington, DC: National Black Child Development Institute.

Buysse, V., Wesley, P. W., & Winton, P. (2006). Evidence-based practice: What does it really mean for the early childhood field? *Young Exceptional Children, 9*(4), 2–11.

Filler, J., & Xu, Y. (2006/07 Winter). Including children with disabilities in early childhood education programs: Individualizing developmentally appropriate practice. *Childhood Education, 83*(2), 92–98.

Jablon, J. R., Dombro, A. L., & Dichtelmiller, M. L. (2007). *The power of observation* (2nd ed.). Washington, DC: Teaching Strategies and National Association for the Education of Young Children.

Trawick-Smith, J. (2009). *Early childhood development: A multicultural perspective* (5th ed.). Upper Saddle River, NJ: Pearson.

CHAPTER 4

Collaborating with Families of Young Children

Learning Outcomes

After studying this chapter you should be able to

- Explain the importance of family involvement in early childhood education.
- Discuss strategies for building and maintaining positive relationships with family members.
- Discuss strategies for helping children feel comfortable in child-care programs.
- List ways to ease transitions as children move from child-care programs to school.
- Identify signs of child abuse and know how to respond.

The children and staff at the State Street Child Development Center had been planning their fall celebration breakfast for weeks. The hand-made invitations had gone home, the decorations were in place, and the muffins and fruit kabobs were ready. Jessica Wilson, the center director, greeted the families as they arrived. She was pleased with the good attendance and proud of the fact that her staff and the families were chatting so comfortably with each other. She remembered her own early days as a teacher and how she had sometimes felt nervous about having parents visit her classroom. Since then, she had come to realize that forging strong relationships with families was one of the most important tasks of an early childhood educator.

DEVELOPMENTALLY APPROPRIATE PRACTICE: THE FAMILY COMPONENT

Developmentally appropriate practice means that educators know not only about children in general but about the individual children in their programs and about the families and cultures in which those children live. You may know a lot about infants or four-year-olds, for example, but family members know things about *this* infant or *this* four-year-old that you need to know in order to do your job well. Even when children attend full-day programs, any individual child will be with you for only a few months or years—and for only part of each day and each week during that time. Family members know about the child's life outside your program, and they will be part of that child's life long after you no longer are. As suggested by Figure 4–1, collaboration with the families of children in your care will (or should) permeate every aspect of your guidance. You become a better teacher, a better caregiver, through your relationships with children's families.

Family involvement in early childhood education is a component of best practices in all professions serving young children and their families. In its guidelines for developmentally appropriate practice, the National Association for the Education of Young Children (NAEYC) requires early childhood programs to establish "reciprocal relationships with families" based on "mutual respect, cooperation, shared responsibility and negotiation of conflicts toward achievement of shared goals" (Copple & Bredekamp, 2009, pp. 22–23). The Division for Early Childhood of the Council for Exceptional Children advocates *family-based practices*—that is, practices based on collaboration and shared responsibility between families and professionals (Trivette & Dunst, 2000). Accreditation standards for family child-care homes emphasize the primary importance of relationships in high-quality programs and identify specific criteria related to building trust and respect as well as communication and involvement with parents and families (National Association for Family Child Care [NAFCC], 2003, pp. 9–10).

Family members know about the child's life outside your program, and they will be a part of that child's life long after you no longer are.

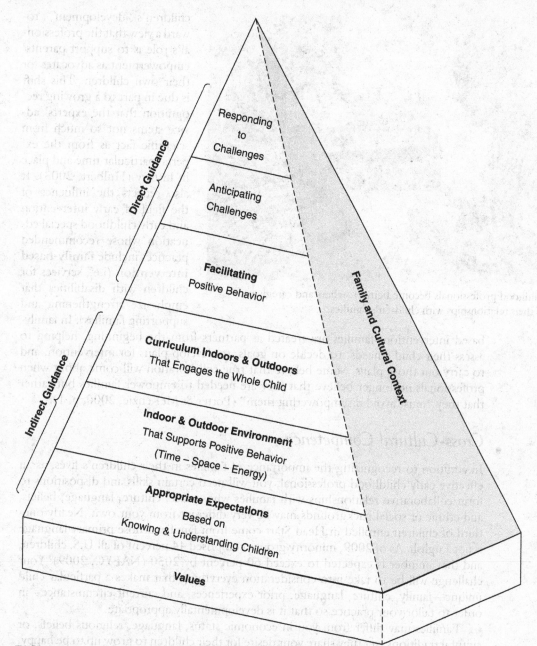

Direct Guidance

Responding
to
Challenges

Anticipating
Challenges

Facilitating
Positive Behavior

Curriculum Indoors & Outdoors
That Engages the Whole Child

Indoor & Outdoor Environment
That Supports Positive Behavior
(Time – Space – Energy)

Appropriate Expectations
Based on
Knowing & Understanding Children

Values

Indirect Guidance

Family and Cultural Context

FIGURE 4–1 The guidance pyramid: Family and cultural context

Shifting Focus from Child to Family

While collaboration has long been important to the professions identified with early care and education, there has been a steady shift in recent years from the view of professionals as "experts" whose job is to teach parents how to support their

children's development, toward a view that the professional's role is to support parents' empowerment as advocates for their own children. This shift is due in part to a growing recognition that the experts' advice stems not so much from scientific fact as from the experts' particular time and place in history (Hulbert, 2003). It also reflects the influence of the field of early intervention and early childhood special education whose recommended practices include **family-based intervention** (i.e., services for children with disabilities that emphasize strengthening and supporting families). In family-

Early childhood professionals become better teachers and caregivers through their relationships with children's families.

based intervention, families are treated as partners from the beginning, helping to assess their child's needs, to decide on goals, to develop plans for intervention, and to carry out those plans. Some believe that true collaboration will come about when professionals no longer believe that they are needed to empower families but rather that they "must avoid disempowering them" (Porter & McKenzie, 2000, p. 1).

Cross-Cultural Competence

In addition to recognizing the importance of families in their children's lives, as an effective early childhood professional, you will need certain skills and dispositions to form collaborative relationships with families whose race, culture, language, beliefs, and ethnic or social backgrounds may be very different from your own. Nearly one-third of children enrolled in Head Start come from families whose primary language is not English. As of 2009, minority groups comprised 44 percent of all U.S. children, and that number is expected to exceed 60 percent by 2050 (NAEYC, 2009). Your challenge will be to take into consideration everything that makes a particular child unique—family, culture, language, prior experiences, and current circumstance—in order to tailor your practice so that it is developmentally appropriate.

Families may differ from you in economic status, language, religious beliefs, or cultural traditions, yet they share your desire for their children to grow up to be happy, competent adults. A study involving focus groups of low-income parents found that they share many values with early childhood professionals: They want a child-care setting that is "warm, cheerful, calm, and inviting," and they want to know that "their child is loved in their absence" (Paulsell & Nogales, 2003, p. 32).

The ability to form relationships with people who are different from you in some significant way is called *cross-cultural competence* (Klein & Chen, 2001). In an increasingly diverse society and global marketplace, cross-cultural competence has become a necessity in nearly every field, and the early childhood profession is no exception. How, then, does an early childhood professional establish and maintain these exciting, productive relationships? Probably the most important step is a genuine desire or disposition to be open to new ideas and respectful of differences. Be aware that "cultures are not superior or inferior. They just are" (Exton, 2000, p. 5). As noted earlier, it is essential to know something about the families you serve—their beliefs, customs, and hopes for their children. There are many available resources (e.g., Hildebrand, Phenice, Gray, & Hines, 2007) to help you acquire basic knowledge about family diversity, but you must realize that no source will tell you everything you need to know. In your quest for knowledge about particular groups, be careful to avoid perpetuating stereotypes. Families from all cultures share many things in common, while individuals within a particular culture can differ widely from each other.

Encountering differences between yourself and others can create a "cultural bump" (Barrera, 2003). Exploring those differences is a way to achieve a deeper understanding of diversity. Check the accuracy of what you may have read about someone's culture by talking about what you have read and asking whether it is true for a particular family. Admitting that you don't have all the answers and understanding and respecting the possibility that someone else's way of seeing things can be as valid as your own sets the stage for examining viewpoints that are acceptable to both parties and perhaps reaching a compromise. This is a process that will take time. You may not reach agreement in one, or even many, conversations. The important thing is to keep the door open for continued dialogue.

❈ Talk It Over ❈

Think about your answers to the following questions: Should infants learn to soothe themselves and sleep alone? Should one-year-olds be allowed to feed themselves? When should children begin to learn to use the toilet? Should you provide special food for a three-year-old who doesn't like what is on the menu? Is it all right for children to make a mess and get dirty as they play? What should adults do when children "misbehave"? Compare your responses with those of your classmates and note whether you encountered any "cultural bumps." Role-play a situation with someone whose answers to a question differed from yours, with a goal of finding a compromise that you can each accept.

What should teachers do when family rules are at odds with classroom rules? Children may hear adults using profanity at home and repeat those words at school. They may have been told to stand up for themselves and hit back when provoked by other children. Accepting family differences does not mean that you have to give up what you believe is right. Many potential conflicts can be avoided by using diplomacy. Young children—and their parents—are capable of understanding that classroom rules may be different from home rules. The important thing is to state those differences without discrediting home life. You can say, "We don't use those words at school. You can say *pastrowzi* (or some other nonsense word) when you are angry."

You can tell a child, "My job is to keep everyone safe. I can't let you hit, and I won't let anyone hit you either. Tell Frederico that you were still using the shovel."

More complicated situations (e.g., when to begin toilet training, or whether children should "clean their plates" at lunch) will require dialogue with families to arrive at solutions that are comfortable for everyone. Remembering the strategies for moving beyond these differences of opinion will help you negotiate the "bumps." Dialogues are much easier and more likely to occur when the parties involved have already established a cordial relationship. The rest of this chapter outlines suggestions for laying the groundwork for collaborative relationships with families, for initiating those relationships with new families, for maintaining them throughout a family's association with your program, and for facilitating families' establishment of new relationships beyond your own program.

STRATEGIES FOR BUILDING AND MAINTAINING RELATIONSHIPS

Laying the Groundwork: Program Philosophy and Goals

Parents who inquire about a program and those who subsequently enroll their children in it may all be served if the center has a carefully prepared written statement of its philosophy and goals. Such a written statement will help parents determine whether a given center has the type of program they want. Having a written statement will also help maintain consistency among various staff members when questions arise after a child begins attending. The basic concept that the early childhood program is framed around the developmental needs of children should be stressed so that families know that you share their wish for the best possible start in life for their children.

Be careful, however that your written materials do not inadvertently convey a sense of excluding some families. Something as simple as an enrollment form with separate blanks for "mother" and "father" names can make lesbian or gay parents, single parents, or grandparents raising their grandchildren feel marginalized. Families who don't speak (or don't read) English will appreciate receiving handbooks and forms translated into their language. When attempting to provide translations, however, some caution is in order. Words that have the same dictionary meaning may carry connotations that can seem rude or insensitive to native speakers of a language. Families may speak a language that is different from the one they use for reading and writing, or they may actually prefer to receive written communications in English. It's a good idea to ask about these preferences and to enlist the help of bilingual family members when the need for translation arises. As more programs move to paperless systems of communication, it's important to remember that families without access to computers will need hard copies of materials.

Initiating Relationships

Children enter new groups for a variety of reasons. A mother's maternity leave expires, and she places her child in an infant-toddler center so she can resume her job. An infant who learns to walk is moved from an infant group to the toddler room. An early intervention team determines that a three-year-old with cerebral palsy will benefit from spending several mornings a week in a neighborhood child development program. Many early childhood programs exist as a service to working parents and, therefore, operate year round. New children enter the program any time openings are created through the departure of other children. A new child enters an ongoing group and gradually becomes part of that group. In other programs that operate only during the school year, the entire group may consist of new children each fall.

The aim in each of these situations is the same: to help children and families become comfortable and happy in the new setting. Each setting offers its own advantages and limitations for achieving that aim, however, which means you will need to tailor your efforts to suit particular circumstances. Furthermore, while you may be able to implement some of these suggestions as a new caregiver or teacher, others will require administrative decisions beyond the scope of your authority. By learning about these ideas now, you will be preparing yourself for the day when you are the administrator, setting policies that will impact children's first days in your program.

Your aim is to help families and children become comfortable and happy in your program.

❋ Talk It Over ❋

In class, describe the first days of school you remember—your own, your siblings', or those of children in early childhood programs. What feelings are prominent in children during those first days of school? How do parents feel? What can teachers do to make the initial period easier? Divide your class and role-play some of these situations. Discuss the feelings expressed.

Think of the point at which a child enters your program as one of the first steps toward building those relationships. Recognize that meaningful relationships take time and that the time you invest at this crucial time will have long-term benefits. Wise managers of child development centers build in opportunities to spend this time, and they strive to reduce staff turnover so that caregivers have years, rather than weeks, to cultivate relationships with children and families. What are those relationships? Of course, you will have a relationship with each child. You will also build relationships with each child's family members and with other adults who care for the child, including your colleagues. Children will develop relationships with each other, and families will develop relationships with other families. This complex network of relationships enriches everyone involved, extending and creating possibilities that would not exist in isolation.

Considering continuity, group size, and ratios. If you think of what you've learned about child development, you will realize why many people feel that relationships are at the heart of early childhood education. After all, it is only through nurturing relationships that children develop trust and learn to feel secure enough to be able to devote energy to the work of growth and development. The importance of this trusting relationship is one reason for the idea of assigning a **primary caregiver** in infant-toddler centers—one person who feeds, diapers, and tends to a child's other needs—so that adult and child can really get to know and bond with each other. It is also the reason behind the limited group sizes recommended for high-quality programs: in most cases no more than 8 infants, 12 toddlers, or 18 three- and four-year-olds. It is simply humanly impossible for one person to meet the needs of children, or build strong relationships with families, when numbers are overwhelming.

In some instances, the best way to help a child is to eliminate the need for adjusting to a new setting. Thus, some infant-toddler program managers have rethought their policies of moving children from room to room as they reach developmental milestones. Instead, they keep children with the same group and caregiver for as long as three years, allowing relationships with both families and children to deepen. Early intervention specialists bring services such as physical or speech therapy to child development centers instead of requiring children with disabilities to adjust to several different settings over the course of a week.

Preparing to welcome a child. One of your main goals as you prepare to welcome any child or group of children into your program is to learn as much as possible about each child and family. That way, you can strive to create the best match possible between the needs of each child and family, on the one hand, and what your program is able to offer, on the other. You may accomplish this through interviews at the center, during home visits, or by asking each family to complete a questionnaire. At the same time, family members are getting to know you and your program and are deciding whether you will meet their needs. These early efforts, in addition to helping you and the family determine whether you make a good match, will lay an important foundation for the enduring relationships that are an important part of any child development program.

❀ Talk It Over ❀

Suppose a family, after observing your program for several hours, has decided to go ahead with the enrollment procedure. Your job is to interview the family members to learn more about the child as well as what the family expects of your program. Brainstorm a list of questions you might ask. Compare your list with examples of enrollment forms used by early childhood programs in your community.

Conducting the initial interview. Getting acquainted with family members as friendly adults is the first step to building a relationship. You don't have to begin by reciting the school's program or the agency's policies. It's probably much more important—and productive—to listen, to find out what families are seeking from your program, and to find out what issues they confront as they try to balance work and family life. Families shouldn't be feared. Many families in this highly mobile society are isolated from their extended families. They may long for someone to talk to about their parenting concerns. They are likely to appreciate someone who will listen as they make inquiries about their children. Some are lonely for adult conversation.

Remember that, as a family child-care provider, early childhood teacher, or early interventionist, you may be the family's first contact with social service and education systems. If family members have experienced their own school days as unpleasant, threatening, and unproductive, they may bring negative feelings with them as they approach the early childhood teacher. They may have many negative associations with social service agencies and thus mistrust an early interventionist coming into their home. Most families need and appreciate reassurance that their child is developing as expected and that they are doing a good job.

Welcoming family members on site. Programs that operate year-round and accept individual children at any time during the year can strongly encourage parents of prospective enrollees to visit the program, spending enough time to get an idea of the type of care and education provided. After a brief orientation visit with the program administrator, family members should be welcome to sit unobtrusively in the classroom, "just watching" the ways children interact with each other and with adults. This observation period should be followed by another opportunity to meet with the administrator for clarification of any questions that might have arisen during the visit. The child should not be present during this first visit since family members need to devote their full attention to observing the center, free from concern for meeting their own child's needs.

Family members should be welcome to make several such visits if they wish; they should not be pressured to make a decision immediately. Once they have made a tentative decision, however, the administrator or another staff member can conduct an introductory interview to gain some basic information about the child as well as the family's expectations of the center.

Programs that operate only during the school year and enroll an entire group of new children at one time can use the same procedure and invite next year's families to come in and observe all or part of a day's session before the end of the school year. Spreading the observations over a month or so will ensure that the program is not disrupted by having too many family members in the classroom on any single day.

Making home visits. Another way to forge relationships with families is to make home visits. In fact, many programs, such as Parents as Teachers (PAT), home-based Head Start, and early intervention services, are delivered exclusively through home visits. As an early childhood professional in one of these programs, your job might be to help teenage mothers develop competence and confidence or to help

families cope with raising a child who has disabilities. Research findings differ about the effectiveness of such programs and about possible reasons for variable outcomes, but it is generally agreed that success is more likely if goals are realistic and if administrators, staff, and families are all clear on the intended purpose (Hebbeler & Gerlach-Downie, 2002; Roggman, Boyce, Cook, & Jump, 2001).

A home visit to get to know the child and family before school starts sets the stage for a comfortable introduction to the program.

In a center-based program, the purpose of the home visit is to set the stage for a comfortable introduction into your program. Children and parents are often more at ease meeting new people in familiar surroundings, and teachers can develop a better understanding when they see where families live and how they interact with one another. The fact that teachers know where they live helps children feel more secure in their new school, and they often greet teachers on their first day with a delighted, "You were at my house!"

Of course, home visits should always be scheduled by appointment at the family's convenience, and families should always have the right to say whether or not they want someone to visit them. For some families, a visit can seem like an invasion of privacy or a threatening inspection of their way of life. Families usually are less reluctant when visits are explained as a way of getting to know each other and helping children feel more comfortable. Focusing the conversation primarily on the child and on topics the parents wish to discuss helps avoid any concern about the quality of furnishings. Visits scheduled before the child actually enters school carry no hint that teachers are coming to discuss problems or misbehavior. At such an early date, parents are the ones who know the child and have information to give.

Teachers in one program for four-year-olds found that home visits made after school began were more pleasant and meaningful when families had a part in planning them. One year they invited each child to plan a special activity to do with the teacher during the home visit. The children played games, shared snacks, made cookies—their ideas were almost limitless. The teachers made sure that children knew they could use school materials for their activity so that family members were not pressured to buy things they might not be able to afford.

These initial steps toward getting to know one another, often before the child sets foot in the center door, help set the stage for families—and, therefore, for their children—to feel welcome in your program. You can magnify the welcoming effect by enlisting the help of families whose children already attend the program, perhaps asking them to host a potluck supper during which they can share their knowledge of the program with incoming families. This not only lightens your burden but begins to build a supportive network of relationships between families, so that new families begin to feel part of the group from the very beginning.

Maintaining Relationships

Acceptance. Accepting families as they are is a key to communicating with them. People are different, and each family is different, too. The "traditional" family with a father who goes to work and a mother who stays home with the children is no longer the norm. Many children live in single-parent families, in families headed by gay or lesbian couples, and in families in which both parents work. Increasing numbers of children are being raised by their grandparents or by foster parents for various reasons. Whatever the families you work with are like, you will be more warmly accepted if you refrain from judging them or attempting to change them. All families have strengths—good points—and early childhood professionals can look for these to help appreciate families.

It is especially important for teachers and caregivers of young children to avoid entering into a competitive relationship with family members who may already be feeling guilty about leaving their child in someone else's care, particularly when published reports of mediocre quality lead child development experts to counsel them that staying home with their children is preferable (e.g., Greenspan, 2003). A casual remark that a child "never acts that way for me" can raise anxiety and cause family members to question their competence. Early childhood professionals must work to support, not undermine, children's relationships with their families.

Some children might be referred to your program by professionals who will be able to provide you with helpful information as part of the referral process. An example might be a child referred for care by a department of social services as part of a plan to help a family break a cycle of child abuse. Children with disabilities or developmental delays may be referred to your program by a team of professionals working with parents to create Individualized Family Service Plans (IFSPs) for facilitating each child's optimum development.

The model form for the IFSP provided by the U.S. Department of Education (2011) includes the following information:

- The name of the service coordinator from the profession most immediately relevant to the child's or family's needs, who will serve as the single point of contact for carrying out the plan
- A statement of the child's present levels of physical, cognitive, communication, social or emotional, and adaptive development
- A summary of the family's resources, priorities, and concerns related to enhancing the child's development
- A list of desired outcomes or goals, stated in measurable terms, and the criteria, procedures, and timelines used to determine progress as well as the need for any revisions

Once a child enters your program, you become part of a team that works together to achieve the developmental goals established in the plan. If you have not already

High-quality programs are open to visits by families before and after the child is enrolled.

been invited to do so, you can ask permission from the child's parents to be included in future team meetings when the plan is reviewed and updated.

Whatever the reason for a family's referral to your program, it is important that you be careful not to prejudge or stereotype that family.

Freedom to visit. High-quality programs are open to visits by parents before and after the child is enrolled. Freedom to visit without a prior appointment indicates openness and honesty. With this policy, families will feel that your everyday manners are the same as your company manners. Working parents especially may find it difficult to arrange for visits but may make a number of short observations if encouraged to drop in when possible.

While it should be easy for family members to drop in to visit when they happen to have a few minutes, it is also important to protect the program from disruptive intrusions. Centers can let families know when children are sleeping so they can plan to visit when they won't disturb them. You can ask that they save questions to ask the director after their visit rather than distracting teachers from the children in their care. Families thinking about enrolling their own children are likely to appreciate knowing that such protections are in place.

Ongoing communication. Families want to be informed about your program, and there are many ways to accomplish this. Of course, telephoning to give or receive urgent information is important. Families should realize that this is a two-way system. Whoever answers the phone at the center must be helpful even when it is not feasible to call the teacher at that moment. A careful record of the question and phone number, including date and time, should be made so the teacher can call the family member at the earliest possible time.

Centers, particularly those serving infants and toddlers, often have a routine of sending home information on a child's day, using a simple form that is sent home with the child each day. These sheets typically list information about what and how much food or formula the child consumed, diapering and toileting, how long or how well the child slept, and something the child did during the day. More personal notes can be added to these routine reports as needed. Some programs use email and attach digital photos to make these sorts of reports more instantaneous and meaningful for

Artful displays of children's work with an accompanying narrative document the life of the children and adults who share the space and communicate to children and their families the sense that children's thoughts and feelings are important. Families can check the board when they pick up their children and have something to talk about on the ride home.

busy parents, provided that they have access to the technology. Some give families a choice regarding the format they prefer.

Conferences.   When families feel free to call the teacher, impromptu telephone conferences can be helpful for receiving news of family activity or a crisis that may affect the child in the school. Teachers can also set the stage for calling parents when the need arises. Brief face-to-face conferences can take place as families bring their children to the center and pick them up each day. When issues arise that need more time, it's best to make an appointment for a longer conversation—in person or by phone—at a time that is convenient for both the parent and the teacher.

Longer conferences at regularly scheduled intervals provide opportunities for more in-depth discussion of how the program is working for everyone. The teacher should be well organized for these conferences so that they can be productive. A short note, asking family members to bring a list of their questions and concerns to the conference, shows that you are interested in what they have to say as well. Keeping in mind the ultimate goal of building solid relationships with families, it is important to view conferences not "as a time for teachers to report to parents about a child's academic progress, but as a way for the important adults in a child's life to share not only academic information, but also social and emotional information" (Lewis & Forman, 2002, cited in Giles, 2005, p. 4). Remember that while your training and work experience have provided you with a lot of knowledge about young children in general, the family members are the experts about their own particular child.

In one program, the teacher sets aside a regular hour or so each week for a ritual the center has come to call "muffin day." When a family signs up for a particular muffin day, the child helps prepare muffins and sets a small table. When family members arrive, they enjoy a relaxed visit with child and teacher; they leaf through the child's portfolio as a starting point for conversation. Usually the child leaves to play after a brief time, and the adults are free to have a more extended discussion. Again, if serious issues arise, the teacher may ask to schedule a more private appointment.

Newsletters. Many centers produce monthly, weekly, or even daily newsletters. Computer desktop publishing programs make it relatively easy to produce attractive, reader-friendly newsletters, including photographs or images of children's creations. Again, these can be produced in hard copy or in digital format on a password-protected section of the program's website. Content can include routine announcements of vacations or special events as well as curriculum innovations—the what and why of a certain event or activity, for example. Some teachers send home a "daily journal," composed with children's help as part of the curriculum. Besides informing parents directly, these newsletters can spark conversations between children and their families about what happens in your program.

Group meetings. In addition to individual contacts, programs often invite families to meet as a group. An orientation session at the beginning of the year, when school is not in session, provides an opportunity for families to view the environment, receive pertinent information, and meet one another. Some programs prepare video-tapes of a typical day to show parents at this meeting. Scheduling such a meeting in the spring gives the individual families the summer months to think about what they have learned and to build their child's positive anticipation for going to school in the fall.

Group meetings at regular intervals throughout the year will probably be more productive if the families have a voice in organizing them. They will be able to tell you what days and times work best for them, as well as what topics hold the greatest interest. Sometimes family members want to hear from "experts" about aspects of their children's behavior that trouble them. Sometimes they appreciate simply having the opportunity for informal dialogue with others who might share similar experiences.

Food is usually a good drawing card and a way to set the stage for a relaxed gathering. Potluck meals, such as picnics or indoors gathering, are popular. Some families enjoy trying some of the activities their children have done; others find it easier to converse with teachers as they work together on a project, such as building playground equipment or cleaning a storage room. Taking photographs of children as they work and play and displaying those photographs around the center along with explanations of what they depict, will spark interest and conversations among family members. The early childhood programs of Reggio Emilia, Italy, have developed this method of communicating about their programs in visually pleasing, highly informative *documentation panels* that are being emulated by many programs in the United States.

Effective meetings require planning, but it is also important that you remain flexible and willing to listen to the families who attend. You may be eager to share all you know about emergent literacy, but your audience will not hear you if they are more concerned about a child who seems to be bullying all the others. Keep your eyes and ears open and view group meetings as an opportunity for you to learn as well as to teach.

COLLABORATING WITH FAMILIES TO HELP CHILDREN FEEL COMFORTABLE IN CARE

When families see that their children are comfortable in your program, they can relax and feel comfortable themselves. There are several strategies to make the child's initial adjustment go more smoothly. Having made one or more brief visits supported by family members, a child can begin attending the program for longer periods of time. As always, remember that these suggestions are general: They must be adjusted to meet the needs of particular children and their families. Not every child will need a lot of time to acclimate to the new setting, and not every family will be able to spend time away from work in order to help with this transition. In general, the younger or more immature the child, the more support is needed.

Adjusting Attendance Patterns

Attending with a family member.   Some programs encourage a family member to accompany the child for the first several days (or, in countries with paid parental leave policies, several weeks). This procedure is most likely to occur in programs for infants and toddlers, although it is also helpful for a three-year-old with no experience being away from home. From the safety of a familiar lap, the child gradually becomes familiar with the adults and other children in the new setting. Eventually, the family member can withdraw from the setting, saying "good-bye" to the child and leaving for a few minutes one day, gradually increasing the length of the absences. These brief separations help the child learn that family members can be counted on to return.

A few children at a time.   In new groups, especially those starting in the fall, the teacher may choose to start only a few children at a time so there will be ample time for the teacher and the assistants to interact with each child individually, showing each one the routines and equipment. Parents may stay if needed, or they may tell their child they are leaving and then leave, thus giving their child practice in being self-sufficient for a while. After each group has had its day or two of introduction, the teacher brings the entire group together on a regular basis.

When there is no choice.   The procedures just described may sound like idealistic ways to introduce children to their first school experiences. Because this is such an important new step, it is good to make it as free of anxiety for as many children as possible. While many families can make time for this gradual introduction to the school if the program helps them plan it this way, there are many parents who may be unable to take time off from work or other commitments in order to introduce their children in this supportive manner.

Be Intentional About Interactions

Approaching and welcoming a child.   The way you act during a child's first moments in your classroom or day-care home can go a long way toward making children, families, and you more comfortable with this transition. With very young infants, for example, it is probably safe to take them in your arms and speak softly and warmly to assure them that you will take good care of them. However, once babies become aware of strangers (at around five or six months), the same strategy is likely to bring on tears or screams of fright. Instead, you need to avoid direct eye contact, perhaps focusing your attention along with the child's on some interesting toy that will allow you to relate indirectly. As children become a little older, their strong tendencies to explore and conquer their environments begin to outweigh their wariness, so you will be able to count on a supply of interesting toys to help children relax and become involved in their new setting. If children are entering your program at around age two, you will need to take into account their emerging drive toward independence and make it very clear that the choice of what and how to play is theirs.

These guidelines are based on typical patterns of child development; you will need to adjust them to meet the needs of individual children. Researchers at the Far West Laboratory for Educational Research and Development (1988) offer the following general principles:

1. Move slowly, allowing time for the child to feel comfortable. The amount of time will vary not only with the child's age, but with temperament, background, life at home, and your behavior.

2. Keep your distance until the child feels comfortable enough to let you come closer. Stay 12 to 15 feet away for the first few minutes; let the child remain in the family member's lap; create psychological distance by putting something between yourself and the child.

3. Use indirect contact with children over six months, focusing your attention and the child's on some interesting object or activity as a way of gradually working up to more direct interaction.

For three- to six-year-olds, a visit to the child development center prior to attending begins to build a feeling of confidence in the new situation. The child can explore the environment, indoors and outdoors, with family members staying close. It is helpful if the visit can take place when other children are not there, or perhaps while they are outdoors. In this way, the new child can survey the physical setting and try out various pieces of equipment without becoming involved with the other children. The child can see the cubby, carefully labeled with his or her name, which will be a personal space for clothes and treasures brought from home. Using a child's name frequently helps ensure each that he or she feels personally valued. The child can see the nap area and cots, perhaps even try out the bathroom (a visit that may hold some anxiety, especially if the parents have been told that the child must be toilet trained in order to enroll). With an unhurried visit, the school will usually hold sufficient interest that the child will look forward to attending.

Past experience with babysitters or out-of-home settings will facilitate the transition for some children. One program sends each new child a letter of welcome from the currently enrolled children, including a digital photograph of the new playmates. Parents report that their children are thrilled to receive such mail, and teachers observe that children in the group are equally excited as they anticipate the new arrival. "Is today the day that Consuela comes?" they ask. And when she does arrive, several eager volunteers stand ready to show her where things are, help with small tasks, and explain the program's rules.

Helping the child with separation.   It is a rare child who can say to his parents, "I'm ready for you to leave." You and the child's family members should make the decision, anticipating as many rough spots as possible, and dealing with the situation decisively when the time comes. Often, family members who hesitate or delay departing upset their child more than is necessary. Some gentle guidance and recognition that the separation may be difficult may be needed. You can help both parent and child by establishing routines for beginning the day: Putting coats or belongings in cubbies, "signing in" on an attendance chart, washing hands, and sharing a favorite storybook or puzzle before saying good-bye can become a ritual that eases the transition into the day for both.

In spite of all your efforts, some children will be left behind whether or not they are ready for their family members to go. In a difficult separation, the teacher who has the best rapport with the child should step in to ease the situation and help occupy the child. At this point, a new, unknown teacher who tries to help may only compound the problem. Encourage the parent to wave good-bye, so the child knows the parent is really gone, and then console the child in whatever way seems appropriate. Discourage parents from trying to slip away unnoticed because the child may become even more upset upon discovering the parent's absence. The child usually adjusts rather quickly. Most often, it is the parent who suffers by carrying this image of a crying child throughout the day at work. You can help by volunteering to call the parent midmorning, when you will most likely be able to report that the child is playing happily.

You can help children feel comfortable after their family members leave by allowing them to use various transition objects or reminders of home. A favorite stuffed toy or blanket can be a great consolation, and for older children, the reminder can even be something intangible. One mother kissed her son's hand as they parted company and told him that whenever he felt lonely he could make himself feel better by rubbing his cheek and remembering her love. Lilian Katz calls this offering "ideas a child can put in his psychological pocket" (Katz & Katz, 2009, pp. 25–28). Photographs of family members near a child's crib or on a child-height bulletin board, perhaps even a tape recording of a family member singing a familiar lullaby— anything that helps the child feel connected to home—will probably have a soothing effect. This

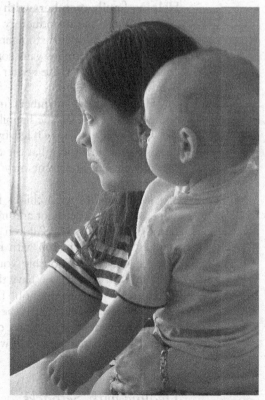

Saying "goodbye" to departing family members from the arms of a trusted caregiver can help ease the pain of separation.

technique proved remarkably effective in one program where staff could not console a new toddler because they did not speak her language.

If you follow the child's cues, you may be able to hold an anxious child on your lap. Speak softly and reassuringly, expressing your confidence that the child will be all right, and don't press for answers to questions. It may be helpful to remind children that "Mommy will be back after we play outside." Pointing out available choices of things to do may help a child become engaged, or you can encourage other children to include the newcomer into their play.

Older children might regain composure if you take them away from the group to "help" with some task. Sweeping a sidewalk or polishing the bathroom mirror might bear just enough similarity to activities at home to ease the transition. Some children will relax if they hear a story or record. Others may find painting or water play relaxing.

Whatever strategy you use, it is important that you acknowledge and accept the child's feelings. Some teachers find it helpful to hand a child a toy telephone as a prop for an imaginary conversation with the family member he or she is missing. Other children put their feelings into writing, scribbling, dictating, or drawing messages to home. Cajoling children to "cheer up" or using heavy-handed attempts to distract them can send the message that you think their feelings are trivial or unacceptable.

Helping family members with separation.   Family members may also need help going through the introductory stage. They may feel guilty about the necessity of leaving their child with strangers. Through the visits and other strategies described in this chapter, families gain confidence in a program and its staff. Once they become confident that the center is a good place for their child, leaving can be less painful for everyone.

Helping family members understand children's behavior can alleviate stress. Sometimes a child can be happily adjusted if the mother brings the child to school but will be very unhappy if left by the father or a carpool driver. The father may then jump to the conclusion that the child is not enjoying school. The teacher can explain that any change in routine may upset the child, including having a different parent drive to school.

Some families see a child's hesitation to join the group, perhaps riding a trike alone, as unusual behavior and may interpret it as meaning that the child is unhappy. If you have seen many children go through this phase, you will be able to reassure families that participation with the larger group will come as the child feels ready. Once again, the relationship you are building with the family will make it possible for them to trust that you have the child's best interest at heart and will remain close by and supportive throughout the period of adjustment. You and the families will recognize your success when the "new" child greets a returning family member with something made in school or a demonstration of a newly acquired skill on the playground. Help families to acknowledge and support these joyful signs of adjustment.

Dealing with Setbacks

Often, even after children have been attending a program happily for some time, something will happen to cause a recurrence of their initial anxieties about separation.

Absences due to illness or vacations can have this effect. Generally this anxiety will be overcome far more easily than the original separation from family. Another potential setback in your relationship with a family can occur when staff members feel unable to deal with a child's disruptive or potentially harmful behavior. Stressful events in a child's life, such as divorce, moving, or serious illness of a family member, can cause changes in behavior. The relationships that you have been developing since your first contact with the family will make it more likely that you will be aware of such events and that you will be able to work with family members to help the child overcome the problem. The topic of coping with challenging behavior will be discussed in greater detail in Chapter 11. The emphasis in this chapter is on building relationships with families before problems arise because without such relationships, it is unlikely that you will secure the cooperation needed to address the issue.

❀ Talk It Over ❀

Role-play the following situation with your classmates: An epic theatrical production is coming to town, and during a group meeting, some families urge you to take your group of three- and four-year-olds to see it. One parent expresses discomfort with the scary content of the production; another objects that she has already purchased tickets to attend an evening performance as a family. You are aware that the special performance for school groups is scheduled during your program's time for morning outdoor play. How will you decide what to do? How will you communicate that decision?

STRATEGIES FOR SUPPORTING FAMILIES AS ADVOCATES

Family Members as Teachers

Family members are teachers, too. They are their children's first teachers, and they'll be there long after the children leave your program. While all families provide a wealth of stimulation and experiences that encourage learning, families with greater educational and financial resources are often able to do this in ways that seem to fit better with school expectations. Some researchers have demonstrated that lending toys and books to low-income families and giving ideas about how to use them with their children is an effective way of providing similar advantages for *all* children. Several cautions are in order, however.

First, as we have emphasized in this chapter, it is not the job of early childhood educators to remake parents in their own image. It is more important to recognize that there are many ways that families help children develop the qualities they value. Next, family members may not always approach the tasks sent home by teachers in ways that are likely to enhance children's literacy, particularly if their image of learning includes sitting still, listening, and producing right answers on command (Hearron, 1992). Finally, teachers must be sensitive to the fact that family members may lack literacy skills themselves, and insisting that they read to their children may cause embarrassment or stress. The more you get to know the families in your program, the more you will be able to tailor your suggestions to meet their particular needs and their individual styles of interacting with their children. The goal is to help families take advantage of the learning potential in everyday activities, not to get family members to act more like teachers (Dunst et. al., 2000). If you learn that family members have problems with reading and writing, you can find tactful ways to help them tap into community resources that provide literacy training. The public library is a good starting point—and it is free of charge!

Families as Policy Shapers

In cooperative nursery schools, Head Start centers, and many other programs, family members are elected to the policymaking boards. They help with selection of goals and may make decisions regarding the distribution of resources. Their input allows the programs to reflect more accurately the needs of the children they serve. From this experience of active participation in governing a child development program, many gain confidence in their ability to effect change on a larger scale. They may run for school boards or other elective offices in the community. You can foster such personal growth by asking permission to nominate individuals for various posts or by asking them to accompany you to community meetings.

Family members' participation in policymaking boards help programs reflect more accurately the needs of the children they serve.

Links with Community Resources

As you come to know the families and the community you serve, you will be in a key position to help families locate needed services. Sometimes you will provide this information at the request of a family; at other times you may be the one who notices a problem and suggests that the family seek assistance. For example, you might become concerned that a toddler does not babble or respond to sounds, and you might share this concern with the child's family, providing them with information about where they can have the child's hearing tested.

Preparing for What Comes Next

Just as you make efforts to smooth a child's entrance into your program, you should also help families make the transition to the next phase of their child's life. For example, you can help a family share what you have learned together about their child's development as that child moves on to a new program.

This chapter has focused on the beginnings of your relationships with children and families and the importance of those beginnings in setting the tone of your subsequent interactions. But ultimately, there will come a time when every child will move on to another setting, and your role will be to help make that transition as smooth as possible. Families may ask you whether their child is "ready for kindergarten." **Readiness** is a concept that has long been a concern of early childhood educators. Interestingly, many who would question children's readiness for kindergarten have no such concerns about the same or even younger children spending 9 or 10 hours a day in a child development center. Developmentally appropriate programs for young children look at readiness from another angle. Instead of asking children to be "ready" for a predetermined program, they expect programs to be "ready" to meet the wide variety of individual needs that will exist within any group of children.

Of course, you cannot control the curriculum in the programs that children go to after leaving you. But you, as an advocate for children, can speak out for developmentally appropriate curriculum. You can help families become informed about the hallmarks and importance of such appropriateness, and you can encourage them to ask questions of the teachers and directors in their new settings. Resist pressure to do inappropriate things (e.g., workbook exercises for four-year-olds) with children this year because they'll need to do it next year. You also help by getting to know more about the programs that children will be entering so you can share information with families. And you can prepare children for transitions by talking about their "new school" in positive terms, by taking them to visit the school, or by inviting a teacher or an older sibling to visit your classroom to talk about "big school."

As you prepare for the future, don't neglect the children's need for closure with your program. Helping to clean or prepare the environment for the next group of children makes the upcoming change more real and can provide a positive way of coping with feelings of anxiety. Children in the Diana School in Reggio Emilia, Italy, composed a book of advice for newcomers at the end of their three years in the school. Surely the process of doing so helped them deal with their feelings of sadness at leaving their old school, as well as any feelings of apprehension they might have had about entering the new one.

DETECTING AND REPORTING CHILD ABUSE

Throughout this chapter, we have emphasized the importance of building positive, accepting relationships with families. As you work toward those relationships, it may be difficult to acknowledge that, for a variety of reasons, some children are abused or neglected by their families. You may not want to believe that someone could injure a child, and you may want even less to become involved in reporting suspected abuse to authorities.

Probably no action by an adult is as harmful to a child as abuse—physical, sexual, or psychological. Abused children often grow up believing that living with abuse is the norm. Thus, they don't complain. They are also likely to suffer long-term consequences, including school failure, depression, substance abuse, and delinquency (Berk, 2012, p. 403). They are more likely to exhibit aggressive behavior, and consequently their path toward being rejected by their peers is established by the time they are in primary school (Bolger & Patterson, 2001). Researchers agree that there is no single explanation for child maltreatment. Factors within the family, such as a child's difficult temperament or parental stress, can trigger abuse. Families may not have access to support from relatives or other sources in the community—either because those systems do not exist or because families do not trust them. Rising crime rates and widespread acceptance of violence are cited as aspects of a social-cultural environment in which abusive behaviors become commonplace and tolerated (Berk, 2012, pp. 401–404).

While the topic of abuse is distressing, you can be encouraged to realize that, as an early childhood professional, you are part of the solution. High-quality programs for young children are part of a support system for families, helping them to shoulder the burden of parenthood, often providing respite for those who may have difficulty coping with the many demands of young children on a daily basis. Furthermore, you can share information about typical patterns of development to help parents form realistic expectations for children's behavior. And you can share good news about a child's accomplishments so that parents see their child, and their own competence at child rearing, in a more positive light.

Besides reporting suspected abuse to authorities and taking steps to make sure that no abuse occurs in child-care centers, early childhood educators can play an important role in fostering children's resilience or ability to cope with stressful experiences. Your warm relationship with a child may make the difference between a life that is happy and productive and one that is permanently scarred because of traumatic events. You cannot always change a harmful home environment, but you *can* give children opportunities to feel valued for what they contribute to the group and to develop skills and abilities that will be lifelong sources of self-esteem (Weinreb, 1997). These are just some of the ways that your work can help prevent the occurrence of abuse and lessen its harmful effects.

What are symptoms of abuse? When you observe bruises, burns, or a child's sudden discomfort or pain during urination or bowel movements, these are causes for concern, particularly if the parent's explanation is implausible. Some things, such as obvious cigarette burns, strap marks, or numerous bruises in various stages of healing are also red flags. Figure 4–2 lists some warning signs of possible abuse or neglect.[1]

FIGURE 4–2   Warning signs of possible abuse or neglect

Consider the possibility of physical abuse when the **child**: • Has unexplained burns, bites, bruises, broken bones, or black eyes • Has fading bruises or other marks noticeable after an absence from school • Seems frightened of the parents and protests or cries when it is time to go home • Shrinks at the approach of adults • Reports injury by a parent or another adult caregiver
Consider the possibility of neglect when the **child**: • Is frequently absent • Begs or steals food or money • Lacks needed medical or dental care, immunizations, or glasses • Is consistently dirty and has severe body odor • Lacks sufficient clothing for the weather • States that there is no one at home to provide care

Consider the possibility of sexual abuse when the **child**:
• Has difficulty walking or sitting
• Is suddenly reluctant to be changed or to participate in physical activities
• Experiences nightmares or relapses in toilet learning
• Experiences a sudden change in appetite
• Demonstrates bizarre, sophisticated, or unusual sexual knowledge or behavior, such as
  • talking about phenomena associated with adult sexual activity (e.g., ejaculation)
  • explicit drawings
  • sexual aggression toward younger children
  • attempted sexual activity with peers, adults, animals, or toys
  • excessive masturbation (non-stop, to the point of injury, involving insertion of objects into the vagina or anus, or accompanied by groaning sounds or thrusting motions)

Consider the possibility of emotional maltreatment when the **child**: • Shows extremes in behavior, such as overly compliant or demanding behavior, extreme passivity, or aggression • Is either inappropriately adult (parenting other children, for example) or inappropriately infantile (frequently rocking or head-banging, for example) • Is delayed in physical or emotional development • Appears unattached to the parent or guardian

Source: National Clearinghouse on Child Abuse and Neglect Information, U.S. Department of Health and Human Services, 2007; Child Welfare Information Gateway, n.d.

---

[1]Although the majority of child abuse occurs in the home, child-care centers have been charged, and some individuals working in those centers have been found guilty of child sexual abuse. In an effort to prevent such occurrences, many centers have established a policy that doors to all rooms are left open. Toilets have no doors behind which indecent acts could take place. No staff member is allowed to take a child anywhere alone. Visitors and volunteers are carefully screened. Any evidence of indecent conduct within a center must be reported immediately to licensing authorities.

Teachers and caregivers are required by law to report suspicions to the local protective services agency. Many early childhood programs have established procedures for making such reports. Individual teachers or caregivers report to a director, who contacts the agency. You may feel uncomfortable "telling" on a parent—particularly someone with whom you have built a relationship over many weeks or months. You may be unsure whether your suspicions are founded. You may worry that the parent will guess that you made the report and perhaps even pull the child from your program. Nevertheless, you are required as an early childhood professional to report any evidence that leads you to suspect that children in your care have been abused and to let the protective services system do its job. It is important to remember that the health, safety, and perhaps the very life of the child are at stake.

Although the law requires that the identity of reporting persons remain confidential, it is not uncommon for families to infer that a report came from staff at the child development program. They may become angry and withdraw their child from your care. Nevertheless, it is your professional responsibility to comply with the law and to be up front with families about that obligation. Most programs include a statement in their policy handbook indicating their obligation to report suspected abuse or neglect.

While being alert for signs of abuse or neglect, you must also be aware that the subject of child abuse is fraught with the "cultural bumps" mentioned earlier in this chapter. "Coining," for example, is a practice in some Asian cultures, involving the application of heated coins to treat a child's illness. Your conclusion that the child had been abused would no doubt come as a great shock to the family, which had been acting with the best of intentions. Still, you would not have known without asking. The challenge is to respect cultural differences on the one hand yet not be lulled to a point where you accept harmful or dangerous practices as "just cultural differences" (Gonzalez-Mena, 2007).

YOUR ROLE AS A STUDENT IN THE CENTER

If participation in an early childhood facility is part of your teacher preparation program, you may be wondering at this point about your place in the relationships among staff and families. If you are already a parent, you may feel at ease talking with other parents, many of whom are very much like your friends and neighbors. If you are younger and less experienced, you may hesitate to interact with parents. What should your role be?

It is important for you to learn as much as you can about parents throughout your training. Find out how the teachers and other staff members work with parents. Observe their interaction when possible. You can learn much by observing the attitudes of both the teacher and the parents. How are problems handled? How are parents' individual needs accommodated? This chapter has suggested various ways that centers can interact with parents. If you have opportunities to become involved with parents as part of your teacher preparation program, be careful to coordinate your efforts with your supervisor's help and never usurp the teacher's rights to discuss the progress of individual children with their particular parents. Also, you must protect very carefully the privacy rights of parents and children and never use information about the family outside the professional circle, where, in the context of understanding the child better, the information is an appropriate subject of conversation. Gossiping about a family is never acceptable professional behavior. Be sure, too, that within the professional circle, parents are spoken of with respect and never with scorn or ridicule.

CONCLUSION

The goal of guidance is to help children become well-adjusted, self-directed, productive adults. Neither teachers nor parents can accomplish this alone; they need each other. At no time in a child's educational experience is a close relationship between home and school more important than during the early years. Families can offer a great deal to their child, the teacher, and the school if they are encouraged to contribute. Child development programs can, in turn, do much to support and strengthen families.

A child's entry into your program is a moment full of potential for making a positive impact on that child's development. The time you spend preparing for that entry not only eases the child's first days in your program but lays the foundation for the caring relationships that are at the heart of early childhood education.

Getting to know the child and family and letting them get to know you in your setting as you learn about them in theirs is the first step. Using what you learn about children and families to adjust your program to individual needs, to make it ready for the particular children you serve, is the next step. Allowing children to ease into the new setting and separate from family members gradually is important, as is providing tangible reminders of home and family within the new environment. Educators should acknowledge and accept children's feelings of anxiety or sadness as well as help them cope with those feelings and move on. Just as you help children and families make the transition into your program, you must, as a dedicated early childhood professional, take steps to smooth their transitions when they move on to their next stages of development.

REVIEW: TEN WAYS TO WELCOME FAMILIES AND BUILD STRONG RELATIONSHIPS

1. Accept all families as they are, not as subjects to improve.
2. Learn as much as you can about the unique qualities of families in your program. Get acquainted by making home visits or arranging for families to visit the program.
3. Communicate your program's goals clearly.
4. Ease children's transition into the program by arranging for visits when other children are not present or by arranging the children's attendance for brief periods for the first week or so. Welcome family members to stay with the child for the first several days if they are able to do so and keep them informed about their child's adjustment when they cannot be there.
5. Respect the child's feelings and need for time to adjust to a new setting. Offer support and reassurance but tailor your attempts to the child's developmental stage and personal preferences.
6. Help children bridge the separation from home by allowing them to bring a favorite toy or blanket. Display photographs of family members where children can see them.

7. Make sure that your program is full of enticing, developmentally appropriate toys and activities that will quickly engage children's interest.

8. Maintain relationships with families through ongoing communication via informal contacts, conferences, group meetings, notes, and newsletters. Take into account differences in home languages, literacy skills and technology capabilities among families.

9. Encourage families to broaden their children's home experiences by providing ideas, materials, and information on community resources.

10. Provide information and help families access community resources to meet their needs and to smooth the transition to the next program when they leave yours.

APPLICATIONS

1. Discuss the distinction between *child-based practice* and *family-based practice*.

2. Interview the director of a child development program (or think about a program you may know from past experience).

   a. List the ways the program builds positive relationships with family members. What additional strategies could you suggest, based on your reading of this chapter?

   b. List strategies the program uses to ease children's transitions into the program and to help children and families make the move to school. What additional strategies could you suggest, based on your reading of this chapter?

3. Think about examples from your own personal life or work experience where you have encountered people whose cultural, ethnic, socioeconomic, or linguistic background was different from your own. What challenges arose in your interactions? How did (or could) *cross-cultural competence* help meet those challenges?

4. Imagine that the school board in your community has announced plans to adopt a "schoolreadiness" policy that will admit or exclude children from kindergarten based on their performance in a screening test. Write a letter to the board, explaining why you agree or disagree with this plan.

5. Make a list of some things that would make you suspect abuse or neglect of a child in a center where you work. Describe what action you would take.

RESOURCES FOR FURTHER STUDY

Websites

Zero to Three National Center for Infants, Toddlers, and Families
zerotothree.org
Provides links to resources for professionals and parents, including interactive features with suggestions for how parents and caregivers can support development throughout the first three years of life.

Culturally & Linguistically Appropriate Services
clas.uiuc.edu
Culturally & Linguistically Appropriate Services Early Childhood Research Institute collects and describes early childhood/early intervention resources that have been developed across the United States for children with disabilities and their families and the service providers who work with them. Parts of the site can also be read in Spanish and other languages.

National Black Child Development Institute
nbcdi.org
Provides information about programs and services for African American families, the needs of African American children, and links to other resources, including a quarterly publication, *Child Health Talk*, which offers specific suggestions for parents.

Readings

Allen, J. (2007). *Creating welcoming schools: A practical guide to home-school partners with diverse families.* New York, NY: Teachers College Press.

Banks, R. A., Santos, R. M., & Roof, V. (2003). Discovering family concerns, priorities, and resources: Sensitive family information gathering. *Young Exceptional Children,6*(2), 11–19.

Derman-Sparks, L. (2006). *What if all the kids are white? Anti-bias multicultural education with young children.* New York, NY: Teachers College Press.

Espinosa, L. (2010). *Getting it right for young children from diverse backgrounds: Applying research to improve practice.* Washington, DC: National Association for the Education of Young Children.

Gonzalez-Mena, J. (2007). *50 early childhood strategies for working and communicating with diverse families.* Upper Saddle River, NJ: Pearson.

Keyser, J. (2006). *From parents to partners: Building a family-centered early childhood program.* St. Paul, MN: Redleaf Press and Washington, DC: National Association for the Education of Young Children.

Lee, S. (2006, September). Using children's texts to communicate with parents of English-language learners. *Young Children, 61*(5), 18–25.

Rowell, E. H. (2007, May). Missing! Picture books reflecting gay and lesbian families: Making the curriculum inclusive for all children. *Young Children, 62*(3), 24–30.

CHAPTER 5

Positive Guidance:
Building Human Resources

Learning Outcomes

After studying this chapter you should be able to

- Define the terms *human resources* and *human capital* and discuss their relationship to guidance.
- Define the following terms and list strategies for promoting each:
  - *self-concept*
  - *self-esteem*
  - *self-efficacy*
  - *prosocial behavior*
- Give examples of positive behavior in infants, toddlers, and young children

A group of three- and four-year-old children in a university child development laboratory were indignant about the amount of litter they noticed on their walks around campus and decided to take action. With the help of their teacher, Bruce and Kendra composed a letter to the college grounds supervisor: *We have been finding some litter. We don't want people to litter. If we see some more litter, then we have to pick it up. We want to put up signs all over campus. We want them to say, "No Littering" and "No eating on the steps because you litter if your food is crumbly. Don't eat anywhere without a plate."*

Bruce and Kendra had confidence in their ability to solve a real-life problem, to convince others with their words, and to make a difference in their world. Most observers would say that they each had a positive **self-concept** and positive **self-esteem.** The one thing they surely possessed was positive **self-efficacy.** Although they are often discussed as separate entities, these qualities interact and influence each other in many ways. Together they comprise the individual's sense of self as conceptualized in Figure 5–1.

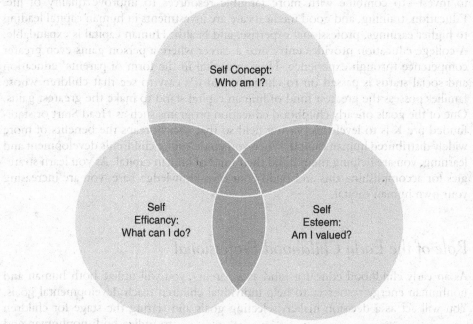

FIGURE 5–1   Three components of the sense of self

Self-concept is your sense of who you are and where you fit in the world; self-esteem is the worth or value you ascribe to your image of yourself and your abilities; self-efficacy is your sense of what you can do, what you are willing to try. Knowing and accepting oneself, feeling competent and capable, and believing in one's own worth are essential resources for becoming a well-adjusted, contributing adult, which is the goal of all our guidance of young children. Along with parents and other important people in children's lives, early childhood educators play a crucial role in nurturing children's development of all these strengths. One of the primary aims of the approach to guidance described in this book is to help you recognize and cultivate these human resources.

WHAT ARE HUMAN RESOURCES?

Resources are the intermediate goods required for making other goods or for achieving other goals. For example, steel is a resource for making automobiles, wheat is a resource for making bread, physical coordination is a resource for walking, and spelling ability is a resource for writing.

We are accustomed to thinking of common resources such as money, fuel, and food. However, people and their talents and knowledge are the most important resources. Without people's knowledge, abilities, skills, and interactions, material commodities could never become resources for making anything. These human characteristics are often referred to as **human capital.** They are the assets available to invest—to combine with more tangible resources to improve quality of life. Education, training, and good medical care are investments in human capital leading to higher earnings, professional expertise, and health. Human capital is expandable: A college education provides entry into a career where a person gains even greater competence through experience. Human capital in the form of parents' education and social status is passed on to children, and it's easy to see that children whose families possess the greatest fund of human capital stand to make the greatest gains. One of the goals of early childhood education programs such as Head Start or state-funded pre-K is to level this playing field so that society reaps the benefits of more widely distributed human capital. When you guide young children's development and learning, you are helping them build their fund of human capital. As you learn strategies for accomplishing this and build your own knowledge base, you are increasing your own human capital.

Role of the Early Childhood Professional

As an early childhood educator (and as a parent), you will utilize both human and nonhuman energy resources to help individual children reach developmental goals. You will act as a decision maker, selecting goals and setting the stage for children to utilize both nonhuman and human resources. The allocation of both types of resources is part of every decision you make.

As you study this course, you are using resources—books, paper, classrooms, libraries, and money—that have been allotted to the goal of preparing you to guide young children. As a teacher, you will marshal nonhuman resources to accomplish the teaching and learning tasks at hand. Teachers of young children are noted for their inventiveness in expanding resources through use of volunteers (human resources) or through "found" materials (nonhuman resources) such as scrap lumber for carpentry or odds and ends for art projects or play materials.

Grandparents pass on their fund of human capital when they share their care, attention, and knowledge with their grandchildren.

Among the human resources tapped by childhood

professionals are good mental and physical health, lots of energy, and emotional stability. Teachers who possess excellent mental ability and are well informed, highly motivated, and well prepared surely achieve more goals for children than those without these resources. A teacher with the ability to relate to all children, to empathize with them, and to love them can be expected to develop more of these abilities in children. Teachers with the skills to facilitate positive behaviors reduce conflicts or disruptions in their classrooms so that children learn more (Morris, Raver, Lloyd, & Millenky, 2009).

Teachers also utilize or set in motion the human resources that are available in children, other teachers, families, and community members. One of your roles as an early childhood professional, in fact, is to help families access and manage their resources so that they can contribute to their children's development goals. Because no program can achieve success without support from families, this resource building must occur simultaneously with your work with children. Chapter 4 offered a number of suggestions for connecting with families. Figure 5–2 lists examples of human resources in early childhood programs.

❈ Talk It Over ❈

Think about an early childhood program you know and list ways in which the staff members, families, and children provided human resources for each other. Compare your list to Figure 5–2. Can you add to the examples listed there?

Prejudice, discrimination, and inequality of opportunity are roadblocks that inhibit or prevent full development of a person's human resources. These inhibitors may exist within a family; within institutions, such as schools or child development facilities; or at more global levels of the state, nation, or world. Individuals can be denied opportunities to develop through accidents of birth—being born black or female or with a disability, for example. While it may be hard for today's college student to imagine, children with mental or physical disabilities were once excluded from the schools and early childhood programs enjoyed by their peers. In a more subtle example of discrimination, a highschool counselor once advised a young woman of color to enroll in a cosmetology program when the student inquired about college programs. Happily, this young woman's determination and persistence led her to obtain a college education, and she eventually became one of the top early childhood educators in the United States. It is now a U.S. government policy to provide equal opportunity and prevent discrimination on the basis of gender, race, religion, or disability. The goal is still a long way from being achieved, but all early childhood professionals should be working to eliminate such roadblocks from their programs, to ensure that each child and family receives equal opportunity and the encouragement to develop all human resources regardless of gender, race, religion, economic status, or ability.

FIGURE 5–2   Examples of human resources in early childhood programs

Early Childhood Educators as Resources for Families

❀ Help families see their children's strengths and accomplishments by communicating carefully about what they do at school.

❀ Listen to families and try to help them achieve their hopes and dreams for their children.

❀ Provide resources (information, reading materials, links to community services as needed).

Children as Resources for Each Other

❀ Model or teach a skill already mastered to another child.

❀ Motivate teachers by responding positively to their efforts.

❀ Extend love, respect, and friendship to teachers and other children.

Families as Resources for Children

❀ Help the child gain a sense of self, a sense of the future and of what it is possible to become.

❀ Teach children what to do and what not to do.

❀ Promote language and cognitive development by talking with children and providing explanations rather than simple commands.

❀ Contribute energy and talent to the child development program:

   ❀ A mother who is a bus dispatcher might invite the children to the bus station to see the bus being washed.

   ❀ A dad who is associated with cable television could arrange for children to appear on television and to observe themselves in action.

   ❀ An aunt who works as a building contractor might supervise the construction of new tricycle paths or building a loft in the room—with labor contributed by committees of women as well as men.

Families as Resources for Other Families

❀ Provide a support system when extended family systems are not available.

❀ Share information in parenting discussion groups.

Volunteers as Resources for Programs

❀ Foster grandparents, retirees give attention, help, and a warm comfortable lap to sit on, and enjoy the feeling of being needed and appreciated that they receive in return.

❀ Cadet teachers, high-school or college students gain experience as they help children learn.

Early Childhood Professionals as Resources for Each Other

❀ Experienced teachers, caregivers, and administrators provide encouragement and advice for newcomers in those same positions, a process called mentoring.

❀ Novice educators compliment mentors and help them gain new perspective on their own practice by asking questions.

THE CHILD'S DEVELOPING SENSE OF SELF

We will now take a closer look at the examples of human resources mentioned at the beginning of this chapter: the healthy self-concept, self-esteem, and sense of self-efficacy that are prerequisites for functioning as a contributing member of society.

Self-Concept

A concept is an idea. When does an infant develop a concept or an idea of him- or herself as an entity separate from his or her parents, siblings, or caregivers? Researchers who have studied this aspect of human development conclude that infants develop a sense of the "I-self" (self as agent or subject) during the first year of life, when they notice their effect on people and objects. Adults come when they cry, smile back, and respond to their cooing; batting at a suspended toy causes it to swing back and forth. During the second year, awareness of the "me-self," capable of observing and reflecting on oneself, emerges. By age two, most toddlers can recognize and give a name to photos of themselves (Berk, 2012, pp. 280–281). They assert their difference from others when they state emphatically that a particular toy is "mine!" For three- and four-year-olds, the concept of self expands to include things like eye color, gender, or prized possessions. From ages five to seven, children become aware of how they are changing and can talk about ways in which they are becoming more grown-up. Self-concept—the answer to the question, "Who am I?"—continues to develop and become increasingly complex throughout childhood and adolescence and into adulthood. It begins with awareness of the physical qualities that make up one's identity and gradually incorporates more abstract attributes (Harter, 2006).

Categorical Self. Watch infants of 16 to 20 months learning to understand and use words. They begin to understand that adults are different from children, and females are different from males. If you say to a toddler, "Take the magazine to Uncle Charlie," the child will deliver the magazine across the room to the adult male. If you say, "Pat the baby," she will select the baby from the family circle for her attention. She is learning categories of people as separate from herself. Pretty soon, the toddler says "me" or "mine," showing recognition of the category of self.

Gender Identity. Gender identity is part of one's self-concept. *Gender constancy* is an idea that young children are only beginning to grasp, and they express their confusion in interesting ways,

Children explore ideas about identity through play, trying on different roles in fanciful ways.

showing that they think they might change from one gender to the other. A boy might laugh when asked whether he would like to try on a dress-up dress and assert, "I don't want to be a girl!" A four-year-old girl, upon seeing her baby pictures where she had short hair, might declare with amazement, "I used to be a boy!" Such comments suggest that children do not yet realize the permanency of being a boy or a girl.

As young children sort through their confusion about identity, they often pass through a phase of extremely rigid thinking about what is appropriate behavior for either gender. It is almost as though they have to

Siblings who are a few years apart in age or of different genders usually have their own interests and sets of friends and thus are less likely to develop competition with each other.

exaggerate the differences before they can begin to see the ways in which boys and girls are alike. One group of three-year-old boys declared firmly, "Girls can't drive," and no amount of questioning by their teacher could shake their conviction at that particular moment. Many professional women have watched in dismay as their young daughters developed a fascination with frilly dresses, makeup, and other stereotypical accoutrements of femininity which they themselves have rejected (Trawick-Smith, 2010).

While children need to explore ideas about gender, adult reinforcement of stereotypical expectations (that boys never cry, for example, or that all girls are dainty) can lead to a distorted self-image and lowered self-esteem. Sadly, children are bombarded by such distorted images in today's media (Levin, 2003, pp. 76–78).

Birth Order.   Birth order and space between siblings can also affect a child's self-concept. Research has indicated that children without siblings generally have high levels of self-esteem. Only children and first-born children have common traits, usually including higher mental abilities, largely because enthusiastic new parents are generally able to invest more time in the child's individual development than are parents with more children.

In a family in which children are close together in age, the children may develop strong rivalries toward each other. The second child may grow up trying hard to catch up with the older sibling. This tendency is often avoided, and competition doesn't develop as readily when the two are of different genders or a few years apart in age so that each has his or her own interests and circle of friends. Depending on the quality of their relationships, older children can be supportive and positive role models for their younger siblings, or they can transmit less desirable behavior patterns such as aggression (Berk, 2012, pp. 507–508).

Supporting Development of Self-Concept.   Babies understand words long before they can use them in their own conversation. When you look into a child's face and address her by name, you are helping to build her self-concept. You can see why diapering, dressing, and bathing—routines that occurs many times each day—offer many opportunities for doing exactly that and why it is important to carry them out gently and in a pleasant social way. As babies get a little older, you can add mirrors and photographs of the children to the environment. Take pictures of children's faces at regular intervals and display them so that children can see how they change over time. Label cubbies with their pictures and names and continue to speak *to* them (not *about* them), addressing them by their names. Enlist family members' help to create a mini photo album for each toddler, clearly labeled with his or her name; filled with pictures of family members, pets, or favorite toys; and stored where the children can access them throughout the day. For older children, this can be expanded to a larger-format binder or portfolio with a photographic record of their participation in projects and activities at school and samples of their work.

Early childhood professionals should counteract gender stereotypes to ensure that no child's opportunities are unfairly limited and try to help children develop more balanced concepts of what it means to be a man or a woman. This requires examining one's own attitudes about gender differences and modulating reactions to children's natural curiosity about their own body and others' bodies. By acknowledging and accepting that curiosity, adults respond in a positive way, teaching children that everyone deserves respect.

Mirrors are fascinating to children as they explore the concept of self.

Awareness of the role of birth order in self-concept formation will help adults understand children's behavior. Children who are bossed by siblings or parents at home may tend to be bossy at school. Children who compete with a sibling at home may carry over this competition at school. Familiarity with each child's family makeup enhances teachers' ability to help children adjust to their home situations.

Self-Esteem

What does the child think of herself, the person (self) that she comes to understand? *Self-esteem is the judgment a child makes about his or her worth in the eyes of others.* Psychologists debate whether self-esteem is a trait (something that remains the same over time, like eye color) or a state (something that fluctuates with circumstances, like feelings) (Harter, 2006). As children move into primary grades, their sense of self-worth is fostered when they feel accepted by the important people in their lives; when they have some control over what happens at home or school; when they feel

Self-esteem is the judgment a child makes about his or her worth in the eyes of others. Adults who show genuine affection and appreciation for children promote feelings of self-worth.

competent; and when they see themselves as "good" (following rules and treating others well) (Trawick-Smith, 2010). Young children with adaptable temperaments, openness to new situations, and good language skills are at an advantage in relating to their peers (Mendez, Fantuzzo, & Cicchetti, 2002).

Self-esteem should not be confused with conceit or inflated ego. In fact, the idea of holding oneself in high regard may conflict with cultural values. As one newly arrived Mexican immigrant mother said, "You can't esteem yourself, you can only esteem others" (Gonzalez-Mena, 1997, p. 61). Lilian Katz, a prominent early childhood specialist, might sympathize with this point of view. She cautions teachers not to confuse self-esteem with narcissism (Katz, 1993). Narcissism is excessive self-love and self-involvement, named for a Greek mythological character who perished after falling in love with his own reflection in a pool. Self-esteem is a genuine sense of one's worth, based on meaningful experiences and accomplishments. Narcissism, on the other hand, generally arises from empty praise that is unrelated to effort or achievement.

Instead of a constant stream of unrealistic, empty praise, adults can do more for a child's self-esteem by making it clear that it is all right not to know or be able to do something and explicitly teaching how to ask for help. Children with the least confidence in their abilities will not seek the help they need, thereby creating a self-fulfilling prophecy of their own incompetence and further eroding their confidence (Marchand & Skinner, 2007, p. 65, cited in Katz & Katz, 2009).

Early childhood educators can have a positive impact on children's feelings of acceptance by building warm, supportive relationships. Listening to children with your full attention, sitting nearby and watching with interest as they build with blocks, and simply smiling to show that you are happy to see them in the morning are all ways of showing children that they have value in your eyes. You foster children's feelings of competence by setting realistic expectations and expressing confidence that children will make good choices and will meet those expectations. Helping children feel successful by pointing out what they are able to do rather than what they are not able to do—in other words, focusing on strengths—contributes to positive self-esteem. You help children build a sense of moral self-worth by using the positive guidance recommended in this book: teaching children what behavior is expected instead of what behavior to avoid. When limits are expressed clearly and stated directly, a child is generally willing to comply and will feel good about fulfilling the adult's expectations.

Valuing Diversity.   Children's judgment about their worth is influenced by their peers. You can set the stage for children to see that they have value in the eyes of other children by promoting appreciation for diversity and acceptance. We know that even toddlers notice physical differences, and much of our teaching of young children involves calling attention to those differences: "This is a fork, and this is a spoon." "That's a dog, not a kitty." Because of our culture's unfortunate history of unfair treatment of people who are different, however, it is likely that even toddlers have already been exposed to many distorted notions about the meaning of differences between people. Bias, or the favoring of one group over another, exists in our culture, and denying its existence will not make it disappear. It may, in fact, have the opposite effect. Even adults who would never consciously teach a child to look down on people who are different can send the message that there is something shameful or bad about the differences children notice if they respond with discomfort when children speak about their observations.

When you are comfortable acknowledging and discussing differences, everyone benefits. Research has shown that all children develop empathy and helping skills when individuals with disabilities are included in their classrooms (Diamond & Stacey, 2000). While children with physical or speech disabilities are likely to be accepted by their peers, those with other types of disabilities (e.g., autism-pervasive developmental delay, attention-deficit disorder) are at risk for rejection and will need your help to develop social competence and friendship skills (Odom et al., 2006). Children from privileged homes or majority ethnic groups may recognize and lose a false sense of superiority while both they and their less-privileged peers gain more realistic self-images and sense of their places in the world. Girls and boys who aren't pressured to conform to gender stereotypes can develop all facets of their personalities.

❀ Talk It Over ❀

Suppose you notice that your block area is dominated by boys, while the girls in your classroom spend all their free time in the dramatic play area. Since you feel that each area fosters different, but equally important, types of learning, you are concerned that both the boys and girls are missing opportunities. Brainstorm with your classmates a list of ways you can make each area more attractive to all children.

The question for early childhood educators, then, is not whether bias can exist in young children but what to do to counteract it. Taking a proactive stance in counteracting bias has been called *anti-bias education*. The four core goals of anti-bias

High-quality early childhood programs strive to foster each child's confident self-awareness and ability to relate to all people with comfort and empathy.

education are to foster in each child (1) confident self-awareness, (2) the ability to relate to all people with comfort and empathy, (3) the ability to recognize unfair treatment of people who are different, and (4) the ability to stand up for oneself and others in the face of bias (Derman-Sparks & Edwards, 2010, pp. 4–5).

As they move toward these goals, children pass through predictable stages, often marked by confused or mistaken concepts about their own identity as well as differences in others. Two-year-olds, for example, might believe that scrubbing will transform dark brown skin to beige. Four-year-olds might shun a classmate who has cerebral palsy out of fear of losing control of their own bodies. Whatever the misconception, it's important to listen calmly to the children's ideas.

Overreacting, either by laughing at children's errors or hushing them in embarrassment, will only teach children that differences are a highly charged subject. On the other hand, you cannot always remain silent, assuming that, with experience, children will eventually clear up their misconceptions—particularly when those misconceptions can be harmful to themselves or to others. When children's unfounded fears cause them to shun a classmate who has a disability, for example, you have a responsibility to step in. For their own good, and for the good of the child being judged, you need to confront the situation directly and tell the children in a calm, nonjudgmental manner why their behavior is not acceptable. Afterward, you can reflect on what happened and think about how to set the stage for more equal treatment.

Facilitating Acceptance.   How can you help all children feel accepted and accepting of others who may be different from them? By observing carefully, you may be able to determine the reason a particular child is rejected or ignored by the other children and can devise strategies to overcome the problem. Some children just don't know how to join in play. If Marcus's plaintive "Can I play?" is repeatedly met with rejection, you can suggest other ways he can try to join in. Perhaps you might suggest a role to Marcus: "Tell them you're the mail carrier, and you have some letters for them." Or you might enter the play yourself and take Marcus with you: "We're some customers for your shoe store. Do you have any shoes in our size?"

Sometimes a child has a disability that makes it difficult to gain entry into play situations. One study found that children with cerebral palsy became more skillful dramatic players after they were given opportunities to practice away from the classroom, with only the teacher and a friend of their choosing (Brown, Althouse, &

Anfin, 1993). In addition to the practice sessions, the researchers used photographs to record play episodes and recorded the children's narration of events depicted in the photographs. The feedback of hearing their recorded voices prompted the children to speak more audibly, making them more understandable to the other children and, consequently, more desirable playmates.

Sometimes the problem is not due to a child's skill but rather to some external circumstance. For example, a child who frequently arrives at the center after children have formed small play groups may have difficulty joining in. You can help alleviate the problem by bringing that issue to the parents' attention and working together to find a solution. Perhaps the child can join a carpool with neighbors, thereby arriving on time and already be part of a small group of potential playmates. This minor adjustment in arrival time might lead to the child becoming more socially accepted and, consequently, having more positive self-esteem.

You can be proactive and promote acceptance by selecting appropriate books and songs, providing plenty of opportunities for cooperative dramatic play, and avoiding competition. Competition has no place in an early childhood program. Even in elementary school, competition can be destructive, leading to such bitter adult memories as being the last one chosen for sports teams.

Early childhood professionals should work to ensure that each child or family receives equal opportunity and encouragement to develop all human resources, regardless of gender, race, religion, economic status, or ability.

Self-Efficacy

Efficacy is the power to produce an effect. Self-efficacy is a personal judgment about one's own ability to produce an effect or to learn a concept or skill. Self-efficacy has been described in detail by Albert Bandura, a social psychologist, who believes that children learn much from watching others in their environments (Bandura, 1986).

You have seen self-efficacy in operation when you have watched a child confidently imitate something a parent or an older child has done. For instance, Marta takes a pencil and makes curly marks in a notebook, as she sees her mother doing. Darnell pokes his fork into a piece of meat after seeing an adult do it. Lucia, a new walker, goes for the stairs every time the gate is left undone, wanting to try the fascinating adventure of stair climbing. Wei Li "reads" the picture book, reciting with inflections the story she has just heard her mother read to her. Each child is showing self-efficacy, a confidence in himself or herself and a belief that he or she can be effective in carrying out an activity.

You've seen self-efficacy among your peers, too. For example, you may have seen a teenager jump on a friend's motorcycle and start the engine without any instruction for driving and stopping safely. Some would say the youth is foolish, while others might say he has great confidence in his ability to ride just like the friend who came on the motorcycle for a visit. Some people can be self-efficacious, or very confident of their abilities, even though a skill is new to them.

❀　　**Talk It Over**　　❀

What could we mention that you've never tried, but you think you could handle comfortably? Acting? Computing? Skiing? Skydiving? Quilting? Mountain climbing? White-water rafting? How would you rate your sense of self-efficacy? What experiences have contributed to it? How have important people in your life supported (or hampered) its development?

Contributing to Children's Self-Efficacy.　　How can you help children develop feelings of self-efficacy? If you recall the guidance pyramid presented in Chapter 1, the following suggestions will come as no surprise. First, start with an image of the child as competent and know enough about typical patterns of child development that your expectations of children are reasonable and age appropriate. Adults who expect three-year-olds to sit still and listen for long periods are setting an unrealistic standard. When the children inevitably wiggle and squirm, adults who hold unreasonable expectations are likely to become frustrated and scold them. If this happens often enough, the children will come to believe that they are, in fact, incompetent—unable to live up to expectations. In contrast, an adult who knows enough about three-year-olds to set appropriate goals will find many opportunities to express pleasure in their success, and the children's sense of competence will grow accordingly.

Next, provide a safe environment where hazards have been removed. If a child gets hurt, an adventuresome spirit and self-efficacy is often curtailed. A baby-proofed room supports self-efficacy because the child is freer to explore without danger, and adults are less likely to inhibit that exploration with constant admonitions to "be careful!" The selection of materials and equipment that you make available to children can promote or inhibit feelings of competence. Materials and equipment should provide enough challenge to attract

For self-efficacy to develop, children need to explore without pressure. The accomplishment of successfully using equipment is its own reward.

and intrigue children without being so difficult that the children become frustrated. Since children vary widely in the rates at which they develop, this means that every classroom should include materials and equipment in a range of difficulty. A selection of puzzles in a classroom for three- and four-year-olds, for example, could include those with only a few large pieces, as well as several more complicated ones, perhaps even some complex jigsaw puzzles. When children with limited manual dexterity will be using the puzzles, you can add some with special knobs for lifting the pieces.

Materials that can be used in many ways, at many levels of ability, are called **open ended**. Examples include sand, water, easel painting, dress-up props, and blocks. To explain using the last example, toddlers or children with little experience with blocks might simply carry them around, or they might dump them into heaps. Older or more experienced children will begin to use the blocks more systematically, creating forms and naming their structures and using them as stages and props for dramatic play. The point is that every child can use blocks with some degree of competence. Your provision of open-ended material helps all children feel competent.

After providing a safe environment, adults promote children's self-efficacy by allowing children to explore and experiment, avoiding constant reminders to be careful. In reality, most children are quite careful of their own safety. You may recall reading in a child development text about experiments showing evidence of a child's natural caution. In one experiment, the investigator placed the small children on a glass table that appeared through the glass to be a steep cliff. Would the small children risk trying to crawl across the glass even with their mothers on the other side? No. At 6 to 14 months, infants showed fear of the cliff and would not crawl across; they were cautious and protected their own safety (Campos, Bertenthal, & Kermoian, 1992).

For self-efficacy to develop, a child needs to explore without pressure. Modeling by others, especially by other children, usually encourages children to try new pieces of equipment. When children are successful in using the equipment, that accomplishment is its own reward. They will practice the skill over and over.

Children with Disabilities.
Like all other children, children with disabilities need a strong sense of self-efficacy. Depending on the nature and extent of their disabilities, you may need to make a little extra effort to help them develop that sense. That extra effort might involve making modifications in the environment, such as providing spoons and forks with built-up handles so that children with physical disabilities can feed themselves independently. Or you might make adaptations in the way materials are arranged for use. A raised platform for block building, for example, will make it more accessible for children who use wheelchairs. Conversely, a loft that is inaccessible by wheelchair will surely decrease feelings of competence for a child who cannot get to it. Adaptive technology for children with communication disorders can range from something as simple as a set of picture cards to sophisticated computerized devices for conveying messages. Because some children with disabilities are less likely than others to imitate their peers, your role might involve direct teaching of specific skills, such as dressing oneself, and building into the daily schedule many opportunities for practicing those skills.

Setting realistic goals, providing adequate support, and stepping back as children become more independent are the keys to fostering self-efficacy in children with or without disabilities. Parents and other experienced professionals, such as occupational and physical therapists, can help you know how to support children and when to step back.

Prosocial Behavior

Yolanda, 18 months old, is lying prone on a small bench in her toddler classroom, sobbing in her dismay at her mother's recent departure. Brittney, the same age, comes over and gently pats her back. When Yolanda continues crying, Brittney brings her own "blankie," along with a favorite board book. She tenderly covers Yolanda and sits next to her, "reading" from the book they have both enjoyed in the past. Slowly, Yolanda's tears subside, as she begins to respond to the solace offered by her young friend.

Prosocial behavior is defined as actions that help another person, regardless of motive. A particular type of prosocial behavior is altruistic behavior, defined as helping another with no expectation of reward (Penner & Orom, 2010). Prosocial behavior builds on qualities of empathy (feeling what one perceives another person feels) and sympathy (feeling sorrow or pity for another person). Sharing, taking turns, being helpful, and being generous to others are all examples of prosocial behavior in early childhood. By taking actions such as offering their "blankie" to a crying friend, children as young as 18 months have demonstrated their willingness to help others achieve some goal (Warneken & Tomasello, 2006). Even younger babies (6 to 10 months), when given a choice between two puppets after watching a little dramatization, show a preference for the puppet that has been helpful (Bloom, 2010). In other words, the roots of prosocial behavior seem to be present in the earliest years of life. The responsibility of parents and early childhood professionals is to nurture those roots without holding children to unrealistic expectations that they share or take turns from day one.

Prosocial behaviors appear to be prominent in children who develop a strong sense of trust during infancy, and they are characteristic of children with healthy self-esteem. Children who show prosocial behaviors relate to others in a manner that makes them acceptable playmates (Trawick-Smith, 2010). Other children show their pleasure when the child is helpful, and they seek out the child as a playmate. This reinforcement contributes to the child's positive self-esteem.

Prosocial behavior is linked to cognitive development, appearing more often in children who succeed at perspective-taking tasks. It is related to self-regulation or the ability to manage one's own responses to another's distress well enough to be able to take action. Patterns of prosocial behavior emerging in early childhood are likely to persist into adulthood (Eisenberg, 2010; Eisenberg, Fabes, & Spinrad, 2006).

Teachers and caregivers can nurture prosocial behavior by creating an environment where it is more likely to occur—one with plenty of interesting materials and ample space so that children don't have to quarrel over resources. They can notice and comment on instances in which one child helps, consoles, or shares with another. They can provide examples for children to emulate, in their own interactions with others as well as in the stories they tell or read to children.

APPRECIATING POSITIVE BEHAVIOR

Even toddlers are capable of positive behaviors such as helping, although their limited skills sometimes thwart their intentions. Appreciating—and thereby encouraging—positive behavior is an important aspect of guidance. It is also self-perpetuating: The more you appreciate positive behavior, the more positive behavior you will have to appreciate. Your value system, which stems from your family and cultural background as well as your own life experiences, will determine what you believe to be positive behavior. Your feelings about yourself and life in general will also color your perceptions. When adults feel positive about themselves, they are better able to understand and accept children's behavior.

In some ways, the line between positive and negative behavior exists in the eye of the beholder. In fact, some positive behavior can appear downright negative! T. Berry Brazelton (1992), a renowned pediatrician, argues that there are predictable times in the lives of all children when their behavior "falls apart," when they seem to move backward in development in ways that perplex and dismay their parents and caregivers. These times invariably signal rapid spurts of physical, cognitive, or socioemotional growth. An example might be a child on the verge of walking, whose frustration at being left behind evokes a sudden change in disposition and screams of rage. Brazelton views these periods not as crisis points but rather as "touchpoints," unparalleled opportunities for understanding and supporting development, if we anticipate them positively and avoid becoming locked in power struggles.

This book is based on the premise that positive behaviors are those which help children move along toward the goal of becoming well-adjusted, fully functioning adults. In other words, behavior that is typical of a particular stage of development, that paves the way for the next stage, is positive. Positive behavior is not, therefore, the same thing as compliance with adult wishes, especially if those adult wishes reflect a lack of knowledge of children's development.

By studying child development and carefully observing the behavior of many children, you can learn to adjust your expectations so that the behavior you expect is within the bounds of possibility for children to achieve. By observing the behavior of a child over time, you can begin to understand what particular behaviors mean for that child. You may begin to see how behavior that seemed irritating to you actually serves a positive function for a child.

Focusing on positive behavior places less desirable behavior in better perspective and develops a more accurate impression of the whole child. It allows you to emphasize strengths and help children overcome weaknesses. Early childhood educators with heightened awareness of positive behaviors will set the stage so that those behaviors can occur and will respond in ways that make these acts occur more often. In other words, they will use techniques of indirect and direct guidance.

Infants

For babies, behavior is the language with which they can tell us what they need. Although we may enjoy babies more when they are sleeping, cooing, and snuggling, babies who cry when they are hungry or wet are also exhibiting positive behaviors. In fact, we worry about an infant who lies passively in the crib and seems to have given up on the world.

Babies are often noisy, although many adults seem to equate a quiet baby with a good baby. Unless they have a disability, babies increasingly use their vocal cords to get attention and express their excitement. They coo and babble to practice sounds and engage in *conversations* with willing partners.

Understanding caregivers willingly give babies their undivided attention during feedings and other intimate moments throughout the day.

Babies thrive on attention and fall to pieces when that attention is withheld. Gurgling, smiling, flailing arms and legs, even screaming in outrage—all are ways that healthy babies exert their influence on us to get the attention they need. Understanding caregivers willingly give babies their undivided attention during feedings, diaper changes, and other intimate moments throughout the day instead of interpreting apparently negative behaviors as "just wanting attention."

Babies with typical development are social. They like people and enjoy the games that people play with them. They form strong attachments to the people who are important in their lives. These attachments are an important part of becoming fully human—even when the tears that follow that important person's departure make your job a little harder. Toys, television, and propped-up bottles should never replace the human touch and voice in a baby's life. To be happy and secure, babies must be loved unconditionally, and this is your responsibility when they are in your care.

Unless they are impeded by some disability, babies are typically active. They roll over, then stand in their cribs, and before long they climb out of those cribs. One of the pleasures of caregiving is sharing their sheer joy in movement. Out on the floor, they scoot along until they learn to crawl, and then they pull themselves up on furniture. Life grows more perilous as they encounter dangerous things that used to be out of their reach—the heater, the cord on a coffeemaker, cleaning chemicals in the cupboard under the sink.

Babies are curious, and their sense of danger is undeveloped. They don't get into things to be naughty or to irritate their tired caregivers. They are merely following irresistible natural urges to explore their environments, seeking the knowledge they need to understand their world. They do this through tasting, touching, chewing, seeing, and hearing. As a caregiver, you may have the privilege of seeing them discover for the first time that one action makes something else happen: that kicking the side of the crib makes the bell on the mobile ring or that pushing a dish to the edge of the highchair tray results in a satisfying crash on the floor and perhaps an interesting response from you. Rejoice in these signs of intellectual growth.

Whereas your job with very young babies is to meet their needs so that they feel secure, your job with mobile babies is to prepare their environments so that they can explore safely and to encourage that exploration. With toddlers, your task is to foster their growing sense of independence and autonomy—including their ability to say "no"—recognizing all these as positive behaviors.

Toddlers

Of course, there's more to toddler behavior than "No!" One positive behavior is that toddlers explore on their own. Toddlers want to use a tricycle, though they may walk it along instead of pedaling it. They like to walk on a balance beam, a curb, a short wall, or something else a few inches from the ground, perhaps holding onto an adult's hand. They may climb onto high places and be unable to get down. They have difficulty changing their minds. For instance, after they've decided they want to eat a peanut butter sandwich, they have difficulty settling for a jelly sandwich. Although the process may be quite messy, they take great satisfaction in feeding themselves, using fingers as well as spoons to get the food to their mouths.

Their language is growing by leaps and bounds. They can ask for help to get a drink of water or say "me do it" when they don't want your help. They can tell a playmate that something is "mine," and they enjoy repeating simple songs or rhymes.

Try visualizing yourself as a toddler to understand the pleasures of toddler life. For example, happiness is getting into things and poking your fingers into things. A cardboard carton from the grocery store makes a toy that you can play with for days—in and out, out and in, sitting down, rising up—a rhythm of exploration. You poke at Grandma's toe through her open-toed shoe and could just as well poke around the electrical outlet if someone didn't watch out for you.

After toddlers turn two and become aware of the toilet, they like handling this alone. Sometimes for fun they sit backward on the toilet so they can hold on to the lid. They like surprising their teacher by going to the bathroom all alone without a reminder and remembering to wash their hands afterward. They like the teacher's individual comments, complimenting them for doing the task alone.

Three- to Six-Year-Olds

For a three- to six-year-old, action is a positive behavior, the key to healthy development, a sign that the child is growing. Physical action means continuous running, climbing, crawling, and hopping. Young children sit still only if it is their decision, and that is why it is preferable to let children choose their activities. They generally know best what their body needs next. If they decide to look at a book or do a painting, their concentration can be quite intense.

Pretend that you are a three- to six-year-old now. Positive behavior is laughing after recovering from the shock of bumping into a playmate while running outdoors. Positive behavior is pretending about a big banner seen across the street, "Yeah! It's a big net and it is winding around us. It's got us! We can't get away!" and having your friends pretend to be caught in the struggle and laugh with you.

Positive behavior is making skis out of the hollow wooden ramps from the block corner, putting your feet in, and walking and having your buddies laugh at the new discovery that they hadn't seen before. Positive behavior is hanging by the knees on the jungle gym and having someone say, "I didn't know you could do that!"

Positive behavior is feeling big enough to say "Bye" to Mom or Dad and joining other children at play. Positive behavior is wrestling with your friend in the grass and knowing you can hold your own and that your friend won't really hurt you. Positive behavior is being glad when Daddy surprises you by stopping by the school to visit for a while and coping with sad feelings when he leaves.

Talking and listening are positive behaviors, although for young children, talking is often more interesting than listening. You will frequently hear conversations that sound like two interviews run together on a tape recorder, with both children talking and neither listening.

Talking—getting your ideas across and telling someone how you feel—is a positive behavior. One child whispers to another, "You're my friend," or shouts, "No! no!" when someone takes a toy. Talking is asking for information: "Why do I have to take a nap?" It is telling the teacher important news before someone else does—"I have a new baby sister!" Talking is sometimes arguing with a playmate about whose turn it is or which is the right way to build a spaceship in the block corner. Through such arguments, young children learn that other people might have different ideas than theirs, which is a big step toward being able to take the perspective of another person.

❀ Talk It Over ❀

Imagine that you work in a child development center, and a co-worker complains to you about a particular three-year-old child in her classroom. "Eduardo never sits still," she says, "and he is always arguing with the other children about whose turn it is to do something. I think he is too young to be in our center." What might you say in response?

All children's behavior has meaning, and an adult's task is to search for that meaning. What do the things children do tell you about them? You can't draw conclusions from one or two incidents but must watch children over a period of time. When you sit down and reflect on the day's events after school, or at home after the children are safely tucked in each day, ask yourself "What positive behavior did I observe today?" Then you can analyze what you did to help or hinder what happened. These can be lessons for the future.

Of course, problems should not be ignored. Always remember, however, that apparent problems may be positive behavior for some children. For example, you might have children who are quiet and withdrawn who then gradually grow to trust you and themselves and begin to stretch and strain the rules. These may be problems for you, but for those children, the actions signify growth. What do you do? Certainly, don't try to control their behavior and push them back into their shells! Ignore them for a while unless someone's going to get hurt because these children may be working through a problem through acts of self-expression. The teacher's goal is to tailor the guidance to children's individual needs. Within a short time, these children will likely be willing to follow the rules again.

CONCLUSION

Resources are potential means to achieving goals. We combine the human resources of energy and knowledge with material resources—such as wheat and tools for farming and food processing—to create another resource—such as bread—which is in turn transformed into more of the human resource energy. An understanding of human resource development helps early childhood professionals view their work as essential, not only for the lives of individual children and families they serve but for the future of society as a whole.

Positive behaviors are resources, the human resources that education attempts to develop. Positive behavior includes making your needs known, expressing your thoughts and feelings, and relating to others. It includes moving, doing, exploring, and discovering. A strengths-based approach to guidance means looking for, and celebrating, positive behaviors. A positive self-concept, feelings of self-efficacy, and a healthy sense of self-esteem are strengths to be fostered if children are to become productive, happy, self-governing individuals who behave in prosocial ways. Self-concept, including gender and ethnic identity, develops along with a child's other concepts of objects, actions, or people. Self-esteem is a child's appraisal of his or her worth, as revealed in the eyes of others. Self-efficacy is a child's own judgment of being able to do a task or to learn a skill or an idea. Working toward the goals of anti-bias education is a proactive approach to fostering self-esteem for all children.

REVIEW: TEN WAYS TO FOSTER HEALTHY SENSE OF SELF AND POSITIVE BEHAVIOR

1. Value the potential in each child for developing human resources of knowledge, skills, and dispositions.

2. Understand and appreciate how all individuals (families, children, educators, community members) can provide valuable resources for each other.

3. Set positive expectations: Study typical patterns of child development so you will know, in general, the types of behavior to expect at various ages. Make sure that your rules and expectations for children are within their abilities. Expect that children will want to cooperate and be helpful.

4. Provide a safe environment with plenty of opportunities for children to do the things that are typical of each age: to move, explore, practice independence, and try new skills.

5. Communicate positive expectations: Point out to children what they can do rather than what they cannot do. Determine what children are trying to do and how it will facilitate their development as competent individuals; then, if possible, help them do it.

6. Let children know when you appreciate their behavior. Recognize a child's elation when accomplishing a task and cheer the child's successes and prosocial behavior.

7. Ignore negative behavior, when possible; when necessary, intervene to stop it and prevent harm.

8. Respect children. Identify each child by name to aid self-concept learning. Treat all equally and avoid comparisons. Assist children in learning to respect and value diversity.

9. Focus on children's strengths rather than on their weaknesses. Start each new day with a fresh slate, remembering that children forget rules easily.

10. Strive to eliminate every hint of prejudice, discrimination, and inequality of opportunity that could inhibit the development of children or parents.

APPLICATIONS

1. If you have had the opportunity to observe a child as part of your study for this course, analyze your notes and look for evidence of human resources:

   a. Give examples of the child's strengths and abilities.

   b. Give examples of the teacher being a resource for this child.

   c. Give examples of the child's parents or other adult caregivers being resources for the child.

   d. Give evidence of the child being a resource for other children or of other children being a resource for this child.

2. Observe children as they carry out routines such as dressing, eating, and toileting. Try to include at least one child with a disability in your observations. Look for examples of the following:

   a. Two instances of self-efficacy

   b. Two statements related to self-concept

   c. Evidence of the child's awareness of, or response to, diversity

   d. Two examples of prosocial behavior

3. As you work with other adults, record statements of two adults that seemed particularly positive in helping a child develop a high level of self-esteem. State your conclusion regarding the meaning of the statements to each child.

RESOURCES FOR FURTHER STUDY

Websites

Center on the Social and Emotional Foundations for Early Learning (CSEFEL)
csefel.vanderbilt.edu

An organization focused on promoting the social emotional development and school readiness of young children birth through age five. Provides links to resources for educators and families, with practical strategies based on current research.

Zero to Three National Center for Infants, Toddlers, and Families
zerotothree.org
Provides links for professionals and parents on topics such as early childhood mental health, as well as the document *Helping Young Children Cope After a Disaster*.

Readings

Bennett, T. (2007). Mapping family resources and support. In D. Koralek (ed.), *Spotlight on young children and families* (pp. 20–23). Washington, DC: National Association for the Education of Young Children.

Day, C. B. (2006). Leveraging diversity to benefit children's social-emotional development and school readiness. In B. Bowman & E. K. Moore (eds.), *School readiness and social-emotional development: Perspectives on cultural diversity* (pp. 23–32). Washington, DC: National Black Child Development Institute.

Diamond, K. E., & Stacey, S. (2000). The other children at preschool: Experiences of typically developing children in inclusive programs. In S. Sandal & M. Ostrosky (eds.), Natural environments and inclusion. *Young Exceptional Children Monograph Series, 2* (pp. 59–68). Denver, CO: Division for Early Childhood Council for Exceptional Children.

Levin, D. E. (2003). *Teaching young children in violent times: Building a peaceable classroom* (2nd ed.). Cambridge, MA: Educators for Social Responsibility and Washington, DC: National Association for the Education of Young Children.

Vaughn, S., Kim, A., Morris Sloan, C. V., Hughes, M., Elbaum, B., & Sridhar, D. (2003). Social skills interventions for young children with disabilities. *Remedial & Special Education, 24*(1), 2–15.

PART II

Strategies for Guidance

CHAPTER 6

Indirect Guidance—
The Role of the Environment in Facilitating Self-Direction

Learning Outcomes

After studying this chapter you should be able to

- Explain the terms *indirect guidance* and *environment as a third teacher*.
- Discuss ways that physical space influences children's behavior.
- List strategies for promoting self-direction through arrangement of space and materials.
- List ways to modify the environment for children with disabilities.
- Describe components of an effective daily schedule for promoting children's self-direction.
- Describe how adults can invest energy effectively to promote children's self-direction.

Kim comes into the playroom and selects a puzzle from the puzzle rack. She puts it on the nearby table and begins to take it apart. Soon she is joined by Josh, whose wheelchair arms slide under the tabletop, allowing him to work puzzles alongside Kim. The two children carry on a pleasant conversation as they work side by side, frequently pausing to check each other's progress or offer suggestions about placing a particular piece. When they finish, they replace their puzzles in the rack and move to another area of the room. Throughout this time, their teacher is occupied across the room, greeting other children as they arrive.

Although it may not be immediately apparent, a great deal of guidance occurred in the situation just described. You will recall that guidance is everything adults deliberately do and say, either directly or indirectly, to influence a child's behavior, with the goal of helping the child become a well-adjusted, productive, self-directed adult. This chapter examines the ways of influencing children's behavior indirectly, setting the stage for successful self-direction.

INDIRECT GUIDANCE

Indirect guidance is the behind-the-scenes work and planning that influences the behavior of a child. Indirect guidance requires the management of the environment—the space, equipment, materials, and human energy that make up the program. Indirect guidance means that the adults make arrangements, set schedules, and make plans that are easy for children to use or follow safely, healthfully, and happily. Indirect guidance does not involve direct interactions with children; it sets the stage for them. Components of indirect guidance include (1) forming appropriate expectations based on understanding of child development; (2) managing space, time, and energy to create an environment that supports positive behavior; and (3) planning a curriculum that engages the whole child. (See Figure 6–1.)

Previous chapters discussed the importance of setting reasonable expectations for children of a particular age and adjusting those expectations in light of children's individual characteristics, backgrounds, and experiences. In this chapter, we turn to the second component of indirect guidance: creating an environment that supports positive behavior through the intentional management of time, space, and energy. The connections between guidance and curriculum (the next tier on the guidance pyramid) will be examined more closely in Chapter 9. We will focus primarily on the indoor environment, recognizing that the principles discussed apply to the outdoor environment as well. The outdoor environment will be discussed in greater detail in Chapter 10.

In the scenario at the beginning of this chapter, both Kim and Josh were able to work independently because their teacher had carefully and thoughtfully selected a variety of puzzles, stored neatly on a shelf near the table and chairs where they were to be used. This arrangement, and raising the table height to accommodate a wheelchair, made it convenient and natural for the children to select and work together comfortably on puzzles that appealed to their interests and were appropriately challenging. The completed puzzles let the children know that they had succeeded, and the rack on the nearby shelf told them where to put the puzzles when they finished. Because the teacher's schedule provided ample time for self-selected activity, and because she had invested her own energy in arranging materials, Kim and

Indirect guidance is the behind-the-scenes work and planning that influence the behavior of children. It means that adults work together to arrange classrooms, set schedules, and make plans that are easy for children to use or follow safely, healthfully, and happily.

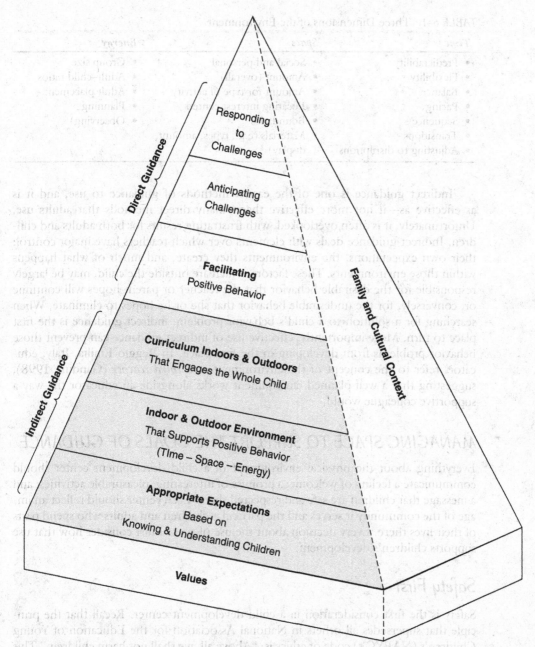

FIGURE 6–1   The guidance pyramid: Indirect guidance

Josh had many opportunities to learn from each other as well as to enjoy each other's company as they worked side by side. Both are growing in independence and self-control, and that growth is being guided by their teacher. Table 6–1 lists key elements of the three dimensions of environment that we will discuss in the rest of this chapter.

TABLE 6–1 Three Dimensions of the Environment

Time	Space	Energy
• Predictability	• Social and personal	• Group size
• Flexibility	• Amount (overall)	• Adult–child ratios
• Balance	• Amount for type of activity	• Adult placement
• Pacing	• Locating interest centers	• Planning
• Sequence	• Boundaries	• Observing
• Transitions	• Materials (e.g., types, amount,	
• Adjusting to disruptions	display)	

Indirect guidance is one of the easiest methods of guidance to use, and it is as effective as—if not more effective than—many direct methods that adults use. Unfortunately, it is often overlooked, with frustrating results for both adults and children. Indirect guidance deals with elements over which teachers have major control: their own expectations, the environments they create, and much of what happens within those environments. These factors, which are outside the child, may be largely responsible for the desirable behavior that the teacher or parent hopes will continue or, conversely, for the undesirable behavior that she or he hopes to eliminate. When searching for a solution to a child's behavior problem, indirect guidance is the first place to turn. More importantly, effective use of indirect guidance can prevent those behavior problems from developing in the first place. In Reggio Emilia, Italy, educators refer to the concept of the environment as a *third teacher* (Gandini, 1998), suggesting that a well-planned environment works alongside an educator the way a supportive colleague would.

MANAGING SPACE TO SUPPORT THE GOALS OF GUIDANCE

Everything about the physical environment of a child development center should communicate a feeling of welcome; a promise of interesting, pleasurable activities; and a message that children are safe and respected there. Each center should reflect an image of the community it serves and the particular children and adults who spend parts of their lives there. Every decision about the use of space must consider how that use supports children's development.

Safety First

Safety is the first consideration in a child development center. Recall that the principle that supersedes all others in National Association for the Education of Young Children's (NAEYC's) code of ethics is, "Above all, we shall not harm children." This means scrupulously following regulations such as those for fire exit placement, playground fencing, and sanitation practices. Equipment must be sturdy and well maintained to prevent accidents. Materials or items that might be dangerous for children must be removed or locked away where children cannot reach them.

State licensing rules spell out these and many more safety requirements in detail. Complying with those rules should be the bottom line for protecting children every day, not something that must be done to pass annual inspections. This compliance is largely the responsibility of the center's manager, but each staff member contributes by sharing in the maintenance or housekeeping tasks and promptly reporting any problems or hazards. Compliance with regulations makes the job of guiding children easier. The children will feel more secure and be able to play freely without reminders of "Don't touch that!" or "Come away from there!"

Amount of Space

Few would disagree that children need room to move if they are to learn and grow. There are widely varying responses to the question of just how much room that takes. State licensing standards set minimums (e.g., 35 square feet per child in Michigan). Anita Rui Olds (2001), an expert in designing environments for young children, argues for at least 42 square feet per child and recommends 46 or 50 square feet. An argument can be made for setting an even higher standard. One study has found that children's stress levels are heightened in environments with less than 54 square feet of accessible play space (Legendre, 2003). Olds cautions that these figures denote only the activity space for children and do not take into account additional needs, such as bathrooms, diapering, adult work or meeting areas, storage, entryways, and corridors. When these space needs are calculated, minimum building requirements become 88 square feet per child. For high quality, Olds recommends 125 square feet per child and notes that this is, in fact, the benchmark achieved by the world-renowned centers of Reggio Emilia, Italy (Gandini, 1998).

As a beginning early childhood professional, you may have little control over the amount of space you are allocated. You will have a say in what you do with that space, however, and the way you manage space will have tremendous impact on children's experience and development.

Social space refers to an area of space that a child feels belongs to him or her. Social space is also referred to as *territoriality*. Cultural differences as well as individual preferences or particular settings account for variations in perceptions of social space. If you grew up on a ranch in Wyoming, you are likely to feel uncomfortable walking down a crowded street in New York or Shanghai. You probably sit or stand closer to other people at a party or family gathering than you do in a job interview. Usually you are unaware of your personal preferences for social space until that space is violated.

Shelves and the movable riser create a protected space in this toddler classroom where children can play without interference from passing traffic. The cars and trucks arranged attractively on the shelf invite children to use them and suggest categories of vehicles. The nearby photos of real trucks and children playing on larger versions of the toys suggest themes for play.

The arrangement of activity centers in child development facilities determines how close together children will be to each other—that is, how much social space each child has. Because children are likely to want to play with other children in the block area or dramatic play corner, these centers need more space than, for example, a library corner where one or two children will curl up with books. As a general rule in early childhood centers, a learning space or environment, such as a seat at an art table or a section of a sandbox, belongs to a child as long as it is being used. Others must respect use of the space until the child leaves. You might say, "Johnny is working there. You can hammer over here." Such guidance defines Johnny's territory or social space.

Crowding violates an individual's social space and is likely to trigger aggression for several reasons. Young children's immature motor skills make it difficult to navigate tight spaces, leading to more accidental collisions. When collisions occur, young children may not have the cognitive ability to recognize that they were unintentional, the emotional maturity to inhibit their angry reactions, or the language skills to voice their objections. Adults can eliminate many guidance problems by avoiding crowding in various learning centers. If there are frequent behavior problems, teachers should analyze the use of space and the number of children using the space.

Some teachers post a number or a sign with a certain number of dots or stick figures to tell children how many are allowed to play in an area. They believe that this helps prevent overcrowding and arguments and gives good experience in counting and comparing quantities as well. The problem is that these numbers, which are arbitrarily determined by the teacher, may not make sense to the children and, worse, they can interfere with children's desire to play with their friends. Furthermore, they deprive children of an opportunity to regulate their own behavior, which is a major goal of guidance. Teachers often find themselves repeating rules like, "Only four children at the sand table" as frequently in May as they did in September. When this happens, it's time either to reconsider the necessity of the rule or to find ways to embed its message within the environment. Does it really matter whether four or six children play at the sand table? As long as there is a sufficient number of other, equally interesting things to do, children who feel crowded will move away. Or, with your support, they will negotiate a solution with each other. If everyone wants to play in the sand, you may need to look at the rest of the room and determine why the other activities are not attracting children. Or you might talk it over with the children and seek their suggestions for a solution if they happen to see it as a problem.

In some cases, too many children participating in a given activity can create safety

As long as there are plenty of interesting things to do, children can decide for themselves to move away if they feel crowded at a water table.

hazards or hamper the ability of the adult to adequately support each child's learning. If you let the environment itself communicate those limits, you will support children's self-regulation and save your own energy. Children can easily understand the rationale for wearing safety goggles at the workbench or smocks while finger painting. If you provide only two pairs of goggles or five smocks, the children will have a logical rather than arbitrary reason to limit their own numbers.

For toddlers, you will be wise simply to provide duplicates of popular activities. For older children, a space to stand and watch or a sign-up sheet nearby (even if the children scribble their "signatures") helps children wait patiently for an opening at a popular activity. Children also need to know that they will have plenty of other chances to use materials so they will not feel that they are missing a once-in-a-lifetime opportunity. Don't follow the example of the teacher who let her four-year-olds play at the sand table only once or twice a year "because they always crowded around it and fought over the toys."

Personal Space

One way to make child development centers seem less like cold, impersonal institutions and more like warm, cozy homes is to provide personal space. Infants in centers have their own cribs; older children have lockers or cubbies. Pictures of family members can be posted near cribs, and a small soft toy from home can be tucked inside to help the infant feel more at home. Lockers and cubbies can be identified with carefully printed names as well as a picture of the child or some other image to help children recognize their spaces.

Some teachers find it useful to label individual spots on the floor for group time or at the table for meals. Some children, too, find it reassuring to know that a particular spot is theirs. This may not be necessary, however, and certainly should never become a rigid constraint. Many children enjoy choosing their own places (and neighbors), particularly after they have become more familiar with the program.

❀ **Talk It Over** ❀

Recall a personal space you had as a child. Was it important to you? Brainstorm some ways personal space might be provided for children who spend their days away from home. How do you think personal space benefits a child?

In addition to personal space assigned to particular children, centers should provide many spaces in which children can experience a sense of privacy while remaining under your supervision. Toddlers will love to crawl into a cave made from an empty appliance carton and peek out through strips of fabric forming a curtained entryway. Older children might find respite from bustle and noise in a book nook or loft. Most early childhood classrooms use a system of low shelves or dividers so that children playing in a particular center see only their immediate area, while adults can see the entire room from almost any point within it. As more children spend greater portions of their lives in institutional settings, these private spaces become increasingly important.

Providing Clues for Behavior

As children look around the rooms or playground, they should be able to tell whether a space is for running and jumping or for working quietly with a puzzle. The furniture and materials in the space and the way they are arranged provide the clues children need. In the vignette at the beginning of this chapter, the arrangement of puzzles, shelves, and table and chairs told children to select a puzzle from the shelf, work it on the table, and replace it on the shelf. On a playground, the equipment tells the children to climb or swing, and the open spaces between the equipment invite children to run and shout. Classrooms sometimes send this invitation inadvertently when the furniture arrangement creates long, clear, pathways that beckon the children to run!

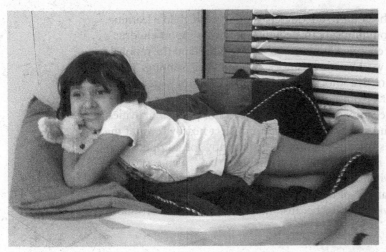

In addition to personal space assigned to particular children, centers should provide many spaces in which children can experience a sense of privacy while remaining under supervision.

Boundaries between areas can be delineated in several ways. Of course, low shelves and portable room dividers show children where one area ends and another begins. They also help create a feeling of intimacy in the smaller spaces they define. Changes in textures underfoot can guide children's use of space: A carpeted area defines the space for building with blocks, for example, while the vinyl flooring that surrounds it creates a road for driving the big trucks. A special reading lamp or light fixture suspended over a library area can create a pool of light that suggests a boundary. Color can also give clues: all the blue chairs around the art table, for example, along with a blue sponge and blue bucket kept nearby for cleaning up spills.

Of course, you will need to augment the messages sent by the environment with your own explanations: "You may drive the truck around the block area; we keep the trucks away from the art corner because their noise bothers us." Because habits take time to develop, it is a good idea to keep space arrangements stable until children have a clear idea of what activities take place and what behavior is appropriate in each space. When you must use the same space for more than one activity, such as having children take their naps in a playroom, lowering the lights and covering the toy shelves somehow will give the clues that children need to know it is naptime, not playtime.

Sufficient Play Spaces

It is important to equip a room and yard with sufficient play spaces for the number of children in the group. It is a simple matter to count the number of possible play spaces to see how many children a room or yard can serve. For example, given 2 tricycles, 2 swings, and a teeter-totter, you have 6 spaces. Indoors you might have 2 play spaces at the easel,

4 in the housekeeping corner, and 4 at the puzzle table, making 10 play spaces. At a minimum, there should be about 50 percent more play spaces than children in order to provide freedom of choice and suitable alternatives if one activity isn't working out for some reason. This means that for 20 four-year-old children, then, there should be *at least* 30 play spaces available. Providing twice the number of play spaces as children (in this case, 40 play spaces) increases children's options and potential for self-direction.

Finally, to keep things interesting for young children, you need to be able to rotate equipment from time to time. A good rule of thumb is to maintain an inventory yielding three times the number of play spaces as children. Children under three years of age will need even more play spaces. They are likely to move more quickly from one activity to another, and they are less likely to be able to wait their turn. Furthermore, they typically explore materials with their mouths, and these items must be removed for cleaning before another child plays with them. Without a generous supply of replacements, there will soon be nothing with which to play unless the teachers spend all their time cleaning. Sufficient well-operating equipment that provides adequate play spaces will help keep harmony.

Attracting Interest

Having materials out and ready to use will invite children to become involved without you telling them what to do. A child will know what to do with an easel that has fresh paper and clean brushes in well-filled paint containers. Dolls seated expectantly in

highchairs will entice children into the dramatic play area, and a selection of dress-up clothing hanging nearby will help them elaborate their play themes. An open book in the library corner or the beginnings of a simple construction in the block area will invite children to continue those activities.

Although children like to know that familiar items will be available to them every day, as noted earlier, it is a good idea to rotate equipment to keep interest fresh. You can put away the items that seem to have lost their appeal and bring out others that the children have not seen for a while. Or you can create a new spark of interest in "old" equipment by adding new accessories—small animals in the block area, for example, or some new dress-up items in the dramatic play corner.

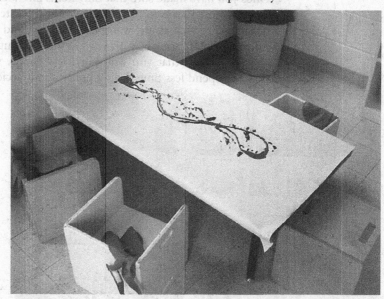

This table has been carefully set up so that three toddlers can finger paint. The table and three cube chairs are just their height, and each child is supplied with a smock. A fourth cube has been inverted for the teacher to sit nearby. A large sheet of paper taped to the table makes the entire surface available for painting. Rather than simply placing blobs of paint in front of each seat, the teacher has created an attractive, intriguing pattern in the middle of the table. Her goal is to encourage encounters among children as well as between children and paint.

Indirect Guidance   **127**

Order is part of indirect guidance and suggests a planned, orderly use of materials. If equipment is displayed in a helter-skelter manner, you can expect children to respond with like behavior. Visually pleasing, thoughtful arrangements of materials can instill an appreciation for beauty and encourage children to notice things and relationships they might otherwise have overlooked.

Promoting Independence and Engagement

When children can go into learning centers and find what they need on shelves they can reach, they can play independently. If they have to wonder whether they may use particular materials or ask for help each time they need an item, their independence is thwarted. Teachers who want to guide children toward independence and self-regulation make sure, first, that everything they put within children's sight and reach is meant to be available for children's use.

Dangerous materials are locked away. Materials that are not meant for children's immediate use are stored out of reach, and preferably out of sight as well. These include toys that you do not want used this week; extra supplies of paper, paints, and paste; and items intended for adult use, such as big scissors or flannel board props for circle time. If your center does not have cupboards or closets with doors that close, you can use sheets or curtains to cover the shelves that you want protected from children.

Once you have made sure that only items intended for children's use are available to them, the next step is to plan where you will locate each interest or activity center. Messy activities—such as art, water or sand play, and cooking and meals—should be located near a water source, with vinyl or tile flooring. This makes cleaning up spills a lot less trouble so that you will spend less energy warning children to be careful, and they will spend less time feeling guilty about accidents, which are bound to hap-

The teacher has prepared this table in the art area with a protective covering and four softened lumps of clay so that children can use it with ease and not worry about messes.

pen. Blocks, dramatic play, and a reading nook will be more inviting on a carpeted surface that muffles sound and makes sitting on the floor more comfortable. Noisy activities such as blocks, carpentry, and dramatic play should be located away from quieter areas for looking at books or writing. Table toys, puzzles, and games can serve as a buffer between the two types of activities. Heavy blocks, trucks, and carpentry that may mar woodwork or furnishings should be stored near where they can be used without the children constantly being cautioned about care of property. Moving carpentry outdoors will take the noise outside as well.

Classrooms for children ages three to five generally do not have the luxury of a space dedicated to sleeping. Instead, cots are stored during the day and set up for naptime after the blocks and other toys are put away. Since babies operate on their own schedules, infant rooms need to devote considerable space to cribs and provide comfortable adult seating for rocking and feeding babies as well as a protected space for crawling and playing on the floor. As babies become toddlers, their play will benefit from the arrangement of simple interest centers for dress-up, blocks, and table activities such as finger painting or playdough. They will probably enjoy dumping things out or carrying items from one area to another, so boundaries should not be rigid. Figure 6–2 illustrates a possible floor plan for a classroom of three- to five-year-old children; Figure 6–3 is a sample floor plan for an infant-toddler classroom.

For each interest center, it is important to provide storage for toys and supplies near the area of expected use and near an appropriate surface. Providing several different levels

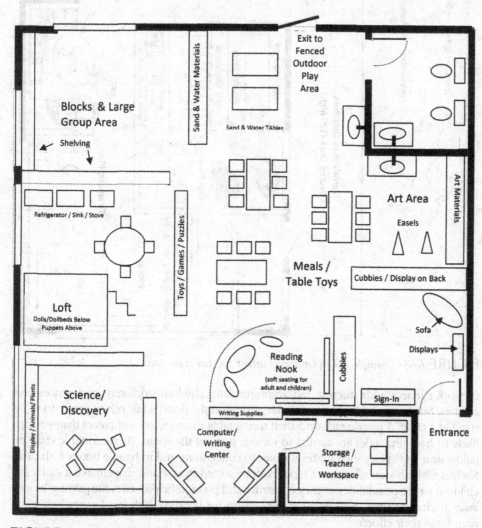

FIGURE 6–2   Sample floor plan for a preschool classroom

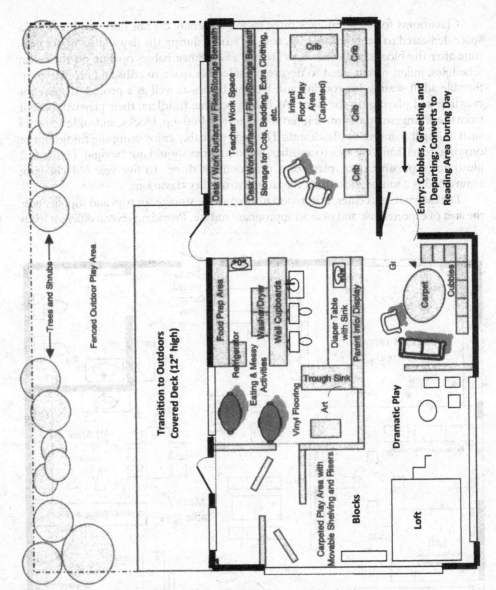

FIGURE 6–3 Sample floor plan for an infant-toddler classroom

of work surfaces adds interest and accommodates children's different preferences and abilities. Some may be more comfortable sitting on the floor, while others prefer to sit or stand at a table. A puzzle rack on a shelf near a table means fewer lost pieces than you are likely to have if puzzles are carried to various parts of the room. A comfortable chair or pillow near the library shelf makes it easier to concentrate and to handle books with care. Shelves with dividers where unit blocks can be sorted by size and shape make it easier for children to see possibilities as they construct and provide helpful cues for putting blocks away at cleanup time. A slightly raised platform for building with blocks may help children focus their efforts.

Sensory Appeal

Children are keenly attuned to their environments, often noticing and responding to things that adults overlook or take for granted. According to Olds (2001), children "live continuously in the here and now, feasting upon the nuances of color, light, sound, odor, touch, texture, volume, movement, form, and rhythm around them" (p. 21). Indirect guidance means thinking carefully about each of these elements and using them to create a tranquil, harmonious atmosphere that will support children's feelings of safety, trust, and self-worth. It means striking a balance between a sterile, impersonal, institutional quality on the one hand and a cacophony of primary colors and commercially produced decorative clutter on the other.

Plain, neutral carpeting and light-colored walls are not distracting and allow the children and their creations to stand out instead of being overwhelmed. Instead of mass-produced plastic objects, an array of baskets, plants, rich fabrics, pottery, and framed artworks, chosen to reflect the lives of children and their families, conveys a homelike atmosphere—what Olds calls a "spirited place." Images of children and their work, artfully displayed with accompanying narratives, document the lives of the children and adults who share the space and communicate to children and their families the sense that children's thoughts and feelings are important (Gandini, 1998, pp. 175–177).

Using Space Efficiently

Adults often complain about a lack of space in child development centers when the actual problem is an inefficient use of the space that is available. From time to time, you should take a good look at how the various areas of your center are used—at any given moment as well as over the course of a day or a week. Some teachers reserve a large, carpeted area of their classroom for large group meetings or circle time, an event that might occupy only a small part of each day or, in the case of toddlers and some other young children, may not occur at all. They make no conscious plans for children to use that area in the much longer time block for self-selected activity or to arrange the space to accommodate several smaller groups. The children—somewhat like molecules filling a vacuum—use the large open area in their play, but they do so haphazardly and not always in ways that please the teacher. This unintended consequence can be avoided by using the large carpeted area to help define a block center. After the blocks are put away at cleanup time, the area becomes available for circle activities and, later, for naptime. Thus, the space can be well used throughout the day, not just during a 15-minute group time.

Adult furnishings pose another challenge to efficient use of space. Early childhood educators seldom teach from a desk in the front of the room, so having a large desk in the room at all times is probably not the best use of the space. If you cannot eliminate the desk, you can make it serve double duty, perhaps by using its surface as a place where children can display interesting items from home. Vertical surfaces on the front and sides might hold displays of photographs or children's art, or, if the desk is metal, provide a surface on which children can use magnetic shapes or letters.

Modifying Environments for Children with Disabilities

Several federal laws require that states provide educational services for children with disabilities in the least restrictive environment and that facilities serving the public (e.g., child development centers) make every reasonable effort to accommodate individuals with disabilities. The prospect of doing this will be less daunting if you recall that it is part of developmentally appropriate practice to recognize that any group of children will contain a wide range of abilities and needs and to tailor a program to the individual needs of those children. When you set up and equip an environment so that everyone can use it comfortably, you are following the principle of *universal design*, a concept that has become increasingly influential among architects and designers in recent years. You may have noticed examples of universal design in your own environment: closed captioning on television programs, traffic signals that emit chirps or beeps when it is safe for pedestrians to cross the street, and kitchen gadgets with large, soft handles that are easy to grip. Universally designed learning materials are "appealing, easy to use, flexible, multi-sensory, and adaptable to a variety of users and situations. They often invite cooperation, and they don't single out or stigmatize the user" (Haugen, 2005, p. 46).

Preparing an environment to meet the special needs of children with particular disabilities is not very different from preparing an environment to promote the independence and self-control of children who are at several different stages of "typical" development. Just as you provide a softer environment for toddlers learning to walk, you provide wider aisles between furniture for children who use wheelchairs to move through your classroom safely. Maintaining a predictable environment where children can find what they need from day to day helps all children feel more secure at the same time as it helps a child with a vision impairment navigate her surroundings. For children with hyperactivity or attention-deficit disorder (ADD), you might try putting fewer choices of materials on shelves, switching from fluorescent to incandescent lighting, and adding very quiet background music to muffle distracting noises (Grisham-Grown, Hemmeter, & Pretti-Frontczak, 2005, pp. 205–206). Visual representations of the daily schedule or the sequence of steps for tooth brushing help all children, particularly those with autism spectrum disorder, function independently (Meadan et al., 2011). The key is to observe carefully and tailor your modifications to the specific needs of the individual children in your care. Table 6–2 provides a list of suggestions to help you broaden the range of abilities you can meet with ordinary equipment.

Just as you provide a softer environment for toddlers learning to walk, you provide wider aisles and higher tables for children who use wheelchairs.

TABLE 6–2 Adding and Adapting Materials to Accommodate All Children

	Broaden Accessibility	Add Sensory Element
Art	Offer a choice of work surfaces (e.g., easel, table, floor)	Add texture (e.g., sand) to finger paint
	Stabilize painting surface (tape individual pieces of paper to table, or cover entirely)	Provide options for children who are uncomfortable with messy hands
	Wrap brush handles with foam for ease of grasping	
	Provide modeling material of varying malleability (e.g., playdough, clay)	
Balls	Various weights, sizes, and bounciness	Various materials (e.g., foam, stuffed fabric, rubber)
	Tethered	
	Inserted into a tube sock for ease of retrieval	With added sensory features (e.g., bells, lights)
Blocks	Various weights and sizes	Variety of materials (e.g., wood, cardboard, plastic)
	With bristles or magnets to help with stacking	
	Platform or table to build on for children who cannot get on floor	With shakers or bells inside
Books	With stiff pages (e.g., cardboard, plastic) or tongue-depressor tabs for easy turning	With textured surfaces, flaps, or cut-outs to stroke, lift, or poke
	Recorded versions for children with vision impairment	With sound effects operated by child (e.g., pressing button, opening page)
	On computer for children who cannot hold a book	
Dramatic play	Tables and other furniture at heights to allow access for children in wheelchairs	Variety of fabric textures (e.g., satin, velvet, plush, fake fur)
	Dress-up clothes with large openings, Velcro fasteners	Sound effects (e.g., microwave that beeps, phone that rings or buzzes)
	Varying realism (e.g., "police uniform" vs. lengths of fabric)	
	Large knobs or handles on cookware and appliance replicas	
Table toys	Variety of difficulty (e.g., number of puzzle pieces, knobs on pieces, size of elements)	Sound effects (e.g., when lotto card is "correctly" matched with corresponding image on board)
	Provide cookie sheets or cafeteria-style trays to help child control small loose parts that can roll out of reach	Items that light up when manipulated in specific ways

MANAGING TIME

The previous chapter mentioned one aspect of managing time as part of guiding young children: allowing teachers to remain with the same group of children from one year to the next so that relationships develop between children, between teachers and children, between teachers and families, and between families. This growing sense of community will make your job easier as you strive to help children become productive members of the larger community. The less time adults and children have together, the greater the skill and competence required of the adults who must interpret the children's needs.

As in the case of space, you may not have control over the amount of time that you and children spend together. Program policies will dictate whether children spend all or part of each day; whether they attend every day, year round, or only a few mornings a week during only a few months per year; and whether they stay with you for all or only part of the period they are enrolled. Again, as with space, what you do with your time with children is what matters most.

You will need a plan for arranging the sequence of events that occur each day in your life with children. With young infants, your plan will consist mostly of following their lead: feeding and diapering when needed, rocking them to sleep, or playing with them when they are awake and alert. Gradually they will consolidate their periods of wakefulness and sleep into something that resembles a schedule so that you will be able to predict when most of the children in a group will be hungry or ready for a nap.

Predictability and Flexibility

A natural outgrowth of the biological rhythm is a regular sequence of daily events that helps children and adults know what to expect and contributes to everyone's sense of security. It does not require that you become a slave to the clock. As long as children know that they can expect to clean up, listen to a story, and have snack after their period of self-selected activity, they will probably not be disturbed if the activity period is stretched a little longer some days to allow them to complete a particularly engrossing block structure. The keys to appropriate scheduling are predictability and flexibility.

Meeting Individual Needs

Other factors you need to consider as you plan a daily schedule include the length of time the children are with you and the way they spend their time before and after your program. If children arrive at the center still sleepy and needing breakfast, your schedule will need to include enough time for eating and for other physiological needs, such as bowel movements and urination, as well as an afternoon nap. On the other hand, children who have slept later will probably neither need nor want a rest time in the middle of their half-day program.

Whatever the objectives of a program, children's physical needs must come first. Some schools plan full-day kindergarten programs in the misguided belief that they will be able to cover more academic material with the children. But even five-year-olds who may not nap need time to unwind and relax. This means that their day must include both slower-paced activities in the classroom and opportunities for physical exertion and socialization outside.

In full-day centers, children may begin arriving as early as 6 a.m., with others coming as late as mid-afternoon. In shorter programs, children may be brought on a school bus and arrive all at one time, or they may arrive individually within about a half-hour time span. Regardless of the arrival schedule, the sequence of events must be flexible enough to allow children to enter comfortably, to be made welcome, and to pick up the thread of activity without feeling strange or left out.

Balancing Activities

A schedule that provides a balance between various types of activities will make life easier for everyone. Providing adequate time for vigorous play means that children are likely to be more willing and able to settle down and listen to a story you want to read to them. "Big body play gets children's blood going and minds moving, or rather, gets the mind settled" (Carlson, 2011, p. 42). On the other hand, having scheduled periods of quieter activities, such as group meetings or singing, can be refreshing for everyone and will help prevent children from overtiring themselves.

Another type of balance to consider is the amount of time in which children are able to select and carry out their own activities—in other words, time for play. Recalling developmental goals for toddlers and young children, you will want to ensure plenty of opportunities for them to exercise their autonomy and initiative. NAEYC guidelines for developmentally appropriate practice recommend "extended time periods in learning centers (at least 60 minutes) so that children are able to get deeply involved in an activity and sustain dramatic play, construction, and other activities at a complex level (Copple & Bredekamp, 2009, p. 153). The Early Childhood Environmental Rating Scale, a widely used instrument for assessing quality of early childhood programs, sets a more stringent standard, requiring that children have access to a variety of free-choice activities for at least one-third of the time (a "substantial portion of the day") in order for a classroom to receive a rating of "good" or better (Harms, Clifford, & Cryer, 1998).

Experience shows that the quality of play increases when children have enough time to develop intricate play themes and have interesting conversations (Christie & Wardle, 1992). A study of early childhood practices in the United States and nine other countries found higher levels of language for seven-year-old children whose preschool teachers had emphasized free choice. Furthermore, less time in whole-group activities and the availability of a richer variety of equipment and materials in preschool were linked with improved cognitive skills at age seven (Montie, Xiang, & Schweinhart, 2006).

It makes sense that pulling children away from their self-initiated activity to do what adults think is important can work against the development of concentration and attention span. This does not mean, however, that "free play" is a "free-for-all." The quality of your interactions with children will influence children's feelings (Hestenes, Kontos, & Bryan, 1993) as well as what they gain from their play (Early et al., 2010). Those interactions are part of direct guidance, which we will discuss in detail in the next chapter; they cannot happen, however, unless you have set the stage with abundant, thoughtfully arranged, interesting materials and adequate time to become deeply engrossed in meaningful play. When you understand the concept of indirect guidance, you will see that you can provide plentiful opportunities for children to accomplish important learning without resorting to the kinds of teacher-directed activities you may remember from elementary school.

Time Block Planning

Using a **time block plan** enables you to achieve your objectives while remaining flexible. Large time blocks can be shortened or lengthened without disturbing children's sequence-of-events orientation. A time block plan readily accommodates children's

Indirect guidance means setting the stage with abundant, thoughtfully arranged, interesting materials and adequate time for children to become deeply engrossed in meaningful play.

needs, the various activities, and the surprises that each day brings without rushing children through their activities.

A part-day program usually includes three blocks of activities: (1) self-selected activity indoors, (2) teacher-directed activity, and (3) self-selected activity outdoors. In a longer day program, one or more of these blocks might be repeated, and additional blocks of time for meals and naps must be included. Children who attend only part of the day, or for a few days each week, often feel that they have missed something when they attend full-day programs and see that other children remain at the center after they go home. If there are enough part-time enrollees, the program should assign them all to one group with a sensitive teacher who makes special short-range plans instead of extended week-long plans. If children have an opportunity to complete projects on their days in the center, they'll feel good about coming back. If they feel they have to leave projects unfinished, they are likely to be dissatisfied.

Table 6–3 provides a sample schedule for a full-day program for three- to five-year-old children. Table 6–4 is a sample schedule for infants and toddlers. The times designated on the sample schedules are not rigid requirements; you should be ready to extend a morning period of self-selected activity if children are particularly involved in some project or to reverse the order of indoor and outdoor play on the morning that children arrive flushed with excitement about the newly-fallen snow. (A reward for your flexibility in this case will be that the children are already dressed in their snowsuits and boots!) Note, also, that self-selected activity outdoors requires the same quality of planning as self-selected activity indoors and that teacher-directed activity can occur in either location.

Transitions

Transitions are those times in the schedule when children move from one activity or location to another. Under the best of circumstances, transitions create a certain amount of added stress for both adults and children, and these are the most likely times for children to appear out of control. For very young children or for children with disabilities such as autism, transitions can be experienced as a threatening departure from routine. You can avoid many of these negative effects in two ways: by eliminating all but the absolutely necessary transitions and by planning very carefully for the transitions that you must include in your schedule.

TABLE 6–3   Sample Schedule: Full-Day Program for Three- to Five-Year-Old Children

Time	Block I—Arrival and Self-Selected Activity Indoors
7:30	Greet children individually as they arrive. Children put their personal items in cubbies and select an activity from books, dramatic play, blocks, or coloring. As more children and staff arrive, additional activities are made available: painting, clay, table games, science area, woodworking, computer. Project work in small groups with an adult is one available choice.
9:00–10:00	Snack available at a small table as a choice; children serve themselves, eat alone or with others, and clean up after themselves.

Time	Block II—Teacher-Directed Activity
10:00–10:15	Clean-up and transition to group time.
10:15–10:30	A combination of conversation, music, and story. The group may be divided into several small groups.
10:30	Transition to outdoor play: Toileting as needed. Dress for outdoor play.

Time	Block III—Self-Selected Activity Outdoors
10:45–11:45	As they finish dressing, children move in small groups to the playground for self-selected activity: large muscle equipment, wheel toys, sandbox, water play, gardening, painting, dramatic play, music.
11:45	Transition to indoors: Children help put away playground toys and return to building. Remove outdoor wraps and place in cubbies. Toileting as needed.

Time	Block IV—Mealtime
12:00	Children gather for quiet singing or story on rug while a few help set tables for lunch.
12:15	Children sent from group to wash hands and sit down at lunch tables. Adults sit with them; children serve themselves some foods family style with adult assistance as needed. Conversation encouraged.

Time	Block V—Naptime
12:45	Transition to nap: While children eat, one adult prepares nap area (gets out cots, arranges blankets, stuffed toys, etc.). When finished eating, each child goes to the bathroom to toilet and wash, then goes to prepared nap area. Adults help children settle by playing soft music, rubbing backs, perhaps reading individual stories.
1:00–3:00	Sleep.
3:00	Transition to Afternoon: Children awaken, use toilet, wash hands, have snack, quiet individual conversation or games. When all have finished snack, dress for outdoor play.

Time	Block VI—Self-Selected Activity
3:30	Outdoor play with choices as described above.
4:30	Clean up play yard and move indoors; toileting as needed.
4:45	Quiet time indoors: table games, coloring, story, singing, or records. Dress and dismiss children as parents arrive.
6:00	All children gone home.

Note: A half-day program would follow the schedule for Time Blocks I, II, and III, adjusting times as needed.

TABLE 6–4 Sample Schedule: Full-Day Program for Infants and Toddlers

Infant schedule revolves around a cycle of feeding, diapering, sleeping, with opportunities for play, exploration, and interaction with others (indoors and outdoors) when child is awake and alert. These times lengthen gradually as the infant matures and the following sequence of events emerges:

Time	Block I—Morning
7:30–9:00	Arrival and quiet play. Each child is greeted upon arrival and helped to separate from parent. Adults read to or play with individual children. Children are diapered or helped with toileting as needed.
9:00	Handwashing and mealtime. Children are invited to help set table; adults and children sit and eat together; children help clear table and wash hands.
9:30–11:00	Self-selected activity indoors and/or outdoors. Children choose from blocks, dress-ups, vehicles, push- or pull-toys, small climbing ramp, materials for dumping and collecting, books, etc. Adults invite a few at a time to participate in an activity requiring more supervision and support (e.g., painting, clay, "goop"). Ideally, outdoor play (water, sand, riding toys, balls, hoops) available as a choice during this time block. Children are diapered or helped with toileting as needed.

Time	Block II—Midday
11:00	Handwashing and mealtime. Children are invited to help set table; adults and children sit and eat together; children help clear table, brush teeth, and wash hands. Diapering and toileting as needed.
12:00	Naptime. Adults sing to children, rub backs, and help them settle on their cots. As children awake from nap, adults provide quiet activities away from children who are still sleeping. Snack served when majority of children are awake. Diapering and toileting as needed.

Time	Block III—Afternoon
3:30–6:00	Self-selected activity indoors and/or outdoors. Children choose from blocks, dress-ups, vehicles, push- or pull-toys, small climbing ramp, materials for dumping and collecting, books, etc. Adults invite a few at a time to participate in an activity requiring more supervision and support (e.g., painting, clay, "goop"). Ideally, weather permitting, outdoor play (water, sand, riding toys, balls, hoops) available as a choice during this time block. Children are diapered or helped with toileting as needed.

Reducing the Number of Transitions. The time block method of planning allows you to eliminate unnecessary transitions because many types of activities occur simultaneously, and no child has to wait for everyone to finish an activity before moving on to play somewhere else. For example, the art materials are available in one of the interest areas throughout the first time block so that a child who finishes in five minutes can move on, leaving the child with a greater interest or attention span to work longer without being urged to hurry because the other children are restless. Some teachers include a simple self-service snack as one of the choices available during this time block, thus eliminating the transitions involved in getting children to and from the table as a group.

Planning Transitions.   Once you have pared the number of transitions in your schedule to the essential few, you can plan to make each transition as calm and orderly as possible. This requires that each adult knows what comes next, knows what his or her responsibilities are, and is at least one step ahead of the children in the process. It also requires that children know what comes next and what their responsibilities are, which means that you will have to tell them (or show them) many times until they gradually learn the routines. As children become more familiar with the daily sequence of activities, they will be less likely to become confused or upset at transition times. When children are playing, they need advance notice of transitions so that they can bring some closure to their present activity and reorient themselves. Be careful about making such announcements to the entire group at one time, however, or you may find that you instigate bedlam, with children knocking over their block structures and running around, shouting "Clean up! Clean up!" You will probably find it more effective to approach children individually or in small groups in the various centers, calmly asking that they begin putting the blocks on the shelves, or hanging up the dress-up clothes.

As children become more familiar with the daily sequence of activities, they will be less likely to become confused or upset at transition times. Adults can help by

Well-planned transitions, such as involving children in songs or finger plays rather than expecting them to wait for what comes next, make life less stressful for teachers as well as children.

reminding children what comes next and by structuring the transitions for them. Avoid telling the children to "hurry up and wait." When moving from group time to outdoor play, for example, you could dismiss children one at a time by name, or you could say that all those with brown shoes should get their coats. One group of four-year-olds particularly enjoyed it when this method was turned into a sort of guessing game: "If you have curly hair, brown pants, and a striped tee shirt, you may go get your coat and mittens." In a room with two adults, one should be prepared to take some children outside as soon as they have their coats buttoned, while the other adult helps the rest of the group.

At cleanup time, both adults might be needed to help the children start the process, but as soon as that is well under way, one adult should move to the next activity with a few children who have finished their cleanup responsibilities. That might mean sitting on the carpet and singing a few songs to initiate group time or starting a finger play with children who arrive at the snack table ahead of the others. Of course, all materials needed for the next activity should be ready. Don't expect children to sit and wait while you hunt for the missing pieces of your flannel board story.

❀ Talk It Over ❀

What transitions have you observed in your own experience in a child development center? Describe how those transitions were handled and offer suggestions for making them go more smoothly.

Daily Plan Sheet

A posted daily plan sheet indicating who is responsible for each activity, such as that in Table 6–5, will help. The less experienced the staff, the more detailed this written plan must be. It is important to remember that the details refer to what is expected of the adults in order to provide certain choices for children. In Table 6–5, for example, the teachers must have prepared (perhaps with children's help on previous days) three sets of cards: one with children's photographs, one with their first names, and one with their "special names" (See p. 146 for a description of the "special names" project.) As you can see, James needs to make sure that these cards are displayed in an organized and inviting way and make himself available to observe what children do with the cards or suggest other ways of using them. Marissa needs to clean and sanitize the table, then (ideally with children's help) set out napkins, cups, the juice pitcher, and a basket of muffins. Children are free to participate in either activity, as they choose, during the times indicated. Marissa will note who has not had snack and give them a "last-call" warning at 9:45.

Disruptions

Once children have learned the schedule, changes can cause discomfort and confusion unless you take special care to prepare children for them. With a little thought and

TABLE 6-5   Sample Daily Plan Sheet (Three- to Five-Year-Old Group)

Time	Class of Activity	Specific Activity	Staff
Time	**Block I—Arrival and Self-Selected Activity Indoors**		
7:30–10:00	**Interest Areas:** Books, Art, Music, Dramatic Play, Blocks, Table Games, Science, Woodworking, Computer	Add people figures to block area; "special names" letters in reading area	LaToyah*
	Project Work (8:30–?)	Matching game with name cards	James*
	Self-Serve Snack (9:00–10:00)	Orange juice and bran muffins	Marissa*
Time	**Block II—Teacher-Directed Activity**		
10:00–10:15	**Clean Up;** transition to Group Time	Special attention to blocks and dramatic play areas	LaToyah
10:15–10:30	**Group**	Read *Mama, Do You Love Me* and any new "special names" letters	James
10:30–10:45	**Transition** to outdoor play; toileting as needed; coats, etc.	Supervise toileting; then help with wraps; take children outside as ready in groups	LaToyah James
		Set up outdoor play areas	Marissa
Time	**Block III—Self-Selected Activity Outdoors**		
10:45–11:45	**Interest Areas:** Large Muscle Equipment, Science, Garden, Sand, Water, Art, Dramatic Play, Music	Tricycles and climber Tubing and funnels in water table	LaToyah James
	Transition: Clean up; go inside; remove wraps; toileting	Easel painting	Marissa
Time	**Block IV—Mealtime**		
12:00–12:45	**Quiet group activity** while a few children help set tables	Fingerplays and songs: *Two Little Blackbirds* (with children's names inserted)	James
	Transition to table; handwashing		
	Lunch and Conversation	Supervise table setting	LaToyah
		Supervise handwashing	Marissa
Time	**Block V—Naptime**		
12:45–3:00	**Transition:** toileting, stories, music, backrubs	Set up cots while children move to table area; then join them	James
	Sleep	Supervise table area	LaToyah
	Transition: toileting, handwashing, snack, individual quiet play, dress for outdoors	Supervise bathroom	Marissa
		Help children settle	All

(Continued)

Table 6–5 *(Continued)*

Time	Class of Activity	Specific Activity	Staff
Time	**Block VI—Self-Selected Activity (Indoors and/or Outdoors)**		
3:00–6:00	**Outdoor Play** with choices as above	Outdoors: large hollow blocks; weed & water garden; bean bag toss	James
	Transition to indoors		LaToyah
	Quiet Play, stories or music		
	Dressing and dismissing children as parents arrive	Indoors: giant floor puzzles; puppets	James
		Greet parents; share details of child's day	Marissa

* LaToyah works 7:30–4:30; James works 8:00–5:00; Marissa works 9:00–6:00. All take 1 hour break: LaToyah: 12:45–1:45; James: 1:45–2:45; Marissa: 2:45–3:45.

planning, you will be able to incorporate changes into your schedule while still meeting the children's needs for predictability and a balance of activities.

Weather. A rainy day may mean that you lengthen the time block for indoor self-selected activity and substitute some type of vigorous indoor activity, or perhaps a walk with umbrellas, during the time block slated for outdoor activity. A cupboard stocked with some special activities for rainy days, including suggestions for stories, songs, or poems, is a great help when it rains unexpectedly.

Special Guests. If an unscheduled special guest arrives, offering an unexpected learning opportunity, the teachers might agree to shelve the scheduled plan for the period and listen to the visitor during the minutes the visitor is available. When prior planning includes a special guest, that person's particular activity will dictate the type of activity to eliminate for the day. For example, a visiting twirler who marches children around the yard could be scheduled for outdoor playtime, whereas a guitarist might be scheduled for the time usually reserved for music. Using these considerations when scheduling events ensures that the children's energy level is appropriate for the type of behavior expected—marching with the twirler or relaxed singing with the guitarist.

Special Events. Field trips, holidays, and local special days such as a community parade may require changes in the schedule. For example, if a field trip requires walking, then restful activities should be scheduled for the periods directly before and after the trip. Or, if children are attending a children's symphony, the schedule could be rearranged to provide an early period of vigorous outdoor activity to help the children's bodies be ready for restful listening. When planning a field trip, if most of the events of a regular day can be preserved—even though abbreviated—the children will have fewer questions about "What do we do now?" and "Where do we go?"

Of course, the primary consideration in planning field trips is children's safety. Teachers should visit the site in advance to make sure that there are no tempting hazards and that the main attractions are interesting enough that volunteer assistants will not have difficulty managing bored children's behavior. Regulations regarding transportation (vehicle inspections, passenger restraint devices, first aid kits, emergency information records, etc.) should be scrupulously followed. Parents must be fully informed and provide written permission for their children to participate in such activities. Because of difficulty ensuring children's safety (and to protect themselves from liability), many programs have discontinued field trips. Creative teachers can take heart in the fact that many interesting "field trips" can consist of short walks within the neighborhood.

Holidays can overtire young children unless teachers are alert to protecting them from too much stimulation. A low-key program at the child development center provides a calming counterbalance when children's home schedules are disrupted with extra shopping trips, late bedtimes, and exciting anticipation. Community organizations often want to provide parties or treats for children's programs during the holiday season. Tactfully encouraging these well-intentioned benefactors to schedule their events later in the year will prevent problems and brighten children's days after the holiday excitement has worn off.

MANAGING ENERGY

Adults often describe children as full of energy, and they are well aware of how much of their own energy it takes to keep up with their charges. Often, adults experience an energy drain because they are working at cross-purposes with children. It takes incredible energy to keep a rambunctious group of three-year-olds sitting still for a story that doesn't interest them or to keep a toddler from poking fingers into forbidden places. Managing energy as part of indirect guidance means getting in sync with children so that you are, in effect, harnessing their energy to help achieve the goals of guidance. Adults who invest their energy in planning exciting group activities for three-year-olds or providing lots of legitimate places for toddlers to explore find their work much less exhausting. Some would say they are working smarter, not harder.

Group Size and Adult–Child Ratio

As we have seen in discussions of space and time, some aspects of energy management will be beyond the control of an individual teacher. Unless you work alone, as a family child-care provider, for example, the adult–child ratio in your program will likely be established by administrators. Still, the numbers of adults and children in a group will determine the ability of those adults to manage energy—their own as well as the children's.

Adult–child ratio refers to the number of children in relation to the number of adults in the group. *Group size* refers to the total number of children. Both are important. In general, the lower the ratio (i.e., the fewer children per adult), the better the quality of care. The adult–child ratio is directly related to how much personal interaction can occur between the teacher and each child and how much energy the teacher can devote to one child without shortchanging another. The ratio also control how enriching the program can be, whether adults can encourage children to use their energy constructively to learn and develop, or whether they must continually fight to keep a damper on that energy.

However, ratios don't tell the whole story. The overall number of individuals in a given space will also impact quality. In a room with 24 toddlers and 6 caregivers, the mathematical ratio is 1:4, just as in an infant room with 12 toddlers and 2 caregivers. However, the human ratio for the caregivers in the first room is three times greater in the larger group because each caregiver would need to know the personalities and needs of 24 children—as well as their families (Ruopp, Travers, Glantz, & Coelen, 1979). And because the toddlers themselves would be interacting with twice as many children and adults, those interactions would be more likely to be stressful and less likely to nurture the kind of relationships needed to support development.

The stimulation of large numbers of children in a single group can be fatiguing for everyone. The younger the child, the smaller the number of children that each child and caregiver should be required to interact with each day. Appropriate group sizes encourage friendships among children and enable adults to interact with individual children. They foster mutual trust among children, teachers, and families.

For these reasons, there are specific group-size and adult–child ratio requirements in the NAEYC accreditation guidelines (NAEYC, 2007b) as well as in most state licensing requirements. Younger children require more adults to care for them and smaller group sizes overall. For example, the recommended ratio for infants up to 15 months of age is 1 adult for 3 or 4 babies, with a maximum group size of 6 or 8. For four-year-olds, the maximum recommended group size is 20 children, with a

Appropriate group sizes encourage friendships among children and enable adults to interact with individual children.

ratio of at least 1:10. Because the NAEYC guidelines define a high-quality program, they usually differ from state licensing guidelines, which are minimum standards.

Early childhood programs have various admission and grouping policies. Some prefer a more homogeneous single-age group, such as all three-year-olds or all four-year-olds. Others advocate a wider age range, such as two to five, so that older children can learn to help younger children, as they would in a family situation. This decision will have an impact on group size and staff–child ratio because mixed ages will increase the range of individual differences among the children and require curriculum materials and equipment with a greater range of difficulty.

Keeping groups intact as children mature rather than promoting the children to a new group and teacher, helps avoid the problems of adjustment to a new group and encourages teachers to work harder to find solutions to children's problems.

Maximizing Energy Efficiency

Numbers of adults do not ensure high-quality programs. Working with young children requires a particular set of knowledge, skills, and dispositions. The more knowledge and experience you have, the more efficiently you will be able to use your energy. Like champion athletes, master teachers make it look easy because they are able to achieve maximum gains with minimum exertion. Your study of guidance is part of your professional preparation to enter the early childhood field. Ideally, you and your colleagues will continue your study throughout your careers. High-quality programs hire the most well-educated staff possible. They provide orientation and training for staff and volunteers without formal training, and they provide regular opportunities for in-service education. They assign those staff to work with smaller groups of children, and they provide mentors to help new or inexperienced staff make more detailed plans until they develop the skills to cope with fast-moving events.

Managing your energy as part of indirect guidance means using your presence to attract children to a particular area of the room rather than admonishing them to leave an area that you feel is overcrowded. It means using your presence to help children control their own behavior. You can sit so you can see the entire room while you help an individual child with a puzzle. You can also sit nearby and show interest in what children are doing rather than standing and talking to another adult until the noise level escalates and problems erupt. Instead of asking children to adjust their behavior, you can sometimes adjust yours. For example, if you notice that children are fussing because they can't see the pictures in the book you are reading, you can move from the floor to a low chair.

Planning and Preparation

Curriculum planning and preparation of materials are part of managing energy as a form of indirect guidance. When adults invest the energy to provide a wide variety of interesting and appropriate activities and respond to children as they participate in those activities, children are more likely to use their boundless energy constructively. On the other hand, if learning experiences are poorly planned or are too easy or too difficult, children may take matters into their own hands in ways that you don't want. Boredom is one of the major causes of misbehavior, and it can lead a previously cooperative child to turn mischievous.

Children who have attended the same center for several years will require special plans. Some of these children have been around longer than the teachers. Also, if children attend school part of the day, they will need a change of pace and opportunities to release pent-up energy in the after-school program. If children are unruly, one of the first things to examine is the richness of the curriculum offerings. The curriculum is far easier to change than the children.

It follows that teachers need paid time away from children to invest their energy in this planning; NAEYC's accreditation guidelines make this a requirement. Serving eight hours a day on the floor with children leaves little time for creative thought, evaluation of past practices, and preparation for exciting learning projects.

❊   Talk It Over   ❊

Name some troublesome behaviors you have observed in child-care settings. Suggest specific ways that these troublesome behaviors could be averted by using indirect guidance techniques—for example, room arrangement; variety, quantity, and accessibility of materials; or scheduling. Tell why you think your suggestion would work.

Observing Children

Observing children at play is another way that teachers' use of energy shapes the classroom environment. In doing so, teachers gain insight into children's particular interests and abilities and generate ideas for a curriculum that builds on those strengths. Let's look at two examples of curriculum planning that stemmed from observations of children's interests.

One family child-care provider noticed that her toddler charges enjoyed prolonging the hand-washing ritual that followed toileting. So she included water play in her plans for the week and watched children spend long periods happily pouring, splashing, and babbling to each other. Another day, noting the toddlers' intense interest in the new infant who had just joined the group, she added dolls, washcloths, and towels so that children could imitate her "taking care of baby."

A group of three- and four-year-olds were fascinated when their teacher read a story in which a mother repeatedly called her child "dear one." Perhaps they were confusing the affectionate term with the antlered woodland animal. The teacher's explanation about special names that people sometimes give their loved ones prompted an animated conversation over lunch as children told each other their own "special names." The observant teacher followed up by making charts of children's "regular" and "special" names, printing those names on cards for children to sort and match with photographs. The children checked themselves by matching names on the cards with names on the chart or cubbies, and made the observation that "the special names are the ones with those funny little [quotation] marks." With the children's help, the teacher composed a note to be sent home, requesting that families send a letter explaining the origin or meaning of their child's "special name." As each letter came in, it was read aloud at group time, to the rapt attention of the children. The collected letters were put in a binder and placed in the book area near the classroom entrance, where children revisited them often—alone, with each other, and with parents or their teacher. Of course, all the usual classroom choices (blocks, dramatic play, puzzles, art, sand, water, etc.) were also in use every day while this project was under way.

CONCLUSION

Indirect guidance influences children's behavior through management of space (including equipment and materials), time, and the energy of the people in the center. Indirect guidance is the behind-the-scenes work and planning that pays big dividends by helping children become self-directed, self-controlled, and independent. Many indirect guidance techniques are carried out when the children are not present. Adults need protected time when they are not responsible for children in order to plan and prepare. Investing time and energy in indirect guidance will help ensure the success of the direct guidance techniques discussed in Chapter 7.

REVIEW: TEN TECHNIQUES OF INDIRECT GUIDANCE

Manage Space, Equipment, and Materials

1. Make safety a priority: Comply with fire and sanitation regulations; store dangerous materials away from children; and monitor equipment for needed repair or replacement.

2. Create a warm, inviting atmosphere by providing personal space and including materials or photographs that reflect the lives of children in the center.

3. Make the environment your co-teacher: Create protected areas where children can work and play without disrupting each other; use furniture or other clues to create boundaries; locate noisy or messy activities away from quieter ones; and arrange materials attractively so that they tempt children to use them and conveniently so that children can use them independently.

4. Provide enough materials so that children can keep busy: at least 50 percent more play spaces than children.

Manage Time

5. Plan a daily schedule that is predictable yet flexible enough to meet individual needs.

6. Provide a balance between active and quiet times as well as between activities selected by children and those that are teacher directed.

7. Ensure that children have ample uninterrupted time to develop complex play themes.

8. Limit the number of transitions in the schedule and carefully plan for those that are needed.

Manage People and Energy

9. Maintain appropriate adult–child ratios and group sizes so that children and adults can form nurturing relationships.

10. Plan a rich and varied curriculum appropriate to the ages and experiences of children.

APPLICATIONS

1. Observe a child development center (either the laboratory site to which you have been assigned or another center in your community). Describe the way the environmental arrangement tells children

   a. What to do with their coats and other belongings

   b. What to do with their cup and napkin after a snack

   c. What to do before or after using the toilet

   d. What to do to be safe in the outdoor play area

   e. Where to paint or draw

   f. Where to be noisy and where to be quiet

   g. Where running is appropriate

   h. What to do when they first arrive

   i. What to do after the snack

   For each example, explain how the environmental arrangement made it easy or difficult for the child to behave as expected.

2. Analyze the daily schedule in the program you observe. What percentage of the day is devoted to children's self-selected activity? How many transitions are built into the day? Evaluate the schedule using the guidelines discussed in this chapter.

3. If the program you observe has one or more children with disabilities enrolled, try to find out what changes in scheduling and room arrangement were made to accommodate those children. If there are no children with disabilities included, suggest modifications that could be made for a child with impaired vision and for a child with autism.

4. Review the section on management of energy in this chapter and list examples of effective or ineffective uses that you noticed during your observation.

RESOURCES FOR FURTHER STUDY

Websites

Center to Mobilize Early Childhood Knowledge
community.fpg.unc.edu/connect-modules/learners
Online learning module on the purpose, use, and potential benefits of assistive technology interventions when working with young children; includes videos, handouts, and activities based on real-life situations.

Community Playthings

communityplaythings.com
Manufacturer of equipment for early childhood programs. The website includes links to resources, including space planning guides preschool and infant-toddler classrooms.

Spaces for Children

spacesforchildren.com
Website of Louis Torelli and Charles Durrett, an early childhood educator and an architect, whose goal is to create "rich places of learning that are child directed and teacher efficient." Includes links to articles as well as photos of renovations and new facilities designed by the team.

National Lekotek Center

lekotek.org
Website for the National Lekotek Center, a not-for-profit organization providing information about toys and play for children with disabilities.

Readings

Ceppi, G., & Zini, M. (eds.). (1998). *Children, spaces, relations: Metaproject for an environment for young children*. Reggio Emilia, Italy: Reggio Children and Commune de Reggio Emilia.

Curtis, D., & Carter, M. (2003). *Designs for living and learning: Transforming early childhood environments*. St. Paul, MN: Redleaf Press.

Deviney, J., Duncan, S., Harris, S., Rody, M. A., & Rosenberry, L. (2010). *Inspiring spaces for young children*. Silver Spring, MD: Gryphon House.

Greenman, J. (2005). *Caring spaces, learning places: Children's environments that work*. Redmond, WA: Exchange Press.

Lally, J. R., & Stewart, J. (1990). *A guide to setting up environments: Infant/toddler caregiving*. Sacramento, CA: California Department of Education. Available online at clas.uiuc.edu/fulltext/cl03267/cl03267.html.

Ostrosky, M. M., Jung, E. Y., Hemmeter, M. L., & Thomas, D. (n.d.). Helping children understand routines and classroom schedules. *What Works Briefs #3*. Champaign, IL: Center on the Social and Emotional Foundations for Early Learning. Available online at vanderbilt.edu/csefel/briefs/wwb3.html.

CHAPTER 7

Direct Guidance—
Interacting with Children to Foster Self-Direction

Learning Outcomes

After studying this chapter you should be able to

- Explain what direct guidance is.
- Explain and describe several techniques of affective guidance.
- Explain and describe several techniques of physical guidance.
- Explain and describe several techniques of verbal guidance.

Antonio is trying to roll out cookie dough and is rolling it to pieces. Seeing his mounting frustration, the teacher, Olga, comes close to him and says, "Let's roll it soft and slow, like this." She gently places her hand on Antonio's hands to demonstrate. As Antonio begins to master the technique, Olga steps back, saying "Now you have it!" In another corner of the room, Olga notices Michaela gazing longingly as Layla plays with the dolls. Michaela seldom speaks and is difficult to understand when she does. The other four-year-olds in her classroom have been avoiding her and complaining that she grabs their toys. Olga walks over and says with a smile, "Layla, when Michaela looks at something like that, sometimes it means that she would like to play with it, too. Let's ask her." With Olga's help, the two girls begin playing together with the dolls. Later, when Layla notices Michaela reaching toward a doll bottle that another child is holding, she says, "She's trying to tell you she wants to play with the bottle."

150

DIRECT GUIDANCE

Direct guidance means the affective, physical, and verbal techniques used to influence a child's behavior. Direct guidance includes facilitating prosocial behaviors, preventing problems by anticipating and redirecting particular behaviors, and using consequences to encourage or discourage particular behaviors. (See Figure 7–1.)

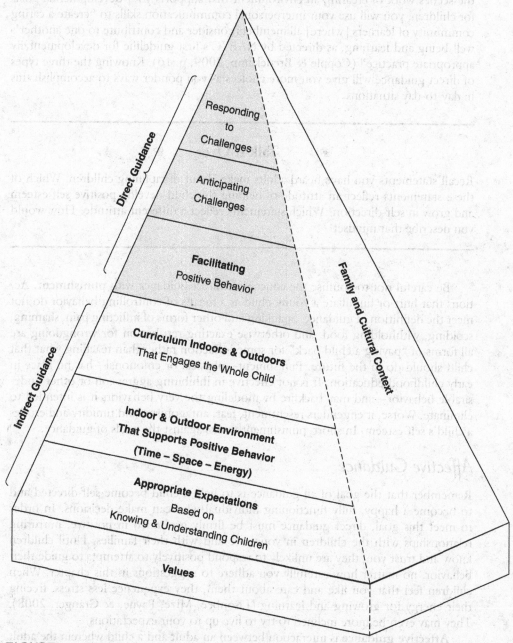

FIGURE 7–1   The guidance pyramid: Direct guidance

There are three types of direct guidance: affective, physical, and verbal. In the example at the beginning of this chapter, Olga was using all three types as she helped Antonio with the cookie making and helped Layla understand Michaela's intentions.

Direct guidance is used in conjunction with, and builds upon, the indirect guidance techniques discussed in Chapter 6. Once you have completed all the behind-the-scenes work of creating an environment that supports your developmental goals for children, you will use your interpersonal communication skills to "create a caring community of learners [where] all members consider and contribute to one another's well-being and learning, as directed by NAEYC's first guideline for developmentally appropriate practice" (Copple & Bredekamp, 2009, p. 16). Knowing the three types of direct guidance will give you more choices as you ponder ways to accomplish this in day-to-day situations.

❀ Talk It Over ❀

Recall statements you have heard adults make about disciplining children. Which of these statements reflect an attitude of helping the child develop positive self-esteem and grow in self-direction? Which statements reflect a different attitude? How would you describe that mindset?

Be careful not to confuse the concept of direct guidance with **punishment.** Actions that hurt or humiliate a young child as a means of controlling behavior do not meet the definition of guidance. Spanking and other forms of inflicting pain, shaming, scolding, withholding food, and otherwise exacting retribution for wrongdoing are all forms of "paying a child back" for some infraction rather than teaching what that child should do in the future. Punishment—physical or emotional—has no place in early childhood education. It is not effective in inhibiting aggression or other undesirable behavior—and may backfire by modeling the very behaviors it is intended to eliminate. Worse, it engenders resentment, fear, antagonism, and timidity and erodes a child's self-esteem. In short, punishment works against the goals of guidance.

Affective Guidance

Remember that the goal of all guidance is to help a child become self-directed and to become a happy, fully functioning individual who can make decisions. In order to meet this goal, direct guidance must be firmly grounded in positive, nurturing relationships with the children in your care and with their families. Until children know and trust you, they are unlikely to respond positively to attempts to guide their behavior, no matter how carefully you adhere to suggestions in this chapter. When children feel that you like and care about them, they experience less stress, freeing their energy for growing and learning (Lisonbee, Mize, Payne, & Granger, 2008). They may even be more inclined to try to live up to your expectations.

Affective guidance is interaction between an adult and a child wherein the adult expresses emotion or feelings to influence the behavior of the child. The word *affective,* of course, has the same stem as *affection* and means guidance that addresses a child's feelings. Affective guidance particularly helps develop the child's positive self-concept. Affective guidance is part of all the techniques that will be suggested, but because it is so important, it deserves separate discussion. Affective guidance includes physical affection, smiles, attention, kind words, encouragement, approval, and when necessary, disapproval.

Getting to Know Children.   If you listen carefully, children will teach you a lot about themselves, about what they are thinking and feeling. They come into the world full of questions and ideas and busily proceed to test their bodies' capabilities and investigate their theories about people and things. Your job is to listen carefully and respectfully—with your ears, your eyes, and your heart—to understand what they are trying to do and adapt your responses accordingly (Mangione, Lally, & Signer, 2001). Avoid the temptation to dismiss what they say or do as "cute" and treat their ideas with the dignity they deserve. Ask about what you don't understand. Vivian Paley, who has been observing and listening to children's play for many decades, finds that children make sense of their lives through the stories they create in their play. She cautions teachers about interrupting play that may seem too rambunctious and suggests instead that they simply ask the children "What's the story here?" as a way of helping children focus (2003). Listening to children communicates that you respect and value their ideas, that you are a partner in their quest for understanding. Listening to them teaches you what you can do to help with that quest.

If listening, observing, and reflecting are the keys to knowing and understanding any child, they are particularly useful if you find yourself feeling negative toward a child. This happens occasionally, and you should cope with such feelings as quickly as you can. It usually helps if you understand the child better. Ask yourself, "What does Sarita do that bothers me?" Be on guard against creating a self-fulfilling prophecy by focusing too narrowly on the child's challenging behaviors. Adopt the mindset that every child has positive attributes and make it a point to look for strengths. Think about how you can build on her strengths to improve your relationship with her. In addition to observing Sarita, this requires a willingness to look inside yourself. Sometimes a teacher's negative feelings occur when a child exhibits one of the teacher's own weaknesses. For example, if you were whiny and unpopular as a child, then children with these traits may now bother you. Realizing the source of negative feelings can help you plan ways to respond to a child's needs. In every way, try learning more about such children and confer with others to get assistance.

Being Genuine.   As you strive to listen and understand children's feelings, remember to communicate your own genuine feelings. Of course, you will manage your feelings in an adult and professional manner, but you should not spend your day pretending to be someone you are not. Children will either sense your insincerity or become confused at the mixed messages your words and body language are sending. When a child deliberately pushes another down, you should not lash out in anger, but neither do you have to put on a fake smile and sugary tone to say "It's not nice to hurt our friends." You can show with your facial expressions and tone of voice that you are upset or even angry. If you have already established a positive relationship with a child, letting her see the disappointment on your face when she does something harmful can be reprimand enough.

Honest expression of feelings means sharing the more positive ones as well. You may share children's delight at conquering a new puzzle, smile at their efforts to help one another, giggle at their jokes, and offer a comforting hug for a child who is missing home or skinned a knee. Musician and songwriter Tom Hunter captures this idea with his description of a teacher whose eyes filled with tears when a particularly angry, defiant child experienced a moment of success at group time: "She had gotten a glimpse of something beyond helping a boy behave appropriately, and 'celebrate' was her word for it—not just getting along with him or co-existing, but celebrating" (Hunter, 2006, p. 2).

Giving Attention. You have probably heard an adult say that a misbehaving child is "just doing that for attention," implying that wanting attention is somehow a fault when in fact desiring attention is perfectly healthy. Giving **attention** helps children know that you are aware that they are there and that you are keeping their needs in mind. Children deprived of attention do not thrive, and children who have experienced only harsh negative attention in their short lives may transgress rules because they feel that even getting negative attention is better than being ignored. Some children who seem to be misbehaving to attract attention can be helped by well-timed doses of attention and positive feedback before they act out to get attention.

Providing Feedback. Give honest **feedback** that provides information children can use. Instead of telling Dominic that he is a "good helper," tell him that you appreciate the way he put all the blocks back on the right shelves because it makes it easier for everyone to find them the next day. Don't tell Marinda to "act right" or "quit clowning around." Tell her to "keep the chair legs on the floor" because you are worried that she will hurt herself when she tips back in the chair. In both these examples, you would be using verbal guidance with an emphasis on feelings.

It is important to keep the focus on the tasks rather than on your approval or disapproval of the child. The goal is for children to become able to judge and control their own behavior, not to be dependent on outside opinions for their feelings of self-worth.

Naming Feelings. Reflecting the feeling a child seems to be expressing and **naming** it helps children recognize their own emotions as well as those of others. It gives them the vocabulary they need to express feelings appropriately. You might say, "It looks like you really feel good about climbing way up there," or

Giving attention before children demand it helps them know that you are aware of them and keeping their needs in mind.

"I can see how sad you feel. You really wanted that toy." Be prepared for a child to tell you, "I'm not sad. I'm mad!" The ability to reflect a child's true feelings comes with observation and practice in being sensitive.

Providing Reinforcement. The idea behind **reinforcement** is that we are all more likely to repeat behaviors that produce rewards than we are to repeat behaviors that are either punished or unrewarded. If you think about it, you have been using this technique in many of your everyday interactions with children. When you smile and compliment Scott for hanging up his coat, you are probably hoping that Scott will hang up his coat again tomorrow because he finds your smile and compliment rewarding. For maximum effectiveness in promoting the goals of guidance, compliments should be framed as encouragement, focusing on the effect of a child's actions or on the child's feelings, rather than empty, generalized praise (a topic we will discuss more fully later in this chapter, in the section on verbal guidance). When you ignore a child's whining, you are using a technique of withholding attention (reinforcement) in an effort to decrease or eliminate (extinguish) that undesirable behavior.

Sometimes adults use reinforcement in ways that work against their goals. Teachers who constantly tell children to "stop running in the classroom" would probably find it more effective to compliment the children who obey the rules and walk, thus rewarding the desired behavior with their attention. Inconsistent (or intermittent) reinforcement produce the most long-lasting effect and is another way in which adults sometimes defeat their own purposes. Children who occasionally get what they want by whining will be more likely to try that method in the future, always expecting that this time it will work.

Your success depends on whether or not the reinforcement you are using (or withholding) is actually something the child values. A child who has known only harsh treatment may not find your smile rewarding, a child who is extremely sensitive to tactile stimulation (touching) may not enjoy a hug, and a child who has been neglected or ignored might gain satisfaction from even negative attention. Only through careful observation and getting to know each individual child will you be able to know what that child finds rewarding or reinforcing. And, since young children change so rapidly as they grow and develop, what serves as a reinforcement one week may change the next. Teachers who routinely dispense stickers or candy for "good" behavior are grossly oversimplifying the concept of reinforcement—and doing little to accomplish the goal of guidance, which is to promote self-direction and self-control.

Until now, we have been discussing guidance techniques that you are likely to find useful with all children. Once you have mastered these techniques, they will become second nature for you, and you will begin to use them automatically, creating an environment in which it is possible for children to succeed, and interacting with children in ways that foster their independence and feelings of self-worth.

There will be times, however, when you need a technique to cope with particularly challenging behaviors—behaviors of children who are developing typically as well as those with emotional disorders or disabilities. That technique, borrowed from the field of special education, is the systematic use of reinforcement to decrease or eliminate undesirable behaviors and to increase behaviors that help a child function in the world. It is important to remember, however, that reinforcement builds on all the other techniques you have learned. It will work only if you have an environment and a program that is developmentally appropriate and full of interesting and pleasurable things for every child to do.

Knowing how reinforcement builds on developmentally appropriate practice and understanding how it is used and misused in everyday situations, you will be ready to extend that knowledge and use the technique when working with children with disabilities or developmental delays. As you put your plan for systematic reinforcement into action, remember that these children have strengths as well as typical needs for belonging and self-worth. Look for ways to extend the guidance techniques you are already using, so that all children in your program can experience the joy of accomplishment. The use of external rewards such as stickers or food might be recommended as a first step with some children, but you should discuss this carefully with the other professionals on the intervention team.

Ideally, since the goal for children with disabilities as well as for those who are developing typically is self-direction, the reinforcement should come from inside: from the pleasure derived from the activity or the sense of accomplishment at completing it. External rewards are a bridge used to help a child reach higher levels of development. This will be possible only if what you expect of the child is developmentally appropriate (i.e., geared to the child's level and individual preferences). Once the activities themselves become pleasurable or satisfying for the child, the external rewards will not be needed. In fact, some research suggests that rewarding children for something they are already doing voluntarily can backfire, leading to a decrease in the activity that was rewarded (Kohn, 1994).

❀ Talk It Over ❀

You observe a group of three- and four-year-old children coming back into their classroom after a story hour in the school library. They all excitedly show you the stickers the librarian has given them for being "good listeners" and argue among themselves about whose sticker is most desirable. When you ask them to tell you about the stories they heard, they do not have much to say.

Do you think this is an appropriate use of an external reward? Why or why not? What internal reward might substitute for the stickers? Discuss these questions with your classmates.

Physical Guidance

Physical guidance means all techniques that employ physical contact or physical proximity to influence the child's behavior. As noted in the previous chapter, the physical proximity of an interested adult helps children follow rules and sustain interest in some learning activities. In one class of four-year-olds, for example, a teacher put a variety of seeds, along with paper and glue, on the art table. When an adult sat with the children and expressed interest in what they were doing, they spent more time and produced more detailed collages than when they were left to explore the materials on their own. In another classroom, the teacher was hesitant to make clay available to the children because two children with emotional and behavioral problems had thrown it at each other in the past. She was skeptical when her college professor suggested that she simply ask her assistant to sit near those children when they used the clay, but she decided to try it anyway. The next week, she reported with amazement and pleasure that it had worked: There had been no throwing of clay.

When adults come close and get on children's level, they communicate their interest and help children follow rules and sustain interest in activities.

Beyond just being nearby, adults guide children's behavior by helping, demonstrating, leading, restraining, and removing. Physical guidance is especially effective for children who are just learning, to speak and for those whose language is different from the teacher's. Children can follow your physical guidance even when they don't understand your words. It's important to keep talking, however, even as you guide children physically. Use key words, and they will soon learn the meaning of the words because of their context.

Individuality in Physical Guidance. Children's needs vary in terms of the amount and type of physical guidance required. Younger children, or children with disabilities, may need more physical assistance until their skills and confidence increase. They may need a hand the first few times they walk up an inclined plane or climb to the top of the slide. Your challenge will be to decide what kind and how much help is needed for each child and to step out of the picture as the child shows ability to do things alone. An occupational or physical therapist can help you decide when and how much help to give to a child with a disability. Even among children with typical development, research indicates a wide variation in independent behavior at each age, and children who have been doing something independently for some time occasionally have days when they want or need your help.

Demonstrating. **Demonstrating**, or **modeling**, for children encourages them to imitate the desired behavior. "See, you do it this way" and "Now you try it" are comments you might make while demonstrating. Whether showing children how to flush the toilet, how to use a spoon, how to latch the gate, or how to step on the scale, if you do it first, children will quickly follow. Your actions help them understand your words.

In addition to following your example, children watch other children and imitate them. They learn through this imitation. Watch them at the art table, in the music room, and at the lunch table. They may first imitate and then do it their own way. Knowing this, you can suggest that a child who is struggling with some task learn by watching a more experienced classmate. "Look, Jacob. Quentin will show you where to put your plate and napkin." Like adults, children watch others for clues about how to behave in unfamiliar situations.

Leading.   **Leading** is a technique that gets children going in the desired direction. Perhaps you realize from various clues that two-year-old Gilberto needs to go to the bathroom. You can take his hand and lead him over the most direct route, speaking quietly to him as you go. If a group is going on a field trip, the children in front especially need someone to take their hands and move toward the goal, to stop at the appropriate corners, streets, and things to see. Children gain comfort and security from holding the hand of a teacher or helper. Wanting to hold hands can be a sign of feeling lonely, tired, or scared. Not wanting to hold hands can mean "I feel big enough to go alone."

Restraining.   Sometimes it is necessary to **restrain** a child to protect that child or others. Restraint may be the simple act of putting your hand on a child's arm as a suggestion to go slowly down the stairs, or it may be intervention to keep the child from hitting or kicking you or others. Restraint has a legitimate place when a child is out of control. A hand on the arm, however, is not handcuffs. The important thing is to stop the harmful or dangerous behavior and then let the child move on. You have a responsibility to protect the child, others, the learning environment, and property. You can couple restraint with verbal guidance. For example, you can say, "I know you are feeling really angry, but I can't let you hit Jonathan. I won't let anyone hit you either. Let's sit over here [e.g., by the art table or puzzle rack] for a while and rest. You can tell me how you feel, if you like." Avoid shaming or moralizing. Don't tell a child that others won't like her; just remain firm, fair, and friendly until the child relaxes and then offer several alternative activities that might be interesting to the child. Show the child that you can be counted on to help her develop self-control. Understand that it is a long-term goal, not something learned overnight.

Removing.   **Removing** a child from a group sometimes helps one who is having trouble accommodating to group rules. A child may only need to be removed from the center of trouble to a place to calm down and regain composure. The teacher can sit nearby, providing a loving, nonpunishing support. Many early childhood programs have "thinking chairs" for this purpose. Other programs arrange two seats and call them the "talking-it-over" chairs, so teachers help children talk over their disagreements. The key is your loving—not punishing—support during this process. A "thinking chair" is not a "time-out chair," and children will see through the deception if you call it one thing and use it as another.

Fatigue or hunger can be behind a loss of self-control, so some effort to meet these needs may be called for. Later, you can take a look at the child's schedule to see if she or he is getting sufficient rest. Some adults worry that a child might learn that being removed is more fun than staying with the group; that is, time with the teacher may be rewarding for the child. A wise teacher who believes this to be the case will evaluate the program carefully and make sure children have plenty of opportunities for one-on-one attention so they avoid losing control.

Using Time-Outs.   Many early childhood educators use the term **time-out** or **time away** to mean removing an upset child from a situation and giving him or her a few minutes to calm down. Special educators use the term **brief time-out** to mean a 10- or 30-second removal from the opportunity for reinforcement in order to decrease or eliminate undesirable behaviors, perhaps by momentarily removing a toy or game that interests the child. Confusion of these two terms may be the reason this technique is so often misused, with self-defeating results. Teachers who send children to the "time-out chair" for every rule infraction become dismayed when it does not seem to work.

When your purpose is to help an overwrought child regain self-control, you need to stay with the child. Your calming presence conveys the message that you will help, not abandon the child to frightening, powerful emotions. This is not the same thing as rewarding the loss of control with positive attention. If four-year-old Angela has temper tantrums, for example, you can quietly but firmly remove her from the classroom to an area where she cannot hurt herself or anyone or anything else. Briefly say what you are doing and then stand or sit nearby until Angela regains control.

A brief time-out might be appropriately used to help a child with a habitual, self-injuring behavior stop hurting himself, for example. In such a case, the time-out periods must be brief (removing a favored toy for 10 or 30 seconds, for example) and immediately followed by an opportunity to return to something that the child finds highly enjoyable. Parents must be informed and give their consent before you use the technique, and you should not reduce or eliminate behaviors without teaching useful skills to replace them.

Using time-out as a generic response to unwanted behavior is likely to be ineffective for several reasons. If children are too young or for some other reason do not understand the rule they have broken, they are likely to repeat the same offenses. Children who know why they have been sent to time-out may decide that once they have paid the price for their "crime," they are free to do it again. Perhaps most importantly, isolating children inappropriately can scare them or erode self-esteem. Young children's notions of cause and effect lead them to conclude that if they are punished, they must be bad. A child who is frequently sent to time-out can develop an image, in her own eyes and in the eyes of the other children, that becomes a self-fulfilling prophecy.

When a time-out chair is used many times a day, or when the same child is repeatedly sent there, teachers should ask themselves whether some other technique might be more appropriate and effective. Looking at the situation objectively is likely to reveal many factors that could be contributing to the misbehavior. These might be part of the individual child's makeup or experience, or they might be aspects of your program, such as the schedule, the environment, an uninteresting curriculum, or your unrealistic expectations of children.

Gesturing.   Getting down to eye level and using **meaningful gestures** helps children understand your guidance. Getting down to the children's level helps them know that directions are meant for them. Using gestures helps if they don't quite understand all your words. If you've ever been in a foreign country, you'll recall how much you depend on gestures and the context or immediate setting to give you clues to what is being said. It is good to get in the habit of sitting on a low chair or squatting or kneeling as you attempt to guide children's behavior. Remember that you tower over small children. Good eye-to-eye contact helps children understand your guidance.

Using Body Language. You can give children messages through **body language**. You can show interest, eagerness, or approval through the use of your body, just as you can show lethargy, reluctance, or disapproval. After being acquainted with you for only a short time, children will know when you are tense, irritable, relaxed, rushed, affectionate, and so on. Your stance, your face, the way you hold your hands, and the way you walk tell others how things are going for you. This is one reason it is so important that teachers of young children get sufficient rest. If you're rested, you'll find ways to cope, but if you're tired, you'll get irritated, and it will inevitably affect the children. Young children may indeed be better at reading your nonverbal clues than understanding your verbal ones.

Verbal Guidance

Verbal guidance means using words to influence a child's behavior. You talk with children to communicate your expectations for their behavior as well as your approval or disapproval of what they do. You talk to explain the reasons for rules and actions. But verbal guidance is not all talk. It begins with listening to children. Following are a number of ways to use verbal guidance effectively.

To encourage a child to talk, sometimes you only need to let the child know you are listening: "Hmmmm." "Is that so?" "Yes." or "I'm interested in that." Such nonjudgmental responses encourage a child to go on sharing ideas and feelings.

Listening Carefully. Listen carefully when children communicate their ideas, questions, and feelings. In your contacts with young children, try to give them many opportunities to communicate their thoughts and feelings. Children may communicate verbally and will also communicate nonverbally with body language. Encourage children to ask questions to get information and to share their joys and sorrows verbally and nonverbally. Teachers and parents can learn to listen with an ear for the words and with sensitivity for the feelings behind the words. To encourage children to talk, first give them your attention by tuning out others, by sitting at the level of the children, and by hearing and observing each child who has something to communicate. It is generally possible for a teacher to listen to one child for a few minutes while still keeping an eye on the rest of the group.

You may at times use **reflective listening** by putting words to the feeling the child seems to be experiencing. For example, Greg tells you, "My brother hits me." You note the fear in his voice and try to put it in words, saying, "You really are afraid your brother will hurt you." Or, Abby tells you, "My kitty died." Sensing her sadness, you respond, "You feel sad that your kitty has died." Another child tells you, "Sandy told me she likes the birthday present I bought her." Reflecting her apparent happiness, you say, "You're really happy that Sandy liked the present you bought for her." In each instance, state the feeling tentatively enough that the child can correct you if you are wrong. Reflective listening helps children know you are understanding their feelings as well as their words. By using reflective listening, or **active listening**, as some call it, you gain deeper insight into how children think and feel.

Use a Natural, Respectful Tone of Voice. It is important to speak to children the way you would like to have others speak to you, using your **natural tone of voice**. There is no need to speak in artificially sugary tones, to shout, or to give brusque commands that would be offensive to you or to someone else your own age.

Make Eye Contact. It is important to speak directly to children as you make **eye contact** with them. If you want children to follow your directions, be sure children know you are speaking to them. It is not effective to call out directions across the yard or room. Unless you have the voice of a drill sergeant, you won't be heard or heeded. Also, children tend to imitate the yelling. It is best to speak to individuals or small groups, using physical closeness and stooping or sitting at their level.

In some cultures, eye contact is not a custom or is even considered to be impolite, especially between children and teachers. So children may be taught at home not to look at an adult. Therefore, you should not be upset if a child won't look at you, and don't try to force the child to look you in the eye. You can keep on using your own eyes and talking to the child to gain as much information as you can. You can be warmly affectionate to the child and make an effort to get to know the family so that you can learn more about their special ways of relating or the ways they expect children to show respect for adults.

Use Short Sentences. It is a good idea to use **short sentences** similar to ones children use until you are sure they can understand more complicated ones. Only the essential words are needed, such as "Inside now," "Cleanup time," and "Hold on tight."

If you are a teacher working with children whose language is different from your own, listen closely with your eyes on the child's. You can smile, encourage verbal expression, and nod your recognition. Try to learn some words from the child's language. Perhaps you can ask the parent or someone from that cultural group to help you with a minimum set of phrases, including *yes, no, good*, and *fantastic*. The child will enjoy your effort.

Give Positive Directions. **Positive directions** work better than prohibiting unwanted behavior. You should tell a child what to do instead of what not to do. Even small toddlers can respond to positive directions, such as "Give me the ball," "Eat your cracker," and "Wave bye-bye." These positive directions tell children what to do and suit their level of language development and intellectual understanding. Positive, or "do," directions are best for all young children.

You have frequently heard adults say, "I told you not to . . . " (perhaps not to touch the light or flowers or stove). Researchers have found that these "not to," or negative, directions are much more difficult for children to follow than positive directions. Psychologists have long observed that young children have great difficulty restraining their responses and following "not to" directions. Improvement begins around kindergarten and first grade, but as Strommen (1976) has pointed out, they still make a substantial number of "errors of commission." Furthermore, telling young children "not to do something that they have already started seemed to intensify what they are doing, rather than deterring them from it, as though, once they have begun a course of action, they have to complete it before they can shift to something else" (p. 55).

Thus, telling a child with an upraised fist "Don't hit!" will not be as effective as firmly saying "Stop!" and placing a hand on the upraised arm (restraining). "Don't" phrases leave a child suspended and uncomfortable. Remember how you feel if you are driving along a freeway, and one of your passengers says, "Don't drive so fast." You probably leave your foot on the accelerator while you look around for the reasons for the advice. Telling children what to do helps them respond quickly, and usually that is what your "don't" commands are designed to do. Instead of saying, "Don't spill your milk," for example, try, "Hold your cup with one hand while you pour from the pitcher." Instead of, "Don't step on Johnny," say "Step over here." The "don't" habit is difficult to break for many adults, but you will find that it is worth the effort because "do" directions help the child become self-directed sooner.

❀ **Talk It Over** ❀

Recall a number of "Don't" commands you've heard adults use with children. Change these into positive directions that tell the child what the adult wants done. Which commands would you rather have people use with you? Why?

Place the Action Clause First.   It is a good idea to place the **action clause** of your guidance statement at the beginning. For example, "Hold on tight" is better than "You might fall out, so be sure you are holding the swing tight." With the longer statement, the child may lose interest or fall before you get to the most important part. If you say "Raise the seat" to Jerome just as he moves to the toilet, you may catch him before he urinates on the seat. If, instead, you give a long discussion, he may urinate in his clothing or on the seat.

Give Few Directions.   It is a good idea to give **few directions**—no more than two—and to give them one at a time, if possible. The younger the child, the fewer the number of directions that should be given at a time. If you say, "Scrape your boots and take them off, hang up your coat, and put your mittens on the register to dry," you should anticipate that you'll be repeating at least the last part, if not all of the guidance, several times before all the tasks are done. The child may forget all the steps when bombarded with so many. Children process directions slowly and need context to suggest next steps; therefore, try to give directions one at a time, or no more than two at a time. When you see that a child is following through with what you have asked, you can proceed to give directions for the next steps.

Give Only Necessary Directions. Give only **necessary directions** children really need and avoid being overdirective and bossy. Having set the stage for behavior through the indirect guidance techniques described in Chapter 6, you can use a little patience and have faith that children will behave acceptably, without a steady barrage of "do this" and "do that" directions. Stop talking and watch. See if they really need you to tell them what to do. You may be surprised at how self-directed they already are.

Give Directions at the Appropriate Time and Place. Give children directions at the **time** and **place** you want the behavior to occur. Children don't keep things in mind for very long, so directions that are in context and of current interest are more likely to be heeded. For example, wait until you are outdoors before giving directions about safety on the playground.

Give Real Choices When Possible. Giving choices promotes self-control and independence, but you defeat that purpose if you don't offer children **real choices**. For example, some adults have a habit of saying, "Would you like to come in?" This question indicates to children that if they prefer to stay outside, the teacher will permit it. If the teacher really expects the children to enter the classroom, a more honest statement is, "Come inside now." You can accomplish both aims (getting everyone inside on time and offering real choices) by saying something like "Do you want to hold my hand or walk by yourself as we go inside?" Instead of "Would you like to take a nap?" you can say "Do you want your teddy bear on the cot with you or next to it?" The point is to offer alternatives that would be equally acceptable to you so that the child is not confused and disappointed by having choices offered and then refused after they're made.

Give Logical Reasons. Give **logical** and **accurate reasons** for requests. Children need to learn why requests are made of them. It is legitimate to say, "I want you to sit quietly at group time so everyone can hear the story," or "Everyone must go outdoors because there is no teacher to stay indoors with the children who want to stay in." In the long run, you want children to be able to apply reasons like this to new situations. Arbitrary "I said so" statements are not reasons. Rules or limits that cannot be explained to children may very well be rules that are not justified.

Children who are given reasons for limits or requests are likely to comply. You'll even hear them inform other children as they play. For instance, you might say, "Juan, drive your tricycle this way along the trike path. When you go against traffic, you'll bump into other children. It could hurt them or damage the trike." Later on, Juan might say, "Hey, we go this way."

If a child at the water table splashes water too vigorously, the teacher should give reasons to stop rather than yelling, "Stop that, Jenny." Simply say, "Jenny, pat the water gently. The other children don't want their shirts and jeans to get wet." It is neither logical nor a good reason to tell a child that "People won't like you if you splash water on them." Such statements are threatening to a child. After all, it is the splashing that others don't like—not the child.

Logical reasons for guidance requests can be presented to children in what psychologist Thomas Gordon (2000) calls "I-messages." An "I-message" results when, using the first-person pronoun *I*, the parent or teacher tells a child how some unacceptable behavior makes that parent or teacher feel. Gordon contrasts "I-messages" with "you-messages," which tend to put blame or shame on children. For example, "You just want to get some attention," "You are being naughty," "You're acting like a baby," and "Shame on you" are all "you-messages." Here are two examples of effective "I-messages":

"When you splash water around the bathroom, I get my feet wet, and I'm afraid I might fall."

"When you tear the pages in our books, I can't read them to the children anymore. It upsets me to have our books damaged."

According to Gordon, an "I-message" has three parts:

1. It describes the behavior (in the examples, water splashing and book tearing) in a nonjudgmental way.
2. It tells the child the concrete effect of the specific behavior ("I get my feet wet," "I can't read torn books.")
3. It tells how that effect makes the adult feel ("I'm afraid," "It upsets me") (Gordon, 2000).

I-messages like this are less likely to engender the kind of resentment that children are likely to feel if you scold or place blame. Instead of spending energy resisting what may seem to them like unjust authority, they can focus energy on taking responsibility for their own behavior.

Clearly State Limits and Follow Through.   It is important to state limits or rules clearly and positively and follow through on enforcing the limits or rules. Limits or rules protect (1) the child, (2) other children and adults in the group, and (3) the learning environment, including furnishings and materials. Tell children clearly what behavior is desirable and that, because it is your job to keep them safe, you won't tolerate unsafe practices, chaos, uncontrolled behavior, or damage to facilities. Limits or rules must be consistently and fairly applied. They should apply equally to girls and boys.

Recall that positive rules are easier for a child to follow than negative rules. You can state limits or rules like the following: "You must stay inside the gate." "Hammers stay at the workbench." and "The tricycles go only this direction around the track." Then give brief, logical reasons for the rule. Because you must follow through on every limit you state to a child, it is imperative that you think carefully about what you say. Some children will need physical guidance. You may need to restate the rule or help or lead these children to follow through on the rule you've stated. In the first example, you follow through by leading the child inside the gate and closing the gate. In the second, see that the child returns the hammer to the workbench and be prepared to assist or take the hammer away, if needed. In the third, ensure that the child either turns the tricycle around and pedals with traffic or stops riding.

You can use your presence, as well as your verbal and physical guidance, to help children remember and follow the rules. For example, simply moving closer to children who appear to be on the verge of overstepping a rule may help them remember to follow the rule they have previously learned, even without your having to restate it. Remember that it takes a number of years for children to develop restraint or inhibiting ability. Even five- and six-year-olds may not have mastered this skill. For children to learn the rules and to follow them consistently takes years of practice and patient teaching by the adults in their lives.

Be Consistent. Consistency in setting limits and following through on limits presents a special challenge when several adults share responsibility for a group of children. Children will quickly notice when the adults in charge have different expectations, and they will spend a lot of energy—yours as well as their own—testing the firmness of each adult's limits. Sometimes adults disagree on appropriate boundaries; other times, one adult simply may not know what the other expects. Whatever the reason, the solution is for the adults to talk with each other. If you are a newcomer (perhaps a student teacher) in such a situation, first learn what the customary practices have been. Confer with the adults who have been there before you, listening carefully to the explanations for the various stated rules or limits. Ask questions if you do not understand. The challenge for a new, inexperienced teacher is to strike a balance between being overly directive, constantly telling children what to do or not to do, and avoiding situations where limits are needed, out of fear that the children won't listen. You may have to play some situations by ear and then discuss them with more experienced colleagues afterward. But the more you can clarify with your colleagues in advance, the more you will be able to anticipate challenges and respond in ways that are consistent with established practices. Consequently, you will be more successful in getting children to adhere to limits.

Teach Problem-Solving Techniques. It is important to teach children **problem-solving techniques**. Conflicts are a part of life. Although they may make you uncomfortable, they actually provide fertile ground for meeting many developmental goals, such as taking the perspective of another and managing one's emotions. Rather than wish that children would never argue, you can use conflicts to teach children productive ways of solving problems. Consider this example: Four-year-olds Jeremy and Antwan both want to use the new dinosaur puzzle. The increasing volume of their argument attracts the attention of Derek, their teacher, who is in the block area the other side of the room. He quickly moves to where the children are and stoops down to their eye level to have this conversation:

Derek: What's happening here? You both sound pretty upset.

Jeremy: I want to use the dinosaur puzzle!

Antwan: I had it first!

Jeremy: No. I was here, and he took it from me.

Derek: So, you both want this puzzle.

Jeremy: I want it!

Derek: I know you want to use the puzzle, Jeremy. And I know that Antwan wants it, too. We have a problem because there's only one dinosaur puzzle. [The boys are tugging on the puzzle, about to spill the pieces on the floor.] I'm going to hold the puzzle until we figure out what to do. Do you have any ideas?

Antwan: I could have the dinosaur and he could have a different puzzle.

Derek: Antwan says you could use a different puzzle while he uses the dinosaur one, Jeremy. Is that okay with you?

Jeremy: No. I want the dinosaur. He had it a long time. He should let me have a turn.

Derek: Jeremy says you had the dinosaur puzzle a long time, Antwan, and you should let him have a turn. What do you think?

Antwan: No. He'll keep it a long time and won't give it back.

Derek: Jeremy, Antwan is afraid you won't give the puzzle back, that you'll keep it a long time. How long do you think you need it?

Antwan: I just want to do it one time.

Derek: And you would give it back to Jeremy right after you finish doing it once?

Antwan: Yeah.

Derek: Jeremy, how does that sound to you?

Jeremy: How about if I let him help me do the puzzle? We could do it together.

Antwan: All right!

Derek: So you two are going to work on the puzzle together. It's new and has a lot of pieces, so it may be hard.

Jeremy: Not if we both help.

Antwan: Yeah. We can do it in no time!

With adult support, and given some say in the matter, children can happily share a popular piece of equipment.

When they are involved in suggesting solutions to a problem, children often come up with workable ideas and readily comply, reminding each other about their decision. It is important to try to get children thinking, not to impose your solution. Given a voice in solving their own problems, children often surprise us with their creativity.

Give Logical. Consequences
Logical consequences (Dreikurs & Cassel, 1972), as opposed to punishments, can help children learn to control their own behavior. The more closely the consequence is related to the behavior,

the easier it will be for children to see the connection and to see the fairness of those consequences. Arbitrary consequences that are not closely related to the offense do not have this teaching value and are likely to create feelings of guilt and resentment.

Sometimes you can let children discover the consequences of their behavior naturally. A child who refuses to wear mittens on a wintry day, for example, will have cold fingers during outdoor play. A large part of your role as a responsible caregiver, however, will be to protect curious, impulsive children from the potentially harmful consequences of their behavior that they cannot foresee.

Suppose children are riding their tricycles in a reckless manner on the playground. A natural consequence of their behavior would be the injuries that one or more is likely to suffer when a collision occurs. An unrelated consequence might be the assignment of extra cleanup duties for the involved parties. The first alternative may well teach them to be more careful, but no early childhood professional can ethically allow harm to come to children. The second alternative is more likely to create negative attitudes about cleanup than to teach safe driving habits.

Assuming that environmental factors are not creating the problem (e.g., too many tricycles in too little space), what is needed is a logical consequence, one that helps children see a connection between their behavior and what happens to them. After explaining the dangers of the situation and making sure the children know the rules for safe driving, a teacher might institute a system of issuing "traffic tickets" for violations such as speeding or deliberately crashing into other tricycles. Children could be told that after three such tickets, they will be banned from the tricycles for the day.

If the problem is so widespread that it involves all the children, the teacher might remove the tricycles entirely for a time. Unless the children understand the reason for this action, however, they might view it as an example of all-powerful adults imposing their wishes on smaller, weaker people.

Encourage Rather Than Praise. **Encourage** children to do things for intrinsic reasons rather than to please you. As you observe adults—perhaps even yourself—interacting with young children, you will hear many examples of praise—"I like the way you are walking down the hall, Sharonda," or "What a good helper you are, Elias"—often said in a syrupy tone of voice. Many adults believe that praise is an effective and humane way of influencing a child's behavior for the good. If you think carefully about the goals of guidance outlined in this text, however, you might question this assumption. After all, praise is an extrinsic reward: It tells children they have pleased you and gives them information about how to please you in the future. If we want children to become self-motivated and self-directed, however, it makes sense to focus on more intrinsic rewards: feeling a sense of accomplishment or just feeling good about trying hard.

Many early childhood experts advocate the use of encouragement instead of praise. Instead of empty generalities, such as "Good job!" you can say what the child did: "Thanks for helping us clean up the block area." Be specific: "You sorted all the shapes onto different shelves." Tell what was helpful or positive about a particular action: "Our block area looks so neat and inviting now, and it's easier to find what we need." Focus on children's feelings about their behavior: "You three looked like you had fun doing that hard job together," instead of "I like the way you cooperated"

Children don't work hard because they are competing with peers. They work hard because it is fun to grow in some ability.

(Kaiser & Rasminsky, 2012, p. 183). The distinction may seem subtle, and old habits are ingrained, so you may hear yourself slipping occasionally, but raising your consciousness about the ways you speak to children is one way to bring your practice into line with your beliefs.

Avoid Competition. You should **avoid competition** and instead motivate children by helping them set new personal goals for achievement. You can tell children about the things they are likely to accomplish next. For example, if Mei Li can make letters, you can say, "Before long, you'll be writing your name." Avoid saying, "Mei Li, I bet you can make your name as well as Terrence does." If Caitlin can make the swing go with help, you can say, "Pretty soon, you'll be pumping the swing all by yourself."

It is not advisable to pit children against peers to motivate them. Growth is deciding to learn something for one's own reasons. Competition breeds anxiety and thwarts friendships. As children move on to kindergarten and primary school, they will become more interested in competing with one another to test their growing skills. Young children know when they have succeeded. They are thrilled to zip their own zipper all the way the first time or reach the top of a rope ladder. Such successes are great because children have accomplished skills that yesterday or last month they didn't have. Children don't work hard because they are competing with peers. They work hard because it is fun to grow in some ability. They don't benefit from being challenged to climb higher, run faster, eat more, sing louder, dance faster, or read better than other children.

PLANNING AHEAD

You can anticipate conditions that might interfere with good relationships among children and suggest or arrange shifts in those conditions. As your experience accumulates, you'll begin to recognize situations that typically interfere with the smooth operation of a group. For example, you can try guiding a latecomer such as Consuela into a play group, when you know she isn't skillful at entering groups, by saying, "Consuela, we've saved a spot here for you to work." Or, realizing that overcrowding leads to disharmony, when you see many children being attracted to a small space, you'll quickly adjust equipment to add more play spaces, or you may arrange an attractive activity nearby to entice some children from the crowded area. Such foresight combines verbal, physical, and indirect guidance.

RECOVERING FROM CHAOS

Chaos inevitably erupts occasionally, even in well-planned programs. Adults can often restore order by using a bit of pretend play to get the children's attention and quiet them. You might, for example, take two children by the hand and whisper, "I'm going on a bear hunt. Shhh, come along." Then tiptoe with them to the next group and repeat the invitation until you have gathered all the children and can proceed with the rest of the "bear hunt." One teacher in New Orleans, noticing that the children's play about Hurricane Katrina had reached a frantic pitch and was invading the entire classroom, responded by entering the drama herself and suggesting new roles for the children as members of the National Guard:

> "Pretend we're the National Guard. Watch me put on my uniform. I'm pulling on my hip boots. Let me see everyone pull on your hip boots. . . . Okay, boots on? Now, we count to twenty so the water can go down. Then we'll clean up all the streets and houses in New Orleans." (Paley, 2010, p. 22)

Some teachers use a special signal, such as a particular chord on the piano or flicking the lights off and on. Children will learn that this means you want attention and will respond accordingly unless you overuse the signal. Perhaps the most important part of any method you use is to keep your voice calm and your movements deliberate so that you do not further excite the children. After things have settled down or the children have gone home, you can discuss what happened with your colleagues. As you reflect on what might have created the chaotic situation, you can plan to avoid it in the future.

CONCLUSION

Guidance is defined as everything an adult deliberately does or says, either directly or indirectly, to influence the behavior of a child. The goal of all guidance is to help children become happy, fully functioning individuals who can make decisions and direct themselves. Direct guidance includes all of the interpersonal communication processes.

Three types of direct guidance have been discussed in this chapter: Affective guidance includes techniques in the realm of feeling; physical guidance includes touching, leading, demonstrating, and the like; and verbal guidance includes techniques for communicating with young children through vocal means. These are important techniques to know and to practice. However, knowing techniques is only the beginning. Techniques are no better than the abilities and judgment of people using them and practicing them without having established a caring relationship with children would not constitute guidance, as we have defined it. Try to become sensitive to each individual child's needs and to apply the techniques in a humanistic and person-centered way that will really be helpful to children. With continued study, observation, and practice, you can help young children grow in independence and guide them toward their full potential.

REVIEW: TEN TECHNIQUES OF DIRECT GUIDANCE

1. Build positive relationships with each child; never use punishment, shame, or humiliation.

Affective Guidance

2. Express feelings authentically: Show affection and positive regard for children as well as concern or displeasure when behavior is dangerous or hurtful.

3. Give attention before the child demands it; encourage effort and express appreciation for jobs done well.

4. Accept, reflect, and label the feelings a child seems to be expressing.

Physical Guidance

5. Get down to child's eye level; use meaningful gestures and body language that help the child feel secure and understand what is expected.

6. Demonstrate the desired behavior or skill or lead the child by the hand to provide direction, reassurance, or assistance.

7. Restrain the child when necessary to protect the child or others; remove the child from the scene, if necessary, to help him or her relax and regain composure.

Verbal Guidance

8. Practice good two-way communication skills: Listen carefully when children communicate their ideas, questions, and feelings; use eye contact; and speak in a natural, respectful tone of voice.

9. Give only directions that a child really needs, at the time and place you want behavior to occur; begin by telling the child what to do instead of what not to do; limit directions to one or two at a time; and make it clear whether the child has a choice.

10. State limits or rules clearly, with logical and accurate reasons; follow through by enforcing them consistently; and use logical consequences for misbehavior when possible.

APPLICATIONS

1. Observe and record three examples of affective guidance used by a teacher or caregiver. Write down what was said and done. Evaluate the effects of the guidance.

2. Observe and record three examples of physical guidance in which an adult leads or otherwise physically touches a child to help her follow a statement of guidance. Write down what was said and done. Evaluate the effects of the guidance.

3. Observe and record three examples of verbal guidance used by a teacher or caregiver. Write down what was said and done. Categorize the guidance according to the examples in the chapter. Evaluate the effects of the guidance.

RESOURCES FOR FURTHER STUDY

Websites

Alfie Kohn

AlfieKohn.org
Alfie Kohn is a widely published author and speaker on human behavior, education, and parenting. His website includes a link to several articles concerning the pitfalls associated with the use of extrinsic rewards such as praise in education, parenting, and business management.

Center on the Social and Emotional Foundations for Early Learning
vanderbilt.edu/csefel
Website for a national resource center to promote positive social-emotional development and enhance school readiness of low-income children from birth to five years of age; includes links to resources and training modules in English and in Spanish.

Readings

Elkind, D. (2001, September/October). Instructive discipline is built on understanding: Choosing time in. *Child Care Information Exchange, 141*, 7–8.

Fox, L., & Garrison, S. (n.d.). Helping children learn to manage their own behavior. *What Works Briefs #7*. Champaign, IL: Center on the Social and Emotional Foundations for Early Learning. Available online at vanderbilt.edu/csefel/briefs/wwb7.html.

Gartrell, D. (2001, November). Replacing time-out: Part One—Using guidance to build an encouraging classroom. *Young Children, 56*(6), 8–15.

Han, J., Ostrosky, M. M., & Diamond, K. E. (2006, Fall). Children's attitudes toward peers with disabilities: Supporting positive development. *Young Exceptional Children, 10*(1), 2–11.

Wien, C. A. (2004). From policing to participation: Overturning the rules and creating amiable classrooms. *Young Children, 59*(1), 34–40.

Wolfgang, C. H. (2004). *Child guidance through play: Teaching positive social behaviors (ages 2–7)*. Upper Saddle River, NJ: Pearson.

PART III

Applications

CHAPTER 8

Guiding Young Children in Personal Caregiving Routines

Learning Outcomes

After studying this chapter you should be able to

- List examples of personal care routines and explain their importance in connection with guidance.
- Explain why personal care routines must take into account individual variations in development and culture.
- List goals and strategies for supporting children's development in each area of personal care: feeding, toileting, and resting.
- Discuss strategies for coordinating with families in the guidance of personal care routines.

Annette, age three, is enjoying a relaxing conversation at the lunch table. She spoons the last morsel of her favorite macaroni and cheese from her plate and relishes the tomato and apple wedges, which she eats with her fingers. She pours herself three small glasses of milk, and with the help of her teacher, Fanny, she wipes up the drops that spill on the table. When she finishes eating, she carries her plate to the kitchen counter and goes to the bathroom, where Fanny waits to supervise toileting and toothbrushing. Then Annette joins her friend, Darnell, and they both lie down on their cots, giggling and talking until Fanny comes to rub their backs and help them settle down. In the darkened room, they drift off to sleep to the soothing sounds of favorite lullabies.

Fanny can enjoy a deep sense of satisfaction, knowing that she is taking such good care of the children entrusted to her. Because of her training in child development, she knows how important these simple activities are—how they contribute to children's learning and self-esteem as well as to their physical well-being. That's why she works hard to make sure that meals, bathroom times, and naps are calm and pleasant, for herself as well as for the children, never rushing through these mundane routines to get to the "real" teaching. She knows that she is teaching just as much during these times as during the rest of the day. You will find that guiding children during personal care routines draws upon every element of the guidance pyramid, from setting appropriate expectations or goals and creating an environment that supports those goals to interacting in positive ways that reflect a sensitive understanding of the values reflected in the way these routines are handled by you and by the families of children in your care. (See Figure 8–1.)

IMPORTANCE OF PERSONAL CARE ROUTINES

The more you work with young children and study their development, the more you will realize that they are learning all the time, not only at the times that you are consciously teaching them. Much of your time in a developmentally appropriate program will be spent helping children with personal care routines that are usually considered to be outside the realm of education: eating, toileting, and resting. The younger the child, the greater the proportion of each day that will be devoted to these routines. Because children learn from every interaction, and because so many of your interactions will be concerned with routines, it makes sense for you to give thought to what you want to accomplish during those routines and how you can best do that.

Individual Variations

For young infants, life is a continual round of eating, sleeping, diapering, playing, eating, sleeping, diapering, playing, and so on. But infants vary widely in the frequency and ease with which they cycle through these activities. One baby is a regular sleeper from the beginning, perhaps taking a couple short naps in the morning, one in the afternoon, and sleeping all night starting in the third month. Another baby may sleep a lot one day and little the next, making it hard to predict a pattern. A baby may attack the bottle with gusto, draining it dry almost without pause, while another squirms and turns away from the nipple at the slightest distraction. One may need to nurse every two hours, while another may wait four hours between feedings.

Remembering that individual appropriateness is a key component of developmentally appropriate programs, you will probably agree that a self-demand schedule is best for babies. This means that they are fed when they appear to need it and sleep when they are tired; they are not made to wait until some magic time on the clock. It is painful to watch exhausted and cranky toddlers, barely able to keep their heads from dropping into their plates, unable to finish a lunch that is served too late to meet their particular needs for food and rest.

Infants need more rest than toddlers do, and they need rest at shorter intervals. Gradually, over the first few months of life, most children begin to consolidate their periods of wakefulness and sleep, staying awake and sleeping for longer stretches of time. Toddlers may be able to synchronize their schedules with others, making it possible to plan a group nap time in the daily schedule. Meanwhile, it is up to caregivers to respond to individual needs and not to force conformity. While it may be challenging to get to know each child well enough to accomplish this, your job will be made easier by the very fact that children do differ. Seldom are all babies in a center awake and demanding food or diapering at the same time. Some sleep longer than others, and some sleep while others are awake, giving you the opportunity to devote your full attention to those who need you.

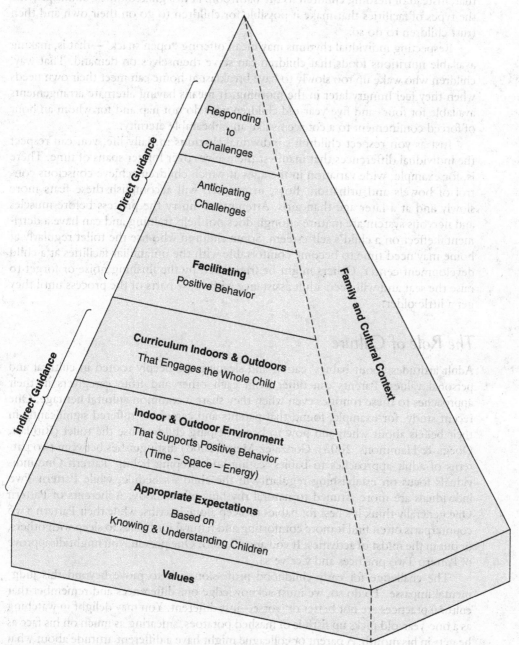

FIGURE 8–1   The Guidance pyramid: Personal care routines

Daily schedules for toddlers and young children should grow out of the natural rhythms that begin in infancy, providing a balance between vigorous and quiet activities and opportunities to eat, sleep, and use the toilet at appropriate intervals. Respect for children's individual rhythms means that schedules should offer large blocks of time when children can choose between quiet and active play. It means that, instead of herding children to the bathroom at designated times, adults provide the types of facilities that make it possible for children to go on their own and then trust children to do so.

Respecting individual rhythms may mean offering "open snack"—that is, making available nutritious foods that children can serve themselves on demand. That way, children who wake up too slowly to have breakfast at home can meet their own needs when they feel hungry later in the morning. It means having alternate arrangements available for four- and five-year-old children who do not nap and for whom an hour of forced confinement to a cot seems like an unbearable eternity.

Just as you respect children's individual rhythms in daily life, you can respect the individual differences that manifest themselves over longer spans of time. There is, for example, wide variation in the ages at which children achieve conscious control of bowels and urination. Boys, in general, will accomplish these feats more slowly and at a later age than girls. Attempts to hurry the process before muscles and nervous system are mature enough does not help training and can have a detrimental effect on a child's self-esteem. Some children who use the toilet regularly at home may need time to become comfortable with the unfamiliar facilities at a child development center. Others might be frightened by the flushing noise or forget to raise the seat and will need adult assistance with these parts of the process until they get a little older.

The Role of Culture

Adult attitudes about babies' eating and sleeping are deeply rooted in cultural and personal values. Parents can differ from each other and from caregivers in their approaches to these routines even when they share a common cultural heritage. One recent study, for example, found that parents and caregivers differed significantly in their beliefs about when and how to begin helping children use the toilet (Ritblatt, Obegi, & Hammons, 2003). Gonzalez-Mena (2008) distinguishes between two patterns of adult approaches to babies' eating and sleeping habits. Pattern One individuals focus on establishing regularity in the child's schedule, while Pattern Two individuals are more attuned to natural rhythms of the body. Adherents of Pattern One generally think it's best for babies to sleep alone in cribs, while their Pattern Two counterparts often find it more comforting and natural for babies to sleep with others, or out in the midst of activities. If you are a Pattern One person, you might disapprove of Pattern Two practices and vice versa.

The challenge for early childhood professionals is to move beyond this judgmental impasse. To do so, we must acknowledge our differences and remember that cultural practices are not better or worse—just different. You may delight in watching as a one-year-old picks up fistfuls of mashed potatoes, smearing as much on his face as he gets in his mouth. A parent or colleague might have a different attitude about what seems a waste of food. Because you value messy, active play, you may be dismayed when families send children to school in hard-soled shoes and fancy clothes, but for them this may be a way to show how well they care for their children.

Sometimes the practical demands of caring for children in group settings must override personal preferences. While the ideal schedule adapts to each infant's bodily rhythms, this is not always possible when one adult must meet the needs of three babies. While some three- or four-year-old children may go all day without a nap at home, they may need to adapt to a different schedule as part of a group so that other children can get the rest they need and so tired caregivers can have a break.

Being culturally responsive means respecting parents' wishes when possible and when those wishes do not create potential harm to a child. Even if you cannot go along with something parents ask of you, you can listen and try to understand their reasons for asking it. Encourage them to talk about what they want for their child in the long run. If you can agree about the goals, it will be easier to talk about the best methods for meeting those goals. If you cannot arrive at a consensus, you can acknowledge that and ask to revisit the conversation another time. Your willingness to talk communicates respect and may open the door to later dialogue. We will return to this topic later in this chapter.

The Child's Perspective

Think back on your own childhood. How often did adults decide whether or when you were hungry or tired, what and how much you would eat, and when you would use the toilet? Who decided what you or others could do with your own body? Were you chastised for touching parts of yourself yet expected to allow others to pick you up, kiss you, and tickle you? Sociologist Frances Waksler (1996) calls these indignities the "little trials of childhood." She argues, however, that these trials are "little" only from the perspective of adults, who, when they reflect honestly upon their own childhoods, sometimes find the memories of such experiences quite painful.

Furthermore, in her interviews in which adults recounted these memories, Waksler found that children are not passive in the face of these trials, but rather they devise all sorts of strategies to regain some control over their own bodies. Adults told stories of coping with demands that they clean their plates by hiding food in a napkin, by swallowing it and then leaving the table to vomit, or simply by going hungry as they sat for hours at the table. They remembered pretending to sleep when they were not tired, even urinating into a wastebasket as a protest to being confined in a room. Waksler concludes that, far from being "mere objects in the social worlds of adults," children are "full-fledged social actors in their own right, possessed of a range of pleasures and pains, knowledge, and methods for achieving their goals" (p. viii).

Waksler's findings are congruent with the belief of the educators in Reggio Emilia that children are "powerful, active, competent protagonists of their own growth" (Edwards, 1998, p. 180). If we share this view, we recognize that guidance is not something that adults do to children to help them become self-directed but rather something that adults undertake in partnership with children. Nowhere is this distinction more important than in the routines that address the bodily functions of sleeping, eating, and toileting.

GOALS FOR PERSONAL CARE ROUTINES

Your ultimate goal as you guide children during these routines, as it is for all guidance, is to help children become well-adjusted, productive, self-directed individuals. As an early childhood educator, you know that this means you must support each child's development in all domains, including the physical, social, emotional, language, and cognitive areas. While feeding, toileting, and diapering might seem to be primarily physical in nature, they actually involve the whole child, in a very literal sense. As children learn to control their bodily functions, they learn particular socially acceptable ways of doing so. Cognitive skills such as remembering things in sequence and new vocabulary are made more meaningful through involvement of multiple senses. In the emotional realm, sensitive, responsive handling of caregiving routines fosters the development of trust, autonomy, and self-esteem.

Supporting development means meeting children's needs and celebrating their accomplishments at their current levels, anticipating but not pushing them toward the next levels. You need to keep in mind all areas of development and not sacrifice an emotional need for independence, for example, in your eagerness to meet a physical need for adequate nutrition. We propose the following six general guidelines for supporting children's growing self-management in feeding, toileting, and resting. The first three are applications of indirect guidance strategies, and the second three involve direct guidance:

1. Know individual children well enough to anticipate needs.
2. Adjust to children's pace; avoid rushing.
3. Organize the environment to facilitate self-direction.
4. Support self-direction with your presence.
5. Model appropriate behavior.
6. Use verbal guidance to direct or redirect behavior.

In the following sections, Tables 8–1, 8–2, and 8–3 provide a few specific suggestions for application of these guidelines in each of the personal care routines. These suggestions are certainly not a prescription for every action you will take as you guide children in their daily lives. Because of the infinite variation among children, as well as among their caregivers, such a prescription would, of course, be both impossible and undesirable. Part of being an early childhood professional is being able to apply principles to new situations, and to make your own decisions about how you will foster children's development.

Goals for Mealtimes

Of course, your overall goal for mealtimes is to ensure that children receive the nutrients they need to grow strong bodies. Equally important, particularly in view of the alarming increase in rates of childhood obesity, is to establish the healthy eating habits that children will need to maintain those bodies throughout life (American Academy of Pediatrics Committee on Nutrition, 2003; Moore et al., 2003). Child-care facilities, where more than half the children in the United States spend substantial parts of their day, are in a unique position to accomplish these aims if they follow guidelines established by the U.S. Department of Agriculture, making sure that each child has enough of the right kind of formula or food and adequate physical activity (Story, Kaphingst, & French, 2006).

Meeting a child's physiological need for food has an impact on other areas of development as well. It provides energy for brain development, and it supports emotional and social well-being, since hungry children may be cranky or lethargic and unable to play well with their peers. Think about all the other aspects of development you can support (or that you might inadvertently impede) during mealtime.

As you feed very young infants, you meet their needs for security, contributing to a lifelong sense of trust that underlies all subsequent emotional development. Attachment, the root of future social relationships, begins to form as babies are held and cuddled by their consistent primary caregivers day after day. When you, as a caregiver, speak softly to babies during the pauses in sucking, you are teaching turn-taking, the fundamental requirement of conversation, and also stimulating sensory and brain development.

As babies become toddlers, caregivers encourage their exploration by offering a variety of foods; caregivers support toddlers' drive toward independence by serving finger food and letting them feed themselves without being overly concerned about messes. Beginning in toddlerhood, and continuing through the early childhood years, children need less food because their rate of growth is slower. By serving a variety of nutritious foods and allowing children to choose what and how much to eat, caregivers help children learn to pay attention to their bodies' signals of hunger and satiation, and perhaps to avoid a lifetime of obesity or eating disorders. Be aware that there can be too much of even a good thing, though. For example, research has found that children who consume excessive amounts of fruit juice are likely to be overweight. Children between the ages of one and six should have 4 to 6 ounces of fruit juice per day (American Academy of Pediatrics Committee on Nutrition, 2001). Children who want more juice because they are still thirsty should be offered fresh water. Whole fruit is preferable to juice because it takes more time to

Children are more likely to try a variety of nutritious foods when they have had a hand in preparing—or even growing—them.

Convenient access to drinking water throughout the day supports children's healthy development as well as their developing self-help skills.

consume and adds fiber to the diet (Story et al., 2006).

You can capitalize on mealtime as an opportunity for building self-efficacy by providing child-sized serving bowls and pitchers, along with your discreet support, so that children can help themselves.

Mealtime can also foster children's feelings of connectedness to each other and to their cultural heritages. Just think of how many of your interactions with other people involve sharing food, whether to mark a happy or sad occasion or simply to enjoy each others' company. Social development is nurtured through the conversations that naturally accompany pleasant meals, your careful attention to the foods you serve, and the behaviors and events associated with those foods.

Perfectly sized tables and chairs allow these toddlers to enjoy their lunch and each other's company.

"Sitting down to [a meal], at any age, should be an invitation to the fabulous banquet that is life" (Reichl, 2007).

When adults try to teach children table manners, they are actually addressing the cultural aspects of food and eating behaviors. While you teach children the mealtime rules in your center, such as keeping food on one's plate, chewing and swallowing food before speaking, and remaining seated throughout the meal, it is important to remember that what is acceptable in one culture or in one family might be seen as rude or snobbish in another. Be careful not to evaluate children's table behaviors as "good" or "bad," since that could sacrifice the goal of fostering self-esteem to the goal of helping a child fit in with someone's idea of polite society.

Health and Safety   Both you and the children need to wash your hands thoroughly before handling food. When serving family-style meals, supervise children closely

---

❀   Talk It Over   ❀

What were the rules in your family about mealtime? Did you eat together at the table? Were you expected to clean your plate? To chew with your mouth closed? To help set the table or clean up afterward? Were mealtimes lively, with lots of conversation, or were you expected to be quiet? How have these experiences affected the way you approach or feel about mealtime today? Which of your childhood experiences would you hope to replicate with children in your care? Which practices might you change? Why?

so that they don't lick the serving spoon or sneeze on the bread basket. Make sure that the amount of food in any serving bowl is small enough for children to manage and thoroughly clean any spilled foods to prevent insect and rodent infestations. Pay attention to safety factors when doing cooking projects with children so that they don't burn themselves on hot electric skillets, for example.

TABLE 8–1   Direct and Indirect Guidance Techniques at Feeding and Mealtimes

---

Know Individual Children Well Enough to Anticipate Needs

❀ Which children are likely to come to school hungry in the morning?

❀ How soon after a bottle is a particular baby likely to be hungry again? How does she or he like to be held during feeding?

❀ Which finicky eater might learn to try new foods if seated next to a more adventurous companion at lunch?

Adjust to Children's Pace; Avoid Rushing

❀ Introduce only one or two new foods at a time until you determine which ones a child accepts.

❀ When a new food is rejected, wait a few days or weeks and try it again.

❀ Let babies enjoy "self-help"—reaching for spoons before they are actually able to fill them with food and carry it to their mouths; "gumming" a graham cracker before they have teeth to chew.

❀ Plan for enough time between meals and snacks so that children are hungry, but not so much time that they are starving.

❀ Schedule some quiet activity to help the children calm down before lunch is served. Allow enough time during meals for children to eat without rushing; encourage those who play with their food or dawdle to move on, but don't scold.

Organize the Environment to Facilitate Self-Direction

❀ Place babies in semi-sitting positions to prevent choking.

❀ Use a small spoon and place food far back on the tongue so the baby doesn't push it out. (Babies have learned to push their tongues out as part of sucking.)

❀ When children are ready, provide cups for liquids and child-sized chairs to sit in.

❀ Make sure each child has a comfortable personal space for eating.

❀ Use family-style service: Provide small serving bowls and spoons so that children can help themselves.

❀ Use small pitchers, partially filled to minimize spilling.

❀ Provide balanced nutrition and let children choose what they will eat. Plan desserts to add to nutritional content to each meal, not as a reward for a "clean plate."

❀ Increase the chances that children will like foods (e.g., serve food at lukewarm temperature or foods that children can help prepare).

❀ Try to offer foods from various ethnic groups to broaden children's experiences as well as to provide familiarity for children from each group.

❀ Provide toast sticks, sandwiches, or vegetable pieces as "pushers."

❀ Serve easily manipulated finger foods like carrot sticks, orange or apple slices, green pepper, cabbage, or tomato wedges; or cook foods until they are soft enough to cut with the sides of a fork.

(Continued)

Guiding Young Children in Personal Caregiving Routines   **183**

Table 8-1 (*Continued*)

Support Self-Direction with Your Presence

❀ Accept infants' signals that they have had enough to eat; wait for their cues that they are ready for more.

❀ Let an older baby hold onto an extra spoon while you use another to feed him or her.

❀ Encourage self-feeding by providing manageable finger foods.

❀ When children are ready to join a group at a table, try to limit the number supervised by one adult to three or four toddlers, or five or six preschoolers.

❀ Sit at the children's level in a position where you can reach each child. Treat accidents calmly; help the child clean up without scolding or punishing.

Model Appropriate Behavior

❀ Plan ahead to divide supervision responsibilities so that each adult can have a relaxed meal too. Take turns, with one adult bringing refills to the tables instead of having every adult continually jumping up and down.

❀ Engage in pleasant conversation with the children at your table, not with adults at other tables; model a quiet voice and "table manners."

❀ Show children what to do: "Cut your meat like this."

Use Verbal Guidance to Direct or Redirect Behavior

❀ Tell children, "Take what you'll eat and eat what you take."

❀ Use short sentences and give one direction at a time: "Feet under the table."

❀ Give positive directions: "Use your bread to push your food onto your spoon." "Chew and swallow your food, Kylie; then you may talk."

❀ Offer choices: "Would you like more milk? Do you want white bread or whole wheat?"

❀ Redirect children who jump up during meals to sit back down. Say, "We get up when we are finished eating."

❀ If a child persists in jumping up during meals, remove the plate (a logical consequence) and say calmly, "It looks like you're finished."

Goals for Diapering and Toileting

Your goals for children in the realm of diapering and toileting will gradually shift as children develop. Keeping children clean and preventing the spread of disease are important parts of a diapering routine, but diapering is also a way of fostering security because it contributes to children's physical comfort. The intimate moments of diapering provide opportunities for pleasant conversations, touch, and eye contact, which build self-esteem and language skills. These opportunities are only available if you give each diapering occasion your full attention. Going through the motions in mechanical fashion while carrying on a conversation with another adult is insulting to children. Imagine a child-care center where the caregivers, as they change diapers, maintain stoic, impassive expressions without meeting infants' gazes or calling them by name. What do you think would be the long-range impact on those infants?

As babies become toddlers, the need for independence emerges alongside the continuing need for cleanliness and sanitation. Your eventual goal, of course, is for children to be able to use the toilet independently. As you work toward that goal, you will be helping children learn to understand their bodies' signals, to control their responses to those signals, to feel comfortable with their bodies, and to take pleasure in their accomplishments.

Gradually, you will be able to teach good hygiene habits, such as how to flush the toilet and how to wash one's hands after using it. Toileting also offers countless opportunities for using small muscles to practice the skills of buttoning and unbuttoning, zipping and unzipping, small triumphs that contribute to self-efficacy. As children learn about their own bodies, they might also begin, in a natural, healthy way, to learn about differences between their bodies and those of their playmates of the opposite sex. Certainly you will want to answer their questions calmly and truthfully and to avoid instilling a sense of shame in children by conveying the impression that there is anything dirty or bad about their bodies or bodily functions.

❋ Talk It Over ❋

What are the various names you have heard parents use to teach their children to indicate their need to urinate or defecate? Why do you think people use these names? Do these names help children learn? What do you think young children think about these bodily functions?

Health and Safety. Caregivers should wear disposable gloves during diapering and any other time they are likely to handle bodily fluids. Thorough handwashing with plenty of soap and warm running water is essential for children and adults after diapering or using the toilet. Infants unable to stand at a sink can be held, or you can clean their hands with a wipe or clean wet washcloth. Because children's tender skin scalds easily, make sure the water temperature does not exceed 120 degrees Fahrenheit in any sink that they might use. Clean up toilet accidents promptly and sanitize with a solution of ¼ cup of chlorine bleach in a gallon of water. (Keep this and any other dangerous material well out of children's reach.) Use the same solution in a spray bottle to sanitize the diapering surface after each use.

Children's Sexuality. Part of your role in guiding children's healthy sexuality development is to promote children's acceptance of their own and others' bodies, as well as of all their natural bodily functions. You accomplish this by being aware of your own feelings about sexuality, by reacting calmly, and by providing factual information at a level children can understand. Teach children through your actions and words that they are proprietors of their own bodies and have the right to accept or reject affectionate touches. Listening to children and respecting their wishes about appropriate touches sets the stage for them to be able to tell you or their parents when someone touches them inappropriately, or in a way that makes them uncomfortable (Chrisman & Couchenour, 2002).

TABLE 8–2 Direct and Indirect Guidance Techniques in Diapering and Toileting

---

Know Individual Children Well Enough to Anticipate Needs

❀ Learn children's signals and special words for toileting so you can respond quickly to prevent accidents.

❀ Talk with parents so that your expectations and methods are similar.

❀ Know which children are likely to become so involved in play that they might forget to stop for toileting and give them quiet reminders.

Adjust to Children's Pace; Avoid Rushing

❀ Take your time with diapering; don't handle it in an assembly-line fashion.

❀ Before initiating toilet-training, wait until children are ready: when they can recognize their bodily signals, control their muscles, and understand what you expect.

❀ Coordinate your efforts to start training when parents are ready to work on it at home as well.

❀ Provide time for children to use the toilet after meals and naps, but make sure children know toilets are accessible at other times as well.

❀ Don't expect all children to conform to your schedule.

Organize the Environment to Facilitate Self-Direction

❀ Keep all diapering supplies ready and within reach so that you can focus on interacting with the child.

❀ Provide potty chairs when children are learning to use the toilet.

❀ Suggest that parents provide clothing that children can pull down and up easily, such as slacks or jeans with elastic waistbands.

❀ Keep extra clothing on hand in case of accidents. Make sure needed supplies (toilet paper, soap, paper towels) are available and accessible to children

Support Self-Direction with Your Presence

❀ Go into the bathroom with children who are learning to use the toilet; stay nearby to encourage children and help them with buttons and zippers.

❀ Sit on a low chair instead of looming over children.

❀ Let children gradually take over more of the responsibility, pulling their own pants down or up, or buttoning one button while you button another.

❀ Handle accidents matter of factly and help parents and siblings to do the same. Help children clean up in private to avoid embarrassment. Tell curious children that "Joe had an accident like some of us do sometimes. I'm helping him get fixed up."

Model Appropriate Behavior

❀ Use appropriate vocabulary for body parts and elimination.

❀ Avoid teasing or conveying messages with your facial expressions that would cause children to feel ashamed of their bodily functions.

❀ Let children see you wash your own hands thoroughly after you help them with toileting.

Use Verbal Guidance to Direct or Redirect Behavior

❀ Gently remind, or invite, children to use the toilet at regular intervals until you know they no longer need such assistance.

❀ Remember that new types of disposable diapers are so absorbent that children may not feel as much discomfort when they are wet as they once did with cloth diapers.

❀ Avoid asking questions for which "no" is not an acceptable answer; instead say, "Time to go to the bathroom."

Some children handle their genitals more than others. Handling of genitals may be a symptom of the need to urinate. Some children seem to be literally holding it back, sometimes because they want to finish a game or some other thing they've started. If you promise to save their place, they may be willing to go take care of their need. Occasionally children have a rash in the genital area that they are merely rubbing. Teachers should be alert to advise parents or the nurse that the child may need medication. Underwear that is too tight or improperly cut can contribute to the child's pulling at it, which may be interpreted by some as masturbation.

Masturbation is a self-stimulating behavior that gives children a pleasurable sensation and is sometimes comforting. In itself is a harmless habit, but it often causes consternation, sometimes even shock, among adults who associate it with adult sexual activity. It's important to remember that this can be a normal form of self-comforting in young children, particularly at naptime. During waking hours, a healthy approach such as focusing on providing other enjoyable activities for the child will be much more effective than more direct efforts to eliminate the behavior. Punishing or admonishing attitudes of adults may actually make it into a problem for the child. Ignoring the behavior is probably best, unless it seems to be so absorbing the child stops engaging in other activities. Masturbation so prevalent that it interferes with the child's ability to participate in other activities can be a sign of more serious problems: injury, infection, and/or possible abuse—all the more reason to refrain from shaming or scolding the child.

Sexual Abuse   While helping a child with toileting routines, teachers and caregivers sometimes observe what they suspect is evidence of sexual abuse. A child who seems to be in pain when urinating or defecating, or who seems to be in pain as he or she is touched or approached, may have been molested. Bleeding from vagina or rectum may also be a result of molesting.

In addition to these physical indicators, children's behaviors can be clues that they have been abused. As a result of your own upbringing, you may feel uncomfortable when you witness behaviors that are part of healthy sexuality development. It is important that you learn what is healthy, however, and be able to distinguish developmentally expected behaviors from the unhealthy behaviors that might indicate abuse.

As part of typical sexuality development, infants and toddlers can be expected to display curiosity about their bodies and to experience genital pleasure. For three- through five-year-old children, typical sexuality development can include masturbation, engaging in various forms of sex play, experimenting with bathroom humor or "bad" words, or exhibiting strong curiosity about their own origins. Children with disabilities may have these experiences later than their peers without disabilities, and they may take longer to understand them (Chrisman & Couchenour, 2002). Figure 4–2 on page 89 listed behaviors that should be "red flags" for you. If you notice any of these signs, be sure to inform your supervising teachers. Child-care providers are legally obligated to report suspected child abuse of any kind, including sexual abuse. Supervising teachers should take responsibility for making reports to authorities or for helping you to do so. In the unlikely event that they do not follow through, it will be up to you to make a report.

In addition to reporting suspected abuse, early childhood professionals have a serious obligation to prevent any abusive treatment of children in their care. Many of the steps to ensure that all staff handle children in healthful ways will also serve to protect those staff members from false accusations of abuse. Most centers require that all doors (including children's bathrooms) be kept open, so that each staff member's interactions with children can be monitored by colleagues. Although these precautions stem from only a few cases involving sexual abuse in child-care centers, even one case is too many, so caring people must be vigilant in ensuring that it never occurs. If you observe any behavior that violates any child's sexuality, you must report that behavior to authorities immediately.

Goals for Rest Times

Sleeping, like eating and toileting, is a physiological phenomenon, and one of your primary goals in guiding children's rest times is to meet the need to restore young bodies after periods of physical or psychological activity. Fatigue develops when there is insufficient rest and sleep; it interferes with growth and disturbs the child's social relations. The frayed nerves of a tired child may lead to crying and overreacting to ordinary situations, disturbing the other children and adults. Certainly the exhausted child has no energy to devote to learning. This is another example of the ways in which all areas of development are interrelated: Physical needs spill over into emotional, social, and cognitive domains.

Your guidance during rest times can contribute even more directly to the ways rest fosters these other areas of development. Loving, cuddling, conversation, and singing at nap time make it a pleasant and happily anticipated event, one that contributes to the sense of security that is so important for babies as well as for older children who may be feeling anxious in their new environments. Babies like to lie in their cribs and play with mobiles, rattles, or toes when they are not sleeping. They often practice vocalizations during this time, and you can foster this language development by responding with smiles and quiet conversation.

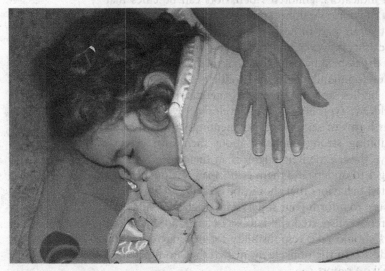

Perhaps one of the most important goals for rest times in an early childhood program is to promote children's confidence in their ability to regulate their own emotional and physical states. It is especially important to make sure that other needs or sources of discomfort are alleviated before putting children to bed; then children can learn the valuable skills of calming themselves and regulating their own entry into sleep states. This ability for self-regulation—knowing how to calm oneself, to breathe deeply, to get comfortable, and

A cozy cot with a favorite stuffed toy and a gentle caress make nap time a pleasant event that contributes to a child's sense of security while meeting the physical need for rest.

to relax into sleep—may be a goal for older children as well if they have not developed it in infancy.

Obviously, none of these goals are likely to be met if nap time becomes a battle of wills between caregiver and child, or if cribs and cots are used to confine or punish children. When these unfortunate circumstances occur, it is probably because the adults in charge have not given sufficient thought to their goals—the reasons they schedule naps in the first place.

❀ Talk It Over ❀

What suggestions could you offer to a parent whose three-year-old son seems never to want to go to bed and often appears tired and cranky during the day? How can adults help children learn to relax themselves either to go to sleep in the first place or return to sleep if awakened before they are fully rested?

Health and Safety   Put babies to sleep on their backs. Keep an eye on them as they sleep. Be careful that cots are not blocking exits during nap times and that you and your colleagues know how to get all the children out safely in case there is a fire. This may mean providing an "evacuation crib," designed with extra support so that you can safely transport several babies. Make sure that sheets and blankets used by one child are laundered before they are used by another and that they are always laundered when they are soiled. Cots and cribs used by one child should be sanitized with a bleach solution before another child uses them.

Children with Disabilities

Special educators call the skills that children need to handle personal care routines independently **adaptive development skills** (Noonan & McCormick, 1993). These skills are frequently included among the goals listed in Individual Family Service Plans (IFSPs) or Individualized Education Programs (IEPs) for children with disabilities. You can expect to be called upon to implement such IFSP or IEP goals as more and more children with disabilities are being served in inclusive settings.

By now it should be clear that teaching adaptive development skills to children with disabilities is just an extension of your work in facilitating personal care routines for all children. Your goal for children with disabilities, like that for children without disabilities, is that they become able to handle their own personal care routines to the extent possible. This means that, whether a child has disabilities or not, you and the child will probably move from a point at which you are taking most of the responsibility and providing lots of support to a point where you have gradually reduced that support and the child is taking more and more responsibility.

The difference for a child with a disability might be in the speed with which you move along the continuum and the type of support you offer. You already know that all children vary widely in the speed at which they accomplish new tasks and in the type or amount of help or encouragement they need from you to do so. It is not such

TABLE 8–3 Direct and Indirect Guidance Techniques at Rest Times

---

Know Individual Children Well Enough to Anticipate Needs

❀ Understand and tolerate anxious children's use of self-comforting behaviors.

❀ Know which children are likely to disturb each other's rest at nap time.

❀ Let children who no longer need naps read on their cots or relax with books in another (well-supervised) part of the building.

❀ Know which children do need rest and will probably fall asleep eventually if you invite them to rest and do not insist that they sleep.

Adjust to Children's Pace; Avoid Rushing

❀ Balance quiet and vigorous activities over the course of the day.

❀ Before requiring a nap, consider the total amount of sleep a child is getting.

❀ In a partial-day program, schedule a quiet activity instead of struggling to enforce a formal rest time.

❀ In full-day programs, schedule plenty of fresh air and exercise in the mornings, so that the children will be ready to rest at nap time.

❀ Maintain a predictable schedule so that children anticipate rest time.

❀ Plan quiet transition periods with low-keyed voices and nonhurried routines: toileting, toothbrushing, removing shoes, lying down on cots, and looking at books.

Organize the Environment to Facilitate Self-Direction

❀ Prepare the environment in advance so that cots are ready when the children are.

❀ Provide a clearly identified personal space for sleeping and resting.

❀ Minimize distractions of visible toys or adults coming and going.

❀ Dim lights, draw curtains, play soft music to create a restful atmosphere.

❀ Adjust the temperature for comfort; eliminate drafts.

❀ Provide covers and allow children to sleep with favorite soft toys or blankets from home.

Support Self-Direction with Your Presence

❀ Anticipate transitions from the lunch table by stationing an adult in the bathroom to help with toothbrushing, toileting, and hand washing in preparation for nap time.

❀ Sit near children as they lie on their cots; rub backs, sing softly, especially songs that use children's names.

❀ Support children who might be feeling homesick or anxious by reminding them of enjoyable things that come after rest time and that you will take care of them.

Model Appropriate Behavior

❀ Use a soft, pleasant voice and gentle movements to help children settle down.

❀ Show children that you enjoy helping them to relax.

Use Verbal Guidance to Direct or Redirect Behavior

❀ Encourage children to use the toilet before and after napping.

❀ Try to redirect a child who makes a practice of delaying a nap by getting up frequently to use the toilet. (But give some thought to possible reasons, such as anxiety about sleeping away from home, and try to address those.)

---

a big step, therefore, to imagine the different impact that various disabilities might have on children's ability to handle personal care routines and to adjust accordingly both your expectations and the types of support you offer. Observing closely and conferring with parents and colleagues can ensure that your expectations are appropriate and can provide ideas about how to support a child's growing independence.

Take the example of independent toileting. While the typical age for children to achieve this skill is somewhere between 24 and 30 months, wise parents and teachers know that even three- or four-year-olds may need continued support in the form of easy-to-manage clothing or occasional reminders to go to the bathroom. Now consider how various disabilities might affect the acquisition of this skill. For a child with a hearing impairment, there may be no variation from the typical pattern. A child with mental retardation might take a little longer to remember the procedures or to develop the prerequisite sphincter control. And a child with spina bifida might need to be catheterized every few hours because weakness and loss of sensation in the lower body make independent toilet use impossible. To expect a delay in toilet use for a child with a hearing impairment would be as inappropriate as expecting the other two to achieve total independence by some predetermined age.

Just as expectations vary with the child and the type of disability, the methods you use to help a child must fit the circumstances. For a child whose physical disability makes toileting impossible, you may need to learn the proper way to insert a catheter. For children who do have the necessary physical ability but do not seem either to know what the toilet is for or to recognize bodily sensations that signal a need to urinate, you may need to use direct guidance techniques. For example, you could put them on the toilet for a few minutes at regular intervals, in the hope that they will urinate while they are there. Or you could try to "catch" them just before the times they usually urinate and put them on the toilet. Both of these methods sound very similar to what parents of typical toddlers have been doing for years. The only difference is that, with some children with some disabilities, you might be trying these techniques a little later and for a little longer period of time.

In short, guiding children with disabilities in personal care routines requires the same kind of sensitivity and adjustment for individual needs that we have recommended in guiding all children. When children have severe disabilities or extreme needs, you may need outside help to discover the best ways to respond. Pediatrician T. Berry Brazelton (1992), for example, was able to teach parents how to handle their hyperactive babies very gently, playing with them or feeding them (but not both at once) in a dark, quiet room. As a caregiver, you might be able to adapt this technique with a baby who is hypersensitive as a result of prenatal drug exposure, for example.

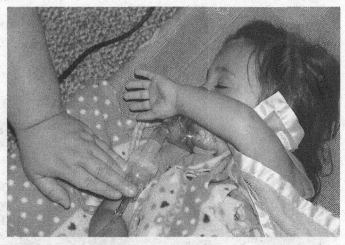

It may be easier to provide treatments children need while they sleep. This child is receiving medication with a nebulizer to alleviate breathing problems.

This book advocates a positive approach to guidance, keeping in mind the whole child as well as the ultimate goals of guidance. A common pitfall in working with children with disabilities is an overemphasis on the things those children cannot do, resulting in a program that teaches small skills in a piecemeal fashion. A child is more than the sum of her ability to use a spoon and toilet correctly; the job of an early childhood educator is to support that larger potential. Here is how one father of a five-year-old boy with autism puts it:

> In general, I believe that the same issues that made it so difficult for Jacob to learn and to connect with others provide him with special gifts. I believe that Jacob, quite literally, experiences and, consequently, organizes the world in a way that is quite different than you or I do. . . . The goal is not to make him normal. The goal is to unleash his special gifts. That is the challenge for all of us. Not simply taking damaged children and making them whole but connecting with their special gifts, enabling them to succeed in their special ways. (Anonymous, 1997, p. 63)

COORDINATING WITH FAMILIES

In no other area of guidance is the connection between home and center more apparent or more important than in the personal care routines of feeding, toileting, and resting. Because they revolve around bodily functions common to all humanity, these routines are deeply imbued with cultural and psychological meanings. The way you handle them will determine whether children feel anxious or secure and comfortable in your care.

It is imperative that you communicate often and openly with family members to learn more about their ways of handling routines at home and to keep them informed about their child's life at your center. The younger the child, the more essential this communication is. Remember that when you disagree with family members about the way to handle a particular routine, it does not mean that either of you are wrong. It does mean, however, that you will have to take the time to talk over the reasons behind each viewpoint and try to arrive at a workable solution. Chapter 4 provides a detailed discussion of ways to foster positive relationships with families. What follows are brief suggestions for coordinating your efforts with family members when guiding children's personal care routines.

Most families of infants or toddlers will want a daily report covering food intake, bowel movements, and rest patterns. Some programs use a two-way journal, kept in a child's diaper bag, in which family members and caregivers can communicate with each other about these and other pertinent facts.

Family members will be more inclined to hear your point of view if they feel that you have listened to theirs with an open mind.

Knowing that a child was up part of the night because of a new tooth coming in may help a caregiver understand the cranky behavior of a usually cheerful baby. When parents know that a child took a longer nap than usual, they can anticipate a slightly later bedtime and plan their evening accordingly.

Changes in routines, such as the introduction of solid foods or beginning toilet training, need to be discussed with family members beforehand. This is not only in the best interests of children and families; it makes your job easier. Getting a child to use a potty chair at the center will be more difficult and take longer if using diapers is still the custom at home.

When Disagreements Arise

Sometimes you and a child's family will have different opinions about how a routine should be handled. When that happens, it is important that you listen carefully to what family members are asking and try to understand the reasons behind their requests.

You have an ethical responsibility to avoid anything that would be harmful to a child, but you also have a responsibility to support the child's family, supplementing, not supplanting, their care. Although your ideas about what is best for children are probably based on a storehouse of knowledge about typical patterns of development, you need to remember that most families also want what is best for their children.

Sometimes what is good for a child is what is good for the whole family, and your supportive cooperation could make a real difference in the family's well-being. More than one caregiver has been asked to shorten a child's nap so that tired family members don't have bedtime struggles to deal with after a hard day at work. When you can reasonably comply with such a request without harming a child, it is probably a good idea to do so.

❈ Talk It Over ❈

Suppose Cameron's father tells you that he wants Cameron to take a shorter nap in the afternoon. He says that Cameron is staying awake until all hours of the night, which is a problem for Cameron's mother, a nurse, who has to wake up at 4 a.m. to get to work on time. You feel that Cameron should be allowed to sleep until he awakens naturally. And besides, you are worried that he will wake all the other children if you get him up early. Role-play this situation with a classmate, with one of you taking the role of Cameron's father and the other taking the caregiver's role. Try to understand the other person's point of view rather than convince that person of yours.

Sometimes your disagreement with a family member might stem from cultural differences. Ideas about how and when children should be fed or toilet-trained are deeply imbued with cultural beliefs and traditions. You won't know what lies behind your apparent disagreements unless you admit that you don't have all the answers and listen to what families have to say with an open, respectful attitude. Certainly, families will be more inclined to hear your point of view if they feel you have listened to theirs with an open mind. Perhaps you'll be able to arrive at a solution that can satisfy everyone, whether that means that one of you learns something that changes your mind or you arrive at a compromise that combines both viewpoints. Even when agreement is not reached, as long as you and the family members have a trusting relationship and focus on what is best for the child, you can end the conversation on friendly terms with a commitment to revisit the issue in future conversations (Gonzalez-Mena, 2008).

CONCLUSION

Eating, sleeping, and toileting are important parts of life for young children; in addition to meeting physiological needs for nutrition, rest, and elimination, they serve many developmental goals. Early childhood educators make wise use of the time and energy they spend in guiding personal care routines when they plan with those developmental goals in mind. In addition to knowledge of typical developmental patterns, caregivers need sensitivity to individual differences and respect for each child's bodily rhythms if they are to help each child achieve independence and control of these bodily functions. Methods of handling personal caregiving needs are rooted in cultural values and practices. Caregivers must be aware of different ways of handling these simple routines, knowing that no one way is always right. The intimate nature of personal caregiving requires close coordination with family members, based on open and honest communication.

REVIEW: TEN WAYS TO PROMOTE DEVELOPMENT THROUGH PERSONAL CARE ROUTINES

1. Remember that the goal is a child's self-regulation and independence.
2. Know the potential of personal care routines for fostering all areas of development (i.e., cognitive, social, emotional, and physical-motor) and plan ways to enhance that potential.
3. Allow plenty of time: Don't rush children through daily routines or expect them to do things before they are ready.
4. Know typical patterns of development so you have an idea of what to expect and when to expect it: that most children establish a regular sleep pattern by about three months, for example, or that many five-year-olds no longer need a nap.
5. Expect wide variations among individual children and respect those differences through self-demand feeding, for example, or by offering choices among a variety of both quiet and vigorous activities.
6. Organize the environment to make it easier for children to manage their own routines. For example, provide personal space for meals and naps, use small serving bowls and utensils, and install child-sized toilets and sinks.
7. Support children's growth toward self-direction and independence by staying nearby, watching closely, and offering encouragement and assistance as

needed. For example, hold a cup as a child pours, rub a back at naptime, and sit on a low stool and help with buttons or zippers in the bathroom.

8. Model appropriate behaviors, such as good table manners.

9. Redirect inappropriate behavior when necessary, using short, concrete statements, such as "Keep all four chair legs on the floor, please."

10. Communicate with families so that you can coordinate your efforts and offer helpful suggestions, as needed.

APPLICATIONS

1. Observe a typical morning in an infant or toddler classroom and another in a classroom for three- and/or four-year-old children. Record how much time the teacher or primary caregiver spends in personal caregiving routines. Compare your findings for the two classrooms. What differences do you note? Based on what you observed, how well did the program you observed meet the goals for personal caregiving routines discussed in this chapter?

2. Assist with one of the caregiving routines (e.g., diapering/toileting, feeding/mealtime, nap/bedtime) for at least two children either at home or at school. Evaluate your guidance of these routines in terms of the goals discussed in this chapter. What did you do well? What would you do differently another time?

RESOURCES FOR FURTHER STUDY

Websites

American Academy of Pediatrics
www.aap.org
Provides children's health and child-rearing information and resources that have been reviewed and approved by more than 57,000 pediatricians.

U.S. Department of Agriculture
nal.usda.gov/childcare/
Information for child-care providers; includes recipes, nutrition, and food safety guidelines and resources. (Click on the link for providers.)

National Food Service Management Institute
nfsmi.org
Includes recipes for child-care food programs, information about food safety and allergies, resources for family child-care home providers, and a newsletter in both English and Spanish.

Sexuality Information and Education Council of the United States (SIECUS)
siecus.org/pubs/RightFromTheStart.pdf
Provides a link to *Right from the Start: Guidelines for Sexuality Issues, Birth to Five Years,* a publication of this national nonprofit organization that "affirms that sexuality is a natural and healthy part of living."

Readings

Anderson, J. (2006 May/June). A comprehensive approach to addressing childhood obesity in early childhood programs. *Exchange, 169,* 41–45.

Bailey, B. (2000). *I love you rituals.* New York, NY: Harper Collins.

Baker, B. L., Brightman, A. J., Blacher, J. B., & Heifetz, L. J. (1997). *Steps to independence: Teaching everyday skills to children with special needs.* Baltimore, MD: Paul H. Brookes.

Birch, L. L., Johnson, S. L., & Fisher, J. A. (1995, January). Children's eating: The development of food-acceptance patterns. *Young Children, 50*(2), 71–78.

Butterfield, P. M. (2002, February/March). Child care is rich in routines. *Zero to Three, 22*(4), 29–32.

Duffy, R. (2006, September/October). From a parent's perspective: Sex and sexuality. *Exchange, 171,* 66–68.

Gonzalez-Mena, J. (2010, July/August). Cultural responsiveness and routines: When center and home don't match. *Exchange, 194,* 42–44.

Oshikanlu, S. (2006, May/June). Teaching healthy habits to young children: Handwashing, toileting, and toothbrushing. *Exchange, 169,* 28–30.

CHAPTER 9

Guidance and Curriculum— *Interdependent Elements of Appropriate Practice*

Learning Outcomes

After studying this chapter you should be able to

- Explain how guidance is supported by, and in turn supports, an engaging curriculum.
- Identify developmentally appropriate goals for experiences in art, language arts, science, and math.
- Discuss indirect and direct guidance strategies for supporting those goals.

After tracing an outline of their very tall student teacher, a group of three- to five-year-olds named it "The Big Body" and watched intently as their teacher fastened the drawing to the wall. When asked what they needed to do next, the children shouted, "Make the insides!" and spent the next several weeks using yarn, markers, drinking straws, sticks, and other materials to create veins, blood cells, a heart, a "grinder" for digesting food, bones, facial features, hair, and glasses. When some parts they had glued to the silhouette began to fall off, they carried the Big Body to an improvised doctor's office in the art area. They stretched it out on the floor and tenderly ministered to it for nearly an hour. The copious "doctor's notes" they produced on clipboards included a diagnosis ("He has a broken heart") and orders to come back "every day for 24 days." After the patient was taken away, one girl held an imaginary telephone to her ear and inquired, "Are you feeling better, Big Body?" A visiting artist, whose own sculpture used found materials in imaginative ways, pronounced the children's creation worthy of display in any gallery.

The Big Body was certainly an elaborate long-term art project, one that involved every member of the class in some way before it was completed. It was also a rich experience in science, math, and language arts. The children used books, computer images, and their observations of their own bodies to carry out their investigations. They calculated how many fingers and toes the Big Body needed and concluded that the "food tube" had to be longer than the "breathing tube" in order to reach the "grinder." They discussed their theories about bones, blood cells, and even how the brain sent "messages" telling the various parts of their bodies what to do, and they represented their ideas in drawings and writing. In other words, the project was an example of **integrated curriculum**. The teacher supported children's learning by providing a rich assortment of materials and plenty of time and space to use them. She helped keep interest levels high by encouraging children to talk about their additions to the project during group time, and she provided resources or suggestions for children to follow up on their own questions. In short, she used indirect and direct guidance strategies to further her teaching goals.

GUIDANCE AND CURRICULUM

This chapter and the subsequent one address the ways in which guidance and curriculum intersect. Because you are probably learning about curriculum in other courses you take as part of your professional preparation, you might think that the topic does not belong in a textbook concerned with guiding children's behavior. Nonetheless, we have important reasons for including this information here.

First, as discussed in Chapter 1, we believe that an engaging curriculum that involves the whole child is a fundamental part of appropriate guidance. Children who are busy moving, talking, playing, exploring, and learning in a well-designed environment will be much less likely to "get in trouble." Instead, they will be expending their energy constructively, acquiring the knowledge and practicing the skills they need as fully functioning members of society. More importantly, they will be using their knowledge and skills in ways that foster dispositions such as perseverance and intellectual curiosity (Katz, 2007). Instead of spending your time and energy telling children what to do (or, worse, what not to do), when your curriculum is based on investigations of topics that matter to them, you have real conversations about the interesting things you and the children are learning. When you shift the focus of your interactions from how the child is behaving to what he or she is thinking, you are building the

Children who are busy moving, talking, playing, exploring, and learning in a well-designed environment will be much less likely to "get in trouble."

kind of relationship that is fundamental to effective guidance (Katz & Katz, 2009). Thus, curriculum supports the goal of guidance, which is to help children become well-adjusted, self-directed, productive adults. The guidance pyramid in Figure 9–1 is intended to convey the idea that an engaging curriculum, supported by a well-planned environment, is a fundamental component of guidance.

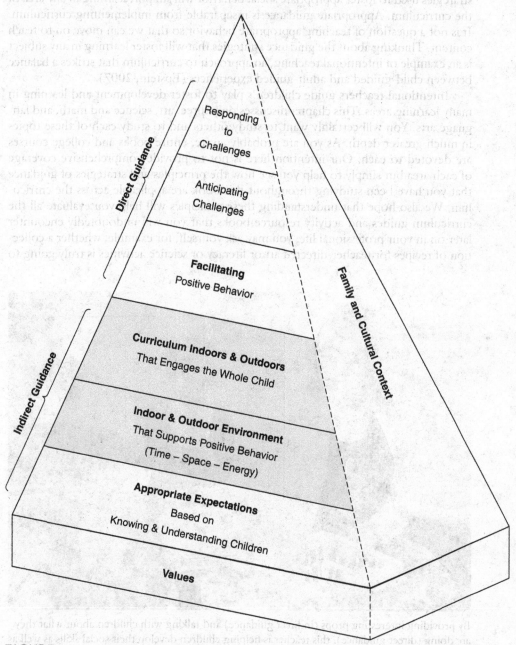

FIGURE 9–1   The guidance pyramid: Play and learning

Second, teachers use indirect and direct guidance to support the goals of curriculum. We know that development is holistic across all domains; we believe that it is impossible to influence development in one domain without tapping into and influencing development in all the others. We guide children's cognitive development as surely as we guide their social-emotional development. The same principles and strategies used to foster appropriate social behavior will support learning in any area of the curriculum. Appropriate guidance is inseparable from implementing curriculum. It is not a question of teaching appropriate behavior so that we can move on to teach content. Thinking about the guidance strategies that will foster learning in any subject is an example of intentional teaching, an approach to curriculum that strikes a balance between child-guided and adult-guided experiences (Epstein, 2007).

Intentional teachers guide children's play to foster development and learning in many learning areas. This chapter discusses only three: art, science and math, and language arts. You will certainly want to study others and to study each of these topics in much greater depth. As you are probably aware, entire books and college courses are devoted to each. Our intention here is not to provide comprehensive coverage of each area but simply to help you see how the principles and strategies of guidance that you have been studying throughout this book are applicable across the curriculum. We also hope that understanding these principles will help you evaluate all the curriculum guides and activity resource books that you will undoubtedly encounter later on in your professional life; you may ask yourself, for example, whether a collection of recipes for teacher-directed art or literacy or science activities is truly going to

By providing interesting props (indirect guidance) and talking with children about what they are doing (direct guidance), this teacher is helping children develop their social skills as well as the vocabulary and concepts that will support future literacy.

help you achieve worthwhile goals for children's learning and development.

We chose to organize the content around subject areas rather than classroom interest centers in order to underscore the fact that various types of learning can occur in any part of the classroom. While the chapter focuses on experiences that typically occur indoors, we hope you will be able to see how many of the basic ideas apply outdoors as well. Many early childhood professionals hold that almost anything that can be done indoors can be done equally well—or even better—outdoors. In Chapter 10, we will take a closer look at guiding children's outdoor play and learning.

Goals for art might include improving hand-eye coordination, encouraging sensory exploration, and learning simple concepts.

GOALS FOR LEARNING EXPERIENCES

The first step in planning how you will guide children's learning experiences in any curriculum area is to be clear about your goals. What is your vision for how the learning experiences you offer will help children become well-adjusted, self-directed, productive members of society? Tap into the best thinking of researchers and educators who specialize in these areas to help you think beyond the immediate and obvious. For example, goals for art might include improving eye–hand coordination, encouraging sensory exploration, and learning simple concepts (e.g., colors, shapes). At a deeper level, goals for art also include learning to use materials such as paint, clay, or drawing pens as "languages" to create and communicate meaning (Gandini, 2005), developing an awareness and appreciation of beauty, solving complex problems, and learning to see things from multiple perspectives (Eisner, 2002).

With regard to language arts and literacy in particular, much has been written about the need to foster children's interest in the sounds and rhythms of speech (phonological awareness), their understanding that print conveys meaning (print awareness), and their ability to draw connections between letters and sounds (alphabet knowledge) (National Reading Panel, 2000). The overall goal that lends meaning to all these components is to enhance children's ability and—just as importantly—their desire to understand and use oral and written language.

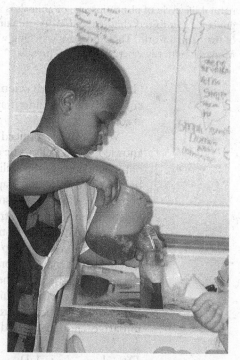

Providing a water table with containers of various sizes encourages children to explore mathematical concepts, comparing quantities such as "empty versus full."

A classroom environment enriched with opportunities to observe the natural life cycle of plants, insects, or animals is an example of indirect guidance that fosters children's curiosity, thinking skills, and knowledge of the natural world. These boys are watching with fascination as a Monarch butterfly emerges from its chrysalis.

Goals for mathematics in early childhood include developing a concept of number, one-to-one correspondence, counting with meaning, sorting and classifying, comparing quantities, identifying shapes, and describing spatial relationships. The overarching goal is to foster in children a "search for sense and meaning, patterns and relationships, order and predictability" (Richardson & Salkeld, 1995, p. 23). Success in mathematics is not only the ability to "do math" but also confidence in one's ability and willingness to apply that ability critically.

Goals for science in the early childhood classroom include fostering children's innate curiosity about the world, broadening their knowledge of the natural world in particular, and helping them develop skills for investigating and thinking about what they observe. Kilmer and Hofman (1995) use the verb **sciencing** instead of the noun *science* because they perceive science for young children as an active process rather than a body of knowledge to be absorbed.

You probably noticed that each of these sets of goals includes not only specific knowledge and skills to be gained but also dispositions such as eagerness to figure things out, confidence in the ability to gain new knowledge or use new skills, and what might be described as a joyful approach to learning. They require you to look beyond the immediate, short-term results toward the lifelong impact of the experiences you provide for children. These goals transcend artificial boundaries between subjects and remind us to view learning as a holistic process. Remember, too, that in addition to these subject-specific goals, you can help children meet more general developmental goals through the learning experiences you provide. The child playing before a mirror in the dress-up corner who discovers she is still the same person, no matter how she transforms her face or alters her appearance with costumes, is establishing **identity**, a major task of early childhood. Regardless of topic, children who set their own tasks and carry them out are practicing **initiative**, another major developmental goal in early childhood.

Developmental Perspective

A developmental perspective on curriculum means that you keep in mind important principles of development as you think about what you want children to learn or be able to do and how you go about achieving your aims. Recall from our discussion in Chapter 3 that two basic principles of development are that (1) development follows a predictable sequence, and (2) development across domains is integrated or holistic. This section provides a brief review of how these principles apply to the curriculum areas that are the focus of this chapter.

Art.   Children feel the silky coolness of finger paint as it slides over the slick paper. They smear large puddles of glue and watch in fascination as it drips from their fingers. They crow with delight as colors bleed and run together at the painting easel. They squeeze wet clay and inhale its earthy scent. If we don't watch them carefully, they taste the clay and paste. They hum softly as they work. They seem to revel in the sheer joy of motion as they scribble across the page. All their senses are engaged, and their attention is absorbed.

For the youngest children, or for those who have had few opportunities to do these things, this sensory exploration seems satisfaction enough. Very soon, however, children begin to take delight in creating something—if only a mark on a page. The important thing is that it is their mark, their creative expression. According to Rhoda Kellogg, who made a life's work of studying millions of children's drawings, children are powerfully motivated to continue drawing, in large part because of the pleasure they take in seeing the lines and shapes they have created. Kellogg's (1979) research has shown that even toddlers have definite ideas of composition and placement of their scribbles on the page. She has documented the predictable stages that children generally go through as they progress from basic scribbles to simple shapes and then complex patterns. If you are familiar with these stages, you will be less likely to worry that the self-portraits of your three- and four-year-olds look like tadpoles.

While Kellogg focuses on the drawings produced by children, Kolbe (2005) focuses more on the process through which children produce their drawings. She sees children's drawing as moving from simply making marks to making meaning. She says that young children enter into a dialogue with their drawings, making more marks in response to the marks that have appeared on the page. At some point—which adults may not notice because it happens too quickly or they don't understand what the child is saying—they perceive something in their drawing, perhaps a representation of an object, a person, a movement, or a sound. Once they have made the discovery that marks stand for something, they can begin to use marks in this intentional way.

For young children, sensory exploration of art materials provides satisfaction enough.

Language Arts. We use the term **language arts** to encompass speaking, listening, reading, and writing, as well as the thinking that is central to all these activities. A toddler who picks up a block and pretends to eat it, with great smacking of lips and a big grin, is using the block as a symbol of food and is using lip-smacking as a symbol of eating. Because words are symbols, too, the child's first use of symbolic play is viewed as a milestone in language development. For older children, dramatic play is spontaneous play in which they decide for themselves whether to join in, what role to take, and how to interpret that role. The focus of the play moves from random actions to specific roles characterized by particular language and eventually to the relationship between roles (Bodrova & Leong, 2007b). That is, at the most mature levels of play, a child not only acts and talks like an ambulance driver but also makes sure the other players properly fulfill their roles of patient, police officer, doctor, and so on.

Dramatic play is spontaneous play in which children decide for themselves whether to join in, what role to take, and how to interpret that role.

As children become aware of written language, they refine their skills in ways that are reminiscent of their early use of spoken language. Just as babies babble in their cribs, practicing sounds long before they speak recognizable words, young children scribble, making distinctions between the marks they intend as writing and those they intend as drawing, and older children use their own rules to invent spellings of words before they learn conventional forms (Whitmore & Goodman, 1995). Thus, all aspects of language are connected to each other, and they all have roots reaching back to the earliest stages of development. Babies listen with their bodies, making eye contact during feeding and diapering, turning away when overstimulated, and crawling or toddling to the adult who calls them. Toddlers pick up books, pretending to bite the picture of a juicy red apple or patting the picture of the "doggy." They flip through the pages or hold the book out for an adult to read to them. The scribbles of young children include key elements of adult writing, including repetition and recombination of basic forms.

The term **emergent literacy** refers to the ideas that children in literate cultures are actively working to make their own sense of print from infancy onward, that there are no hard-and-fast lines between knowing that books contain stories, that a story is in the printed part of a book, and that this particular part of that print stands for this particular sound. Each of these understandings emerges from children's earlier understandings and their repeated encounters with print.

Math. Have you ever counted aloud the children in a group and, upon reaching "four," heard a chorus of voices announcing, "I'm four"? Clearly the children who want you to know that they are four years old have a different meaning of the word *four* in mind. The child who truly has a concept of number would realize that *four* does not name this object or describe a quality of this person. That child also knows that four pennies will remain four pennies whether they are stacked on top of each other or spread out in a row.

Constance Kamii (1982), one of several prominent early childhood experts who base their work on Piaget's theory, says that "teaching" number is impossible; children must reinvent the concept of number for themselves. You have probably noticed that many young children can recite numbers from 1 to 20 or 30 or even more, but when they "count" items, they often skip about, perhaps counting one item several times or not at all. For these children the number words have no more meaning than if they were reciting "eenie, meenie, miney, mo."

According to Kamii, the only way for children to be able to develop this understanding is by handling lots of materials that allow them to compare quantities and notice similarities and differences in those quantities. And it is only after they have formed the concept of number that they can represent their understanding by mak-

Children in literate cultures actively work to make their own sense of print from infancy onward.

ing four marks, for example. Printing the numeral 4 is an even more abstract representation. To do so with meaning, a child needs to understand what *4* represents and be able to control a pencil or crayon—and these are two separate accomplishments.

❀ Talk It Over ❀

Recall your observations of children playing with unit blocks. How did they explore concepts such as part–whole relationships, comparisons of length or height, patterns, and symmetry? What qualities of the unit blocks seemed to support their exploration of these mathematical concepts?

Integrated, Holistic Development. Developmentally appropriate curriculum activities build on children's strengths, providing opportunities for them to extend what they already know and to use their skills for real purposes. Developmentally appropriate

Children develop an understanding of the concept of number by handling lots of materials (e.g., playdough) that allow them to compare quantities and notice similarities and differences.

early childhood programs use an integrated approach, meaning that opportunities for using the knowledge, skills, and dispositions associated with any curriculum area are embedded throughout the daily routines and activities, not taught as isolated subjects. Table 9–1 enumerates some of the ways that experiences in art, language arts, and science and math draw upon as well as enhance children's development in all domains.

Space and Materials. Indirect guidance involves your organization of the environment, selection and display of materials, and arrangement of group size. If you want to foster children's aesthetic sensibility, for example, you will strive to maintain a beautiful and orderly environment, taking care to arrange materials carefully, creating visually appealing displays of children's work, high-quality art objects, and items from nature. You will consider the aesthetic quality as well as the safety and educational value of any item you add to the environment. Because you want children to notice these aspects of their environment, you will remove unnecessary clutter and avoid stereotypical, commercially produced decorations. You will change displays from time to time and provide attractive mats or other surfaces to highlight children's work. Objects that children bring to school can be artfully arranged, perhaps on a special piece of fabric, or in front of a mirror, to invite closer inspection and study (Seefeldt, 2002).

If you want to foster children's fascination with written language, you provide a **print-rich environment** (Neuman, Copple, & Bredekamp, 2000), one in which print is used in ways that are both meaningful and obvious to children. Some teachers advocate labeling every item in a classroom, believing that children will learn to read the word *door,* for example, if they see it printed on a card that is taped to the actual door. Others believe that print used in this way will simply fade into the background so that children no longer notice it. More authentic uses of environmental print include using the children's names on their cubbies or to label photographs of them that are posted at their eye level. Children think of their initial as "their letter," or a symbol for themselves, and they use the letters of their own name as springboards to reading and writing (Whitmore & Goodman, 1995). A large wall calendar can also stimulate interest in print if used for authentic purposes—the way adults actually use calendars to remind themselves of upcoming events—instead of monotonously counting off days every morning. Children will be eager to see their names printed

TABLE 9–1   Curriculum Areas and Developmental Domains

	Physical	Social	Emotional	Language	Cognitive
Art	Using art materials develops control of the small muscles in hands and fingers. As children paint and draw, cut and paste, or pinch and mold materials, they learn to control the tools that they will later use for writing. As they look at the marks they make, their brains must coordinate information from their eyes and hands, a complex task that stimulates further development.	Most art projects are social in nature, in that children share materials around a common table and take turns with various items of equipment. They negotiate with each other about how to share the glue or the fuchsia-colored marker.	Art activities offer emotional release: pounding clay, painting with broad, exuberant strokes. Children take pleasure in their work and its results, which builds confidence. They express things that they are not yet able to put into words.	Being mutually engaged in an absorbing activity makes conversation flow. Children are inspired by, and borrow ideas from, each other. They talk about what they are doing, or what they see someone else doing. With their drawings, paintings, and clay creations, they communicate ideas for which they don't yet have words.	Practice in drawing lines and shapes prepares children to notice differences between the marks they will encounter on the printed page. Making marks with meaning is the beginning of representationals. Children have to think, remember, and make predictions as they solve problems such as how to make a clay animal stand upright or mix a particular shade of green.
Language Arts	Dramatic play involves the use of large and small muscles as children act out various roles, running, climbing, riding tricycles, and buttoning or unbuttoning dress-up clothing.	Children make friends through dramatic play, learning the give-and-take of a small social group. They share, take turns, and respond to rules of family life and school as they take on various roles. They show what they think about how the world works as they negotiate the rules of play: "You have to obey the police officer," or "I'm the mother, you're supposed to do what I say."	Children express joy, fear, anger, or happiness during spontaneous role playing. The drama may become so powerful that they need to reassure themselves that it's only pretend. Children who feel weak may assume a powerful role. Occasionally a frightening incident in the neighborhood, such as a robbery or a fire, gets acted out through dramatic play.	Language development is fostered in the give-and-take of playing the role and reciprocating the social exchange. Creative development is fostered as children elaborate the play and work out solutions to the action that takes place. Some plots or themes develop suspense. Some may relate to stories the children have heard or to television shows or movies they have seen.	Children play out their understanding of the roles of various people they remember. They learn to make decisions while choosing among roles, deciding which dress-up clothing to wear or which group to join.

(Continued)

TABLE 9–1 (Continued)

	Physical	Social	Emotional	Language	Cognitive
Science and Math	Children use small muscles and eye-hand coordination with tools for investigating interesting things and recording the results of those investigations. They use large muscles when working problems of balance in block construction or determining how far and fast they can run.	Arguments about issues of fairness, such as who has more blocks or mashed potatoes, involve comparing quantities, an example of mathematical thinking. Making a seesaw work satisfactorily takes cooperation and builds knowledge of basic physics.	Curiosity and feeling a connection with nature are aroused as children wonder when the butterfly will emerge from the chrysalis. Tackling scientific problems such as balancing a block structure builds confidence. Children become social scientists in dramatic play as they reenact and increase their understandings of people and activities in their community, nation, and world.	Children use language with real purpose as they discuss and defend their ideas about problems involving scientific or mathematical concepts: How can we make this pulley work? Whose card "wins" in this game? How many cookies may each person take?	Putting out one plate and napkin for each person at the table uses the concept of one-to-one correspondence. Talking about the different tastes, textures, and temperatures of foods at lunch involves the scientific tools of observation and comparison. Sorting and classification occur when children help put blocks or other materials away.

on their birthday dates or the date of their turn to take the classroom bunny home for the weekend.

If you want to foster children's confidence in their ability to apply mathematical skills, you will provide lots of materials that invite counting and comparison of quantities. In addition to the manufactured cubes, beads, and plastic teddy bears usually thought of as math materials, these might include collections of found materials such as pinecones, seashells, and bottle caps, as well as sand and water tables stocked with containers of various sizes. You will provide opportunities within the daily schedule for children to help with tasks, such as setting the table, that involve one-to-one correspondence or to decide how to divide a pizza fairly. If you want to support children's innate curiosity as budding scientists, you will create an environment where discoveries are possible in many areas, not just in the science center. And you will stock the room with things that stimulate that curiosity, such as plants, living creatures, scientific tools (e.g., scale, magnifying glass, microscope), and simple machines to take apart and reassemble.

GUIDING CHILD-DIRECTED ACTIVITIES

Once you have set the stage with a variety of enticing interest centers, the learning is up to the children. Using centers should be their choice, not something that they are forced or coaxed to do. Children are free to use the various tools and materials in ways that challenge without discouraging or overwhelming them. In art, for example, some children have very low tolerance for tactile sensations. While smearing finger paint on paper may be fun for you, it may be torture for them. But if allowed to try the activity in their own tentative way, they just might learn to enjoy it. Your interaction with the children will make the difference between an experience that meets your objectives and one that just fills the time. You use direct guidance as you interact with children during their self-selected activities as well as during adult-directed activities.

Affective Guidance

Probably the most important thing you can do is to respect children's work, to take their efforts seriously. You show respect for children's work through physical guidance when you sit with the children and show with your eyes and body language that you are interested in the way they are painting or building with blocks.

Children will often ask you how you like something they have made. If you gush over every dab of paint and stack of blocks, they will soon learn that your praise is insincere. They may begin churning out products with little or no thought, just to get your praise. At the other extreme, if you wax enthusiastic over only those products that meet your standards, you may send the message that the end result is more important than the process of creating it. This risks robbing children of the ability to gauge their own efforts as well as frustrating those who cannot meet your standards. Neither of these options will help you meet the objectives of learning experiences. It is more effective to acknowledge effort and persistence, perhaps to express awe at the difficulty of the tasks children set for themselves. Certainly you can show your delight in colors, textures, and shapes or notice attributes such as size and symmetry of their structures, without implying that one child's work is superior to the work of another. And you can always put the question back to them. When they ask "How do you like my picture?" you can tell them, "You're the boss of your own picture. Tell me how you like it."

❋ Talk It Over ❋

Imagine that you are struggling with some creative endeavor, such as decorating an elaborate birthday cake, designing and creating a costume, or performing a particular piece of music. Suppose someone with expertise at the task were in the room. What could that person do that would be most likely to help you accomplish the task and feel successful? What types of assistance would interfere with that outcome?

Another aspect of affective guidance is accepting and responding appropriately to children's feelings. During dramatic play, for example, you might learn something of the life situation for the children at home with parents and siblings. For example, if children dominate at school, they may be gaining strength to cope with their home situation, where they are dominated. Releasing negative feelings during dramatic play may help children. Rather than disapproving or telling them they are "naughty" when they express strong feelings, reflect the feeling ("You get angry when . . . ") and see how they respond. You may sometimes see children who spank the dolls and shout at others during their play episodes. Realizing that the children are acting a role that may have deep meaning for them personally, you allow them to express these strong feelings as long as they do not harm other children.

Physical Guidance

Sitting nearby and observing without intervening until assistance is called for positions you to catch clues that help in understanding the inner thoughts and feelings of children, as well as their understanding or misconceptions regarding concepts. For example, children might pretend to shoot or otherwise injure others when they are playing the role of police officers or ambulance drivers, revealing that they didn't understand what they saw on television. Observing this, a teacher might schedule a visit from a real ambulance driver to provide more accurate information. By listening to conversation during dramatic play as well as throughout the classroom, you may get ideas of things children are interested in that would make worthwhile projects or field trips for the future.

When help is needed, you use physical guidance in a number of ways. You demonstrate techniques to help children achieve their aims. For example, you can show a child who is frustrated by the paint dripping down the paper how to wipe the brush on the edge of the jar, and you can show children how to press down with the rolling pin to flatten the clay more effectively. You can help stabilize a block structure for children who do not yet understand the concept of balance. You might put your hand over a child's to guide a puzzle piece into place if the task has become frustrating. You can add props to expand children's dramatic play. You can provide a model for children whose only strategy for joining others in play is to keep asking, "Can I play?" which nearly always guarantees a "No." Watch to see what help the children need and give only that, not more.

Sometimes physical guidance consists of what you do **not** do rather than what you do. Avoid making models for the children to copy, whether in art, blocks, or sand. (One exception to this would be to print out names or words for children to copy when they ask you to do so.) In general, the children's thought processes are what is important, not their reproduction of your ideas about how something looks or works. The book *The Hundred Languages of Children* (Malaguzzi, 1998) suggests that children's drawings, sculptures, and block structures are integrally connected to their thinking. Drawing or building for a child, then, would be tantamount to thinking for a child—certainly not something that an early childhood professional would want to do. This does not mean that you cannot help children who have set a particular representational task for themselves and are not satisfied with their efforts. When children develop a sudden passion for dinosaurs, for example, you can suggest that they handle realistic plastic figurines and examine them closely to get a better idea of how to draw them. Or you might show children images of dinosaurs created by professional artists. You can encourage them to observe and talk about the curving tails, long necks, or jagged fins, but you should be careful not to suggest that theirs must look just like the professional's.

Verbal Guidance

As you sit with children, you will be conversing with them, emphasizing their right to decide what to do with the materials. For example, you might ask, "You can decide: Do you like long strips or shiny pieces?" Introduce words such as *behind, below, above,* and *beside* as you comment on what the children are doing in the block area or on the playground. You can draw children's attention to phenomena such as the speed of objects rolling down inclined planes at various angles or to interesting phenomena that lend themselves to further observation and study. "Look at the buds on this bush," you might say. "Were there as many here last week?" "What do you think will happen next?" "How can we find out?" Draw children's attention to the particular attributes of table toys, perhaps their shape or color, and be accepting of the child's discovering a new use for a toy, such as stacking the parquetry blocks or sorting them by color and shape rather than creating patterns.

Ignite curiosity by asking authentic questions—those that you wonder about yourself. Or listen for children's questions and enlist the group's help to find answers. One group of four-year-olds decided to find out which kinds of fresh leaves their guinea pig preferred, so they offered a selection harvested from their outdoor play area (which was pesticide free) and carefully observed what happened. This particular guinea pig had a passion for dandelion leaves, which led to further sciencing—sorting and classifying—as children searched out all the dandelion leaves they could find.

Conversations with Children

Most of your interactions with children should be conversations—not directing or reprimanding their behavior. A room full of meaningful conversations is far more desirable than a quiet room. Being a skillful conversation partner involves physical, verbal, and affective guidance. You sit close by, look at children, show that you are listening, respond to what they say, speak clearly and respectfully, and show your approval and interest with your face and gestures. As we mentioned in Chapter 8, diapering/toileting, feeding, and resting all offer priceless opportunities for you to have one-to-one conversations with children. The materials and experiences you make available during the self-selected activity period will also generate many conversations among

Your goal is not to replace a child's home language but to recognize it as an asset and encourage families to help the child maintain it.

children or between you and the children. You will find that children naturally have a lot to say when your conversation centers around something interesting that they are doing at the moment. It is also easier for them to process what you are saying so that they can focus more energy on learning language (Girolametto & Weitzman, 2006).

Your role is to be a conversational partner, not to correct speech and grammar or "teach" language. You are sure to put an end to a conversation if you interrupt to make a child say something "the right way." Focus on what the child is trying to tell you. When you truly do not understand, you can say so, but if you have an idea of what is being said, you can check its accuracy by asking the child whether that is what he or she meant. If you are watching the child closely, reading all the signs of expression, you'll usually understand.

When children make mistakes, it is sometimes a sign that they are using their minds to try to understand the rules of their language. When a child says, "I eated sghetti," for example, you should recognize the intellectual accomplishment of figuring out that -*ed* is used for past-tense verbs. You can agree with what the child means and tactfully model the more conventional form by responding, "Yes, that's right. You ate all your spaghetti." Such an atmosphere of acceptance will contribute to children's confidence in using language to make their needs known. If children are treated with respect, they will try to communicate. If they get answers to their questions, they will ask further questions. If they find teachers who listen, they'll tell stories of events that are important to them.

Some children may have difficulty with pronouncing certain consonants or with faltering speech. Such problems are not uncommon in young children, and most will be outgrown. Consonants, such as *s, v, t, r,* and *l,* and blends of two or three consonants, such as *cr, str,* and *bl,* are frequently difficult for children and may not be articulated clearly until children are seven or eight years old. If a child is encouraged to communicate freely, these errors will diminish. If a three- or four-year-old child does not talk at all or cannot be understood, you should confer with the child's family members to see if they are observing the same problem. If so, you can provide information about community resources where the child can be screened and receive appropriate services, if needed. A speech-language specialist may consult with you and offer suggestions for ways to help the child in natural, unobtrusive ways. It is important to refrain from pressuring a child because doing so is likely to make problems worse.

English Language Learners

In an increasingly multicultural society, for many children the home language is different from the one spoken in their child development programs. Considering the culture shock you would feel in a foreign country will help you appreciate the feelings that a young child may have when first immersed in a group whose language is different from that spoken at home. Your goal is not to replace the child's home language but to recognize it as an asset and encourage families to help the child maintain it, recognizing that language embodies culture, which is a way of viewing the world that has evolved over generations. Losing a language means losing the connection with those roots (Belt, 2007). Furthermore, children will be able to transfer skills attained in their home language to the new language. Remember that children whose vocabulary seems limited in comparison with their English-proficient peers are probably also in command of a far more extensive vocabulary in their home language. An accurate gauge of their verbal skills must reflect this cumulative accomplishment (Moore & Perez-Mendez, 2007).

Ideally, a program will seek to hire at least one staff member who speaks the same language as each of the children and families they serve. When there are helpers in the classroom who speak their language, children's needs may be more comfortably met. Research has found that Spanish-speaking children in bilingual classrooms with teachers who spoke Spanish more often were less likely to be teased or bullied by their peers and more likely to be viewed as having a close relationship with their teachers. In contrast, those whose teachers spoke English more often were more likely to be rated as having low tolerance for frustration, problems with conduct, and learning difficulties (Chang et al., 2007). Hiring native speakers may not be practical, however, especially if not one but many languages in addition to English are spoken in a particular community. But even if you don't share a language, you can make an effort to learn some words in the children's and families' language. Make a list of key words used around your center and ask a family member to provide the corresponding words in the child's home language. Post the words where you can see them and be reminded to use them. Try learning songs in the family's language. Fortunately, body language can communicate across cultural and language barriers to express love and respect even when verbal language isn't well understood.

Steve Hildebrand (personal communication, 2003), who teaches English classes for young children in Prague, the capital of the Czech Republic, reassures early childhood professionals:

> If you don't speak the child's language, don't worry, because during the early childhood years actions speak louder than words. That is, at this age, smiling, hugging, leading or demonstrating what you want done are the strongest forms of communication, and these actions are recognized by young children of all languages. Children love to watch what other children do and quickly try it, or they catch on to what the teacher wants or what the situation requires and make an effort.

In observing children, you will notice that they talk about what they see, touch, and feel, and they almost always have the translation at hand in terms of a physical object. All children love established rituals—such as snack, outdoor play, and singing—including those learning English. Your words are translated by the actions and activities involved. Pictures, objects, and gestures with smiles are an international language that can be used to help make everyone comfortable with what is going on. Young children don't all catch everything that is going on and, unlike adults, aren't bothered by not knowing everything. Most children need to have things explained to them numerous times in numerous ways.

Like all other children, English language learners need a loving, encouraging audience for practicing and developing their skills. As with all other children, the focus should always be on the meaning of what they are trying to communicate. Mistakes in vocabulary and pronunciation are not problems for long when the learners have lots of opportunities to play with children whose native language is English. Children are quick to correct each other, sometimes not as diplomatically as we would like, but often effectively. Your job is to provide many ways for children to participate and show what they know or can do and to help them remain connected to their home language and culture while supporting their acquisition of another language (National Association for the Education of Young Children [NAEYC], 2009).

Cleaning Up

What you do when self-selected activities are drawing to a close can be just as important as setting the stage at the beginning for furthering the learning experiences. It is no less crucial to think about what you want to accomplish and why—to be intentional—at this point than at any other time of the day. It is a given that classroom interest areas won't stay neat for long after the children arrive. Art is messy. Dramatic play can involve rummaging through all the dress-up clothing to find just the right costume. Serious block building often results in every block being pulled from the shelves and pressed into service. It is easy to forget that the whole purpose of providing these materials is for children to use them and instead to become discouraged at the prospect of putting things back where they belong. Unfortunately, adults often convey that discouragement along with an expectation, stated or implied, that children will not willingly assist with restoring order. Of course, children pick up on this attitude and act accordingly. Here are some suggestions for making cleanup more pleasant for everyone:

- Allow sufficient time. Instead of adding to your stress by rushing through cleanup in order to begin circle time, start a few minutes earlier so everyone can relax and work at a more leisurely pace.

- Remember that children are learning during cleanup: Classifying and sorting are math skills, whether children are using table toys during playtime or putting those toys away during cleanup; matching items to pictorial or printed labels on shelves involves literacy; figuring out how to mop up spills is a form of scientific problem solving; and the entire process provides occasions for lots of conversation (i.e., language learning).

- Rather than just supervising or cajoling, work alongside the children and let them see you take pleasure and satisfaction in jobs well done.

- Make it clear that cleanup is a shared responsibility of everyone in the group. A rule that you must clean up the block area if you play there can backfire and cause children to avoid the area or restrict themselves to the simplest constructions.

- Make cleanup easier by providing clear, logical places for everything and locating necessary tools near where they will be used (e.g., a small broom and dustpan near the sandbox; sponges, buckets, and towels near messy areas; baskets and hooks for dress-up clothing and accessories).

- Have fun. Sing songs like "Pickin' up toys, put them on the shelf" to the tune of "Paw-Paw Patch," or challenge children to try carrying a particular number of blocks at a time.

- Note that washing paint brushes can be as much fun as pretending to wash dishes during playtime, and that children enjoy the sense of empowerment that comes with doing "real work."

- Avoid extrinsic rewards or praise for a "good job." Instead, thank children for their contribution to a more pleasant environment. Comment on the beauty of the organized block shelves or the fact that the group can go outside earlier because everyone's help made quick work of cleanup.

- Be aware that drawing undue attention to children who avoid cleanup can make them more firmly entrenched in their resistance as well as recruit more children to their ranks. Focus instead on the joy of being part of a group that is working together. Plan ahead to entice reluctant cleaners with special jobs.

ADULT-DIRECTED LEARNING EXPERIENCES

We now turn our attention to experiences that usually involve more adult direction: reading and telling stories, singing, and doing science experiments and cooking projects. Success in these experiences where you are front and center will depend in large part on planning and preparation beforehand, on being intentional about what you are doing and why. As you read the following sections, you will note how much intentional teaching relies on the guidance principles and strategies you have studied throughout this book.

Stories

Reading and telling stories are key experiences in children's acquisition of literacy. The pleasure to be found in a good story is a prime motivator for learning to read. These experiences can occur informally with individual children or with small groups during the self-selected activity period, or they can be the focus of circle time for the entire group. Because literature experiences are so important for learning to read later, teachers should do everything in their power to make books interesting for children. One important way to develop this interest is to make sure that children have plenty of time to enjoy books during self-selected activity time. Children who have become acquainted with a story in the book corner are likely to enjoy hearing it again in the group context. They will enjoy retelling stories using flannel board figures or revisiting familiar stories that have been tape-recorded by their teacher. In short, the more pleasurable encounters children have with stories during their self-selected play, the more likely they are to expect group storytimes to be pleasurable—an expectation that becomes a self-fulfilling prophecy.

Selecting Appropriate Books.   For infants and young toddlers, books may contain single items on a page for them to point out and name. Next are those with one idea on a page, like the classic, *Busy Timmy (Jackson, K. and B., 1948)*. Books of this level typically depict action familiar to a child who is not yet worldly enough to have many experiences that relate to reading matter.

Through the third year, books should be short and personally oriented for a child. In a group situation, it is better to read several short books to three-year-olds than to try a longer one and realize in the middle that the children are not understanding the book. When reading to one child, an adult can digress and explain a point, but that is often difficult when reading to a group of children because those who don't need the explanation may lose interest.

Four-year-olds will enjoy longer books if they have had solid earlier experiences where they learned to associate books with the pleasure of being cuddled and basking in one-on-one attention. If you have trouble keeping children's attention at storytime, check to be sure you are selecting appropriate books. If anything, err on the simple side; you can always embellish the story yourself if you sense that children are ready for more detail. Once you have established a pattern of attentiveness, you may then be able to move on to more difficult books. Good storytime guidance begins with selecting the right books.

Organizing Story Groups. The ideal introduction to stories occurs while sitting on the lap of a caring adult. For children fortunate enough to have had that experience at home, the transition to listening in a group is likely to be easy. Infants and toddlers, as well as older children from homes where there are no books and they have never been read to, usually respond well if one adult shares a book with them and allows them to react to the pictures they see. Once they have had many opportunities to enjoy story reading individually and in small groups, children are more able to benefit from large group storytimes. Because early childhood groups typically have several teachers as well as volunteers, it is usually possible to organize small story groups.

Reading and listening to stories are key experiences in the acquisition of literacy, made all the more memorable when associated with the pleasure of snuggling in the lap of a trusted caregiver.

When reading stories to the whole group, if more than one adult is available, those who are not reading should station themselves strategically throughout the group, where they can model listening by showing their own enthusiasm for following the story and perhaps gently place a hand on the shoulder of a fidgeting child should the occasion arise. If there is a child who simply will not sit still for a group story-time, even when given a special place by the teacher, a volunteer should be engaged to read to that child individually. Let the child select the books to read or listen to a recorded story. Such individual experiences lay the groundwork for the possibility that the child will eventually be able to enjoy the group storytime. Teachers who find themselves spending most of storytime reprimanding or reminding children to be still should evaluate why they are devoting time to the activity. Teachers who use extrinsic rewards, such as stickers or praise for "good listeners," are forgetting that the real reward for listening is the pleasure of hearing a good story.

Preparing for Storytime.   None of the goals for storytime are likely to be met when an adult grabs a stack of ragged books on the way to circle and expects to muddle through the next few minutes without preparation. Storytime needs to be planned. The teacher must know the books well and have some idea of how they will affect the children. Judicious use of props, such as puppets, flannel board figures, or pictures, can help the children understand better. Part of the preparation includes planning transition techniques, such as finger plays or songs that have a quieting effect. After a few of these transitional techniques, you can open a book and read. You will dampen enthusiasm if you make the children wait a long time, sternly announcing that the story cannot begin until "everyone is listening." Variety will make storytime more interesting, and children will look forward to what surprises have been planned.

Reading or Telling a Story.   When you know the story well, you will feel free to allow children to respond because you will have confidence that you can resume the story, maintain interest, and keep the group together. By seating children with their backs to the window, you can prevent glare from interfering with their seeing the pictures. Situating the group away from distracting toys, perhaps using a portable screen to shield toys from view, is a form of indirect guidance. You can help maintain interest by altering your voice as you speak for the various characters, but you should avoid making them sound too harsh or scary.

Acting Out Children's Stories.   Children take special delight in storytime when it consists of acting out stories they have dictated to you during playtime. Vivian Paley developed this approach during many years as a preschool teacher in Chicago and has written several delightful books about what she has learned about children's thinking in the process. One theme that appears repeatedly is the power of shared stories—whether arising in pretend play or dictated at the story table—for creating community and making room for everyone in that community. Children seem to understand and accept a child who is different, announcing that they are "friends of everybody in the story." "And when you tell someone your story," Paley concludes, "that person enters the story and becomes your friend too" (2010, p. 90).

❀ Talk It Over ❀

Visit your school or town library and select four or five children's books. Evaluate each book and tell why you believe it would (or would not) be a good candidate for reading aloud to children. For what age do you think it is suitable? Why? Would you recommend reading it one-on-one or to a group? Why?

Singing

Singing easily dovetails with storytime. A period of singing can precede a story and help settle the children for listening. Make a list of a wide variety of songs and musical finger plays in order to be able to choose those that are most appropriate on a given day. Variety is important, for all children will not enjoy the songs equally. They may tire of certain songs, and if asked specifically, "Do you want to sing . . . ?" they may say, "No." It is usually best if teachers know the songs they want children to learn and simply sing them through at a lively tempo, accepting children's suggestions as they come up incidentally. Asking children to choose songs often slows down the event, and some may get bored waiting for others to come up with a choice or may argue about the selection instead of singing. You can discuss choices of songs with children at other times, such as during meals, and then have those songs ready to sing at the next group time.

While all children enjoy learning new songs, singing can be especially helpful for English language learners, who will enjoy repeating familiar songs and may be unaware that in doing so they are gaining valuable practice in language. Rhyme patterns in song are another aid to learning. By age six, children can often sing as many as 100 different songs. This repertoire provides the child with several hundred sentences and patterns for sentence structure, grammar, word meaning, and pronunciation of words that might not be encountered in everyday experience.

Teach a new song using a normal tempo. Sing it for several days until children catch on to it rather than wearing out the children by making them try to learn it all in one day. You can locate some new songs by browsing websites such as pandora. com, and recalling songs you enjoyed as a child. Words to songs are a good resource to add to your file of ideas to use in teaching.

Problem Solving and Experiments

Problem solving is an important part of science and mathematics, but perhaps even more important than solving problems are the ability to recognize or find interesting problems and having the patience and perseverance to keep trying until you solve them. Your guidance can help children cultivate these qualities if you refrain from rushing in whenever you anticipate or encounter a difficulty. Instead of fixing an unstable block structure that threatens to tumble, you can call the children's attention to the problem and help them think through possible alternatives for solving it.

In addition to taking advantage of such naturally occurring opportunities, you can arrange for planned experiences to stimulate children's interest in materials and phenomena that might not arise spontaneously. Be careful when planning experiments to choose phenomena that will make sense to young children and to avoid presenting scientific principles as though they were magic. There is wonder enough for children in the natural world, without taking advantage of their immature reasoning skills in an effort to dazzle them.

Unfortunately, many published science curricula suggest preplanned experiments that are supposed to demonstrate abstract concepts such as gravity, air pressure, and magnetism. Children should be able to see (or figure out) what happened and draw their own conclusions from any science experiment. Their conclusions might differ from yours (or from the "right" one), but making mistakes is part of the scientific process. Hypotheses are made to be proved or disproved. All too often, when adults think they are teaching scientific principles or facts, children are learning in a superficial, rote way. Since we know that young children rely on their senses for information, it is unlikely that they will understand invisible phenomena the way that adults do, but you can learn a lot about their thinking by asking them to draw or otherwise represent their theories.

If you think about it, you'll have no shortage of appropriate experimental subjects. Things that seem commonplace to you are full of possibilities for children to investigate. "What happens to a bucket of snow if you bring it indoors?" "Will a small ice cube melt sooner than a big one?" "Will the doll clothes dry more quickly outside or inside? In the sun or the shade?" "What happens to my shadow when I stand closer to the light?" "Why is the potted plant drooping? What will happen if I give it some water?" "If I boil a seashell, will it get soft like the macaroni shells that we have for lunch?" All these are appropriate subjects for scientific experiments in an early childhood program.

Cooking Projects

Cooking projects might be viewed as a special category of science experiment—one that has the extra advantage of edible results!

Participation is the key, so plan for small groups of children to engage in food projects at one time. Avoid asking the entire group to be spectators while a few do the activity. Find ways to let each child stir a little, pour a little, or carry the pan. Teach children to cut safely with a little knife on a cutting board. Try to allow them to eat the product the same day for maximum recall of the total project. For example, gelatin can be set with ice cubes to hurry the jelling process so children can eat it the same morning or afternoon it is made.

Part of your planning and guidance will foster good health habits by requiring children to wash hands before going to the cooking table. Because hot pans can be dangerous, special care should be taken to protect children without introducing unnecessary fear. An electric skillet is a useful utensil for making things like applesauce, scrambled eggs, pancakes, and the like. Place it on a low table so children can see it and position the table near an electric outlet so that they don't have to step over the cord.

Encourage children to recall the sequence of production as they eat what they have made. They can relate this to other concepts they have already learned. Use pictures to depict the project on a bulletin board so that parents can see what you and the children did and so children can be reminded of the experience later on.

Technology

Opportunities for using technology to foster children's cognitive development abound in early childhood environments. Children use inclined planes to send small cars racing across the room; they use pumps in the water table, pulleys and levers in the block area, and wind power to lift kites on the playground. You can increase the learning potential of these spontaneous uses of simple technology by asking questions that help children focus on the process. "What did you do?" "What happened when you did X?" "What do you think will happen if you do Y?" Through experiences with pulleys, pendulums, wheeled toys, siphons, waterwheels, and the like, children construct what Piaget called "physical knowledge." In the resources listed at the end of this chapter, you will find dozens of suggestions for enriching your environment with simple technology.

More advanced forms of technology are also becoming increasingly commonplace in early childhood programs: computers, video cameras, and printers are a few examples, as are the many forms of assistive-technology products designed for children with disabilities. It is your responsibility as an educator of young children to make sure that any technology is used in developmentally appropriate ways.

According to a position statement of the NAEYC (1996), it is important to use technology to support and extend—not to replace—more traditional materials and experiences. "Painting" on a computer screen is not a substitute for the actual experience, with all its sensory, tactile, and aesthetic qualities. Nor is passively watching an animated video version of a favorite story equivalent to hearing that story and being able to interject your own comments about it as a real live caring adult reads it to you.

Given that computers and other forms of technology pervade all our lives, it is no longer a question of if but rather how you will use these resources in your early childhood program. You must continue to use direct and indirect guidance to ensure that computers and other technology are used in ways that promote children's health and well-being and enhance their development. This means selecting technology that is geared to the ages, abilities, and cultural or linguistic characteristics of children and ensuring that those resources are used in playful, active, engaging ways that integrated with the rest of the curriculum (National Association for the Education of Young Children, 2011b).

Avoid glorified worksheets that do little more than encourage children to guess at one "right" answer or games that promote violence or negative stereotypes based on gender and race. Make sure that all children in your classroom have opportunities to use the equipment and that the computer does not become a boys' domain or the exclusive property of the few children who happen to feel more comfortable with computers because they have them at home. Use technology to promote the inclusion of all children. For example, teacher educator George Forman (1997) recommends using videotape of children at play to help them examine their social interactions, perhaps to notice that they are excluding a particular child. They can then discuss the situation and, with your guidance, make appropriate adjustments.

Specialized assistive technology makes it possible for children with disabilities to participate in a program. One example is a hamburger-shaped recording device that can store short words or phrases. A child with a speech or language disability presses the button to generate a verbal request for "more" at mealtime. One center uses the device to enable a child with cerebral palsy to join the game in which children take turns singing about what they are wearing. The child's classmates record the appropriate words, and he pushes the button to play them when it is his turn at circle.

CONCLUSION

This chapter has looked at guidance in relationship to the curricular areas of art, language arts, and science and math, with an emphasis on the holistic, integrated nature of learning and development in early childhood. Goals outlined for each subject area include the acquisition of specific types of knowledge and skill as well as the cultivation of dispositions such as curiosity, perseverance, and confidence that transcend arbitrary boundaries between subjects. We have shown how intentional teachers think through the ways they can use elements of indirect guidance (e.g., arranging environment, supplying materials, providing adequate time) to support children's learning. We have also discussed applications of the various types of direct guidance, including suggestions for scaffolding children's language and play.

REVIEW: TEN WAYS TO GUIDE CHILDREN'S PLAY AND LEARNING

1. Be aware of the many developmental goals that are facilitated through all learning activities so that you can use indirect and direct guidance to further those goals.

2. Structure the environment to support children's experiences: Provide spaces where children can explore and work without interference from other activities; arrange materials so that they are orderly, accessible, and visually appealing.

3. Provide a rich variety of materials that children can explore freely; including age-appropriate books, high-quality art supplies, and real objects that they can handle and use for experimenting.

4. Provide adequate time for children to explore material and complete projects of their own choosing.

5. Support children's learning with your presence and encouragement:
   - Facilitate the use of blocks as a medium for learning about the physical world (e.g., balance, symmetry, weight).
   - Help children explore concepts of volume and measuring as they play with water, sand, or modeling clay.
   - Encourage children to compare quantities and to notice patterns during everyday activities (e.g., setting the table for snack, recording food preferences or shoe styles on graphs).

6. Use daily routines and activities as opportunities to have respectful, face-to-face conversations with children and to encourage their conversations with each other; focus on the intended meaning rather than on the form of what they say and write.

7. Use physical and verbal guidance to help children accomplish the tasks they set for themselves:
   - Suggest or demonstrate techniques for using materials.
   - Ask questions and make comments to focus children's attention and challenge them to think.
   - Suggest roles for children who have difficulty entering dramatic play situations.

8. Plan a wide variety of activities that challenge children's thinking, observing, and generalizing:
   - Investigate natural phenomena such as animals, plants, earth, sky, seasons, weather, day, and night.
   - Plan daily opportunities for reading or telling stories, for music, and for creative movement activities.
   - Plan cooking experiences related to children's eating interests.
9. Make sure that whole-group experiences are engaging, appropriately paced for all children, and balanced with frequent opportunities for children to have hands-on experiences in small groups.
10. Model the qualities you want children to develop:
    - Use conventional forms in your own speech; rephrase children's statements when you respond.
    - Use writing for authentic purposes and explain what you are doing ("Your mom told me that your uncle would be picking you up today. I'm writing that down so I don't forget.")
    - Wonder about what might happen (e.g., if you mix particular colors of paint or offer the pet guinea pig a new kind of food).
    - Let children see that you don't have all the answers and show them how you look for information in books or on the Internet.

APPLICATIONS

1. Observe two or three children as they use art materials. Carefully write down details of what each does and says. Look for examples of each child's knowledge of color, shape, and so on. How do the children use language? How did the arrangement of space and materials support the children's experience? If an adult provided any direct guidance, how effective was it in promoting goals?

2. Observe two or three children using materials and equipment such as blocks, beads, or puzzles. Write down details of what each says and does. Could you tell that the child was testing for size, color, or fit? How? How does each child use memory while describing something that has occurred in another place or at another time? How did the arrangement of space and materials support the children's experience? If an adult provided any direct guidance, how effective was it in promoting goals?

3. Observe two or three children playing in a dramatic play area such as the housekeeping corner or the block corner. Record what the children do and say. List the sentences spoken by the children and note the average sentence length, vocabulary, and number of questions asked by one child and directly answered by another. What conclusions can you draw about dramatic play and children's language? How did the arrangement of space and materials support the children's experience? If an adult provided any direct guidance, how effective was it in promoting goals?

RESOURCES FOR FURTHER STUDY

Websites

International Reading Association
reading.org
Provides a link to position paper "Literacy Development in the Preschool Years" and a report, "Making Every Moment Count," an argument for integrated curriculum supported by eight national educators' associations, representing mathematics, geography, science, and social studies as well as school librarians and principals.

National Council of Teachers of Mathematics
nctm.org
Provides a link to access to the Standards and Principles for Mathematics Education in grades pre-K through 12.

National Science Education Standards
nap.edu/readingroom/books/nses
Online access, through National Academies Press, to standards developed by the National Committee on Science Education Standards and Assessment of the National Research Council for grades K–12.

Readings

Bowman, B. (ed.). (2002). *Love to read: Essays in developing and enhancing early literacy skills of African American children*. Washington, DC: National Black Child Development Institute, Inc.

Elkind, D. (2006). *The power of play: How spontaneous, imaginative activities lead to happier, healthier children*. Cambridge, MA: DaCapo Press.

Gandini, L., Hill, L., Cadwell, L., & Schwall, C. (eds.). (2005). *In the spirit of the studio: Learning from the atelier of Reggio Emilia*. New York, NY: Teachers College Press.

Haugen, K. (2000, September/October). Using creative dramatics to include all children. *Exchange, 135,* 56–57.

Helm, J. H., & Katz, L. (2010). *Young investigators: The project approach in the early years*. New York, NY: Teachers College Press.

Kolbe, U. (2007). *Rapunzel's supermarket: All about young children and their art*. Byron Bay, Australia: Peppinot Press.

Topal, C. W., & Gandini, L. (1999). *Beautiful stuff: Learning with found materials*. Worcester, MA: Davis Publications.

Worth, K., & Grollman, S. (2003). *Worms, shadows, and whirlpools: Science in the early childhood classroom*. Portsmouth, NH: Heinemann; Newton, MA: Education Development Center; and Washington, DC: National Association for the Education of Young Children.

CHAPTER 10

Guiding Young Children's Outdoor Play and Learning

Learning Outcomes

After studying this chapter you should be able to

- Explain why outdoor play is an important component of guidance.
- Discuss the benefits of outdoor play for children's development across domains.
- List ways to use indirect guidance to support children's play and learning outdoors.
- List ways to use direct guidance to support children's play and learning outdoors.

Cassandra finds a worm in the pine needles next to the sand box where she and some other children are playing. "Look, a baby worm!" she shouts as she picks it up the worm and carries it over to show Koji, Elena, and Bruce. She attempts to put the worm in Koji's hand so that he can hold it, but the worm falls to the ground. "It's going home to his mommy," Koji says, adding, "It needs a home." The four children immediately begin working together to dig a hole under the pine needles. Soon the worm disappears in the soil, but the children don't seem to notice this and continue digging. Bruce says that the worm will be happy because he has a home. "Yeah," Cassandra agrees. They continue digging for about 10 minutes.

This brief incident during outdoor play reflects the children's development in all domains. Cassandra made the connection between the fact that the worm is tiny and her prior knowledge that babies are also small—an example of cognitive skill. Koji also used his prior knowledge to conclude that the "baby" worm must have a mommy. The children showed their understanding of the role of parents as they tried to take care of the baby worm. Cassandra used fine motor skills to pick up the worm very gently, and all the children used gross motor skills to dig and to coordinate their movements with each other. Social skills came into play as Cassandra shared her discovery with her playmates and the children collaborated to build the "home" for the worm. They took the perspective of the worm and hypothesized that it was happy because it had a home, signifying both cognitive growth (moving beyond what Piaget referred to as *egocentrism*) and development of the emotional-social quality of empathy (imagining the feelings of another). Finally, the children's acceptance and enthusiasm for each others' ideas probably contributed to their development of self-esteem.

The emphasis on outdoor play varies among cultures and is shaped by societal values as well as climate conditions. In Norway, for example, many children attend programs conducted entirely outdoors, while in Jordan programs are largely conducted inside to protect children from sun and heat in summer or heavy rainfall in winter (Dietze & Crossley, 2003). Unfortunately, throughout the world today, children's access to outdoor play is steadily eroding due to changing lifestyles. In the United States, for example, 70 percent of mothers reported playing outside every day when they were their child's age, while only 31 percent provided that opportunity for their children (Clements, 2004). To make matters worse, when children who spend large parts of their lives in group care settings do have time for outdoor play, it commonly occurs in barren expanses of gravel or woodchips, surrounded by chain-link fencing, devoid of trees or vegetation, and dominated by gaudy commercial structures of limited versatility. Richard Louv (2005) coined the term "nature-deficit disorder" to call attention to what is happening to current generations of children for whom computers and television are replacing the pleasures of mud, water, grass, trees, and all the living things that inhabit the outdoors. Recently, a growing number of advocates have begun calling for increases in both the quantity and quality of outdoor play experiences for young children (e.g., Oliver & Klugman, 2005; Wike, 2006). When you understand what can be gained when children play outdoors—and what is lost when they cannot—you may adopt the rallying cry "No child left inside" (Nelson, 2006). This chapter describes how to apply the same guidance principles and strategies that you use indoors to facilitate outdoor play experiences that foster every aspect of a child's development.

❊ **Talk It Over** ❊

How much time did you spend outdoors as a child? What did you enjoy doing? Where? With whom? How do you think the experience of young children today differs from yours?

BENEFITS OF OUTDOOR PLAY

Most people associate outdoor play with letting off steam in vigorous physical activity. With a little more thought, you will readily see its potential for enhancing not only physical but also emotional, social, and intellectual development. And you will see once again how each of these strands of development intertwines with all the others. It is important to note that we are discussing *potential* benefits of outdoor experiences. Simply taking (or sending) children outdoors may not be enough to encourage adequate amounts of vigorous physical activity. A review of research on the physical activity levels of children aged two to six years found that only about half engaged in active play for an hour a day and that girls were generally less active than boys (Tucker, 2008). In order for the potential of outdoor play to be realized, experiences must occur in high-quality environments with supportive adult interactions. In other words, guidance principles and strategies must be applied outdoors as well as indoors, and you must begin with a clear vision of what you hope to help children accomplish.

Physical Benefits

Healthy Growth and Development.   Fresh air, sunlight, and exercise, which promote good health, are all important benefits of well-planned outdoor play opportunities. Nature provides vitamin D through sunlight's activation of a substance on the skin. Vitamin D is essential for the growth of strong bones and teeth. Because infants and young children have important growth to achieve in bones and teeth, they need regular doses of vitamin D. By spending some time outdoors in the sunshine each day, a child can receive this health-giving vitamin. Because too much exposure to sun causes skin damage, regular use of sunscreen is essential.

Fresh air, sunlight, and exercise, which promote good health, are all important benefits of well-planned outdoor play activities.

Oxygen, which is of course found in fresh air, is essential for life. Oxygen is essential for the brain to function, and a deficiency of oxygen causes brain injury. Young children use much more oxygen for a given volume of brain tissue than do adults. The benefits of fresh air make it well worth your effort to bundle up babies and take them outside in a stroller for at least a few minutes every day. Once children become mobile, exercise fosters their deep breathing and oxygen intake. And a little fresh air helps adults stay healthy, too!

Exercise is essential to aid all of the body's inner systems to grow, develop, and function as they should. Respiratory, circulatory, digestive, and elimination systems all function more fully when a child has adequate exercise. In the United States, more than 10 percent of children between the ages of two and five are overweight, and more than 20 percent are at risk for being overweight (Ogden, Flegal, Carroll, & Johnson, 2002) and thus more likely to be overweight as adults. Obesity is associated with a host of other health problems, including diabetes and high cholesterol levels (American Academy of Pediatrics Committee on Nutrition, 2003). Its effects spill over into other domains as well: Obese children are teased by their peers; viewed as less attractive, energetic, and competent by adults; and placed at a disadvantage in competition for college admission and financial support (Frost, Brown, Sutterby, & Thornton, 2004). Exercise and fresh air help create healthy appetites and, in combination with good nutrition, can help counteract this alarming trend, and the effects are long lasting: Children who establish healthy patterns of physical activity early in life are less likely to be overweight in adolescence (Moore et al., 2003). The outdoor environment is more conducive to play involving vigorous physical contact, which children enjoy and need. Outdoors there is more space to run and wrestle and less chance of bumping into sharp corners on furniture.

Motor Skills.   Outdoor play spaces provide settings and equipment that motivate children to practice using their bodies and holding their bodies erect, walking, running, climbing, pedaling, pushing, and pulling. Physical education experts tell us that the fundamental motor skills learned in early childhood form the basis for the specialized use of those skills in games and sports, which provide opportunities for building confidence and friendships—an example of how physical development is related to emotional and social qualities. The enjoyment, camaraderie, and health benefits are reaped not only in the school years but throughout life. Motor skills are classified as (1) body management or stability skills, (2) locomotor skills involving movement through space, and (3) manipulative skills, including projection (e.g., throwing, kicking) and reception (catching) (Gallahue & Donnelly, 2003).

Social-Emotional Benefits

Self-Efficacy.   You will recall from Chapter 5 that self-efficacy means a child's judgment of what he or she can do with a skill (Bandura, 1986). It is a personal characteristic of self-judgment that parents and educators should cultivate in young children. Self-efficacy, particularly in motor skills, can be readily observed during outdoor play, and the feelings of self-efficacy gained as children master climbing or pedaling will spill over into other aspects of life. Children who are free to explore, observe, and imitate develop confidence. Children with high self-efficacy tackle challenges and try several strategies until they succeed. Children with low self-efficacy doubt their abilities and quit trying.

Adults promote children's self-efficacy by allowing them to try things that interest them and by seeing that they do not get hurt. They hamper self-efficacy by being overly cautious or expressing worry over children's safety, thus limiting opportunities to explore. They give children the gift of time to explore and to stick to a task or skill until they master it rather than hurry them away to do something adults consider to be safer.

Expressing and Handling Feelings.   Children need opportunities to express all types of feelings, from joyful exuberance to frustration and anger at a playmate's lack of cooperation. They need to learn to manage their feelings, to control their anger, and to understand that sadness or disappointment can be temporary. Studies have shown that exercise combats depression and reduces anxiety in adults (Reynolds, 2011), and it is certainly reasonable to think that the same benefits would apply to children.

Probably the most important aspect of outdoor play for promoting emotional well-being is contact with nature. Just carrying a fussy baby outside can engender calm. Bohling-Philippi (2006) suggests that for children who might be angry, frightened, or depressed, nature can help heal in several ways. Experiencing firsthand the reassuring

cycles of nature, where spring follows winter and sunshine follows rain, helps children accept the ups and downs of their own feelings. Children, like adults, find solace in gardening. Caring for creatures smaller than themselves casts children in a new role, where they learn they are capable of responsibility, tenderness, and empathy.

Gardening is an outdoor activity rich with possibilities for sensory experiences and scientific discoveries. Watching the cycle of growth from seed to plant to harvest brings children into connection with nature.

Getting Along with Others. Living in harmony with other human beings may be one of the outstanding challenges for the whole human race, and the skills for doing so begin in childhood. The skills and dispositions children practice with plants and animals outdoors can apply in their relationships with others. Games and explorations that are not possible inside invite encounters among children, often bringing together those who do not usually play with each other, thus creating opportunities for new friendships. Group games such as tag and hide-and-seek are often an exciting part of outdoor play. In addition to the physical exertion involved in chasing one another and the mathematical skills required to "count to 100," such games often require children to hammer out rules about what is fair or unfair and about who wins. They must also learn to take the perspective of another as they search for a hiding place from which they cannot be seen.

Feeling Connected to Nature. Even more important, and more lasting, than the factual information you provide to children about the outdoor world are the dispositions toward it that you cultivate; some examples are curiosity, awe, love, reverence. These qualities seem inborn in children, but Rachel Carson (1965/1998), a pioneer in the environmental movement, argues that, in order to keep these dispositions alive, a child "needs the companionship of at least one adult who can share it, rediscovering with him the joy, excitement, and mystery of the world we live in"(p.55). She encourages adults who may feel inadequately prepared for this job by emphasizing that "it is not half so important to *know* as to *feel*." According to Carson,

> If facts are the seeds that later produce knowledge and wisdom, then the emotions and the impressions of the senses are the fertile soil in which the seeds must grow. . . . It is more important to pave the way for the child to want to know than to put him on a diet of facts he is not ready to assimilate. (pp. 55–56)

For many people, the relationship with nature that they develop in early childhood provides a spiritual sustenance that shapes and nourishes their entire lives. Jane

Goodall (1999), who has devoted her life to the study of wild chimpanzees in Tanzania and now advocates for humane treatment of animals throughout the world, traces her profound love of nature and enduring belief in the meaning of life to a childhood spent outside "playing in the secret places in the garden, learning about nature" and to a mother who nurtured that passion and empathy for living things (p. 6).

Cognitive Benefits

The physical benefits of outdoor play support learning directly: Rae Pica, a children's physical activity specialist, explains, "While sitting increases fatigue and reduces concentration, movement feeds oxygen, water, and glucose to the brain, optimizing its performance" (2006, p. 112). Physical exertion in combination with the experience of being in nature helps the brain to focus, as a group of neuroscientists found on a rafting excursion where they were cut off from the digital distractions of modern life for a few days. David Strayer, a University of Utah psychology professor who led the trip, argues that nature refreshes the brain. "Our senses change. They kind of recalibrate—you notice sounds, like these crickets chirping; you hear the river, the sounds, the smells, you become more connected to the physical environment, the earth, rather than the artificial environment" (Richtel, 2010, p. 2).

Self-Regulation.   Self-regulation, as noted in Chapter 3, is an essential quality for success in school and life with roots in earliest infancy. Because it involves the ability to inhibit behaviors, it is typically discussed in the context of social-emotional development. Because it includes the ability to focus one's attention (National Research Council and Institute of Medicine, 2000), it contributes to cognitive development in a fundamental way: Children who can focus their attention are clearly at an advantage for learning. To understand this connection, we need to look more closely at the concept of attention. Psychologist William James (1892/1962) proposed two categories of attention: voluntary and involuntary. Voluntary attention involves intentionally focusing on a problem or task; it requires effort and can be fatiguing. Involuntary attention is a more passive response to something an individual happens to notice in the environment. Experiences calling upon involuntary attention are thought to serve as a respite, during which the capacity for voluntary attention is restored (Kaplan, 1995). Outdoor play is rich with possibilities for this restoration to occur. Children don't have to work to concentrate on their play or on all the things within the natural environment that are intrinsically absorbing. The rest from the rigors of voluntary attention is refreshing and ultimately strengthens their ability to use it for tasks like listening to stories or solving problems. This is particularly true for the more than 2 million children in the United States with attention-deficit/hyperactivity disorder (ADHD) who have to work even harder to pay voluntary attention and thus need more chances to rest and recover (Taylor, Kuo, & Sullivan, 2001).

Symbolic Play.   Symbolic play shows us where children are in their cognitive development and provides the means by which they progress to higher levels. At the earliest stages, children need very realistic props to support their pretending. As they gain experience and proficiency, they are able to substitute objects that resemble the real thing less and less, until finally they can pretend with only their words and gestures. They are using mental representations to stand for objects that are not present. When two or more children engage in this type of play together, they need to come to agreement about what particular objects or actions will represent—an accomplishment that involves taking into account another person's point of view, also known as *cognitive decentering*. Mental representation and cognitive decentering are two prerequisites for academic learning, according to Russian psychologist Daniel Elkonin, a student of Lev Vygotsky (1977, 1978, cited in Bodrova & Leong, 2004). Research demonstrates that children engage in more symbolic play and complex interactive dramatic play outdoors than indoors (Frost, Wortham, & Reifel, 2012; Shim, Herwig, & Shelly, 2001). We can conclude that outdoor play promotes cognitive development not only by providing children with a break from thinking, as noted earlier, but also by evoking more of the type of activity that involves high-level thinking.

Curriculum Content: Art.   Because it includes exposure to the natural world and access to the same sorts of art materials found indoors, a high-quality outdoor play area provides ideal conditions for meeting the goals for art that were mentioned in the previous chapter: The natural world is a feast of sensory input: colors sparkling and fading in shifting light; warm sunshine and cool breezes caressing the skin; sounds of birds or crickets and leaves rustling in the wind; the scents of newly mown grass and fresh rainfall; the sweet taste of cold water after strenuous play. The infinite and subtle variations of colors and shapes invite children to notice fine distinctions and stretch their thinking. Is the sky always the same shade of blue? Is it even always blue? How many shades of brown or green are found in a garden or wooded area? Children who marvel at the symmetry of a spider's web glistening with dew are developing an awareness and appreciation of beauty, just as the artists throughout history who have found inspiration in nature. Because there is usually more room and messes are more acceptable outdoors, children can use materials such as paint or clay more freely. A length of newsprint stretched out along a fence elicits more exuberant brushstrokes and perhaps grander intentions than do confining sheets on an easel. It may also invite children to paint alongside one another, providing opportunities to see things from multiple perspectives as they make their ideas visible.

Curriculum Content: Language Arts.   Language explodes outdoors, perhaps because there is so much to talk about or perhaps because children are freed from the constraints of four walls and reminders to "use inside voices." Children delight in singing games and chants that are full of rhymes and repetition and thus are natural ways to cultivate the phonological awareness so essential to literacy. As we mentioned earlier, dramatic play, which provides fertile ground for developing the abstract thought and mental representation skills required for language and literacy, is more likely to occur outdoors than indoors—a finding that holds true regardless of overall program quality (Frost et al., 2012; Shim et al., 2001). Vocabulary growth surges as children learn words for what they observe and take on particular roles in their play. It is said that children begin their journey toward literacy by "learning to read the world" (Rosenkoetter & Knapp-Philo, 2006, p. 1)—in other words, by learning to make sense of their environment and experiences. The sights, sounds, smells, and textures they encounter outdoors furnish the richest possible text for them to read, and they tackle it with zeal. If you have observed children watching insects, you know that their universal fascination with natural phenomena motivates keen observation and extended concentration—the same skills that children use to decipher printed texts.

Curriculum Content: Science and Math. An outdoor play area is an environmental laboratory for learning about nature, weather, plants, animals, and insects and about such concepts as number, speed, gravity, height, weight, and balance. A laboratory is a place in which one tries things out. It is action packed, not quiet like a library. It is full of experimental situations that are ideal for supporting math and science goals. Children sort

Children's universal fascination with living creatures motivates keen observation and extended concentration.

and classify leaves and rocks, compare quantities or size when they notice whose pail has more sand or which caterpillar is biggest, and practice one-to-one correspondence when they play games like "Duck, Duck, Goose." They use language to describe spatial relationships when they talk about being "above" everyone on the climber or "behind" the tree. When they argue about who ran farthest or fastest, they are demonstrating their growing ability to "do math" as well as their confidence and willingness to apply that ability critically. From the puddle that freezes over on the first cold night of fall to the crocus bloom in spring, the outdoor environment is replete with things to stimulate children's innate curiosity about the world. With the help of their teachers, children can investigate things that capture their interest, thereby acquiring thinking and problem-solving skills as they broaden their knowledge of the natural world.

❀ **Talk It Over** ❀

How much time do you spend out in nature (e.g., hiking, camping, gardening)? How would you describe the physical or psychological effect of these experiences on your life?

THE OUTDOOR PLAY ENVIRONMENT

How is outdoor play treated in programs where you have observed or worked? Do adults see their role as limited to setting up the equipment and supervising from the sidelines, stepping in only to solve squabbles or prevent injuries? Is outdoor playtime viewed as no more than an opportunity for children to let off steam while teachers relax a little? Unfortunately, a number of studies have shown that this is frequently the prevailing attitude (Brown & Burger, 1984; Davies, 1996, 1997; Jones, 1989). Given the huge potential of outdoor play for supporting children's development in every domain, we hope that you will agree that outdoor play deserves the same investment of your time and energy as your indoor classroom. At least one study has shown that children engage in more constructive play in high-quality outdoor environments with more natural elements, as opposed to more repetitive, functional types of play in lower-quality environments (Hestenes, Shim, & DeBord, 2007). One tool you might use to evaluate and improve the outdoor experiences you offer children is *The Preschool Outdoor Environment Scale* (POEMS) (DeBord et al., 2005). Research has demonstrated a strong correlation between higher scores on this instrument and children's cognitive and emotional development (Kintner-Duffy, Mims, Hestenes, & Hestenes, 2011).

Planning

Adults should give as much attention to planning outdoor experiences as they do to planning any other part of the curriculum. All activities should be varied and challenging. Equipment should be rearranged or new items introduced often enough to maintain children's interest and entice them to explore. A daily balance of quiet and vigorous activities should always be planned. At times, virtually the whole curriculum can take place outdoors. Children enjoy having art, music, and literature outdoors. These activities allow children quiet interludes that keep them from becoming fatigued. Each child's motor needs should be considered, and equipment should be arranged to challenge and test skills. Many scientific concepts can be learned outdoors, and these should be planned on a regular basis. Spontaneous interests may supersede the plan, but plans must be made, or a program will surely stagnate.

Time for Play

How much time should you plan for outdoor play? How often? National Association for the Education of Young Children (NAEYC) accreditation standards mandate daily opportunities for outdoor play except in cases of severe weather or other health hazard (2007b). This means that you should take children outside unless the one of the following conditions exist: windchill at or below 15 degrees Fahrenheit, heat index at or above 90 degrees, or smog alert issued by local authorities (American Academy of Pediatrics et al., 2002). DeBord and her colleagues (2005) recommend that, at a minimum, children go outside for 30 minutes of play twice a day. It would take double that amount of time to meet guidelines established by the National Association for Sports and Physical Education (NASPE, 2002), which state that preschool-aged children should have daily opportunities for *at least* 60 minutes of physical activity in unstructured settings as well as another 60 minutes of structured activities. Research suggests that children in early childhood programs average less than 8 minutes of moderate to vigorous physical activity per hour of attendance (Pate et al., 2004). This means that children in care for eight (or more) hours per day would accumulate no more than half the targeted amount of exercise, and it is unlikely that busy families would be able to provide another hour each evening after work in between supper and household chores. Ideally, then, a full-day program would schedule two hours of outdoor play per day and make sure to include both plenty of time for self-selected activity as well as some adult-initiated games or physical motor challenges.

Spaces to Support Play

Children need open space and room to move quickly without interfering with others. Accreditation standards stipulate at least 75 square feet of play space per child, with a total area sufficient to accommodate at least one-third of the program's total enrollment at any one time (NAEYC, 2007b). Anita Rui Olds (2001), the child-care design expert first mentioned in Chapter 6, recommends that at least 56 of that 75 square feet per child consist of green space. She adds that high-quality programs will exceed this minimum, providing 200 square feet of outdoor space per child, with about three-fourths of that devoted to green space. Like the indoor environment, the outdoor environment should provide a variety of play opportunities, including spaces for privacy and solitary play, as well as spaces to accommodate small and large groups of children. Ideally, there will be a variety of ground cover in addition to appropriate cushioning in fall zones, including grass, pebbles, or mulch, as well as paved surfaces for riding toys. In addition to sand and water play areas, natural elements such as earthen mounds, trees, shrubs, nonpoisonous plants, and spaces for observing animal life (e.g., bird feeders) will make the space more inviting for children and adults (DeBord et al., 2005).

Safety and Health

For the well-being of all children, a playground should meet the guidelines established by the local licensing agency, by the American Academy of Pediatrics, and by the *Public Playground Safety Handbook (U.S. Consumer Product Safety Commission, 2010*). These guidelines protect children by establishing safety standards, such as minimum amounts of cushioning material under and around climbing equipment.

The space should be enclosed by a sturdy fence, with clear pathways from one area to another, well outside the "fall zones" of swings or climbing equipment. It should be well drained and should be at least partially shaded. While there are many benefits to sunshine, too much of a good thing can be harmful. Protect children from overexposure to the sun by providing shade on the playground and scheduling outdoor playtime for the mornings or late afternoons rather than the hours when the sun is at its highest. Use sunscreen and encourage children to wear hats.

Children—and adults—need access to clean drinking water outdoors. An outdoor drinking fountain will promote the healthy habit of getting plenty of water before, during, and after exercise. It will make supervision easier as well because adults won't have to leave their posts so often to accompany thirsty children indoors. In lieu of a drinking fountain, you can carry water outside in a large thermal jug, but then you will have to choose between generating waste with disposable cups or figuring out how to manage reusable cups in a safe and sanitary manner. Of course, a natural consequence of consuming lots of water is making frequent trips to the toilet, suggesting that the ideal outdoor play area is equipped with toilet facilities that are easily accessible and supervised.

While adults are responsible for ensuring that playgrounds are safe for children, they must also recognize children's need to be challenged. It is helpful for planners to distinguish between the concepts of challenge and hazard. Child development professionals know and celebrate the fact that children are inherently risk takers. Children seek challenges and purposely try to test the limits of their abilities. When faced with a boring or insufficiently challenging environment, they are likely to create their own challenges by using the equipment in ways that adults deem inappropriate (Frost et al., 2004). Confronted with a toddler-sized climber/slide, many four-year-olds will repeatedly scramble up and leap off or dive down headfirst, despite repeated admonitions by their frustrated teachers to "slide down on your bottom."

Hazards, on the other hand, are dangers resulting from conditions over which a child has no knowledge or awareness—usually poor design or poor maintenance. Hazards include protrusions that can catch clothing and lead to strangulation; openings wider than 3.5 inches and narrower than 9 inches—in other words, large enough for a child's torso but too small for the child's head to slip through; unenclosed heights from which children can fall; hard surfaces beneath climbing structures; and equipment that can pinch or shear fingers. With careful planning, it is possible to reduce, if not eliminate, hazards while still meeting children's need for challenges. "What more," asks Olds, "can we wish for our children than that they live self-confident in their ability to enjoy the mystery and fascination of conquering the unknown?" (2001, p. 411).

❀   **Talk It Over**   ❀

Have you observed children taking risks in their outdoor play? Give examples. Do (or would) you feel comfortable supervising them in such a situation? Why or why not? What steps could you take to support children's need to challenge themselves without compromising your responsibility to keep them safe?

Beauty

The beauty of an outdoor play area—or lack thereof—will greatly influence its ability to deliver all the benefits we have described in this chapter. Certainly, it will be difficult for children to absorb a sense of the order and symmetry of nature in a barren, ugly space. Cluttered spaces and neglected equipment do little to promote feelings of tranquility or stewardship toward the natural world. Beautiful spaces invite us to linger; they delight without overwhelming the senses. Far from being a luxury or frill, beauty is an essential element of what Olds (2001) calls "the spirit of place" (p.15). She cautions us, however, to think carefully about the meaning of beauty in an environment for children and strike a balance between function and aesthetics. A typical early childhood playground focuses almost entirely on function, making sure that the area is securely fenced, that equipment is properly anchored, and that fall zones are covered with protective cushioning. Well-meaning adults sometimes attempt to make a basic safe playground more attractive by adding climbing structures or play stations in the bold, intense colors that we assume children prefer. Olds argues that these "arbitrary aesthetics . . . overwhelm children—[leaving] little room for personalization (p. 23).

Another alternative is to use aesthetics to support the function of the outdoor space. Imagine a playground, for example, where, instead of a metal or plastic sliding board plopped in the middle of an expanse of wood chips, there were a long grassy slope with a built-in chute for sliding down and stairs alongside it for climbing back to the top. This is a case of using an appealing curve in the

The beauty of an outdoor play area—or lack thereof—will greatly influence its ability to deliver all its potential benefits.

natural environment to satisfy children's urges to climb, to survey their surroundings from above, and to experience the exhilaration of hurtling down an incline. And it does all this with a greater degree of safety because building it into the hillside means there are no places from which to fall.

Once a basic outdoor play space has been created with an eye toward beauty, your part will be to help maintain that quality by modeling and teaching children to put things back where they belong and to pick up litter. Even if you have inherited a barren, unattractive playground, you can introduce elements of beauty, perhaps adding flowers or shrubs or erecting a sunshade in a soft, natural hue over the sandpit. Whenever adding to or changing an outdoor environment, think carefully about the purpose or function of what you propose. What goals for children will it promote? It is probably second nature for early childhood professionals to think at the same time about how those goals can be accomplished in the safest possible way. Thinking about beauty in the early childhood environment has not been as ingrained in our consciousness, so it may take some time to develop that habit. It may help to remind yourself that the early childhood facility is where you and the children spend many of your waking hours—where you live. Surely the outdoor play area deserves the same attention to beauty that many would shower on their patio or garden at home.

Equipment

The same guidelines for determining an adequate number of play spaces apply outdoors as indoors. If children are having an unusually large number of disagreements on the playground, then the number of play spaces may not be sufficient—perhaps there are 15 places, and 25 children are using the yard. Or perhaps the playground has the wrong kind of equipment. If the sandbox is overcrowded, perhaps the group needs two places to dig. If the swings have too many customers, perhaps the group needs more swings or needs the type where two children can work one swing together. Tricycles double their capacity when equipped with trailers that enable two children to cooperate.

To augment the anchored play equipment and wheeled toys that may already be provided in your outdoor play area to foster large motor skills, consider adding a balance beam, a crawl-through tunnel, jump ropes, hoops, batting tees, and, of course, a variety of balls. A woodworking bench and large hollow blocks will inspire constructive play as well as provide additional opportunities for gross motor development. One or more picnic tables will be useful for outdoor snacks; as work surfaces for painting, drawing, or sculpting with clay; or simply as a setting for small group conversations. Platforms or puppet stages encourage dramatic play. Think about how you can enrich the space with windchimes or colorful banners (DeBord et al., 2005).

In addition to manufactured equipment, children will need equipment to make full use of the natural elements of the outdoor area, including a variety of containers for pouring, carrying, and straining or sifting water and sand. Plastic toy shovels are probably adequate for sand play, but real, high-quality tools (e.g., rakes, shovels, trowels, hoes) are needed for gardening. Hoses and sprinklers support science experiences and are just plain fun. Table 10–1 lists suggested equipment for supporting children's motor skill development.

Well-planned outdoor play areas accommodate the needs of *all* children for fresh air and exercise.

Including All Children

It is important to remember that all girls and boys need fresh air and outdoor play—that is, infants and toddlers as well as older children and children with disabilities as well as those who are developing typically. This means that your outdoor play area may need a protected space for crawlers to feel the grass under their knees or for toddlers to try their emerging skills without being run over by the older children. Other alterations will support the inclusion of children with disabilities. These include surfacing on pathways to accommodate wheelchairs, ramps to provide alternate access to elevated play decks, back support on swings and bouncers, and elevated sand tables, garden beds, or work surfaces so that children in wheelchairs or standers can play alongside their peers.

Many features of the outdoor play environment are particularly beneficial for children with various types of disabilities. We have already mentioned how children with ADHD seem to function better outdoors. Balance beams and tricycles can be therapeutic for children with motor coordination difficulties, and swinging is both fun and helpful for children with sensory

TABLE 10–1 Supporting Motor Skills in Early Childhood

Type of Skill	Examples	Suggestions for Support
Body management skills	❁ bouncing on a trampoline, jumping board, or mattress ❁ hopping with eyes opened and closed ❁ walking a balance beam forward and backward ❁ climbing and descending ladders and stairs ❁ suspending from climbing structures	❁ pretend games (be a snake, frog, kangaroo, or duck) ❁ movement challenges (sit and rolling forward, backward, and around)
Locomotor skills	❁ crawling ❁ walking backward and forward ❁ running toward a goal, with a stop-and-go signal, on tiptoes ❁ jumping ❁ galloping ❁ hopping	❁ games (tag, Simon Says) ❁ hurdle jumping (bamboo pole, placed with one end on the ground and the other end propped up on a sawhorse, so that each child can select the appropriate height
Projection and reception skills	❁ throwing ❁ kicking ❁ batting ❁ catching	❁ big balls and beanbags with large targets such as wastebaskets ❁ plastic bats and balls ❁ batting off a tee ❁ adult partner for young child to minimize frustration (A child who can't throw straight isn't a good partner for one with minimum catching skills.)
Mechanical skills	❁ pedaling ❁ pumping	❁ variety of wheel toys appropriate to each age and ability level ❁ a paved "one-way" pathway encircling the yard to keep wheel toys out of other children's way ❁ swings that two children can push and pull, or ❁ a ramp under swings (children hold tight to the swing chains and with the swing behind them walk backward up the inclined plane as far as possible, then sit on the swing and let gravity carry them forward) ❁ adults stand in front, and children can reach out toward adults' hands with their feet

problems. Conversely, nearly any improvement you make for children with disabilities will enhance play for everyone. For example, one program incorporated a "Sound Path" into its playground so that a child with congenital blindness could participate more fully in outdoor play. The program staff created six stations by installing items that children could strike to create a variety of sounds. Examples included three inverted metal washtubs and a series of copper pipes in various lengths, suspended from a strong string. Children could strike these instruments with their hands, dowels, or other implements. A semi-submerged loop of ridged drainage pipe marked a path around the playground, with breaks at each station. The child who was blind pushed a small cart along the path, guided by the sound of the wheels rubbing against the ridges in the pipe. These additions enriched the playground for all children (Kern & Wolery, 2002).

Including children with disabilities is as much a matter of attitude as it is retrofitting a playground. Universal design is a concept widely applied today in everything from architecture to clothing and Web page design. The idea is to devise "products and environments to be usable by all people, to the greatest extent possible, without the need for adaptation or specialized design" (Center for Universal Design, 2010). Boundless Playgrounds, a national nonprofit advocacy organization dedicated to promoting barrier-free playgrounds, reminds us that playground equipment that makes it possible for children with and without disabilities to play together is fun for everyone (National Center for Boundless Playgrounds, 2008).

Storage

Carefully selected outdoor equipment represents a sizable investment. That investment will be wasted if the equipment is never used because teachers and children cannot get at it easily. It will be wasted if equipment is damaged through exposure to the elements or careless stacking and thus unable to serve the intended purpose of supporting children's development. A storage shed or closet should be conveniently located and well organized so that it is easy for children as well as for adults to get equipment out and to put it away again. Inadequate storage for equipment is often a factor in teachers' distaste for outdoor duty. If they must lift heavy items into place or stumble over a tangled heap of tricycles to reach the balls, they are likely to dislike the task.

Once a satisfactory storage arrangement is achieved, staff must agree about who will put away equipment. Many harmonious relationships can be disrupted if staff members slip away just when this hard part of the day arrives. This is far less likely to happen if the storage is organized so that every item has a designated space. Shelving with large bins or baskets, clearly labeled, makes it easy to sort and retrieve loose items such as balls or sand toys. Garden tools, hoops, and hoses can be hung on hooks along the wall. If the lowest shelf is sufficiently raised above the floor, the area beneath can be divided into designated parking spaces for tricycles and wheeled toys, making it easier to access the entire facility. These steps make the task more manageable and thus less odious for adults and children alike. As a consequence, adults are more likely to model a positive attitude that will make children want to help with the chore.

Maintenance

Regular, careful inspection and maintenance of outdoor play equipment is essential for several reasons. State licensing regulations may mandate that program staff conduct monthly inspections with written documentation of any problems noted and solutions put into place. Outdoor equipment is expensive, and maintaining it is a way to protect your investment. Because outdoor equipment is subjected to weather and heavy use, safety hazards regularly crop up on even the most well-planned playgrounds. Wood structures splinter, bolts loosen or disappear, and gates sag on their hinges, creating gaps that can entrap inquisitive children, all of which make a play yard unsafe. Moreover, careful maintenance is a wise investment of your energy as you strive to guide children's behavior. Recall from Chapter 6 that indirect guidance includes providing an adequate number of play spaces so that it is easy for children to remain constructively occupied. A tricycle or another toy that doesn't work frustrates children and does not contribute to the play space, so oil wheel toys regularly and repair or replace broken parts. Most adults can learn to use pliers to make minor repairs. Children like to help. Remove nonworking toys that need more extensive repairs and bring them to the attention of the maintenance staff.

ADULT GUIDANCE: TEACHING WHILE SUPERVISING

Your guidance of outdoor play begins with your own positive attitude and enthusiasm for it. Teachers who find excuses to keep children indoors—ignoring the resources of the playground and of nature—or who relegate playground duty to their colleagues are missing valuable opportunities to support children's development. All teachers—male and female, novice and experienced—should participate in all aspects of the program. Beginning assistants are frequently given lots of time on outdoor duty. One student teacher said, "Somehow I always get sent out there with the children. I wonder if the other teachers are afraid they might get cold." The student went on to relate what a marvelous time he had playing with the children in the snowy yard. He had helped them examine snowflakes under the magnifying glass, knocked snow from branches, and made snow angels "just like Peter in *The Snowy Day*." Those other teachers may have thought that playground duty was being done by the "low person on the totem pole," but this intelligent young man hadn't allowed himself to treat the children as though it were.

You may remember playground supervisors from your own childhood just standing around, waiting until something unpleasant happened and then trying to do something about it. Research indicates that adults spend more time watching rather than engaging with children outdoors (Hestenes et al., 2007). Given what you have learned about the power of indirect guidance, it should come as no surprise that teachers more frequently support and facilitate children's experiences on outdoor environments rated as higher quality (DeBord et al., 2005). Certainly supervision to ensure safety and intervene before accidents happen is a big part of the adult's job during outdoor play—just as it is during indoor play. But supervision means more than merely watching children (Sull, 2003). An early childhood professional must also interact with children, stay close to them, and listen to what they say, what they ask, and what they need. Alert and responsive adults are able to make adjustments, as needed, to prevent or solve

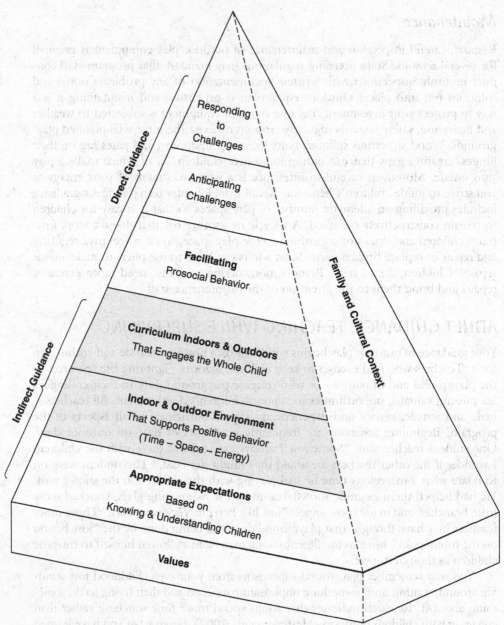

Responding
to
Challenges

Anticipating
Challenges

Facilitating
Prosocial Behavior

Curriculum Indoors & Outdoors
That Engages the Whole Child

Indoor & Outdoor Environment
That Supports Positive Behavior
(Time – Space – Energy)

Appropriate Expectations
Based on
Knowing & Understanding Children

Values

Direct Guidance

Family and Cultural Context

Indirect Guidance

FIGURE 10–1   The guidance pyramid: Play and learning

difficulties. For example, as a young toddler begins using the play yard independently, an adult will stay close by to lend a supporting hand when necessary, thereby avoiding some tumbles that might discourage further exploration. The adult can also prevent one child from inadvertently bumping or pushing into another child, causing a fall. Because young toddlers have a low center of gravity, they tumble easily. Fortunately, they are also well padded, so the falls usually don't hurt, and an adult need not say much more than "Oops! That must have hurt. Hop up and brush off the dirt," and the child will be on the go again.

Even on play equipment that is set up to be reasonably safe for the ages of the children using it, responsible adults must stay nearby while children try their skills. Having enough adults present and interacting with children on the playground makes exploration possible for children who may not always understand the possible consequences of their actions. Adults should stop a behavior only when it is potentially dangerous to a child or to others. As suggested by the guidance pyramid in Figure 10–1, a curriculum that engages the whole child—body, mind, and feelings—prevents problems.

Preparation

Dressed for the Job. One important way for adults to enjoy the outdoors is to dress for it—warm clothes in the winter and cool clothes in the summer. Early childhood professionals are among the lucky few who may wear casual clothing to work. Nothing else is as practical for working with young children. Comfortable shoes give you firm footing on walks, in the yard, on stairs, and when carrying children and equipment. Warm scarves, mittens, boots, and a coat that can take the rugged use it will get are important in winter climates. Hoods attached to jackets mean that hats are always handy. When programs allow it, teachers should feel free to dress in modest shorts with cool shirts in summer and warmer climates. A hat will shield eyes and face from the sun. You will meet the outdoor period with the same enthusiasm as the children if you are properly dressed and if you also use the time outdoors to get refreshed.

Helping Children Get Ready. Getting dressed to go outdoors is one of the personal care routines that will occupy much of your time as an early childhood educator. Like feeding, toileting, and resting, you can treat it as something to be gotten out of the way as quickly as possible, or you can recognize its potential for enhancing all types of development and plan accordingly. The results are likely to be much happier, for you as well as for the children in your care, if you choose the latter course.

What types of development are fostered during dressing and undressing? Certainly, pulling on jackets and manipulating zippers provide opportunities for children to use their large and small muscles. Dressing or undressing "all by myself" can promote a sense of self-efficacy and set the stage for spontaneous discussions about dressing for the weather that will be much more meaningful than the contrived activities so often included in circle or calendar time. In addition, if children are encouraged to assist each other with buttons and zippers, the dressing and undressing ritual can provide chances to practice cooperation and helpfulness.

As with all other personal care routines, your role is to offer just the right amount of support and assistance while encouraging children to do as much as they can for themselves. You may do most of the work when dressing infants or children with severe disabilities, but if you talk about what you are doing and pause to give them a chance to participate, even they can help, by holding still, perhaps, or by extending an arm. As children become a little older or more skillful, the balance shifts, and you provide more encouragement and less physical help. You might tell a three- or four-year-old, "I'll start your zipper, and you pull it up." You might show them the "magic trick" of spreading their coats on the floor in front of them with collars at their feet, slipping arms into the sleeves, and flipping the coats over their heads. Or you might simply remind them that snowpants go on before boots and jackets before mittens. In your zeal to promote independence, however, don't forget that tenderly helping to fasten a coat or tie a scarf is a prime opportunity to connect with individual children and show them that you care. Encouraging children to help each other with these tasks serves the double benefit of giving them pleasure and practice while taking some of the burden off your shoulders.

You use indirect guidance to facilitate these routines in several ways. Taking time and not rushing through them is an important step. This means planning extra time for the transition to outdoor play as weather turns colder and children begin wearing more clothing. It also means having an adult ready to go outside with a few children as soon as they are ready so that the other adults can take the time to help children who need it. This avoids the stress of overheated and impatient children as well as overburdened adults. And knowing that they can go outside immediately provides a powerful motivation for children to learn to dress themselves. Teachers can take turns setting up the outdoor learning environment each day and going out with the children who are dressed for their outdoor period while others are still struggling with zippers and mittens.

Indirect guidance also includes managing the environment and materials. Caregivers can provide individual spaces for children to keep their outdoor clothing and enough room on the floor for them to dress without hampering each others' efforts. They can encourage parents to provide clothing that is appropriate for the weather, suitable for outdoor play, and easy to manage (e.g., large zippers, elastic waists). Centers can keep a supply of extra clothing and boots on hand for emergencies and suggest sources for inexpensive clothing (e.g., thrift stores, consignment shops) to families for whom money is a problem.

Physical-Motor Skills

Adults often find vigorous outdoor activity as enjoyable and tension releasing for them as it is for the children. Playing follow the leader, walking in the "giant's tracks," flying like a bird or an airplane, and playing ball or some version of shadow tag can be as much fun for you as for the children. Teachers serve as models for children and can help establish a pattern of delight in vigorous activity that will have lifelong benefits. Some children need to be taught how to relate to the outdoors, while others seem to teach us. As one renowned author and educator put it, "When people ask me how long I've been teaching movement, dance and rhythms to young children, I tell them, 'I've never taught one child how to move or dance! My claim to fame is moving, dancing, laughing, and celebrating with them! They already know!'" (Chenfeld, 2007, p. 2).

The urge for independence and achievement can be a highly motivating drive for a child. When children challenge themselves on climbing structures, for example, they usually climb only as high as they feel safe, but some may be tempted to exceed their limits when urged on by other children. Wise teachers stay close by and never urge one child to achieve a particular height or speed just because another child has. They help children identify appropriate challenges for their emerging skills. For example, saying, "Since you can climb this ladder, Jim, you might try the tree house tomorrow" encourages a child to continue developing his climbing skills.

Imitating Peers. Modeling or imitation is an important method of learning. Outdoor play provides an opportunity for children to imitate peers and to compare motor skills with others on an informal, noncompetitive basis. If something looks like fun, children will want to try it and won't need any encouragement from adults. Adults can help by having several pieces of equipment available so that one child does not have to give up a place to allow a novice to try. For example, a skillful tricycle driver may lead those who are less skillful, or a child dangling by her knees on the jungle gym might encourage others to try the "trick."

The urge for independence and achievement can be highly motivating for children. When they challenge themselves on climbing structures, they usually climb only as high as they feel safe. Teachers can help children identify appropriate challenges for their emerging skills.

An adult may need to protect less skillful children from the ridicule of the more skillful with comments such as, "After Carlos practices a while, he'll be able to do it like you," or "Don't you remember only a short time ago when you were learning?" or "Yes, Joan is taking longer, but that's all right. She's learning." This helps the beginner to know that other children were once beginners, too. It is never good to motivate children by comparing them to their peers. Avoid statements like, "Victor climbed up here; you try it," or "See if you can beat Andrea to the top of the climber." The child might be secretly admiring Andrea, but this places the child in open competition, which may leave both children quite uncomfortable.

❀ **Talk It Over** ❀

What are some ways adults guided you as a child that fostered or inhibited your motor skill development? Do you think you were encouraged or discouraged from particular activities based on your gender?

Social-Emotional Development

Outdoor play allows children to express their feelings, let off steam, shout, run vigorously, or rest as desired. Children need to be free to shout and run. In guiding their behavior, you should keep these needs in mind. The time spent outdoors should be simpler and less confining than indoors. The rules you state and the behavior you stop must be important. During rough-and-tumble play, for example, an adult should stay nearby and make it clear that the goal is to have fun, so participants should agree to stop if one says "Up." On the other hand, there are usually few reasons for limiting children's noise outdoors. Just as you do indoors, you can help with social learning outdoors by guiding children to work together. For instance, you can encourage one to ride sitting in the trailer while another child pedals the tricycle. Avoid structuring the time so tightly that they have no opportunity to do what they want. If a child does not want to socialize, permit playing alone. If a child prefers climbing to carpentry, then allow that decision. Be sensitive to children's need for quiet places to experience a little downtime. A swing can be such a place to escape. The sandbox can be a restful area. An autoharp under a tree or storybooks to look at and to read should meet the needs of children who like things less active or who become tired from vigorous activity.

Children need to learn the rules of using and caring for the outdoor environment, property, and equipment. These rules are important to protect children, to facilitate individual learning, and to preserve what you have for tomorrow and for future classes. Rules and reasons for all rules can be short and factual, given in a positive tone that anticipates that the child will follow your guidance. You needn't apologize for setting limits or for refusing to allow a child to do something. Explain that tricycles won't last long if they are abused by being run into each other, that wooden blocks will split if dropped from heights, and that painted surfaces will chip if hammered. Teach them that the carpentry bench, rather than a fence or a part of the building, is the place for hammering, and be sure to follow through, enforcing your rules consistently.

Just as indoors, direct guidance outdoors should be very personal; that is, it should be addressed to a specific child in quiet, reassuring tones. Shouts across the play yard are usually ineffective. Children don't know that the shouts are meant for them, and they may not actually hear what is said. Rules or limits related to safe use of equipment often must be repeated numerous times before they become effective in children's actions. Memory is required, and the rules must be recalled at the right time. Use verbal guidance such as, "Both hands on the climber," "Drive the tricycle this way around the circle," and "Play inside the fence." These are samples of rules you may be stating to children to help them remain safe and sound on the playground. Rules stated in positive form, in short direct sentences, help the child know the behavior that you want. Because the children might not understand all the words you say—"inside," "behind," "around"—you will also lead or gesture to give them further clues about what you'd like them to do.

The point is to use guidance in a fair manner, with a suggestion for an acceptable alternative that fits in with the mood or need of the child. The child who wants to drop something from the top of the treehouse can make paper airplanes and fly them from there. The child who wants to paint the building can paint with water. The child who wants to climb high must do it on the jungle gym instead of on the storage shed. Children will be guided by a confident teacher who has an honest explanation and a helping hand.

Sharing. Sharing is a social skill that can be fostered in outdoor play, perhaps because many materials used outdoors, such as water and sand or leaves, twigs and pinecones, exist in such abundant supply. Sharing is a spontaneous act stemming from feelings of generosity. You may hear adults tell children, "You have to share," but if the adults are forcing children to divide something, is it really sharing? Think about your own feelings when you share something with a friend, and think about how those feelings would be different if someone forced you to divide your possessions with another. In the following example, Olivia demonstrates genuine sharing:

> Sherry joined the children at the sand pile after the sand shovels had been divided by the three children present. Sherry said nothing for a while, just watched as the three children scooped and filled their containers. Olivia looked at her and said, "Oh, you don't have a shovel. You can have one of mine." Ben said, "She can't have none of mine." Darnell, the third child, said nothing. Sherry played happily with the shovel Olivia gave her.

The teacher, standing nearby, said simply, "Olivia, it was kind of you to share one of your shovels." By labeling the behavior, the teacher helped the children learn something about the concepts of sharing and kindness and let them all know that these were valued. As a means of encouraging such prosocial behavior, this subtle message was probably much more effective than preaching or reprimanding Ben for his unwillingness to share.

Children, like all the rest of us, have to feel that they "have had enough" of something before they can feel generous about sharing it. Ben and Darnell probably had reasons for not sharing. "Enough" is individually defined. Forced sharing is likely to make a child feel that adults are on the other child's side. Children who have difficulty sharing should be helped to have long, sustained experiences with equipment and supplies that no one forces them to relinquish, so they can finally feel that they have "enough."

Taking Turns.   Sharing means giving up part of something you have, while taking turns requires that you relinquish it entirely for a period of time or wait for someone else to finish. Just as the feeling of having enough is prerequisite to true sharing, the ability to wait your turn requires assurance that you will, in fact, have a turn. Consider this example of negotiations among a pair of four-year-old boys who each wanted to use the last available tricycle: Nathaniel and Jose were gripping opposite ends of the tricycle's handlebars. Their teacher, Genevieve, stepped over and took hold of the trike:

Genevieve: I can see you both really want this tricycle.

Nathaniel: I want it!

Jose: I want it!

Genevieve: I don't know what to do. This is the only one left. I need you to help me figure out this problem.

Nathaniel: He should let me have it. I was here first.

Jose: You were not. I want it.

Genevieve: You both want the trike. We have two boys who want to ride and only one trike. Do you have any ideas for solving this problem?

Nathaniel: Let me have it for a while and then Jose can have it.

Genevieve: So you think you could take turns? Is that all right with you Jose?

Jose: He'll keep it too long.

Genevieve: Nathaniel, Jose thinks you'll keep the tricycle too long. How long do you think you'll ride it?

Nathaniel: Two times around the track.

Genevieve: What do you say, Jose?

Jose: Okay.

Given the opportunity to fulfill his wish, Nathaniel willingly dismounted after two turns. The teacher anticipated another crisis when Jose declared that he wanted 10 turns, but decided to see what happened as the children worked through their own solution. After his first turn around the track, she asked him how many turns he had taken so far. "Five," he replied without hesitation. Asked again, after one more circuit, he said, "10," and promptly relinquished the coveted tricycle for another rotation of turn-taking. Genevieve knew that children need to know that their needs will be met and that their rights will be respected if they are to learn to respect the rights of others.

Taking turns with a popular item of equipment may be beyond the developmental capability of some children. With toddlers, for example, the wisest course is simply to provide duplicates of popular items. Some teachers try to help children manage turn-taking by providing a timer and arbitrarily declaring that each turn with the tricycle, for example, will be five minutes long. As noted previously, however, children need to feel that they have had enough of something before they can willingly share it with another. When the time limit is established by the adult, a child may spend the entire five minutes worried about the impending bell rather than enjoying the ride. When teachers simply point out that another child is waiting a turn, however, and let the rider decide when to give up the tricycle, they are often surprised at how promptly and cheerfully the child gives up the toy.

Cognitive Development

Spontaneous experiences that nurture a child's sense of inquiry are significant and, because they grow out of a child's own interests, can be worth far more than many planned group experiences. Sometimes an episode occurs outdoors that is meaningful for one child and can be developed or repeated so that the total group benefits from it. Science experiments should be planned frequently for the outdoors to supplement the experiments that may be going on indoors with somewhat different equipment. Observations done indoors can be checked outdoors and vice versa. Gravity, the properties of inclined planes, and balance are concepts for which teeter-totters provide excellent examples. Labeling these concepts indoors and again outdoors helps children learn that knowledge carries over from one situation to another.

Planting seeds and bulbs in a garden or flower bed makes a challenging learning experience. Children get to observe the natural cycle of planting, sprouting, blooming, ripening, and harvesting; they begin to see how their actions have an effect on that cycle and to appreciate how we depend on it for our food and well-being. These are all concepts that are part of "ecoliteracy" (Capra, 1999), which many believe to be an essential quality for humans to achieve a sustainable existence on this planet. Children will learn from you whether a colorful beetle is something to admire and wonder at, something to recoil from in disgust, or something to be promptly squashed under-foot. If creatures—such as bees or hornets—are potentially harmful, then you should teach children to respect them and keep a safe distance. More often than not, it is the children who might harm the creature in their eagerness to examine it. Teach them to observe without touching when possible, to be very gentle when they do touch, and to return the worm or insect to its "home" safely.

Recalling that science is as much a process as a body of information, adults will encourage children's exploration and experimenting, asking questions such as these: "What would happen if we . . . ?" "How did you make it do that?" "Tell me what happened. What do you think the [worm, bird, squirrel] is trying to do?" The important thing is that the teacher be alert to the child's activity. Commenting on something a child sees, picks up, or even fears can provide an excellent learning situation. Children will encounter many things that are new to them in the natural world and will need to know the accurate names for each. Of course, these conversations with children will promote language development. You can also encourage literacy by providing field guides (to birds, rocks, butterflies, etc.) and letting children see you using them to look up interesting factual information.

Children enjoy singing, counting, and clapping games like "Farmer in the Dell," "One Potato, Two Potato," and "Miss Mary Mack." You may remember such games from your own childhood and can pass them on to the next generation. If not, try interviewing an older relative about his or her memories of childhood games. Some-times children, particularly those whose cultural origins differ from yours, will be able to teach you their own rhymes. All children are delighted if you take the time to write down their chants and will be highly motivated to "read" what you have written, a task made easier because the words are repetitious, and the children already know what they say. Providing a basket stocked with clipboards, paper, and fine-point felt pens will encourage children to record their songs or their observations of natural phenomena, thereby fostering their emerging writing skills.

EMERGENCIES

Emergencies can occur both indoors and outdoors. There should be few serious emergencies if the playground design follows safety guidelines, if equipment is well maintained, and if a sufficient number of adults (based on the number and ages of the children) station themselves at strategic intervals throughout the play yard so they are indeed interacting with children as discussed earlier.

Safety must be a prime concern of all adults. Adults must never leave chil-dren unattended. If someone feels that an activity is dangerous, then it should be stopped until the staff can decide whether it should be permitted. Of course, chil-dren should not be smothered by adults to keep them safe, but being on the safe side is the best rule.

When you are a new teacher, you may occasionally wonder if the children should be permitted to do something. The best procedure is to take a child by the hand and say, "Let's ask [the lead teacher] if it is all right for you to do this." This way, your guidance fits in with established rules.

If a child falls or appears to be hurt, a teacher's calm behavior is a first requirement. If you get hysterical, the child—and probably the whole group—will get hysterical, too. It will be easier to remain calm if you know and follow a plan for emergencies that has been established prior to the admission of children. Such a plan should include:

- Having names of parents and their telephone numbers at home and at work conveniently located at each telephone of the school and in the teacher's pocket for use on field trips
- Having the name and phone number of each child's doctor
- Obtaining written permission to contact an emergency medical service if parents cannot be reached

Many programs have teachers carry a fanny pack that contains a cell phone and emergency supplies, such as tissues and bandages, on the playground and on field trips. The minor bumps and scrapes that are an inevitable part of childhood can often be handled with a sympathetic word or hug. When a more serious accident or injury occurs, have the child stay quiet and do not jerk the child to standing or into your arms. Reassure the hurt child and advise helpers how they can help. Perhaps they can call the parent or doctor or both. Tell them what to say and do. The person whom the child knows best should provide comfort and reassurance until the parent arrives.

Someone must be delegated to continue guiding the rest of the children, who will likely need a calm explanation of what has happened and how the hurt child is feeling. A quiet time for talking about the times when they have been hurt may be called for. The incident will be meaningful, as some may have experienced such accidents before. Children may be extremely fearful and need reassurance.

FIELD TRIPS

Field trips expand the range of outdoor experiences and offer innumerable opportunities for observing, asking questions, posing problems, and collecting data. They need not be elaborate: A walk around the block can be an adventure for toddlers (and older children as well) if you approach it in a spirit of discovery. Your community may have parks, an arboretum, a botanical garden, or a butterfly garden where professional naturalists are happy to help you create interesting encounters for children.

Moving outside the carefully prepared environment of a center or school adds an element of risk. Some schools have eliminated field trips to avoid liability, but careful planning can ensure that excursions are safe and have true educational worth. The more elaborate the field trip, the greater the preparation and planning required. A basic necessity is a sufficient number of adults so that each one is responsible for not more than four children and keeps constantly alert to their whereabouts. Preparation for the field trip includes visiting the site ahead of time and then briefing all helping adults about points of particular interest.

Riding in cars and buses presents some hazards. Adults and children must use seatbelts or appropriate restraints in private cars and vans and in hired buses if they are available. Children must remain seated and be reasonably orderly to avoid distracting the driver. It is important to have a second adult in the car besides the driver. When visiting animals in zoos or on farms, children must be kept a safe distance from fences or pens until you are sure the animals are harmless, and they should wash their hands or use a sanitizing solution afterward.

During the field trip, you and the other adult helpers may have to interpret the words of guides employed at the site, who may not be familiar with the children's level of understanding. Encourage children to ask questions and be sure that you respond to them factually—including saying "I don't know; let's ask" when appropriate. Some teachers like to help children prepare a list of questions in advance, and they assign responsibility for finding answers to those questions to particular individuals or small groups. Another strategy for helping children focus their observations is to provide each child with paper on a clipboard and a pencil, and ask that they draw some specific feature of the site. Record children's comments and use them as discussion starters to help children reflect on their experience back in the classroom.

CONCLUSION

Outdoor play has rich potential for enhancing children's development in every domain. In particular, it promotes health by establishing patterns of vigorous physical activity. It fosters knowledge and appreciation of the natural world. It offers myriad opportunities for children to practice social skills and manage feelings. Finally, it supports cognitive development, directly through exposure to rich content and indirectly by providing needed respite between periods of mental exertion. To meet the objectives for outdoor play, teachers should give special thought to the opportunity and responsibility they have in guiding children's activity there each day. They should use all of the guidance principles discussed in Chapters 6 and 7 and apply each one in a creative way. Children are individuals, with differences in development. The teacher's challenge is to support children where they are on the development ladder and to be ready to help each child reach the higher rungs as he or she is ready.

REVIEW: TEN GUIDES FOR SUPPORTING DEVELOPMENT THROUGH OUTDOOR PLAY

1. Schedule at least one generous period for outdoor activity for all children every day except in very severe weather. (Observe children carefully and shorten their time outside in accordance with windchill or heat index factors.)

2. Make sure the outdoor play area includes grassy surfaces, trees and shrubs, and materials found in nature, such as wood, stone, soil, and water, to give children opportunities to learn about nature and to develop a sense of connectedness with it.

3. Expand the possibilities of classroom activities such as painting, dramatic play, or block construction by providing the needed props and materials outside. Bring parts of the outdoors (leaves, pinecones, a bucket of snow) back inside for further exploration.

4. Foster feelings of self-efficacy by arranging the environment to maximize challenges while minimizing hazards by encouraging children to try things and respecting their choices; never try to motivate them through competition with others.

5. Plan outdoor activities and arrange equipment to foster development of physical-motor skills (e.g., body management, locomotor, projection, reception) as well as social, emotional, and cognitive skills.

6. Make sure children have plenty of time for spontaneous play and unplanned discoveries.

7. Be sure that you and the children are protected with warm clothing, sunscreen, and/or mosquito repellant, as warranted by local conditions, so that everyone can enjoy safely participating in the outdoors in every season.

8. Participate actively in children's learning and in their vigorous activity, as a teacher, not just as a supervisor, while remaining aware of the whole group.

9. Model the qualities you hope to see in children: Teach and follow rules of safety for protection of individuals and property; demonstrate curiosity, wonder, and respect for natural phenomena (rather than distaste or fear).

10. Broaden children's experiences with nature through field trips to nearby parks, botanical gardens, natural history museums, planetariums, and children's science museums.

APPLICATIONS

1. Observe a child during outdoor play at a child care center. What is the child's judgment of his or her motor capabilities (i.e., self-efficacy)? State your evidence for your decision. What motor skills, social skills, and language skills did the child practice? What and with whom does the child play? What similarities or differences do you notice with regard to children's ages, genders, or ability levels?

2. Evaluate the outdoor play area, using the guidelines discussed in this chapter. Does it provide adequate space for children to move freely and quickly? Are there a sufficient number of play areas to accommodate the group? Are there areas for children to relax and play quietly, alone or with just a few others? Are there any safety hazards? Is the space planned to meet children's health needs (e.g., shade, drinking water)? Are there natural, aesthetically appealing elements?

3. Observe and record a teacher or caregiver helping a child learn a skill. What types of physical and/or verbal guidance does the adult use? Was the guidance effective in getting the child to do the desired thing? Explain.

RESOURCES FOR FURTHER STUDY

Websites

Boundless Playgrounds
boundlessplaygrounds.org
Website of national nonprofit organization whose mission is to help "communities everywhere create extraordinary barrier-free playgrounds where children with and without disabilities can develop essential skills for life as they learn together through play"; includes guidelines and links to resources.

Earthplay
earthplay.net
Website of Rusty Keeler, who consults with programs to enlist participation of families and communities in the design and construction of appropriately challenging, environmentally friendly outdoor play spaces that appeal to all of children's senses.

Natural Learning Initiative
naturalearning.org
Website of a research and extension program of the College of Design, North Carolina State University, Raleigh, North Carolina, whose purpose is to promote the importance of the natural environment in the daily experience of all children, through environmental design, action research, education, and dissemination of information.

Readings

Greenspan, D., Miner, N., & Kudela, E. (1995). *Backyards and butterflies: Ways to include children with disabilities in outdoor activities.* Brookline, MA: Brookline Books.

Kamii, C., & De Vries, R. (1980). *Group games in early education.* Washington, DC: National Association for the Education of Young Children.

Meyer, A. P. (1997, March). More than a playground: Accessible outdoor learning centers. *Child Care Information Exchange, 114,* 57–60.

Moore, R. C., & Cosco, N. (2003). *Developing an earth-bound culture through design of childhood habitats.* North Carolina State University, Department of Landscape Architecture. Available online at childrennatureandyou.org/.

Pica, R. (2006, May). Physical fitness and the early childhood curriculum. *Young Children, 61*(3), 12–19.

Rivkin, M. S. (1995). *The great outdoors: Restoring children's right to play outside.* Washington, DC: National Association for the Education of Young Children.

CHAPTER 11

Understanding and Addressing Challenging Behavior

Learning Outcomes

After studying this chapter you should be able to

- Propose possible reasons for children's challenging behaviors.
- Describe strategies for preventing or reducing the occurence of challenging behavior.
- Describe strategies for addressing challenging behavior after it occurs.
- Explain how to develop a behavioral intervention plan in collaboration with families.

Seth, age three, had been attending the child development center for only three weeks and, although he appeared eager to join the other children's play, he didn't seem to know how to do so. Often he would charge into the classroom, march over to a small group that was engrossed in some activity, and either shove a child or knock over something the children were building. At times he became so angry at something another child said or did that he lashed out with blows and ear-splitting screams. The other children had started cowering at his approach and protesting vehemently, "No, you can't play here. You'll knock it down!"

Seth's behavior was interfering with the work of the school. He destroyed the other children's learning environment. At times he had even hurt children. Most troubling in the teacher's mind, Seth was beginning to be a scapegoat in the group. Whenever quarrels or mishaps occurred, the other children were quick to blame them on Seth. Something had to be done. Unfortunately, that "something" for an alarming number of children like Seth has been expulsion from school. A recent study of nearly 4,000 state prekindergarten programs found that they expelled children at a rate more than three times that for elementary and high school students (Gilliam, 2005). The purpose of this textbook is to help you avoid such drastic measures by providing strategies for preventing troublesome behavior and for dealing with it when it occurs. The aim of this chapter is to help you understand challenging behaviors within a context that includes a child's overall development, family expectations and interactions, and environmental factors so that you can address those behaviors more effectively. Remember that the goal is to use indirect and direct guidance to build on children's strengths, to help them become well-adjusted, self-directed, productive adults—not merely to "stamp out" behavior that you deem troublesome.

MEANINGFULNESS OF BEHAVIOR

Children who knock things over or hit children are telling us something with their behavior. They are saying as clearly as they know how, "All is not right in my world. Help me." Children may exhibit challenging behavior because they are tired or hungry, feel insecure, need attention, or have some other unmet need. They may simply not know how to behave in the unfamiliar group setting or how to get along with other children. They may have a disability or developmental delay that makes it hard for them to do what is expected. Or the program itself may be eliciting the undesired behavior because it does not have in place the elements of guidance discussed in this text: developmentally appropriate expectations, an environment (including the classroom arrangement, daily schedule, and adult availability) that facilitates positive behavior, and curriculum that engages the whole child in the learning process alongside a caring community of adults and other children.

Regardless of the source or type of challenging behavior, child development professionals are in a unique position to help a child become more self-managing, particularly if they get to know each child as a unique individual. They can strive to understand what factors may be contributing to the behavior and look for ways to address them.

For some children, the challenging behavior occurs regularly, part of the child's repertoire of responses to life in general. For others, it may be more transitory, often as a response to stress. Stress is a part of every life, but individuals vary in their **resilience**, or ability to cope with stress. Some children seem to thrive despite circumstances that seem intolerable, such as extreme poverty or chaotic home lives. Others have trouble adjusting to any change in their daily lives. Because stress is largely a matter of perception, it is impossible to say that one child has more reason to feel stressed than another. Nurturing the quality of resilience will help all children meet the inevitable challenges and setbacks they will face in life. Research has shown that responsive care (i.e., meeting a child's needs predictably) and warm relationships with important adults contribute to the development of resilience (Bowman, 2006).

Confronted with the behaviors of a child such as Seth, therefore, a wise early childhood professional asks several questions:

- *Is this just a bad day for this child, or does he do these things with regularity?* All children have days when they are tired or cranky and thus more prone to lash out at others. Adults who understand this help the child regain control without making a mountain out of a molehill. When the behavior occurs repeatedly, however, it's time to ask the next question.

- *Is this behavior likely to be harmful to the child, to other people, or to the environment? Or is the behavior simply an irritation or a bother to adults?* Sometimes adults simply have expectations that are unrealistic for the age of the children, or they expect the children to know something that no one has bothered to teach them. As shown in the guidance pyramid depicted in Figure 11–1, appropriate expectations based on understanding of child development patterns form the

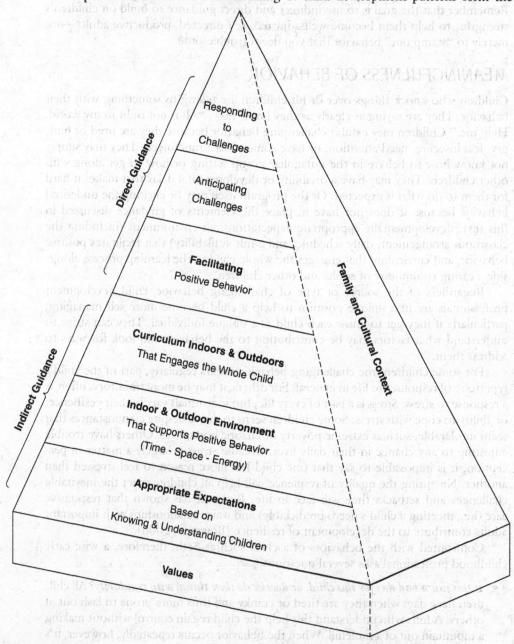

FIGURE 11–1   The guidance pyramid: Preventing and addressing challenging behavior

254   Chapter 11

foundation of all guidance. Many so-called troublesome behaviors are actually simply manifestations of typical development. Some children will come closer to being typical than others. Some typical behaviors may also be troublesome, but adults should not make these behaviors worse through their treatment of the child. For example, toddlers are frequently chastised for saying "no" or for their intense curiosity, which makes them want to handle every loose object in sight. Three-year-olds are scolded for their shyness or for hiding behind their parents' legs when someone, especially a stranger, approaches them. Four-year-olds are considered problematic when they act brashly, talk loudly, or make up fantastic stories.

❀   Talk It Over   ❀

What types of children's behaviors really bother you? Does the child's age or gender make a difference in the way you feel about particular behaviors?

If adults are honest with themselves, they might realize that a particular behavior they find challenging is actually nothing more than their own "pet peeve" and that, except for grating on the teacher's nerves, it poses no threat to the well-being of anyone or anything. Depending on your personal preferences, crying, pouting, whining, tattling, and even an occasional toddler temper tantrum could be included in this category. Some adults are put off by extreme shyness or bossiness. If your careful observation convinces you that a behavior is truly harmful or potentially so, the next step is to try to understand that behavior—its meaning for the child and the factors that might be contributing to it.

- *Are there factors pertaining to the child's development, health, or environment outside the school or center that contribute to the behavior?* Take the example of Seth at the beginning of this chapter. He may be short tempered when hungry or tired. His language skills might lag behind those of the other three-year-olds so that he communicates his wishes by hitting or shoving to get what he wants. Due to inexperience or immaturity, he may lack the social skills required to diplomatically enter play situations with other children. He may not have developed the emotional skill of controlling his temper or inhibiting his responses to frustration. He may live in a household where shoving and hitting are accepted means of getting what one wants. He may be regularly exposed to violent actions in his neighborhood or through television, movies, and video games. Understanding these possibilities does not mean that we blame the child or conclude that we cannot help him learn appropriate behaviors. It does mean that we tailor our intervention strategies to suit the particular situation. And that leads to the next question.
- *Are there factors within the child development program that contribute to the problem, either eliciting or rewarding the behavior?* Sometimes children's challenging

Engaging activities, an adequate supply of materials, and time to enjoy them can prevent much challenging behavior.

behaviors are reactions to circumstances within their immediate environment: Are there enough adults to supervise the room adequately and, by their very proximity, help Seth inhibit his urges to strike out? Does the child enjoy a close warm relationship with at least one of those adults, or do all their interactions with him consist of reprimands and orders? Does the daily schedule accommodate physical needs for rest and snacks? Is there enough equipment so that children do not have to compete for toys? Is the equipment appropriate to the ages of children in the program? Do the materials provided reflect children's lives and interests enough to engage their minds? Is there enough space so that children can build without accidentally bumping each other's structures? Do they have enough time to play so that they don't feel they must grab toys before the window of opportunity closes? Do they have enough time for exuberant outdoor play? Sometimes adults create situations or act in ways that inadvertently encourage children to persist in their challenging behaviors: Does Seth get a teacher's attention only when he misbehaves? Does hitting or pushing "work" for Seth? Does it give him entry into the play group? Do the other children give him what he wants? Is the excitement of their anguished cries more interesting than anything else going on in the program?

- *Does the child know what behavior is expected?* Do the adults in the center teach the children appropriate ways to get what they need and help them practice those strategies? Young children with little or no experience in group settings must learn how to navigate the situations they encounter. Do adults view children's misbehavior as evidence that they need to teach alternatives, or do they react with irritation and frustration?

Careful observation and reflection can provide answers to these questions, can help you to understand the problem more fully, and, consequently, can help you to deal with it more effectively.

We place this chapter about dealing with challenging or problematic behaviors at the end of this book because we are convinced that effective use of all the positive guidance techniques discussed thus far will prevent many problems entirely and help keep those that do occur within manageable limits. As you read through the rest of this chapter, we hope you will see that everything you have learned about guidance so far comes into play when analyzing and coping with problems that arise.

PREVENTING OR REDUCING CHALLENGING BEHAVIORS

As we noted at the beginning of this chapter, the most important tool in your repertoire for dealing with challenging behaviors is the relationship you develop with each child. Children's feelings of attachment to the important adults in their lives motivate them to please those adults and want to be like them. It may take extra work on your part to cultivate closeness with children whose social or ethnic background differs significantly from your own because they may not behave in ways that you have been conditioned by your culture to expect (Ray, Bowman, & Brownell, 2006). You may, in fact, be predisposed to judge those children harshly, to interpret perfectly reasonable behavior as negative. We know, for example, that the teaching population is predominantly white and female (Ray et al., 2006). We know, too, that African American children have higher rates of expulsion from preschool than their white peers, and we know that boys who are expelled outnumber girls more than 4 to 1 (Gilliam, 2005). Just as adults misunderstand children who are different from them, some children, accustomed to what may seem to you to be harsh treatment at home, could misinterpret a more gentle approach as overly permissive or even uncaring (Ballenger, 1998). It is crucial that you be honest with yourself about potential biases and strive to surmount them if you are to build a warm, supportive relationship with every child. Your ability to provide effective guidance as well as the child's future success in school and life depend on that relationship.

Even though you might not see immediate results, your effort and dedication could make a crucial difference in a child's life. One teacher tells of being hugged by a "stranger" passing her on the street one day who told her, "I remember you. You're the teacher who used to hug me every day!" Puzzled at first, the teacher remembered that, years earlier, she had worked in a therapeutic nursery school where, every day for months, she had to restrain a little girl to keep her from hurting herself or others during violent tantrums (Weinreb, 1997). Certainly that teacher must have felt deep satisfaction to know that she had been able to deal with a child's negative behavior in a way that the child, now grown up, could remember so positively! The important thing is to have faith in children, treating each one as an individual and never giving up your efforts.

Setting and Enforcing Appropriate Limits

Understanding troublesome behavior does not mean accepting it. Adults are responsible for establishing the behavioral limits or boundaries that are necessary for the safety and healthy development of children in their care. This means that children should be prevented from (1) hurting themselves; (2) hurting others, either physically, psychologically, by teasing, or by infringing on others' rights; and (3) destroying property. If you think about it, these limits can encompass all the "rules" that typically govern early childhood programs. Confining your list of classroom rules to a minimum number that clearly relate to these essential limits has several advantages:

- The fewer the number of rules in place, the easier it is for children to learn those rules and the fewer occasions for children to transgress those rules.

- Fewer transgressions mean that adults can spend the time and energy they would have spent reprimanding children in more positive interactions with them.
- Fewer reprimands mean fewer assaults on children's self-concept and feelings of self-efficacy.
- Instead of teaching children to memorize and conform to a list of arbitrary prohibitions, adults will be teaching them the reasons for the rules.
- Helping children understand that rules safeguard the rights of everyone helps them move beyond blind obedience to acting out of a sense of justice and fair play—in other words, to taking their part in a democratic rather than a totalitarian society.

Limits must be communicated to children in ways that they will understand and remember. Recall from the guidelines for direct guidance given in Chapter 7 that, in addition to having few rules, it is most effective to state those rules succinctly and positively. Thus, the three basic limits can be stated as follows:

- Be safe.
- Be kind to others.
- Take care of our room (or school).

Adults can teach the meaning of these concepts by noticing and appreciating examples of positive behaviors.

- "You're using both hands on the climber, Maria. That's a good way to keep yourself safe."
- "It was kind of you to let Jeb have a turn on the tricycle, Eduardo."
- "Thanks for picking up that paper, Kamiko. It makes our playground look really nice."

Adults can also point out, calmly and nonjudgmentally, the times when children transgress these limits:

- "When you tip your chair back like that, Bosah, you could fall and hurt yourself. Be safe and keep all four chair legs on the floor."
- "Pinching hurts. See? Ava's crying."
- "I'll help you pick up the puzzle pieces from the floor, Jerome. If they get lost, we won't have those puzzles to play with. We all need to take care of our school."

Adults must be realistic about how closely or how quickly they can expect children to comply with limits. A young toddler's version of "be kind" might include giving a favorite "blankie" to a crying playmate. But it might not preclude taking an exploratory nip on that playmate's arm, just to see the interesting reaction. Four-year-olds, eager to test their growing physical prowess, will probably need many reminders to "be safe," particularly if their environment offers no opportunities to challenge their growing abilities or contains inappropriate hazards, as discussed in Chapter 10. Wise adults consider learning about limits to be a work in progress for young children, a goal toward which they constantly strive, though they may never reach it completely.

No matter how carefully you establish and enforce limits, there will be children who, for one or more of the reasons discussed earlier, will be unable to comply with them. Their challenging behaviors will require all your knowledge, skill, and tenacity. Remember that while your immediate goal may be to stop the undesirable behavior, your long-term goal is to help children reach their potential to be well-adjusted, self-directed, productive adults. This means there is no one-size-fits-all solution, no magic bullet that will work in every situation to eliminate a troublesome behavior.

Authenticity.   The way an adult responds to a child's challenging behavior is crucial. Some adults become so intent on stopping the problem that they begin to act more like jail keepers than teachers, scowling constantly and speaking to children only to issue commands or reprimands in harsh tones. Children need to feel that adults care about them before they can care what the adults think of their actions. A warm smile, a gentle touch on the shoulder before problems occur can build children's sense of emotional connection to you and help them want to do the right thing. Some adults go to the opposite extreme, however, seeming to believe that they must wear an exaggerated smile and speak in sugary tones at all times. "That's not nice to hit your friends," they croon through clenched teeth. Children are quick to sense this phoniness and will react accordingly.

It is possible to let children know in respectful and authentic ways that you are upset by their actions. Get down on their eye level, perhaps holding their hands or shoulders so that they face you. Let your facial expression and body language reflect the fact that hurting other children is not acceptable to you. Tell them so and be sure to add that your job of keeping children safe extends to them as well.

The following are never appropriate responses to a child's challenging behavior because none of them accomplishes the goal of guidance to help children become well-adjusted, self-directed, productive adults:

- Punishing a child verbally or physically
- Giving a child a negative label
- Shaming the child
- Creating competition or comparing the child with others
- Threatening the child with expulsion or with calling the child's parents or some other authority figure

ADDRESSING CHALLENGING BEHAVIOR TO PROMOTE SELF-MANAGEMENT

Observation

Observation is a first step toward understanding and dealing with challenging behavior. First and most importantly, unless you observe closely, you will be unable to notice or appreciate positive behavior—to find the good or the strength that all children possess. Where does he play? With whom does he play? What good things does he do? Next, observation can tell you when and where misbehaviors occur most often so you can begin to think about why they happen. This is where the ABC analysis discussed earlier comes into play. Figure 11–2 is an example of an event sample collected by teachers over a three-week period because they were concerned about a child (Jeb)'s aggression toward other children. As they reviewed their findings the teachers concluded that Jeb was using aggression (hitting, pushing, grabbing toys) in order to get or maintain access to play materials or to get other children to comply with his wishes. They noted, furthermore, that his aggressive acts usually "worked" for him—that is, he was able to keep playing with the item, get another to stop doing something that annoyed him, or take a coveted role in a group game. They considered whether the environment might be contributing to Jeb's behavior by providing insufficient materials or space for play. But they knew that the classroom area, as well as the quantity and variety of materials, exceeded basic requirements by a substantial margin. They decided that either Jeb did not know other, more acceptable, ways of getting what he wanted or that he had simply learned that his way was a reliable method of achieving desired results.

In contrast to Jeb, Seth (the child we met at the beginning of this chapter) did not seem to be getting what he wanted through his behaviors. Rather than being allowed to join children at play, he was increasingly excluded. As the teachers continued to observe and share their thoughts about Seth, they concluded that he had many strengths. He wanted to play with other children and loved games of chase on the playground. He could be very careful and precise in controlling his body—he once spent over an hour building an elaborate block structure, moving so carefully that he never bumped or knocked over a single block even though other children's buildings were very close to his. The other children seemed to be afraid of him at times; yet at other times they relished being chased by him. He showed that he could take a leadership role when, on a walking field trip to a favorite park several blocks away, he surprised the teachers by giving accurate directions to "go this way," and "cross here." Although he had some language delays and was being served by a speech therapist who visited him at the center weekly, he could communicate quite clearly about topics that interested him. One morning, for example, a street sweeper passed in front of the center and several excited children rushed to the window, exclaiming about the "tractor." Seth, with some indignation, corrected them: "That's not a tractor. It's a sweeper-machine."

The teachers also observed the environment as they sought to understand the meaning of Seth's behavior. They wanted to know if anything in that environment was contributing to the problem: perhaps a room arrangement that offered no space for Seth to get away by himself at times or made it impossible to supervise all children visually? Perhaps a schedule with too many transitions during which Seth lost his self-control?

Throughout this process, the teachers made it a point to think about times when Seth behaved appropriately and to recall the things that he did well. When teachers zero in on behavior *problems*, they frequently neglect the kinds of individualized observation that can reveal the very strengths that will help a child correct a difficulty. Whether a problem is minor or severe, the child's strengths should be assessed first.

As they observed, the teachers developed their theories about the reasons behind Seth's behavior. First, and perhaps most obviously, he did not know how to get other children to let him join their play, and his disruptive attempts to do so were met

Date/Time	Antecedent Event	Behavior	Consequence
2/27 (T) 9:37 free play	J is building a car with Legos. B takes one of J's Lego pieces.	J stands up and slaps B and takes back the Lego piece.	B looks at J and resumes building. J, sits back down and continues building.
2/27 (T) 3:22 free play	K is making an "sss" noise and J says, "Stop making that silly noise." K continues.	J hits K with a spoon.	K keeps playing, but stops making the "sss" noise.
2/27 (T) 4:15 free play	Some boys are building a hospital with hollow blocks. B comes over and takes J's block. J says, "That's mine," and pulls on the block. B hits J.	J takes block in both hands and forces it forward so that it hits B a few times.	Adult tells boys to keep hands and objects to themselves; that they will have to find something else to do if they cannot; and that they should use words when angry. Both resume building.
3/1 (R) 11:30 outdoor play	J and B are playing "freeze tag." B tells J he cannot be the "unfreezer."	J runs toward B and kicks him in the leg.	B cries and boys immediately resume game with J as "unfreezer."
3/4 (M) 9:05 free play	J is playing with toys; a boy comes over and reaches for toys.	J stands up and pushes boy.	Second child leaves the area and J continues playing with toys.
3/4 (M) 10:00 free play	C and J are playing with table toys and both reach for the same item.	J hits C on the arm a few times.	C leaves the table and J continues playing.
3/6 (R) 9:00 free play	J and C are playing with Legos. C takes one of J's pieces.	J whines, "Hey, that's mine!" The boys scuffle and J hits C on the arm.	C leaves area and J resumes playing.
3/6 (R) 11:20 outside play	J is playing football with C and D. They keep throwing the ball away from J. He screams, "Stop! Let me have it."	J tackles C to the ground, sits on him and grabs the ball.	Adult talks to boys about ways to share the ball. Tells J to express anger in words instead of hitting. Boys resume playing with J in control of ball.
3/7 (F) 9:00 free play	J and B are playing with blocks. B moves a block that J has put into place. J moves it back and B moves it again.	J says, "No, B!" and hits B on the arm.	B starts to hit J back but an adult intervenes and tells the boys to "play nicely." J replaces block in original position and resumes play.
3/10 (M) 11:30 outside play	J and JA are in sandbox. JA takes a shovel from J and walks away.	J stands up and hits JA in the middle of his back with his fists.	JA throws the shovel at J's feet and runs away. J resumes digging with shovel.
3/18 (T) 10:45 outdoor play	J is playing "police" with B and T. N is riding the bouncy ball.	J pushes N off bouncy ball and grabs it away when she falls.	Teacher tells J that we don't push people off toys and goes to get ice for N's nose. J rides away on bouncy ball.

FIGURE 11–2   Example of an ABC event sample to analyze a child's aggressive behavior

Children can use props like a dollhouse with miniature people to act out feelings and gain some control over them.

with rejection. Second, the teachers wondered whether his outbursts of screaming or hitting other children might stem from his misinterpretation of their approaches as threats rather than signals that they were trying to play with him. Finally, he might not know how—or he might not be developmentally ready—to manage his strong feelings at the perceived encroachment. Armed with these theories about the meaning of Seth's behavior, the teachers could target some of the underlying causes of the challenging behavior. They could show Seth that building a similar structure alongside the group of children he wanted to join might lead to an invitation to combine efforts once they realized that he was not going to destroy their creation. They could model ways he could contribute to the ongoing play, perhaps offering a particular block or dramatic play accessory appropriate to the scenario. They provide words to help both Seth and the other children understand each other's actions: "Maybe Darius wants to be the bus driver for the people in your apartment building when he drives up close like that." Or, "Tell Darius to be careful of your building and that you don't want to play bus driver right now." Meanwhile, they could continue their efforts to embed the goal of emotional development throughout the curriculum for all the children.

Helping Children Manage Their Feelings

According to Stanley Greenspan (1997), a child psychiatrist who has studied children's emotional development extensively, one of a child's earliest tasks is to learn to integrate feelings into a sense of self—to know that a person can move from playful joy to anger, and back to joy, all while remaining the same person (pp. 68–73). Here are some suggestions for helping children recognize, understand, and manage their feelings:

- *Give children words for their feelings.* "You're angry because Josh took the wagon you wanted." "It looks like you're feeling sad about saying goodbye to your mom this morning." "I can see that you're so excited about spending the weekend at your dad's that it is hard for you to settle down for nap."

- *Make learning about feelings a part of the curriculum.* Read books about feelings in general or about children coping with particular feelings. Use puppets or dolls to present vignettes of common situations, such as a child taking a toy from another, and ask children how they think the character might feel. Practice self-calming techniques.

- *Encourage children to reflect on their own feelings.* For example, help them make personal books with pages captioned "I felt sad when . . . ," "I felt happy when . . . ," and so on. Be sure to include the full range of feelings, both positive and negative. Children can illustrate each page with a drawing, or you can take digital photographs of them acting out the facial expression corresponding to each feeling. Children will enjoy looking at themselves in a mirror as they try out these expressions.

❁   **Talk It Over**   ❁

Build your emotional vocabulary. Brainstorm as many words as possible for the range of emotions that children might experience. Try to go beyond the simplistic "happy, sad, angry." Think about the actions, words, facial expressions, or body language that might allow you to infer that a child was feeling a particular emotion. Practice using these words with the children (or adults) in your life (e.g., "It looks like you're disappointed that cleanup time came so quickly"). Give them a chance to correct you if you have misinterpreted them.

Frustration.   Frustration is frequently the initiator of troublesome behavior, and it takes a considerable amount of time for a child to learn to cope with it. Frustrations arise

- When the child is stopped or thwarted in some desired activity—when the child is riding a tricycle and another child builds a barrier in the road, for instance
- When the child fails to get something that she has waited for—when a child has waited for a turn to hold the bunny and a quick spring shower requires a shift of children and activities indoors, for example
- When there are insufficient toys and equipment and the child doesn't see anything to use as a substitute for the desired one
- When the child attempts or is encouraged to attempt activities that are too difficult for him or her
- When a change in familiar routines, people, or activities occurs

Children (like adults) have varying thresholds of tolerance for frustration. Like adults, they respond to frustration in different ways. Some children react by withdrawing for a while and then seem unable to regain their momentum. Psychologist Jean Piaget (1962) explained that once young children make up their minds about something, they get "centered" and find it very difficult, if not impossible, to think of another solution or to change direction. A frustrated child often cries, gets angry, and may strike out, either to get whatever is desired or just to relieve tension. Anger is a common response to frustration. Angry children may hit, push, bite, cry, scream, or have temper tantrums.

Of course, it is unrealistic to think that children could, or even should, go through life without experiencing frustration. Acquiring the ability to cope with frustration is an important part of emotional development. Adults who seek to guide that development, however, do have a responsibility to help keep the level of frustration within manageable limits for the particular children in a given setting. Knowing that two-year-olds can probably tolerate less frustration than four-year-olds, you will make sure to have several duplicates of popular toys in a toddler room. On the other hand, you might expect the four-year-olds to be able to wait for their turns with the new wagon.

Furthermore, you will tailor your age-based expectations to the particular characteristics of the children in your care. While turn-taking may be an appropriate goal for four-year-olds in general, many factors might make it less appropriate for any particular four-year-old. Children who have never had opportunities to play with other children, for example, or children who have never had their own toys might find sharing especially difficult. A child whose coping skills are already taxed by a disability or by an abusive home life may have a much lower tolerance for frustration than a child without these challenges. Remember that the ability to share requires a feeling that one has enough of whatever is being shared.

Once you are sure you have eliminated sources of unnecessary or extreme frustration, you should then concentrate on ways to help children learn to manage their reaction to frustration. Recognizing children's feelings and encouraging them to express those feelings are good starting points. After children have become calm, you can help them think of strategies for coping. For example, children can sometimes wait a turn more patiently if they "sign" their names on a waiting list for a popular toy, thus assuring that they will be next.

Anger.   Anger is a normal human emotion, although its experience is often frightening, both for the person who is angry and for those who witness the anger. Some adults, perhaps because of their childhood experiences with their own or others' anger, are particularly disturbed by anger in children. Nevertheless, children have a right to feel and express anger. It is our job to help them learn how to manage their anger so that it does not overwhelm them. It is also our job to intervene when children lose control of their anger and become violent or aggressive, so we need to make a clear distinction between children's feelings of anger and their behavior.

Goleman (1995) reviewed several research studies and concluded that a cooling-down period, away from the situation that triggered the anger, can help get feelings back under control—but not if the angry person uses that time to rehash the reasons for the anger. One popular strategy for helping children manage their anger is to teach them the "turtle technique," that is, to "take time to tuck [inside an imaginary shell] and think" instead of reacting immediately when something happens to make them angry (Hemmeter & Fox, 2007).

Some people find that vigorous activity, going off alone to a tranquil place, or becoming engrossed in some enjoyable activity can serve to defuse anger. Depending on the particular child, you might try suggesting one of these alternatives, but only after you have recognized and accepted the child's feeling as legitimate. The idea, in other words, is not to cajole a child to snap out of an emotional state, but to help the child gain enough control to be able to express that emotion appropriately.

Note that the suggested activities defuse anger because they absorb the child's attention, gradually moving it away from the angry thoughts, not because they provide a way to vent the anger. A popular notion, many years ago, was that venting, such as pounding clay or hitting a doll, served as a kind of safety valve for letting off steam. According to Goleman, however, such ventilation serves the opposite effect, increasing rather than decreasing angry feelings (Goleman, 1995).

As an early childhood professional, you will use the principles of indirect guidance to minimize circumstances that evoke anger. You will use direct guidance to teach children how to express anger in appropriate ways and will gently help them do this when they do become angry. As we noted earlier, stories and picture books can provide models of children coping with strong feelings. Or you can help children role-play situations using small figures, puppets, or dress-up clothes, so that they have some idea of how to respond when things irritate them in real life.

Finally, you will intervene when their anger boils over into actions that harm themselves or others. It may sorely challenge your professional skills, but you need to remain calm. Becoming angry yourself will only make things worse. Keep your voice low and quiet, squat down, and look the child directly in the eyes. Remind the child of the limits she has overstepped, staying nearby to assure that the behavior stops. Make it clear that it is the behavior that is the problem; you are not rejecting the child personally, nor are you condemning the child's feelings.

You may need to remove the child from the group with an explanation like, "Komiko needs some time to think." Tell the child, "I'll listen if you want to tell me about what is bothering you." When the child begins to regain control, you can suggest alternative play activity based on your knowledge of what the child likes, does well, or finds rewarding. Mentioning that "the green tricycle is waiting for someone to ride it," or "the children in the sandbox are making birthday cakes," can redirect a child's activity and change the focus to appropriate alternatives. Avoid rushing the child back to the situation in which the problem occurred.

Remember that it will take time for children to develop the skills you are trying to teach them, and you will probably have to repeat the above sequence many times. You should see some progress, though. A child who appears constantly angry or who makes no progress toward self-control should prompt you to look for reasons. Are your responses to the angry outbursts somehow rewarding for the child? Is some aspect of your program or environment creating tension? Is there something going on in the child's life outside of your program that is creating turmoil?

Helping Children Manage Their Behavior

We turn our attention now from children's feelings to their actions. Children's challenging behaviors can take many forms, from aggression toward others to self-comforting habits such as thumb-sucking that are probably more troubling to adults than harmful to children. As you respond to each type of behavior, remember that the goal is not merely to eliminate a troublesome behavior, but to help children manage their own actions in the long run.

Oppositional Behavior. Sometimes a child seems to defy every request made by an adult for no reason. She may refuse to stop playing and come to large group. In the actual moment of refusal you are faced with making what Lilian Katz (Katz & Katz, 2009, pp. 13–16) called a "least worst error." You may feel that allowing her to continue playing and "sit out" large group will encourage other children to join the rebellion. On the other hand, if you force her to come to group, she is likely to disrupt it, distract other children, and reduce the enjoyment for everyone. The odds are that if you are doing meaningful things of real interest to the children at your large group, they will not be tempted to join the recalcitrant child. Acting out children's stories or sharing what individuals and small groups have learned or accomplished in connection with class projects are both likely to captivate children's attention. You may even find the child who had refused to come to group gradually inching closer to be able to hear what's happening.

❈ Talk It Over ❈

Four-year-old Kim had frequent, violent temper tantrums in the classroom—throwing dramatic play props across the room when the call to clean up interrupted her play, for example. Kim's mother expressed the opinion that the teacher was "too soft." She said that she spanked Kim or sent her to her room when she misbehaved at home. What would you say or do if you were the teacher in this situation?

Aggression.   Aggression is the use of force to express feelings or to obtain what one wants, without regard for the rights of others. There is a distinction between aggression, which is destructive, and assertive behavior or standing up for one's rights, which is healthy and constructive.

As always, your first step in dealing with behavior that you believe to be aggressive is to observe carefully. Not every act that results in tears or an injury to another is aggressive. Infants occasionally hurt others by pushing too hard or striking another with a hard toy held in a wobbly, uncertain grasp. Toddlers, new to walking upright, might trod on the fingers or toes of their creeping peers. And four- or five-year-old children often knock each other down because they are too absorbed in their play to notice someone coming across their path.

All of these are accidents, and it is your job to use indirect guidance techniques to help prevent them. Make sure that all toys you provide for infants are soft and that there is enough room for children to move freely, without hurting each other. When the inevitable accidents do occur, tend to the injured child while calmly telling the other that, "It hurts when you step on Cameron's toes." Even very young children can feel empathy and will probably be concerned that a child is crying, although the connection between their actions and those tears is not yet clear to them. Asking the "guilty" party to help, perhaps by bringing you a tissue, may help restore positive feelings on both sides. Apologies seldom help, and demanding that children say they are sorry may merely teach them to be insincere.

In some forms of aggression, children hurt each other or damage property because they don't know another way to get what they want. Or they are so full of pent-up feelings that they lash out at whatever is closest to them. Some toddlers might even bite, out of simple curiosity. While these actions are intentional, they are not done out of malice, so blame and punishment are inappropriate. Certainly you would never try to teach the child a lesson by showing him what it feels like to be bitten or hit!

Your first responsibility is to stop the hurtful action, gently restraining the child if necessary, and perhaps removing him or her to a quiet place away from the group. Say, "I can't let you kick Josh. It hurts him. And I won't let anyone kick you, either." If the child is old enough to talk, you can wait until he or she calms down a little and then find out what precipitated the action so you can begin to teach alternative ways of getting what one wants or expressing strong feelings.

With most troublesome behaviors, your energy will be better spent preventing these types of actions than in dealing with them after they occur. Too many children in a room with too few toys and too few alert adults is a sure-fire recipe for lots of biting, hitting, and kicking, as children are forced to rely on their own devices for meeting their needs. The pressure of an inappropriate curriculum or schedule can create tension that is likely to erupt in violence. Are the activities so difficult that they frustrate children or so simple that they leave the children bored and unchallenged? Are children tired or hungry? If so, perhaps you need to make a change in scheduled mealtimes and naptimes. Attention to such factors will probably reduce the overall number of situations that require your intervention.

Direct guidance techniques provide additional preventive tactics. Teach the problem-solving techniques discussed in Chapter 7 so that children develop the skills they need to resolve conflicts before they erupt into violence. Real-life issues, such as how to make sure everyone has a fair chance at riding the tricycles, are potent topics for lively group discussion at circle time. During children's play, move close to them and show interest in what they are doing before their encounters escalate into violence. Sometimes just your reassuring presence helps children focus on constructive play and keep their disagreements in check. Act as a coach, providing cues for more appropriate ways that children can get what they want: "Tell Megan that you'd like a turn with the tricycle" or "Tell Todd that you are using those blocks now." Act as an interpreter for children who are unable or unwilling to express themselves verbally: "It looks like Jerome doesn't like it when you bump your truck into his" or "I think Lakeisha feels crowded when you sit so close to her." A child who continues to hit or lash out at others can be temporarily removed from a chosen play area as a logical consequence of the unacceptable behavior.

The final, and perhaps most troubling, form of aggression is hostile aggression, in which a child derives satisfaction from hurting another or doing damage. Dealing with this form of aggression will take all your skills as a sensitive observer, trying to discern the reasons behind the child's actions. You can deal with the individual acts of aggression using the techniques described above, but you would also be wise to seek the assistance of a professional counselor or psychologist as well, for children who take pleasure in inflicting harm are probably in some sort of psychological pain themselves.

Perhaps they have witnessed some form of violence in their home or community. Perhaps they have been a victim of abuse. Perhaps they have a disability that somehow makes them unable to feel empathy. Or perhaps they have too many stressors in their lives at this point in time. Your job is not to diagnose or assign blame, but rather to observe carefully and respond compassionately. Consultation with parents and other professionals will be essential to devise a plan for coping with these challenging situations. Appointing one teacher to take primary responsibility for working with the child may help to maintain consistent rules and consequences.

Teasing.　　Teasing is a form of verbal aggression that develops in the fourth and fifth years, as children become more skillful with words. If your goal is to teach children self-esteem coupled with empathy for others and a sense of fair play, you will certainly want to address this behavior when you observe it, particularly if the teasing involves issues related to race, ethnicity, disability, or disfigurement.

Although adults often dismiss teasing as an insignificant and inevitable rite of passage, children see it differently. In one study, children with cancer rated teasing about their appearance as more painful than any medical treatment. Tell the teasers that their behavior is hurtful and that you won't let them continue it. If they are old enough, children being teased can be coached through role-play to stand their ground, perhaps conceding matter-of-factly, "Yes, I suppose I do look strange with my hair gone." This throws teasers off guard and deprives them of satisfaction so they eventually stop teasing (Ross, 1996).

Disrupting the Learning Environment.　　Disruption of the learning environment is disturbing to the other children, to the teacher, and often even to the perpetrator. Appropriate room arrangement, as described in Chapter 6, will help avoid accidental disruption of the learning environment: Protected space out of the traffic lanes for block building, a table for doing puzzles, and a quiet nook for enjoying books away from noisy activities all make it less likely that any child's natural exuberance will interfere with others. Within a carefully planned environment, a rich, engaging curriculum, full of projects and investigations that grow from children's interests and tap the unique skills that each one brings to the group, will keep children so engrossed with their own pursuits that they don't have time to interfere with others. Finally, the adult can use direct guidance to help children navigate the environment successfully. For example, adults can coach children who want to join others already at work so that they can enter the play in an acceptable manner instead of barging in or whining plaintively, "Can I play?" Also, a child can watch for a moment to see what the others are doing and then find a way to make a contribution to the play, perhaps by offering a special accessory for the spaceship they are building. Adults can also work with the group of children to develop agreements about things like who gets to knock down a block structure—ideally, that should be only the person who built it.

Destroying Property.　　Children can learn respect for property and understand that destroying materials means that there will not be toys for other days. While adults should not allow intentional destruction or careless neglect of equipment, they must realize that there is normal wear and tear on equipment: Paint gets chipped and toys get broken, for example. Still, children can learn not to hasten these processes by driving tricycles into the walls or using blocks as hammers.

Use caution when dealing with such actions. Ask yourself whether they were intentionally destructive or accidental. Children who are just learning to steer tricycles may not yet be able to control them. Children who are first encountering blocks may not realize how they are to be used. If you are sure that the destructive behavior is neither accidental nor the result of ignorance, use logical consequences to deal with it. Logical consequences are those that are clearly related to the offense. Ideally, logical consequences involve restitution rather than retribution; that is, they give children a means of restoring what has been destroyed rather than simply paying them back for their misdeeds. A child who has destroyed another's block structure can be encouraged to help rebuild it. Children also need to know what the alternative is, should they fail to stop their destructive behavior. Tell a child, "Blocks are for building. Pounding with them hurts everyone's ears and will ruin our blocks. If you can't use them to build, you will have to play somewhere else." Tell a child who intentionally crashes the tricycle, "You have to drive safely if you want to use the tricycle. If you crash into walls, you are showing me that you can't do that, and you'll have to play somewhere else today." Of course, it is important to follow through on your warning if the child repeats the behavior. It is also important to start each new day afresh. Never deprive children of the use of a material today because they might have misused it yesterday or last week. Children, like all the rest of us, need many chances to learn new ways of behaving.

Attention Seeking. Some children resort to unacceptable behavior to get attention. They seem to be saying that even negative attention is better than no attention at all. They may seek help when they could do a task themselves. They may seek reassurance. Their behavior clearly says, "I want you to notice me." Recognizing that the attention is something that every human needs, your job is to provide the attention *before* the child resorts to acting out to get it. Greeting children personally each day with a brief conversation about something that others don't know about, such as something you've learned on a home visit, is a good way to show children that you know and care about them as individuals. Using a child's name frequently in working with him helps him know you are talking to and noticing him. Keeping groups small also makes frequent individual attention possible. Denying attention does not improve attention-seeking behavior. Children must be allowed legitimate ways to shine and increase their self-confidence in order to cast off their attention-seeking devices.

❀ Talk It Over ❀

Three-year-old Malcolm has been attending a part-day program for a little over a month. His teachers are frustrated because he doesn't sit still at storytime and, during free play, they have to remind him repeatedly to "go down the slide on your bottom." What advice would you have for these teachers?

Lying and Fantastic Tales. Lying and telling fantastic tales are closely related. Young children often spin fanciful tales. Some may be designed to get attention or make the child feel powerful. Others may be wish fulfillments, as in the case of a child who told many stories in which his absent father played heroic roles. You may be able to help keep reality in check by reminding a child, "That's one of your pretend stories, isn't it?" Forcing a young child to admit that a story is a lie will probably do little more than make the child feel bad. Children may also deny doing something, either because they did not perceive it as wrong at the time or because they are afraid of incurring your displeasure. The adult may contribute to lying of this sort by the way questions are asked. The child's natural inclination is self-defense; therefore, when asked, "Did you dump out the puzzle?" the child may say, "No." If you saw the child dump the puzzle deliberately, you can say so. Otherwise, asking "Who did it?" is probably a waste of time. The important message for a child to learn is that people will stop believing a person who tells lies.

Tattling. Tattling is troublesome to some teachers, and children who tell on other children are often unpopular with their peers. Still, there are times when adults obviously appreciate having problems they may not have noticed brought to their attention. Families, too, may inadvertently encourage this behavior by placing older siblings in charge of younger ones. This ambivalence confuses children about whether or when they should tell on their peers and siblings.

One thing that can be said for children who tattle is that they know the rules and can verbalize them. Adherents of Vygotsky's theory of development argue that this attempt to regulate the behavior of others is an important step in acquiring self-regulation (Bodrova & Leong, 2007a). One response to a child who tattles is, "Don't worry, I'll take care of Ana Maria, if you take care of . . . ." (using the child's own name). Be aware, however, that if you respond by immediately going to check on Ana Maria, you are rewarding the tattling.

Swearing and Name Calling. Swearing and name calling can be a habit learned at home or from older children in the school or neighborhood. Many adults, who swear themselves believe that children should be punished for doing so. Clearly, that is a double standard. In general, the words do not mean the same things to the children using them that they do to adults, so it is important to determine what the language means to the child before trying to squelch it. Your overreaction will only serve to teach children how powerful these words can be. Ignoring isolated occurrences will probably be much more effective than any long lecture about proper language. Of course, ignoring may not always be possible, because other children, who are also deeply interested in the power of words, will inevitably come to tell you that "Jessie said a bad word." You can agree with them that "we don't use those words at school," without making a federal case out of it. And you can capitalize on children's fascination with language by teaching some playful substitutions: "Oh, pastrowzi!" or "Fiddlesticks!" It may be surprising how young children adapt to the standards of the school. One school bus driver noted that the children used pretty strong language en route to and from school but seldom used the same words at school. The driver had not heard anyone correct the children; they just adapted to the customs of the new environment.

Self-Comforting Behaviors. Thumb sucking and nail biting are habits that may grow out of tension and a need for comfort. They may relax a child or relieve stress and, unless they interfere with a child's participation in play or other activities, should probably be ignored. Even when they seem excessive, rather than attempt to deal with such behaviors, you should look for the cause of the tension in the child's life. Unless the pressure that is causing a behavior is removed, stopping one behavior usually results in starting another. Shaming or calling these behaviors naughty is usually counterproductive. The same advice applies to masturbation, another self-comforting behavior, unless it is excessive or precociously imitative of adult sexual activity, in which case it might indicate that the child has been sexually abused. (See Figure 4-2 on page 89 for guidelines to help you make an objective determination about this.)

Quiet and Withdrawn Behavior. You may not think of quiet and withdrawn behavior as challenging, yet it may be the most difficult behavior to deal with. In large groups, quiet and withdrawn children may actually move through the day almost without notice because the assertive and aggressive

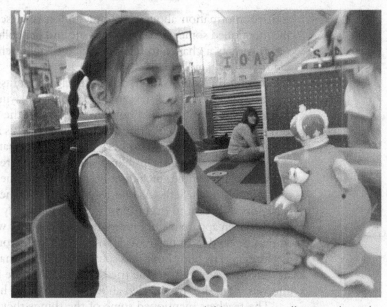

In large groups, quiet and withdrawn children may actually move through the day almost without notice because the more assertive children receive all the teacher's time and energy.

children receive all the teacher's time and energy. In such groups, if you were to ask a teacher for a character sketch of each child, the quiet and withdrawn children are the ones most teachers would likely forget or have little to say about.

Some shy or withdrawn children may need help from their parents in making the initial adjustment to school. Parents may have to bring them for only short periods for several weeks or stay in the classroom with them until they become comfortable in their new setting. The reassuring presence of the same adult every day usually helps the withdrawn child cope with the school situation. Adults also help by refraining from pressuring a child to participate in any particular activity and acting as a buffer to keep others from approaching a withdrawn child too quickly. The adult can invite a child to play with some appealing material and then gradually recede into the background as the child becomes engrossed and other children join in.

COLLABORATING WITH FAMILIES TO CREATE A PLAN OF ACTION

Let's return to the story of Seth, the child we met at the beginning of this chapter. Seth's teacher had already established a friendly relationship with Seth's mother and stepfather during regularly scheduled conferences and home visits. They had talked about his mother's job, how things were going for Seth and the new baby, and so on. These contacts had paved the way so that the teacher felt comfortable asking to meet with Seth's parents and knew it was unlikely that they would react with worry or anger that their son was "in trouble." At the meeting, the teacher was careful to share the positive information about Seth, in addition to describing his disruptive behaviors. She mentioned some of the strategies she and her colleagues had tried. Then she gave Seth's parents a chance to tell whether the same behaviors were occurring at home and how they handled it.

During the conversation, it became clear that, as an only child until the birth of his new sibling, Seth had next to no experience playing with children his own age, so it made sense that he would not have developed the skills to get children to let him into their play or to recognize their playful overtures as invitations. Furthermore, the teacher learned that Seth had been spending alternate weekends with his biological father and several older stepsiblings. Apparently there were very few limits on behaviors in that household, including no regular bedtime, and the older children played very roughly with Seth. As she listened, the teacher realized that Seth's problem behaviors did seem to occur most often immediately after a weekend, a pattern that had not been apparent since it did not happen every week. Seth's mother also reported that he tended to be crankier and react more strongly to any frustration when he was hungry. His body build was somewhat smaller than his age-mates and he typically ate very little at meals, so she tried to ensure that he had nutritious snacks at regular intervals. Still, she was puzzled about what to do to help him control his outbursts.

The teachers mentioned some of the things they had been teaching all the children about how to use words to express feelings, or how to stop, take a deep breath, and count to five to regain control when upset. As they continued to talk, the teachers and Seth's parents formulated a plan. Seth's mother said she would try to encourage him to practice the self-calming technique when he became upset at home. She also agreed to talk about the problem with his biological father and to alert the teacher the next time Seth was spending the weekend with him.

The teachers agreed to remind Seth when the center's open snack was made available, realizing that some mornings he was so busy playing that he skipped snack. They would refer to him by name frequently, making sure to acknowledge the positive things he did, and they would use modeling or prompts to help him learn more effective ways of joining other children at play and to recognize when other children wanted to engage him in play. They would try to make sure he knew he could refuse those invitations and how to respond with words rather than screams or blows. Finally, they would make sure that someone would stay near Seth on the days immediately following his weekends with his dad. In addition to reacting (i.e., stopping his problem behavior firmly, as needed), the teachers decided to plan activities that Seth particularly enjoyed and to let him know that they had done so. If Seth lost control, an assistant would continue the activity with the group so the lead teacher could stay near Seth.

Teachers and parents agreed to keep each other informed about how the plan was working and to schedule another meeting if needed. They put in writing the plan resulting from their discussion. (See Figure 11–3.) The teachers made a point of sharing the positive things that Seth had done each day when his family came to pick him up. Soon Seth began acting up less often and other children became more accepting and less fearful of him. The problems didn't disappear entirely, but improvement was evident.

A troubled child like Seth must be helped, or the entire group will be affected. Some would say that Seth was getting more than his share of the teacher's time,

Positive Behavior Support Plan

Child's Name _____ **Date** _____

Behavior interfering with development or learning:
> *Disrupting children's play (knocking over block structures); hitting and/or screaming at minor provocations by other children.*

This is a problem for the child because:
> *Children are unwilling to play with him, meaning that he is missing out on important opportunities for learning. They are beginning to blame him for any mishap that occurs which can lead to damaged self-esteem if he begins to see himself as a "bad boy."*

How often does it happen? When?
> *Several times a week, sometimes several times a day; often on Mondays after spending weekend at home of biological father.*

What seems to trigger it?
> *Desire to join children at play: will sometimes knock over a block structure or disrupt a dramatic play scenario*
> *Being approached by another child while he is occupied.*

What does the child gain from the behavior?
> *Attention from adults; avoidance by other children.*

What possible substitute behaviors are acceptable?
> ❋ *Playing alongside others until invited to join, or offering interesting additions to existing play scenarios, rather than barging in.*
> ❋ *Using language to express strong feelings*
> ❋ *Using self-calming strategies (deep breath, count to five)*

How will these behaviors be taught or supported
> **at school:** *continue to incorporate emotional skill building in curriculum for all children (stories, modeling, reflecting children's feelings); provide individual coaching for Seth on effective ways to enter play groups and to recognize and respond appropriately to approaches from other children; monitor snack intake; assign one adult to help him regain control when outbursts occur; be particularly vigilant on days after weekends with dad*
> **at home:** *help Seth practice self-calming strategies at home; speak with dad about possibly maintaining a more normal routine on weekend visits*

When and how will results be communicated? *Updates as needed at arrival and/or departure; meet again in one month to review progress and revise plan if necessary.*

Participants:

Family Member(s): _____

Center Staff: _____

FIGURE 11–3   Example of a plan for addressing challenging behavior

but the other children were glad to have him more relaxed and able to control himself. They didn't vie for the head teacher's time when Seth needed attention. One precaution wise teachers follow is to avoid blaming parents or putting them on the defensive regarding a child's behavior. After all, the child's troublesome behavior may not be a parent's responsibility. The behavior could be a reaction to the school—to teachers, children, the schedule, curriculum, crowding—or it could be related to other factors. Even if the basis of the problem is in the home, the parents often cannot do anything about the behavior exhibited at school. Certainly parents lecturing the child is not likely to be effective. And punishments administered at home, hours after the infractions occur at school, are likely to cause resentment, confusion, and even more misbehavior. In cases where challenging behavior seems to be caused or exacerbated by something in the home environment, early childhood professionals can help most by putting families in touch with counseling services or other appropriate assistance.

Four things helped the situation with Seth: (1) observation, to be sure of what was actually happening; (2) a conference with the mother and stepfather to arrive at a plan; (3) staff follow-through in carrying out of the plan; and (4) sincere respect for both the child and his parents.

CHILDREN WITH DISABILITIES

A college instructor was taken aback one day when confronted by a question from a young woman about to graduate from an early childhood teacher preparation program that had included a course in guidance as well as several courses in special education. When asked for feedback about how well the program had prepared her to enter the profession, she said that she would have liked more information about dealing with challenging behaviors of children with disabilities. She seemed to believe that somehow what she had learned about guidance did not apply or was not sufficient where children with atypical development were concerned—a belief that is probably shared by many teachers in the field. We want to emphasize, therefore, that the information presented in this textbook is intended to apply to *all* children. The principles and strategies put forward throughout this book are congruent with intervention practices recommended by the Division for Early Childhood (DEC) of the Council for Exceptional Children (2009). These include setting expectations that take into account the child's age, ability, and cultural background; creating environments and curricula that support positive behaviors; observing carefully; and collaborating with families, all of which should sound familiar to you at this point. The DEC advocates a three-tiered model of prevention and intervention approaches, beginning with "universal practices" to promote communication and social skills for all children and then adding "targeted instruction" in these skills for children who are at risk for delays or problems, and, finally, planning "individualized interventions" for children whose challenging behaviors remain unabated. The intervention should begin with understanding what purpose the behavior serves for the child and how the environment might be eliciting or rewarding the behavior. It should include specific strategies for teaching new skills that can be implemented by family members at home as well as by educators in child-care or other settings (DEC 2009).

Try to map the tiered approach advocated by the DEC onto the guidance pyramid you have encountered in this book. Which parts of the pyramid correspond to the first tier (universal practices to promote communication and social skills for all children)? Which part might encompass the second tier (targeted instruction in these skills)? Finally, where would you put the third tier (individualized interventions)?

Response to Intervention

The DEC's tiered approach to challenging behavior is similar in many respects to a method of identifying learning disabilities cited in the 2004 reauthorization of the federal Individuals with Disabilities Education Act (IDEA). This method, called *Response to Intervention* (RtI), allows school districts to use a child's response to research-based intervention strategies to determine whether a learning disability exists. Previously, identification of a learning disability was based on documentation that a child's achievement did not measure up to his or her potential (e.g., I.Q.), leading some to argue that children had to fail before receiving special education services. The RtI approach means that teachers, in consultation with a team of interventionists, provide extra help in the regular classroom for children who appear to have learning difficulties. For some children, this may be enough to keep them on track and avoid referral to special education. Children for whom the extra help is insufficient may then be identified as needing special education services (National Center on Response to Intervention, n.d.).

The goal of RtI is help children in kindergarten and primary grades succeed in school. A companion model, *Recognition and Response* (R&R, or "RtI for PreK"), developed at the Frank Porter Graham Child Development Institute in North Carolina, addresses the needs of younger children with a similar three-tiered approach:

- *Tier 1:* Setting up an environment and implementing a curriculum designed to help all children acquire important skills.
- *Tier 2:* Working with small groups of children who seem to need extra help with specific skills.
- *Tier 3:* Providing extra support for individual children to practice skills taught in Tier 2 (Buysse & Peisner-Feinberg, n.d.).

While RtI and R&R appear to focus most closely on helping children acquire the levels of literacy and math proficiency needed for success in school, it's important to remember that academic success depends heavily upon the social-emotional skills and self-regulation that are fostered by the guidance strategies presented throughout this textbook. The classroom examples provided on the R&R site (randr.fpg.unc.edu/classroom-examples) are described as having developmentally appropriate practices and overall good quality in place before targeting specific issues such as a child's difficulty paying attention at storybook reading or lags in vocabulary and letter recognition.

Focus on the Child

Even knowing a lot about guidance in general, you may feel insecure because you feel you lack sufficient knowledge about particular disabilities, though it is unrealistic to expect to know in advance all about every possible disability you may encounter. But if you remember that children with disabilities are children first, you will focus on the child, not on the disability. If you remember that children are individuals, you will realize that two children with autism, for example, can be as different from each other as they are from any other children. This means that you can—and must—use all the guidance strategies you have already learned with every child. You must look beyond the label and get to know the unique child to understand what the particular challenging behavior means for that child. Recall the story in Chapter 3 about the little girl with autism who raced around the room and whose teachers discovered a way to enter her world only after observing closely enough to discover her fascination with bright light.

You won't feel so compelled to know everything about every conceivable disability if you remember that you have allies in your work. First, families are the experts about their own children and can help you know the child behind the label. They may have already learned a great deal about the disability that they can share with you, or you can work together to learn more. Next, the professionals who comprise a child's intervention team have specialized knowledge about the disability that you can tap. Finally, there is a wealth of resources available in print and on the Internet that you can access as the need arises.

Learning about a child's disability *as part of getting to know that child* can help you avoid two pitfalls: At one extreme, you might be tempted to blame children for behaviors that are beyond their control because of a disability. Children with attention-deficit/hyperactivity disorder (ADHD) may have great difficulty coping with distractions or sitting still. They are not willfully "misbehaving," and reprimands will do more to damage their self-esteem than to change their behavior.

Whether or not a child has a particular disability, you can—and must—use all the guidance strategies you have already learned with every child. You must look beyond the label and get to know the unique child, to understand what the particular challenging behavior means for that child.

Your time and energy will be better spent looking at how you might modify the environment to reduce distractions. Does the lighting need to be adjusted? Can some sources of extraneous noise be removed or at least softened? The good news is that modifications made for children with disabilities often improve the environment for all the children in the setting.

At the opposite extreme, you might assume that every challenging behavior is simply the result of a disability and therefore cannot be addressed. With your help, children with ADHD whose behavior is disruptive of others can learn coping strategies such as moving to a special quiet area in the room where they can do puzzles or look at books when they begin to feel out of control. Children with autism can benefit from coaching in the play skills we take for granted in other children, such as initiating play or responding to an invitation from another child (Stanton-Chapman & Snell, 2011). Always remember to evaluate general information about a disability in light of what you know about a particular child through your own experience and that of his or her family. This is part of "evidence-based practice" we discussed in Chapter 3 (Buysse & Winton, 2007).

CONCLUSION

While this chapter has ostensibly focused on the tip of the guidance pyramid, we have shown that dealing effectively with challenging behavior actually involves every other segment of the pyramid as well. Adults have to know children well enough to recognize that what is a reasonable demand for one can be overwhelmingly stressful for another. They have to build the kind of warm, supportive relationships with children that motivate positive behaviors. They have to establish clear, appropriate expectations and an environment that minimizes stress. Finally, they have to help children learn alternatives to replace the behaviors that pose a danger to themselves, to others, or to the environment.

We have described some of the challenging behaviors that occur in almost any group. Many behavior problems cannot be ignored, for they interfere with other children's safety and learning. Some extreme behaviors tell us that a child needs help with a problem. You may have been reading this chapter with some degree of skepticism, thinking that the suggestions we have offered sound fine in theory but would never work with a particular child or group of children that you have known. While we certainly concur that guidance will not be equally effective with every child, we remain convinced that many, if not most, challenging behaviors can be addressed through appropriate guidance.

The first step is for the teacher to observe the child over a period of time to be sure that an act is typical for that child. If so, to what extent is the behavior a result of inappropriate expectations, an environment that fails to support positive behavior, or a curriculum that does not engage the whole child?

Through discussions with the parents, a teacher can learn whether the behavior occurs at home, what the parents are doing about it, and perhaps whether home factors are contributing to the tension that may be part of the problem. It is unfair to jump to the conclusion that parents are at fault for the child's troublesome behavior. Nor are judgments about the existence of deep psychological problems within the range of expertise of most early childhood professionals. It is irresponsible for teachers to allow a problem to persist over a period of months without conferring with parents. A collaborative approach that enlists parents' involvement from the beginning and supports their feelings of competence is likely to engender a willingness to deal with the challenging behavior. Blaming will create only resentment and defensiveness.

Following careful observation, early childhood professionals will attempt to create conditions that make it possible and likely for a child to replace the challenging behavior with a more positive one. A plan coordinated among all staff members will help avoid working at cross purposes. Helping the child to find outlets for strong feelings and to talk over behavior may be helpful.

In cases of extremely challenging behaviors, teachers should seek advice from a guidance or mental health professional who might visit the school and offer the staff advice for coping with a troubled child. Parental knowledge and consent must be obtained before any such step is taken. Children's behavior problems that are severe or that are associated with some type of disability require a collaborative and comprehensive approach in which parents and professional specialists set specific goals and determine the best strategies to use.

REVIEW: TEN WAYS TO COPE WITH CHALLENGING BEHAVIOR

1. Remember that the goal is to teach self-control. Focus on children's strengths; catch them being good and ignore minor misbehavior that does not harm anyone.
2. Be sure your expectations are realistic and appropriate for the age group in your care. Be aware of variations among children and within the same child over time; adjust your expectations accordingly.
3. Set few limits (rules) and consistently enforce those you do set.
4. When behaviors present potential harm to the child, to others, or to the environment, try to understand the behavior: Observe and record the time of day, the surrounding events, and with whom a child has problems.
5. Consider that a child's health, hunger, and fatigue may be contributing to the behavior and try to alleviate any problems.
6. Examine the environment and schedule for possible contributing factors (see Chapter 6).
7. Move close to the child to prevent problems; when harmful behavior occurs, use a quiet voice and manner to stop it immediately; explain your reasons and redirect the child.
8. Teach the child alternative modes of behavior (e.g., how to cool down through vigorous activity or how to express feelings in words).
9. Consult with family members and enlist their help.
10. Seek assistance from and collaborate with other professionals.

APPLICATIONS

1. Think of a challenging behavior you have observed in a child-care setting. What message does the child seem to be sending? List possible contributing factors, either in the child's make-up or the environment, and explain your reasoning.

2. Write (or role-play) a scenario in which you discuss the behavior with the child's family in order to understand it better and arrive at a plan of action.

3. Give several suggestions for coping with the behavior with the goal of helping the child become more self-managed.

RESOURCES FOR FURTHER STUDY

Websites

Center for Early Childhood Mental Health Consultation
ecmhc.org/index.html
A multiple-university project designed to develop strategies to help Head Start programs build a strong mental health foundation for their children, families, and staff. Includes links to teaching tools for helping children express feelings, participate in circle time, and follow classroom routines.

Center on the Social and Emotional Foundations for Early Learning
vanderbilt.edu/csefel
Source for "What Works Briefs," articles and PowerPoint presentations on a variety of topics regarding managing challenging behaviors.

DIRFloortime
www.icdl.com
Provides information and strategies for parents and professionals in dealing with autism spectrum disorder based on the work of Dr. Stanley Greenspan.

National Center on Response to Intervention
rti4success.org
Website describing essential components of Response to Intervention, with links to training resources (videos, webinars, etc.)

Readings

Barton, E. E., Reichow, B., Wolery, M., & Chen, C.-I. (2011). We can all participate! Adapting circle time for children with autism. *Young Exceptional Children, 13*(2), 2–21.

Bishop, H. M., & Baird, D. S. (2007, March/April). Challenging behavior. *Exchange, 174,* 26–30.

Kaiser, B., & Rasminsky, J. S. (2012). *Challenging behavior in young children: Understanding, preventing, and responding effectively* (3rd ed.). Upper Saddle River, NJ: Pearson.

Nielsen, S. L., Olive, M. L., Amy, D., & McEvoy, M. (1998). Challenging behaviors in your classroom? Don't react—Teach instead! *Young Exceptional Children, 1*(1), 2–10.

Oliver, S., & Klugman, E. (2003). When play presents problems—Resources for managing common play challenges. *Child Care Information Exchange, 153,* 35–40.

Tyrrell, A. L., Horn, E. M., & Freeman, R. L. (2006, Fall). The role of the family in the positive behavior support process: Team-based problem solving. *Young Exceptional Children, 10*(1), 12–21.

Vance, E., & Weaver, P. J. (2002). *Class meetings: Young children solving problems together.* Washington, DC: National Association for the Education of Young Children.

References

American Academic of Pediatrics Committee on Nutrition. (2001). The use and misuse of fruit juice in pediatrics. *Pediatrics, 107*(5), 1210–1213. Cited in Story, M., Kaphingst, K. M., & French, S. (2006, Spring).

American Academic of Pediatrics Committee on Nutrition. (2003, August). Prevention of pediatric overweight and obesity. Pediatrics, *112*(2), 424–430. Retrieved July 10, 2007, from aappolicy. aappublications.org/cgi/reprint/pediatrics; 112/2/424.pdf.

American Academy of Pediatrics, American Public Health Association, and National Resource Center for Health and Safety in Child Care and Early Education. (2002). *Caring for Our Children: National Health and Safety Performance Standards: Guidelines for Out-of-Home Child Care Programs* (2nd ed.). Elk Grove Village, IL: American Academy of Pediatrics and Washington, DC: American Public Health Association.

Anonymous. (1997, April/May). Jacob's story: A miracle of the heart. *Zero to Three, 17*(5), 59–64.

Bailey, D. B., McWilliam, R. A., Buysse, V., & Wesley, P. W. (1998). Inclusion in the context of competing values in early childhood education. *Early Childhood Research Quarterly, 13*(1), 27–47.

Ballenger, C. (1998). Culture and behavior problems: The language of control. In W. G. Scarlett and Associates. *Trouble in the classroom: Managing the behavior problems of young children.* San Francisco, CA: Jossey-Bass.

Bandura, A. (1986). *Social foundations of thought and action: A social cognitive theory.* Upper Saddle River, NJ: Prentice Hall.

Barrera, I. (2003, May). From rocks to diamonds: Mining the riches of diversity for our children. *Zero to Three, 23*(5), 8–15.

Belt, T. (2007). *A personal perspective on culture.* Presentation at Crosswalks National Institute: Infusing Cultural, Linguistic and Ability Diversity in Preservice Education, Asheville, NC, July 28, 2007.

Berk, L. E. (2012). *Infants and children and adolescents* (7th ed.). Upper Saddle River, NJ: Pearson.

Bloom, P. (2010, May 5). The moral life of babies. *New York Times Magazine.* Retrieved June 7, 2011, from nytimes.com/2010/05/09/magazine/09babies-t.html.

Bodrova, E., & Leong, D. (2004). Chopsticks and counting chips: Do play and foundational skills need to compete for the teacher's attention in an early childhood classroom? In D. Koralek (ed.). *Spotlight on young children and play* (pp. 4–11). Washington, DC: National Association for the Association of Young Children.

Bodrova, E., & Leong, D. (2007a). *Tools of the mind.* Upper Saddle River, NJ: Pearson.

Bodrova, E., & Leong, D. (2007b). *Vygotskian/post Vygotskian research on the development of children's intentional make-believe play.* Presentation at NAEYC National Institute for Early Childhood Professional Development, Pittsburgh, PA, June 12, 2007.

Bohling-Philippi, V. (2006, September/October). The power of nature to help children heal. *Exchange, 171*, 49–52.

Bolger, K. E., & Patterson, C. J. (2001). Developmental pathways from child maltreatment to peer rejection. *Child Development, 72*(2), 549–568.

Bowman, B. (2006). Resilience: Preparing children for school. In B. Bowman & E. K. Moore (eds.). *School readiness and social-emotional development: Perspectives on cultural diversity* (pp. 49–57). Washington, DC: National Black Child Development Institute.

Brazelton, T. B. (1992). *Touchpoints: Your child's emotional and behavioral development.* Reading, MA: Addison-Wesley.

Bredekamp, S. (ed.). (1987). *Developmentally appropriate practice in early childhood programs serving children birth through age 8*. Washington, DC: National Association for the Education of Young Children.

Bredekamp, S., & Copple, C. (eds.). (1997). *Developmentally appropriate practice in early childhood programs serving children birth through age 8, revised ed*. Washington, DC: National Association for the Education of Young Children.

Bredekamp, S., & Rosegrant, T. (1992). Reaching potentials through appropriate curriculum: Conceptual frameworks for applying the guidelines. In S. Bredekamp & T. Rosegrant (eds.). *Reaching potentials: Appropriate curriculum and assessment for young children* (pp. 28–42). Washington, DC: National Association for the Education of Young Children.

Brown, J. G., & Burger, C. (1984). Playground design and preschool children's behaviors. *Environments and Behavior, 16*, 599–626.

Brown, M. H., Althouse, R., & Anfin, C. (1993, January). Guided dramatization: Fostering social development in children with disabilities. *Young Children, 48*(2), 68–71.

Buysse, V., & Peisner-Feinberg, E. (n.d.). Recognition and response. Retrieved August 2, 2011, from randr.fpg.unc.edu/sites/randr.fpg.unc.edu/files/RandR-Overview.pdf.

Buysse, V., & Winton, P. (2007, Spring). Evidence-based practice: Recognizing different ways of knowing. *Early Developments, 11*(1), 4–5.

Campos, J., Bertenthal, B., & Kermoian, R. (1992). Early experience and emotional development: The emergence of wariness of heights. *Psychological Science, 3*, 61–64.

Capra, F. (1999). Ecoliteracy: *The challenge for education in the next century*. Liverpool Schumacher Lecture, March 20, 1999. Retrieved July 18, 2007, from ecoliteracy.org/publications/pdf/challenge.pdf.

Carlson, F. M. (2011). *Big body play: Why boisterous, vigorous, and very physical play is essential to children's development and learning*. Washington, DC: National Association for the Education of Young Children.

Carson, R. (1965/1998). *The sense of wonder*. New York, NY: HarperCollins.

Center for Universal Design. (2010). Principles of universal design. Retrieved November 28, 2011, from www.ncsu.edu/project/design-projects/udi/center-for-universal-design/.

Center on the Developing Child at Harvard University. (2010). *The foundations of lifelong health are built in early childhood*. Retrieved June 7, 2010, from developingchild.harvard.edu.

Center on the Developing Child at Harvard University. (2011). *Building the brain's "air traffic control" system: How early experiences shape the brain*. Working paper no. 11. Retrieved June 20, 2011, from developingchild.harvard.edu.

Chang, F., Crawford, G., Early, D., Bryant, D., Howes, C., Burchinal, M., Barbarin, O., Clifford, R., & Pianta, R. (2007). Spanish speaking children's social and language development in pre-kindergarten classrooms. *Journal of Early Education and Development, 18*(2), 243–269.

Chenfeld, M. B. (2007). *Celebrating young children and their teachers*. St. Paul, MN: Redleaf.

Chess, S., & Thomas, A. (1996). *Temperaments: Theory and practice*. New York, NY: Bruner Mazel Publishers.

Chrisman, K., & Couchenour, D. (2002). Healthy sexuality development: A guide for early childhood educators and families. Washington, DC: National Association for the Education of Young Children.

Christie, J. F., & Wardle, F. (1992, March). How much time is needed for play? *Young Children, 47*(3), 28–32.

Chugani, H. T. (2004). *Fine-tuning the baby brain*. The Dana Foundation. Retrieved June 16, 2011, from dana.org/news/cerebrum/detail.aspx?id=1228.

Clements, R. (2004). An investigation of the status of outdoor play. *Contemporary Issues in Early Childhood, 5*. Cited in Oliver & Klugman (2005).

Collins, R., Mascia, J., Kendall, R., Golden, O., Schock, L., & Parlakian, R. (2003, March). Promoting mental health in child care settings: Caring for the whole child. *Zero to Three, 25*(4), 39–45.

Copple, C., & Bredekamp, S. (eds.). (2009). *Developmentally appropriate practice in early childhood programs serving children from birth through age 8*, (3rd ed.). Washington, DC: National Association for the Education of Young Children.

Cryer, D., & Burchinal, M. (1997). Parents as child care consumers. *Early Childhood Research Quarterly, 12*, 35–58.

Danese, A., Moffitt, T. E., Harrington, H., Milne, B. J., Polanczyk, G., Pariante, C. M., Poulton, R., & Caspi, A. (2009). Adverse childhood experiences and adult risk factors for age-related disease: Depression, inflammation, and clustering of metabolic risk markers. *Archives of Pediatric and Adolescent Medicine, 163*(12):1135–1143.

Davies, M. (1997). The teacher's role in outdoor play: Preschool teachers' beliefs and practices. *Journal of Australian Research in Early Childhood Education, 1*, 10–20.

Davies, M. M. (1996). Outdoors: An important context for young children's development. *Early Child Development and Care, 115*, 37–49.

DeBord, K., Hestenes, L. L., Moore, R. C., Cosco, N. G., & McGinnis, J. R. (2005). *POEMS: Preschool outdoor environment measurement scale.* Lewisville, NC: Kaplan.

Derman-Sparks, L., & Edwards, J. O. (2010). *Anti-bias education for young children and ourselves.* Washington, DC: National Association for the Education of Young Children.

Diamond, K. E., & Stacey, S. (2000). The other children at preschool: Experiences of typically developing children in inclusive programs. *Young Exceptional Children Monograph Series No. 2: Natural Environments and Inclusion*, 59–68.

Dietze, B., & Crossley, B. (2003, Fall). Two cultures/two approaches: Outdoor play in Jordan and Norway. Interaction. *Journal of Canadian Child Care Federation.* Retrieved October 13, 2003, from childcareexchange.com/eed/index.php.

Division for Early Childhood. (1998/2009). *Position statement: Identification of and intervention with challenging behavior.* Retrieved November 28, 2011, from http://www.dec-sped.org/About_DEC/Position_Statements_and_Concept_Papers.

Dreikurs, R., & Cassel, P. (1972). *Discipline without tears.* New York, NY: Hawthorn Books.

Dunst, C., Hamby, D., Trivette, C. M., Raab, M., & Bruder, M. B. (2000). Everyday family and community life and children's naturally occurring learning opportunities. *Journal of Early Intervention, 23*(3), 151–164.

Early, D. M., Iruka, I. U., Ritchie, S., Barbarin, O. A., Winn, D. C., Crawford, G. M., Frome, P. M., Clifford, R. M., Burchinal, M., Howes, C., Briant, D. M., & Pianta, R. C. (2010). How do pre-kindergarteners spend their time? Gender, ethnicity, and income as predictors of experiences in pre-kindergarten classrooms. *Early Childhood Research Quarterly, 25*, 177–193.

Edwards, C. (1998). The role of the teacher. In C. Edwards, L. Gandini, & G. Forman (eds.). *The hundred languages of children: The Reggio Emilia approach—Advanced reflections* (2nd ed.) (pp. 179–198). Greenwich, CT: Ablex.

Eisenberg, N. (2010). Empathy-related responding: Links with self-regulation, moral judgment, and moral behavior. In M. Mikulincer & P. R. Shaver (eds.). *Prosocial motives, emotions, and behavior: The better angels of our nature* (pp. 129–148). Washington, DC: American Psychological Association.

Eisenberg, N., Fabes, R. A., & Spinrad, T. L. (2006). Prosocial development. In W. Damon & R. M. Lerner (eds.). *Handbook of child psychology* (pp. 646–718). Hoboken, NJ: John Wiley & Sons.

Eisner, E. (2002). *Ten lessons the arts teach.* Retrieved June 21, 2007, from naea-reston.org/tenlessons.html.

Elkonin, D. (1977). Toward the problem of stages in the mental development of the child. In M. Cole (ed.). *Soviet developmental psychology* (pp. 538–635). White Plains, NY: M. E. Sharpe. Cited in Bodrova & Leong (2004).

Elkonin, D. (1978). *Psychologija igry* [The psychology of play]. Moscow: Pedagogika. Cited in Bodrova & Leong (2004).

Epstein, A. S. (2007). *The intentional teacher: Choosing the best strategies for young children's learning.* Washington, DC: National Association for the Education of Young Children.

Epstein, A. S. (2009). *Me, you, us: Social-emotional learning in preschool.* Ypsilanti, MI: HighScope Press and Washington, DC: National Association for the Education of Young Children.

Exton, Mary. (2000, Winter). When one culture rubs up against another. *Focus on Infants and Toddlers,* 3–5.

Far West Laboratory for Educational Research and Development. (1988). First moves: Welcoming a child to a new caregiving setting. *Child Care Video Magazine*. Sacramento: California Department of Education.

Forman, G. (1997, April 24). *Negotiated learning for children through technology*. Presentation for the annual meeting of North Carolina Community College Educators, Winston-Salem, NC.

Frost, J. L., Brown, P., Sutterby, J. A., & Thornton, C. D. (2004). *The developmental benefits of playgrounds*. Olney, MD: Association for Childhood Education International.

Frost, J. L., Wortham, S. C., & Reifel, S. (2012). *Play and child development* (4th ed.). Upper Saddle River, NJ: Pearson.

Galinsky, E. (2010). *Mind in the making: The seven essential life skills every child needs*. New York, NY: HarperCollins.

Gallahue, D., & Donnelly, F. C. (2003). *Developmental physical education for all children* (4th ed.). Champaign, IL: Human Kinetics.

Gandini, L. (1984, Summer). Not just anywhere: Making child care centers into particular places. *Beginnings*, 17–20.

Gandini, L. (1998). Educational and caring spaces. In C. Edwards, L. Gandini, & G. Forman (eds.). *The hundred languages of children: The Reggio Emilia approach—Advanced reflections* (2nd ed.) (pp. 161–178). Greenwich, CT: Ablex.

Gandini, L. (2005). From the beginning of the atelier to materials as language: Conversations from Reggio Emilia. In L. Gandini, L. Hill, L. Cadwell, & C. Schwall (eds.). *In the spirit of the studio: Learning from the atelier of Reggio Emilia* (pp. 6–16). New York, NY: Teachers College Press.

Giles, H. C. (2005). Three narratives of parent–educator relationships: Toward counselor repertoires for bridging the urban parent–school divide. *Professional School Counseling, 8*(3), 228–235. Retrieved May 30, 2011 from EBSCO*host*.

Gilliam, W. S. (2005). *Prekindergarteners left behind: Expulsion rate in state prekindergarten systems*. New Haven, CT: Yale University Child Study Center. Retrieved July 23, 2007, from fed-us.org/PDFs/NationalPreKExpulsionPaper03.02_new.pdf.

Girolametto, L., & Weitzman, E. (2006). It takes two to talk—the Hanen Program for parents: Early language intervention through caregiver training. In R. McCauley & M. Fey (eds.). *Treatment of language disorders in children* (pp. 77–103). Baltimore, MD: Paul H Brookes.

Goleman, D. (1995). *Emotional intelligence*. New York, NY: Bantam Books.

Gonzalez-Mena, J. (1997, September/October). Independence or interdependence? Understanding the parent's perspective. *Exchange, 177*, 61–68.

Gonzalez-Mena, J. (2008). *Diversity in early care and education: Honoring differences*. New York, NY: McGraw-Hill.

Goodall, J. (1999). *Reason for hope*. New York, NY: Warner Books.

Gopnik, A. (2009). *The philosophical baby: What children's minds tell us about truth, love, and the meaning of life*. New York, NY: Farrar, Straus and Giroux.

Gopnik, A., Meltzoff, A. N., & Kuhl, P. K. (1999). *The scientist in the crib: What early learning tells us about the mind*. New York, NY: HarperCollins.

Gordon, T. (2000). *Parent effectiveness training: The proven program for raising responsible children*. New York, NY: Three Rivers Press.

Greenspan, S. I. (2003, July/August). Child care research: A clinical perspective. *Child Development, 74*(4), 1064–1068.

Greenspan, S. I. (with Benderly, B. L.). (1997). *The growth of the mind and the endangered origins of intelligence*. Reading, MA: Addison-Wesley.

Grisham-Brown, J., Hemmeter, M. L., & Pretti-Frontczak, K. (2005). *Blended practices for teaching young children in inclusive settings*. Baltimore, MD: Paul H. Brookes.

Gunnar, M. R., Dryzer, E., Van Ryzin, M. J., & Phillips, D. A. (2010). The rise in cortisone in family day care: Associations with aspects of care quality, child behavior and child sex. *Child Development, 81*(3), 851–869.

Hall, E. L., & Rudkin, J. K. (2011). *Seen and heard: Children's rights in early childhood education*. New York, NY: Teachers College Press.

Harms, T., Clifford, R. M., & Cryer, D. (1998). *Early childhood environment rating scale* (rev. ed.). New York, NY: Teachers College Press.

Harter, S. (2006). The self. In N. Eisenberg, W. Damon & R. M. Lerner (eds.). *Handbook of child psychology* (pp. 505–570). Hoboken, NJ: John Wiley & Sons.

Haugen, K. (2005, January/February). Learning materials for children of all abilities: Begin with universal design. *Exchange, 161,* 45–48.

Hearron, P. F. (1992, January 3). They said to make a college: Families' perceptions of kindergarten homework tasks. *Proceedings of Qualitative Research in Education Conference, University of Georgia, Athens, GA.* Retrieved November 19, 2011, from coe.uga.edu/proceedings/Quig92_Proceedings/index.html.

Hebbeler, K. M., & Gerlach-Downie, S. G. (2002). Inside the black box of home visiting: A qualitative analysis of why intended outcomes were not achieved. *Early Childhood Research Quarterly, 17*(1), 28–51.

Hemmeter, M. L., & Fox, L. (2007). *Promoting young children's social competence addressing challenging behavior: Implementing the teaching pyramid.* Center on the Social and Emotional Foundations for Early Learning. Presentation at NAEYC National Institute for Early Childhood Professional Development, Pittsburgh, PA, June 9, 2007.

Hemmeter, M. L., Joseph, G. E., Smith, B. J., & Sandall, S. (2001). *DEC recommended practices: Program assessment: Improving practices for young children with special needs and their families.* Denver, CO: Division for Early Childhood of the Council for Exceptional Children and Longmont, CO: Sopris West.

Hestenes, L. L., Shim, J., & DeBord, K. (2007). *The measurement and influence of outdoor child care quality on preschool children's experiences.* Presentation at Biennial Conference of the Society for Research in Child Development, March 2007, Boston, MA.

Hestenes, L. L., Kontos, S., & Bryan, Y. (1993). Children's emotional expression in child care centers varying in quality. *Early Childhood Research Quarterly, 8,* 295–307.

Hildebrand, V., Phenice, L., Gray, M., & Hines, R. P. (2007). *Knowing and serving diverse families* (3rd ed.). Upper Saddle River, NJ: Pearson.

Horton-Ikard, R. (2006, September). The influence of culture, class, and linguistic diversity on early language development. *Zero to Three, 27*(1), 6–11.

Hulbert, A. (2003). *Raising America: Experts, parents, and a century of advice about children.* New York, NY: Alfred A. Knopf.

Hunter, T. (2006). *Visits to the heart of education: Remembering what's important. Essays by Tom Hunter.* Bellingham, WA: The Song Growing Company.

Jackson, K. and Jackson, B, (1948). *Busy Timmy.* New York: Simon and Schuster.

James, W. (1892/1962). *Psychology: The briefer course.* New York, NY: Collier Books.

Jones, E. (1989, December). Inviting children into the fun: Providing enough activity choices outdoors. *Exchange, 70,* 15–19.

Kaiser, B., & Rasminsky, J. S. (2012). *Challenging behavior in young children: Understanding, preventing, and responding effectively.* Upper Saddle River, NJ: Pearson Education.

Kamii, C. (1982). *Number in preschool and kindergarten.* Washington, DC: National Association for the Education of Young Children.

Kaplan, S. (1995). The restorative benefits of nature: Toward an integrative framework. *Journal of Environmental Psychology, 15,* 169–182.

Katz, L. G. (1993). *Distinctions between self-esteem and narcissism: Implications for practice.* Clearinghouse on Early Education and Parenting, University of Illinois at Urbana-Champaign. Retrieved November 19, 2011, from ceep.crc.uiuc.edu/eecearchive/books/selfe.html.

Katz, L. G. (1996). Child development knowledge and teacher preparation: Confronting assumptions. *Early Childhood Research Quarterly, 11,* 135–146.

Katz, L. G. (2007, May). Viewpoint: Standards of experience. *Young Children, 62*(3), 94–95.

Katz, L. G., & Katz, S. J. (2009). *Intellectual emergencies: Some reflections on mothering and teaching.* Lewisville, NC: Kpress.

Kellogg, R. (1979). *Children's drawings, children's minds.* New York, NY: Avon Books.

Kern, P., & Wolery, M. (2002, Spring). The sound path: Adding music to a child care playground. *Young Exceptional Children 5*(3), 12–20.

Kilmer, S., & Hofman, H. (1995). Transforming science curriculum. In S. Bredekamp & T. Rosegrant (eds.). *Reaching Potentials: Transforming Early Childhood Curriculum and Assessment* (pp. 43–63). Washington, DC: National Association for the Education of Young Children.

Kintner-Duffy, V., Mims, S., Hestenes, L. L., & Hestenes, S. L. (2011). *Comparisons among quality measures in child care settings: Indicators of quality in relation to child outcomes.* Presentation at Society for Research in Child Development, Washington, DC. Retrieved November 19, 2011, from ncrlap.org/Resources/.

Klein, M. D., & Chen, D. (2001). *Working with children from culturally diverse backgrounds.* Clifton Part, NY: Delmar Thomson Learning.

Kohn, A. (1994, December). The risks of rewards. *ERIC Digest.* ED376990. Retrieved November 19, 2011, from eric.ed.gov.

Kolbe, U. (2005). *It's not a bird yet: The drama of drawing.* Byron Bay, Australia: Peppinot Press.

Legendre, A. (2003, July). Environmental features influencing toddlers' bioemotional reactions in day care centers. *Environment and Behavior, 35,* 523–549.

Levin, D. E. (2003). Teaching young children in violent times: Building a peaceable classroom (2nd ed.). Cambridge, MA: Educators for Social Responsibility.

Levitt, P. (2009). *Keynote address.* National Smart Start Conference, Greensboro, NC, May 20, 2009.

Lewis, A. E., & Forman, T. A. (2002). Contestation or collaboration? A comparative study of home-school relations. *Anthropology & Education Quarterly, 33(1),* 60–89.

Lisonbee, J. A., Mize, J., Payne, A. L., & Granger, D. A. (2008). Children's cortisol and the quality of teacher-child relationships in child care. *Child Development, 79(6),* 1818–1832.

Louv, R. (2005). *Last Child in the Woods.* Chapel Hill, NC: Algonquin Books.

Lubeck, S. (2000). On reassessing the relevance of the child development knowledge base to education: A response. *Human Development, 43,* 273–278.

Malaguzzi, L. (1994/2005). Your image of the child—Where teaching begins. *Exchange, 96,* 52–56; reprinted online 2005. Retrieved May 18, 2011, from secure.ccie.com/resources/view_article.php?article_id=5009652&action=view.

Malaguzzi, L. (1998). History, ideas, and basic philosophy: An interview with Lella Gandini. In C. Edwards, L. Gandini, & G. Forman (eds.). *The hundred languages of children: The Reggio Emilia approach—Advanced reflections* (2nd ed.) (pp. 49–97). Greenwich, CT: Ablex.

Mangione, P. L., Lally, J. R., & Signer, S. (2001). *The next step: Including the infant in the curriculum* [DVD booklet]. Sacramento, CA: CDE Press.

Marchand, G., & Skinner, E. A. (2007). Motivational dynamics of children's academic help-seeking and concealment. *Journal of Educational Psychology, 99(1),* 65–82.

Maslow, A. (1968). *Toward a psychology of being* (2nd ed.). New York, NY: D. Van Nostrand.

Meadan, H., Ostrosky, M. M., Triplett, B., Michna, A., & Fettig, A. (2011). Using visual supports with young children with autism spectrum disorder. *Teaching Exceptional Children, 43(6),* 28–35.

Mendez, J. L., Fantuzzo, J., & Cicchetti, D. (2002, July). Profiles of social competence among low-income African American preschool children. *Child Development, 73(4),* 1085–2000.

Montie, J. E., Xiang, Z., & Schweinhart, L. J. (2006). Preschool experience in 10 countries: Cognitive and language performance at age 7. *Early Childhood Research Quarterly, 21,* 313–331.

Moore, L., DiGao, A. S., Bradlee, M. L., Cupples, L. A., Sundarajan-Ramamurti, A., Proctor, M. H., Hood, M. Y., Singer, M. R., & Ellison, R. C. (2003). Does early physical activity predict body fat change throughout childhood? *Preventive Medicine, 37,* 10–17.

Moore, S., & Perez-Mendez, C. (2007). *Responsive teaching of culturally, linguistically and ability diverse young children in the classroom.* Presentation at Crosswalks National Institute: Infusing Cultural, Linguistic and Ability Diversity in Preservice Education, Asheville, NC, July 26, 2007.

Morris, P., Raver, C., Lloyd, C. M., & Millenky, M. (2009). *Can teacher training in classroom management make a difference for children's experiences in preschool? A preview of findings from the Foundations of Learning Demonstration.* Retrieved June 3, 2011, from mdrc.org/publications/527/full.pdf.

National Association for Family Child Care. (2003). *Quality standards for NAFCC Accreditation* (3rd ed.). Developed by The Family Child Care Accreditation Project, Wheelock College. Salt Lake City, UT: Author. Retrieved July 17, 2003, from nafcc.org.

National Association for Sports and Physical Education. (2002). *Active start: A statement of physical activity guidelines for children birth to five years.* Reston, VA: Author.

National Association for the Education of Young Children. (1996, September). NAEYC Position statement: Technology and young children—ages three through eight. *Young Children, 51*(6), 11–16.

National Association for the Education of Young Children. (2007a). *Intentionality in early childhood education: 16th National Institute for Early Childhood Professional Development.* Retrieved June 4, 2007, from naeyc.org/conferences/pdf/NAEYC_Institute_Preliminary_Program.

National Association for the Education of Young Children. (2007b). *NAEYC Early Childhood Program Standards and Accreditation Criteria: The Mark of Quality in Early Childhood Education.* Washington, DC: Author.

National Association for the Education of Young Children. (2009). *Where we stand on responding to linguistic and cultural diversity.* Retrieved July 2, 2011, from naeyc.org.

National Association for the Education of Young Children. (2010). *2010 NAEYC standards for initial and advanced early childhood teacher preparation programs for use by associate, baccalaureate and graduate degree programs.* Retrieved May 18, 2011, from naeyc.org/files/ecada/file/NAEYC%20Initial%20and%20Advanced%20Standards%203_2011.pdf.

National Association for the Education of Young Children. (2011a). *Code of ethical conduct and statement of commitment.* Retrieved September 2, 2011, from naeyc.org/files/naeyc/file/positions/Ethics%20Position%20Statement2011.pdf.

National Association for the Education of Young Children. (2011b). *Draft: Technology in early childhood programs serving children from birth through age 8.* Retrieved July 2, 2011, from naeyc.org.

National Center for Boundless Playgrounds. (2008). *About us—Inspiration.* Retrieved January 20, 2008, from boundlessplaygrounds.org/about/inspiration.php.

National Center on Response to Intervention. (n.d.). The essential elements of RTI. Retrieved September 11, 2011, from www.rti4success.org.

National Reading Panel. (2000). *Teaching children to read: An evidence-based assessment of the scientific research literature on reading and its implications for instruction.* Washington, DC: National Institute of Child Health and Human Development, National Institutes of Health.

National Research Council and Institute of Medicine. (2000). *From neurons to neighborhoods: The science of early childhood development.* Committee on Integrating the Science of Early Childhood Development. Jack P. Shonkoff & Deborah A. Phillips (eds.). Board on Children, Youth, and Families, Commission on Behavioral and Social Sciences and Education. Washington, DC: National Academy Press.

National Scientific Council on the Developing Child. (2010). *Persistent fear and anxiety can affect young children's learning and development: Working paper no. 9.* Retrieved November 19, 2011, from developingchild.harvard.edu.

Nelson, E. (2006, September/October). The outdoor classroom: "No child left inside." *Exchange, 171,* 40–43.

Neuman, S., Copple, C., & Bredekamp, S. (2000). *Learning to read and write: Developmentally appropriate practices for young children.* Washington, DC: National Association for the Education of Young Children.

New, R. (1999). What should children learn? Making choices and taking chances. *Early Childhood Research and Practice, 1*(2). Retrieved November 23, 1999, from ecrp.uiuc.edu/v1n2/new.html.

Noonan, M. J., & McCormick, L. (1993). *Early intervention in natural environments: Methods and procedures.* Pacific Grove, CA: Brooks/Cole.

Odom, S. L., Zercher, C., Shouming, L., Marquart, J. M., Sandall, S., & Brown, W. H. (2006). Social acceptance and rejection of preschool children with disabilities: A mixed-method analysis. *Journal of Educational Psychology, 98*(4), 807–823.

Ogden, C., Flegal, K., Carroll, M., & Johnson, C. (2002). Prevalence and trends in overweight among US children and adolescents, 1999–2000. *Journal of the American Medical Association, 288*(14), 1728–1732.

Olds, A. R. (2001). *Child care design guide.* New York, NY: McGraw-Hill.

Oliver, S., & Klugman, E. (2005, July/August). Play and the outdoors: What's new under the sun? *Exchange, 170,* 6–10.

Paley, V. (2003, September 19). *Building community through stories.* Keynote presentation at Price Reading Symposium, Appalachian State University, Boone, NC.

Paley, V. (2010). *The boy on the beach: Building community through play*. Chicago, IL: University of Chicago.

Palmer, P. J. (1998). *The courage to teach: Exploring the inner landscape of a teacher's life*. San Francisco, CA: Jossey-Bass, Inc.

Palsha, S. (2002). An outstanding education for ALL children. In V. R. Fu., A. J. Stremmel, & L. T. Hill (eds.). *Teaching and learning: Collaborative exploration of the Reggio-Emilia approach* (pp. 109–130). Upper Saddle River, NJ: Pearson.

Pate, R. R., Pfeiffer, K. A., Trost, S. G., Ziegler, P., & Dowda, M. (2004). Physical activity among children attending preschools. *Pediatrics, 114*, 1258–1263.

Paulsell, D., & Nogales, R. (2003, March). Parent perspectives. *Zero to Three, 23*(4), 32–35.

Pelco, L. E., & Reed-Victor, E. (2003). Understanding and supporting differences in child temperament: Strategies for early childhood environments. *Young Exceptional Children, 6*(3), 2–11.

Penner, L. A., & Orom, H. (2010). Enduring goodness: A person by situation perspective on prosocial behavior. In M. Mikulincer & P. R. Shaver (eds.). *Prosocial motives, emotions, and behavior: The better angels of our nature*. Washington, DC: American Psychological Association.

Perry, N., & Gerard, M. (2002). The problematic relationship between child development theory and teacher preparation. *Journal of Early Childhood Teacher Education, 23*(4), 343–348.

Piaget, J. (1962). *Play, dreams, and imitation is childhood*. New York, NY: W. W. Norton.

Pica, R. (2006). *A running start: How play, physical activity and free time create a successful child*. New York, NY: Marlowe & Company.

Porter, L., & McKenzie, S. (2000). *Professional collaboration with parents of children with disabilities*. Philadelphia, PA: Whurr Publishers.

Ray, A., Bowman, B., & Brownell, J. O. (2006). Teacher–child relationships, social-emotional development, and school achievement. In B. Bowman & E. K. Moore (eds.). *School readiness and social-emotional development: Perspectives on cultural diversity* (pp. 1–22). Washington, DC: National Black Child Development Institute, Inc.

Reichl, R. (2007 March). Teach your children well. *Gourmet Magazine*. (Cited in ExchangeEveryDay, July 10, 2007, www.childcareexchange.com).

Reynolds, G. (2011, July 6). Why exercise makes us feel good. *New York Times*. Retrieved November 19, 2011, from well.blogs.nytimes.com/2011/07/06.

Richardson, K., & Salkeld, L. (1995). Transforming mathematics curriculum. In S. Bredekamp & T. Rosegrant (eds.). *Reaching Potentials: Transforming Early Childhood Curriculum and Assessment* (pp. 23–42). Washington, DC: National Association for the Education of Young Children.

Richtel, M. (2010, August 15). Outdoors and out of reach: Studying the brain. *New York Times*. Retrieved November 19, 2011, from nytimes.com/2010/08/16/technology/16brain.html.

Rinaldi, C. (2001). Documentation and assessment: What is the relationship? In Reggio Children and Project Zero (eds.). *Making learning visible: Children as individual and group learners* (pp. 78–89). Reggio Emilia, Italy: Reggio Children.

Ritblatt, S. N., Obegi, A. D., & Hammons, B. S. (2003, Spring/Summer). Parents' and child care professionals' toilet training attitudes and practices: A comparative analysis. *Journal of Research in Childhood Education, 17*, 133–146.

Roggman, L. A., Boyce, L. K., Cook, G. A., & Jump, V. K. (2001). Inside home visits: A collaborative look at process and quality. *Early Childhood Research Quarterly, 16*(1), 53–71.

Rosenkoetter, S. E., & Knapp-Philo, J. (eds.). (2006). *Learning to read the world: Language and literacy in the first three years*. Washington, DC: Zero to Three.

Ross, D. M. (1996). *Childhood bullying and teasing: What school personnel, other professionals, and parents can do*. Alexandria, VA: American Counseling Association.

Ruopp, R., Travers, J., Glantz, F., & Coelen, C. (1979). *Children at the center: Final report of the National Day Care Study* (Vol. 1). Washington, DC: Department of Health, Education, and Welfare.

Sandall S., Hemmeter, M. L., Smith, B. J., & McLean, M. E. (2005). *DEC recommended practices: A comprehensive guide for practical application in early childhood special education*. Longmont, CA: Sopris and Missoula, MT: DEC.

Seefeldt, C. (2002). *Creating rooms of wonder: Valuing and displaying children's work to enhance the learning process.* Beltsville, MD: Gryphon House.

Shim, S. K., Herwig, J. E., Shelley, M. (2001). Preschoolers' play behaviors with peers in classroom and playground settings. *Journal of Research in Childhood Education, 15*(2), 149–163.

Stanton-Chapman, T. L., & Snell, M. E. (2011). Promoting turn-taking in children with disabilities: The effects of a peer-based social communication intervention. *Early Childhood Research Quarterly, 26*(3), 303–319.

Story, M., Kaphingst, K. M., & French, S. (2006, Spring). The role of child care settings in obesity prevention. *The Future of Children, 16*(1). Retrieved August 7, 2007, fromfutureofchildren.org/usr_doc/07_5562_story-care.pdf.

Stott, F., & Bowman, B. (1996). Child development knowledge: A slippery base for practice. *Early Childhood Research Quarterly, 11*, 169–183.

Strommen, E. (1976). Learning not to: It takes a long time. In *Women and Children in Contemporary Society* (pp. 55–56). Lansing, MI: Michigan Women's Commission.

Sull, T. M. (2003, Spring). Real supervision. *Texas Child Care, 26*(4), 3–5.

Szanton, E. S. (2001, January). Viewpoint: For America's infants and toddlers, are important values threatened by our zeal to teach? *Young Children, 56*(1), 15–21.

Taylor, A., Kuo, F., & Sullivan, W. (2001 January). Coping with ADD: The surprising connection to green play settings. *Environment and Behavior, 33*(1), 54–77.

Trawick-Smith, J. (2010). *Early childhood development: A multicultural perspective.* Upper Saddle River, NJ: Pearson.

Trivette, C. M., & Dunst, C. (2000). Recommended practices in family-based practices. In S. Sandal, M. E. McLean, & B. J. Smith (eds.). *DEC recommended practices in early intervention/early childhood special education* (pp. 39–46). Longmont, CO: Sopris West and Denver, CO: Division for Early Childhood of the Council for Exceptional Children.

Tucker, P. (2008). The physical activity levels of preschool-aged children: A systematic review. *ECRQ, 23*, 547–558.

U.S. Consumer Product Safety Commission (2010, November). Public playground safety handbook. Publication #325. Retrieved November 28, 2011 from cpsc.gov/cpscpub/pubs/325.pdf.

U.S. Department of Education. (2011). *Model Individualized Family Service Plan.* Retrieved September 9, 2011, from ed.gov/policy/speced/reg/idea/part-c/index.html.

Waksler, F. C. (1996). *The little trials of childhood and children's strategies for dealing with them.* London, UK: The Falmer Press.

Warneken, F., & Tomasello, M. (2006, March 3). Altruistic helping in human infants and young chimpanzees. *Science, 311*(5765), 1301–1303.

Weinreb, M. (1997, January). Be a resiliency mentor: You may be a lifesaver for a high risk child. *Young Children 52*(2), 14–19.

Whitmore, K. F., & Goodman, Y. M. (1995). Transforming curriculum in language and literacy. In S. Bredekamp & T. Rosegrant (eds.). *Reaching potentials: Transforming early childhood curriculum and assessment* (pp. 145–166). Washington, DC: National Association for the Education of Young Children.

Wike, J. (2006, September/October). Why outdoor spaces for children matter so much. *Exchange, 171*, 44–48.

Willis, J. (2007, Summer). The neuroscience of joyful education. *Educational Leadership, 64*(9). Retrieved August 9, 2007, from ascd.org.

Wolery, M., Strain, P. S., & Bailey, D. B. (1992). Reaching potentials of children with special needs. In S. Bredekamp & T. Rosegrant (eds.). *Reaching potentials: Appropriate curriculum and assessment for young children* (pp. 92–111). Washington, DC: National Association for the Education of Young Children.

Zimiles, H. (2000). On reassessing the relevance of the child development knowledge base to education. *Human Development, 43*, 235–245.

Name Index

Kaiser, B., 168
Kamii, C., 205
Kaphingst, K. M., 181
Kaplan, S., 229
Katz, L. G., 28, 39, 46, 83, 102, 198, 199, 265
Katz, S. J., 39, 46, 83, 102, 199, 265
Kellog, R., 203
Kermoian, R., 107
Kern, P., 238
Kilmer, S., 202
Kinter-Duffy, V., 232
Klein, M. D., 70
Klugman, E., 225
Knapp-Philo, J., 230
Kohn, A., 156
Kolbe, U., 203
Kontos, S., 135
Kuhl, P. K., 51
Kuo, F., 229

Lally, J. R., 153
Legendre, A., 123
Leong, D., 53, 204, 230, 270
Levin, D. E., 100
Levitt, P., 52
Lewis, A. E., 79
Lisonbee, J. A., 152
Lloyd, C. M., 97
Louv, R., 225
Lubeck, S., 54

Malaguzzi, L., 12, 13, 210
Mangione, P. L., 153
Marchand, G., 102
Maslow, A., 12
McCormick, L., 189
McKenzie, S., 70
McLean, M. E., 29
Meadan, H., 132
Meltzoff, A. N., 51
Mendez, J. L., 102
Millenky, M., 97
Mims, S., 232
Mize, J., 152
Montie, J. E., 135
Moore, L., 180, 227
Moore, S., 213
Morris, P., 97

Nelson, E., 225
Neuman, S., 206
New, R., 27
Nogales, R., 70
Noonan, M. J., 189

Obegi, A. D., 178
Odom, S. L., 103
Ogden, C., 226
Olds, A. R., 122, 131, 233, 234, 235
Oliver, S., 225
Orom, H., 108

Paley, V., 153, 169
Palmer, P., 39
Palsha, S., 63
Pate, R. R., 232
Paulsell, D., 70
Payne, A. L., 152
Pelco, L. E., 50
Penner, L. A., 108
Perez-Mendez, C., 213
Perry, N., 54
Phenice, L., 71
Phillips, D. A., 52
Piaget, J., 263
Pica, R., 229
Porter, L., 70
Pretti-Frontczak, K., 132

Rasminsky, J. S., 168
Raver, C., 97
Ray, A., 257
Reed-Victor, E., 50
Reichl, R., 182
Reifel, S., 230
Reynolds, G., 227
Richardson, K., 202
Richtel, M., 229
Rinaldi, C., 63
Ritblatt, S. N., 178
Roggman, L. A., 76
Rosegrant, T., 18
Rosenkoetter, S. E., 230
Ross, D. M., 268
Rudkin, J. K., 9, 13
Ruopp, R., 144

Salkeld, L., 202
Sandall, S., 29
Schweinhart, L. J., 135
Seefeldt, C., 206
Shim, J., 232
Shim, S. K., 230
Signer, S., 153
Skinner, E. A., 102
Smith, B. J., 29
Spinrad, T. L., 108
Stacey, S., 103
Story, M., 181, 182
Stott, F., 54
Strayer, D., 229
Strommen, E., 162
Sull, T. M., 239
Sullivan, W., 229
Sutterby, J. A., 227
Szanton, E. S., 28

Taylor, A., 229
Thomas, A., 51
Thornton, C. D., 227
Tomasello, M., 108
Travers, J., 144
Trawick-Smith, J., 100, 102, 108
Trivette, C. M., 68
Tucker, P., 226

Van Ryzin, M. J., 52
Vygotsky, L., 230

Waksler, F. C., 179
Wardle, F., 135
Warneken, F., 108
Weinreb, M., 88, 257
Weitzman, E., 212
Whitmore, K. F., 204, 206
Wike, J., 225
Willis, J., 48
Winton, P., 55
Wolery, M., 238
Wortham, S. C., 230

Xiang, Z., 135

Zimiles, H., 54

Subject Index